The
Archaeology
of Home

The Archaeology

of Home

An Epic Set on
a Thousand Square Feet
of the Lower East Side

Katharine Greider

PUBLICAFFAIRS
New York

Published in the United States by PublicAffairs™,
a member of the Perseus Books Group.

PublicAffairs books are available at special discounts for bulk purchases
in the U.S. by corporations, institutions, and other organizations. For
more information, please contact the Special Markets Department
at the Perseus Books Group, 2300 Chestnut Street, Suite 200,
Philadelphia, PA 19103, call (800) 810-4145, ext. 5000,
or e-mail special.markets@perseusbooks.com.

Library of Congress Cataloging-in-Publication Data
Greider, Katharine.
    The archaeology of home : an epic set on a thousand square feet of
the Lower East Side / Katharine Greider. — 1st ed.
       p.   cm.
    Includes bibliographical references.
    ISBN 978-1-58648-712-6 (hbk : alk. paper)
    1. Lower East Side (New York, N.Y.)—Buildings, structures, etc.
2. New York (N.Y.)—Buildings, structures, etc.   3. Buildings—
Research—New York (State)—New York.   4. Lower East Side
(N.Y.)—History.   5. New York (N.Y.)—History.   6. Greider,
Katharine—Homes and haunts—New York (State)—New York.
I. Title.
    F128.68.L6G74 2011
    974.7'1—dc22

                                                            2010052006

E-book ISBN: 978-1-58648-990-8

First Edition

10 9 8 7 6 5 4 3 2 1

CONTENTS

NUMBERED KEY

JOURNEY THROUGH THE EAST SIDE
THE APPROXIMATE LOCATIONS OF FAMILY HOMES

● **AUTHOR'S FAMILY**

1. The author's first home in New York, No. 258 E. 7th Street, was occupied in the 1850s by an Irish-born cartman and his family.

2. No. 239 E. 7th Street, the author's one-time home and the center of our story.

3. The author and her family's current home.

○ **BARNARD FAMILY**

4. The Barnards' home on Broome Street (1840s), before moving to No. 239 E. 7th Street.

◎ **WEINSTEIN FAMILY**

5. The Weinsteins' home, shortly after immigrating, on Attorney Street (mid-1840s); also a synagogue.

6. The Weinsteins' second location, on Houston Street.

7. The Weinsteins' third location, on Avenue C, just before moving to No. 239 E. 7th Street in 1860.

8. Abraham Weinstein, widowed and remarried, moved from No. 239 E. 7th Street to No. 243 (late 1860s).

◉ **PHILLIPS FAMILY**

9. The Phillips's location on Delancey Street (1850s). Levy Phillips's glazier shop was listed in business directories at No. 255 Delancey Street.

10. Levy and Clara Phillips's home on Columbia Street when granddaughter Clara Hart was born (1865); several years later they moved to No. 239 E. 7th Street.

11. Rachel and Joseph Hart's home (1865); Rachel, the eldest child of Levy and Clara Phillips, gave birth to daughter Clara Hart here.

12. Isabella Salomon's home (1910); Isabella, the youngest child of Levy and Clara Phillips, moved here after the death of her mother and after the sale of the property at No. 239 E. 7th Street.

○ **WIEDER FAMILY**

13. The Wieders' location, on Cannon Street (1891–1892), around the time of their son Michael's birth.

14. The Wieders' location, on Columbia Street (1893–1894), around the time of their son Morris's birth.

15. The Wieders' location, on Lewis Street (1897), the same year Simon Wieder, the Wieder family patriarch, petitioned for U.S. citizenship.

16. The Wieders' location, on 6th Street, around 1900.

17. Simon Wieder's trimmings shop, on Avenue C, before and after the family moved to No. 239 E. 7th Street (around 1907).

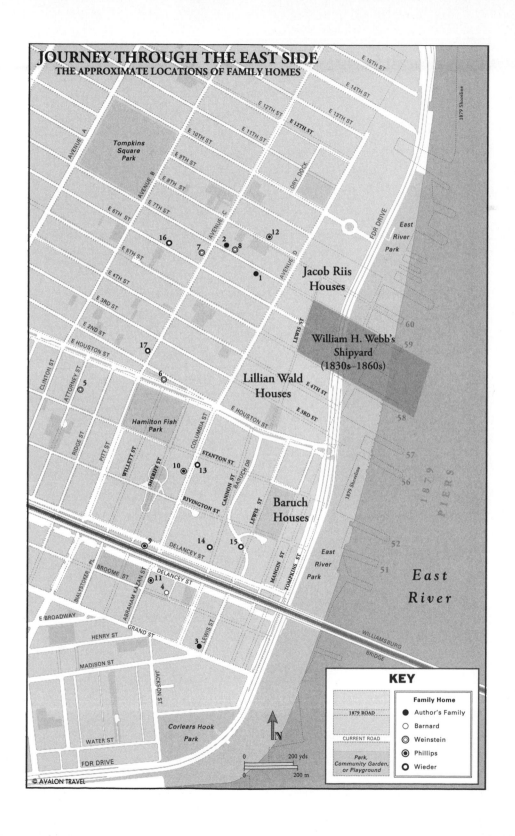

JOURNEY THROUGH THE EAST SIDE
THE APPROXIMATE LOCATIONS OF FAMILY HOMES

E 15TH ST

E 14TH ST

E 12TH ST

E 13TH ST

E 12TH ST

Tompkins Square Park

E 10TH ST

E 11TH ST

E 9TH ST

E 8TH ST

AVENUE A

DRY DOCK

E 7TH ST

AVENUE B

E 6TH ST

FDR DRIVE

AVENUE C

East River Park

E 5TH ST

16 ○

2 ● ○ 8

●12

7 ○

E 4TH ST

● 1

AVENUE D

Jacob Riis Houses

E 3RD ST

E 2ND ST

LEWIS ST

60

E HOUSTON ST

17 ○

59

William H. Webb's Shipyard (1830s–1860s)

CLINTON ST

ATTORNEY ST

6 ○

Lillian Wald Houses

E 4TH ST

5 ◎

E 3RD ST

E HOUSTON ST

58

RIDGE ST

Hamilton Fish Park

COLUMBIA ST

STANTON ST

57

PITT ST

WILLETT ST

SHERIFF ST

10 ◎ ○ 13

CANNON ST

BARUCH DR

56

1879 Shoreline

1879 PIERS

RIVINGTON ST

LEWIS ST

Baruch Houses

52

9 ◎

DELANCEY ST

14 ○ 15 ○

MANGIN ST

TOMPKINS ST

East River Park

51

BIALYSTOKER PL

BROOME ST

11 ◎

DELANCEY ST

4 ○

ABRAHAM KAZAN ST

East River

E BROADWAY

GRAND ST

LEWIS ST

HENRY ST

3 ●

WILLIAMSBURG

BRIDGE

MADISON ST

JACKSON ST

Corlears Hook Park

↑ N

WATER ST

FDR DRIVE

© AVALON TRAVEL

0   200 yds
0   200 m

KEY

	Family Home
1879 ROAD	● Author's Family
CURRENT ROAD	○ Barnard
Park, Community Garden, or Playground	◎ Weinstein
	◉ Phillips
	○ Wieder

The Phone Call

THIS MORNING, I have brought out the box. After dropping the kids at school and David at the bus stop, I hauled it from the back of the hall closet and tore off the packing tape, releasing an odor of dust and mildew.

It's nothing but a box of battered files bearing such dry labels as "Engineers' Reports," "Contractors," "Working Loan App.," "Court Docs," and the somewhat more evocative "Gary's Noise Complaint." I lift out the folders. My throat constricts.

These are the records of what David and I came to call our "real estate debacle." For months, I daily thumbed through the files with an anxiety of the sort the body remembers all too well. How fresh these documents have kept the thing, so that now, years later, they tune me up like a music box, setting off the familiar suite of physical responses—the agitating gut, the sweating palms.

The call came late one evening in January 2002. David was out of town. I had the children in bed with me, and reached over their small, sleeping bodies to answer the phone. It was Ralph, the architect we'd hired to recommend a schedule of repairs for the dilapidated row house we called home. He and his colleagues, a contractor and an engineer, had convened that afternoon to study digital photos taken in the dank crawl space beneath our basement floor. The situation, he told me, was more serious than we had supposed. Indeed, the foundation of the building in which my children and I were even now settling down for another night's rest was in what professionals call a failed condition, its crushed and rotted wooden beams propped up by crumbling brick piles and two-by-fours (these last suggesting an inadequate repair of relatively recent vintage). Ralph said he would wait until Monday morning before reporting this hazard to the City of New York, at which time city officials would almost certainly seal the building. And he left no doubt as to what we should do over the weekend: Get the hell out.

This was the squealing-tires moment, time of slow motion, anesthetized, alert, poppies swaying silently in the breeze. I called David. I ran downstairs to tell the owner of the basement apartment. I buzzed the parlor-floor door until someone answered, and broke the news to its tenants, recent college grads. I told the young couple to whom, only months before, David and I had rented the second floor. She answered the door in her bathrobe. Her mother had recently died of cancer. Yes, I insisted, I'm told it's not safe. There's no time. I'm sorry. I went hurriedly back upstairs, lay down next to my children, and, for the first of what would be many, many times, taunted myself with an image that seemed almost as preposterous as death itself: our building kneeling and falling into the street. Also unreeling in my head was a scenario in which I did the prudent thing, woke the children, hustled them to safety, our breaths misting the night air. I didn't move. That night I slept.

It had been nearly a decade since we'd first settled on this block near the eastern edge of lower Manhattan, 7th Street between Avenues C and D. The last five of these years we'd spent on the top floor of a small, south-facing row house, No. 239, about midway between Tompkins Square Park, always sounding with bongos and barking dogs, and the silently moving waters of the East River. During the mid-1980s this four-unit building had been turned into a financially dodgy and socially fractious co-op; as the owners of the top two floors, we were majority shareholders. It was here we brought our newborns home from the hospital in 1997 and 2000. It was here that the one pink towel David and I had quite happily shared for years turned into an entire set. The place literally held together the family we'd made. The precise elevation of its stairs and angle of its light secretly inscribed themselves on our bodies and gave us comfort in familiarity. The house or, to be precise, our shares in the co-op, were our principal investment, dollars laid up like so many bushels of grain. We were at home there. It was the setting of our imagined future.

Very early on, the roof leaked. On one or two occasions, rain trickled down through a ceiling light fixture in the living room. The building's exposed western wall also proved unable to keep out the weather, so that the interior paint on that side, from our third-floor kitchen all the way down to the vestibule, sagged like aging skin. David and I were not handy. We managed to get the roof replaced by a reputable outfit, but work on the parapet went badly; the guy slashed open his thigh with a circular saw and I sent him off, never to be heard from again, with a sandwich bag of codeine I'd gotten after my C-section. All this was exasperating, to be sure, but I thought I recognized a story line in which the young marrieds bungle their way into a charming wreck where they raise their happy brood amid the peeling paint and loose floorboards.

What we got instead was that phone call. We took a three-month lease in a tenement across the street and moved out. Picture the city version of an Amish barn raising. My parents drove up from Washington and my brother and sister-in-law helped pack boxes, tape things up, break things down. So did the neighbors. Our friend Stanley, also the co-op's lawyer, turned up in gray sweatpants, for him an extraordinary sartorial choice that enhanced the atmosphere of quiet but deep alarm. I remember looking down from the place across the street and seeing my grandmother's sideboard in two pieces on the sidewalk. The potted flowers from the deck sat lined up there, too; a young man, not unkindly, offered to buy them. Some stuff came with us, a lot went into a storage unit in Queens, and other things we simply left behind: a crib, a couch, a stash of holiday paper, a litter of abandoned toys. We didn't know if we'd ever be back. All that day David carried and carried like a mule, propping open the door to No. 239 with the sack of change we'd accumulated over the years, until someone stole it, and the door swung shut.

So began the nearly two years we spent trapped in the airless world of that box. "Dear Stanly [sic]," reads a note from the architect, misfiled in the folder marked "Engineers' Reports" and dated February 4, 2002. "This morning I have informed the Department of Buildings that 239 East 7th Street, is a structurally unsafe building. They have informed me that they are sending an inspector to the building. It is critical that all tenants stay out of the building at all times. Please inform them again." And yet the next day I walked through the building with the inspector himself. I had dressed up slightly, thinking to put across the impression of a responsible matron, an effort that was effectively countervailed by the scene of utter ruin that awaited us in the basement, the floors torn up, the apartment empty save for an enormous television on which, in their own extremis of anxiety, the longtime owner and his companion were in fact watching the *Jerry Springer Show* at top volume. At this point I cried, and the inspector wrote up an extensive violation, and I asked him, "So your only response is this punitive action?" and he wore a bored, irritated expression as he looked at me and answered simply, "Yes."

For the rest of that spring we lived across the street, above a night-club whose dance track produced a regular wee hours' thumping in the solar plexus. Then we went down to suburban Virginia to stay at David's parents' place for four months. In the fall of 2002 we returned to New York—our oldest was to begin kindergarten—and rented a tiny apartment on 8th Street through most of 2003.

It was during this time, as we vacillated unnervingly between looking at No. 239 as the family home to which we would stage a joyful return and seeing it as a moribund shell, that I came to recognize how much it had contained, how laborious it was to shift those contents elsewhere. And it was during this time that a light slowly rose on the darkened tableau of the past. It began with a question: *What happened here?* How was it, for example, that the building we'd bought into only five years earlier, and that an engineer had walked through and pronounced in decent shape, was now essentially kaput?

In my box, sitting on top, I find a familiar spiral notebook, its cover a photograph of a monarch against crimson zinnias. During the worst of it I bought two of these notebooks. David's has water and woods on the cover and is filled with the sweat-drenched dreams that poured out of him during those months. Mine is all phone numbers, lists, and

jabbing, disconnected phrases. "Get to buildings dept. file," I scratched out, and below this, the words, "treasure trove."

By the time I got to this file, as someone—a lawyer? an architect?—had darkly hinted might be the case, certain documents related to goings-on of the last thirty years were missing. I did, however, discover records on No. 239's rear addition. This project had given each floor a small back bedroom, expanding the building's depth from forty-two feet to about fifty-seven feet. It was listed in the Buildings Department computer as ALT-121–75 and dated 1975, which comported with what our co-owners had told us. But when I pulled the original at the municipal archives on Chambers Street, I right away noticed the looping penmanship and black, fluid ink of another age. And there was the date: May *1875*. Surrounded by genealogists at their whirring microfilm spools, I sat there for a long time, studying the permit application. "The present Rear wall to be taken out entirely," it read, "being in a very unsafe condition." So the building had indeed been a wreck, not *five* years ago but 125 years ago. I laughed out loud.

Notwithstanding the advice we were getting from various friends and acquaintances—sue the insurance company, sue the co-op's original sponsor, sue your co-owners, sue the broker who sold you the apartment, sue the engineer who inspected it—the more I learned about the building, the more it seemed impossible to fix blame for our little disaster on anyone in particular, ourselves included. The thing was laid in place by countless acts and omissions and by time itself. I pursued this line of thinking; it was a relief, an escape from my unhappy self-absorption, to learn that many, many others had attached themselves to this very place and been torn loose, after a year or after fifty years, by choice or circumstance, but without exception, and forever. The answers to that question—*what happened here?*—kept coming and coming until it seemed to me that to understand this one place might be the closest I would ever come to understanding the universe.

In the cavernous Beaux Arts public library on 5th Avenue, I hunted after the name on the 1875 permit application: Phillips, John Phillips. Soon I was meeting the family as the census taker found it at No. 239 in 1880. Living in an apartment of less than 1,000 square feet were Levy and Clara Phillips, their daughter, Isabella, eighteen, and son,

Samuel, twenty, and their eldest, twenty-six-year-old Rachel, with her kids, Clara and William, who first appeared to me not as people long dead but as little children near the age of my own. I was fascinated by their pellucid realness, playing there on the stoop between the curlicued iron railings. I saw their mother coming home, carrying packages, bread and sausages and coffee cut with chicory, perspiration between her shoulder blades under the shirtwaist as she climbed the narrow stair in summer. I listened to their earthy, German-inflected English. What, I wondered, did this place mean to them?

But I couldn't seem to find any trace of the John Phillips who'd signed the buildings department papers. Finally—I was thinking about the gum-snapping inspector who'd found my weeping so banal—it struck me: Maybe Levy Phillips had understood something we hadn't. That the buildings department guy is and must remain a stranger. He is not someone to whom you entrust a thing so intimate and authentic as the Jewish name your parents gave you. To him, you are John. I somehow felt that Levy and I, having lived in the same house, were closer than strangers.

So this is a story about that place through time, an attempt—it cannot be more than that—to reconstruct the lost worlds I once so blithely inhabited and to which my own lost world was soon appended. It is a necessarily selective narrative, extrapolated from the spare documents ordinary people leave behind—letters in a few cases, but mostly entries in the census, vital records, directories—and from histories and contemporary memoirs, and from living memory, that of a few former occupants and neighbors of No. 239 as well as my own. I see it as a kind of conversation among a few of us who passed through this place between Avenues C and D, halfway between the lamp-lit elms of Tompkins Square Park and the coursing, salty-smelling estuary of the East River. The talk is about being there.

The patterns that began to draw me in that day in the archives are the ways people mix themselves with a place, bind themselves to it as if to stop time itself. Family, community, property, status, one's past and one's future—these are abstractions we embody in particulars and "put" somewhere. Among the people who have put themselves down

on this piece of ground, who've owned it or lived on it, are a raffish young colonist who loved horse racing and a Puerto Rican mother with her teenage children, a native-born bookbinder turned rent collector and a Hungarian shopkeeper. Strangers. And yet I know *something* about them. I know a place with which they mixed themselves, to which they were, for a time, bound.

There is no person without place, without context. The moment we're born our lungs sift the air or we don't go on. Heidegger called it *Dasein*, the human *being-there*. While we can migrate from place to place, we don't choose to be embedded in place any more than we choose to be born or to hurtle toward death.

Place is a kind of parentage. There is a kinship of place, an alternative genealogy, where instead of sharing the stuff of the body itself, we share the environment each of us, in successive generations, has literally incorporated. The winter sun dropping below the tenement roofs burned down, in a similar pattern, in my eyes and in the eyes of a grocer's daughter, Isadore, who was twelve at the dawn of the Civil War. The stretch of sidewalk from stoop to Avenue C offered the same counterpressure to the legs of a slight man named Simon in 1907 as it did to my daughter's nearly a century later. The feel of the stoop's iron railing was in his hands, now long in the dust, and in his sons' hands.

The most radical incorporation of place is expressed in the word "home." Home, like the body itself, is so critical it disappears from view; it is the place from which we look out. To those of us who made this place home, 7th Street was both a physical and a psychological state; it defined inner and outer, up and down, our orientation toward the city and the world.

All of us impregnated that place with images, dreams, and symbols, and all of us carried something away that went with us wherever we went, a picture of the place, a mental map depicting, at the most basic level, a low place near the eastern shore of a long, narrow island. Over the decades the map took on new elements, while others faded away. Originally it showed a wide-open salt marsh that in the warm months was green and full of good things to eat. Then, for two centuries, this meadow lay in pieces, separate properties divided by ditches, stakes, and imaginary chains. For nearly as long, it has been

the sketch of a highly legible—to use urban planner Kevin Lynch's term[1]—cityscape, a tight grid of paths labeled with numbers and letters, broken to the east by the river and to the west by the open space of Tompkins Square. At first, the neighborhood was at the city's burgeoning northern perimeter—new and uptown; but growth swept past it, making 7th Street old, downtown. The larger district, bounded by cross town thoroughfares to the north (14th Street) and south (Houston Street), was once known as Stuyvesant's swamp, later Kleindeutschland, the East Side, Loisaida, and Alphabet City. Today it's commonly known as the East Village. From the beginning people have read this area as distinct, a topographical zone, and, later, a language and culture island.

It's in the use of a place that people are most attentive to it. Intensively, for centuries, people have used this place near the eastern shore of Manhattan. They have used it to fodder the cattle whose muscle and fat, in turn, fed them. They have traded it for money. By controlling this piece of earth and the improvements on it, they've collected rents and interest on mortgages, taxing the labor of others. They have stored lifetimes of accumulated wealth in the building—equity—and used it in all the usual ways families use wealth, to succor and reward and occasionally to curb and admonish. This place has been a prop in narratives of loss, of gain, and of pitched battle. People have used the building most essentially by living in it; year upon year they have scrubbed the soot of their fires from its walls. In all these ways the building and the land have formed a piece of hundreds of human identities, a small or obscure part in some cases, in others, a defining one.

Each one of us built that environment, and was built by it. Together, as the architects of something perfectly ordinary—our own lives—we became builders of a city so big and various it is beyond knowing. What follows, then, is a creation story of sorts. It is one version of the epic of New York.

Indeed, while people have wrung what value they could from this place, in the end, it isn't so clear whether it's the place or the people who are fuel in the exchange. The latter are consumed in the process. All the city's old buildings are full of ghosts.

By 2010, a modern structure fit to carry new generations through another century had replaced our decrepit old building on 7th Street, all but erasing its memory. And I think what I have been doing these hours in the library is trying to shape a vessel in which to gather, one last time, the dispersed ghosts of that place, not least the ghost of a young mother who carried my name. Some nights I've lain in bed going over the line of title in my head, tapping the syllables together methodically, *Van Corlear, Beekman, Steenwyck, DeLancey, Lewis,* in the steady rhythm of breathing, or walking, as if I could get somewhere, to some beginning maybe, or some finality, down through 7th Street to the place where rock melts, that unspeakable heat at the center of the world.

The Low Green
Prairies of the Sea

O NE AFTERNOON in April 2002, when we'd been out of No. 239 about two months, our fax machine spat out an interesting map. It showed the streets of Manhattan superimposed on the island's original topography, with sinuous waterways draining into the rivers, and hatching where early New Yorkers had extended the shoreline by dumping cartload after cartload of dirt into the East River. A little box marked the approximate location of No. 239. It sat within a marsh, indeed, almost directly astride a former creek.

Richard, the map's sender, was the engineer we'd hired after realizing the extent of the mess we were in—he was expert, eminently practical, also avuncular and wise. Home, he'd later tell us with a shrug, is where you turn the key. The underground stream seemed especially to excite Richard's interest. I could hardly begrudge him that. Nor was the news entirely a surprise to me. Neighbors had often remarked, with that New Yorker's combination of ruefulness and irrational pride, that the whole block was built on a swamp. Still, the swamp had always seemed to me a quaint mythical thing, like the lost island of Atlantis. On the map it swam unpleasantly into focus.

Later I recognized Richard's schematic as an adaptation of a map first published in 1859 by another wise engineer named Egbert Ludovicus Viele and quite famously known as Viele's Water Map. According to the book where I first encountered Viele, *Manhattan in Maps*, city contractors routinely refer to his work to gauge groundwater conditions at proposed worksites. The book even quotes a contractor, Mel Febesh, who testified that, when laying the foundation for the fifty-nine-story Citicorp Center at Lexington and 54th, the crew dug down and there it was—the stream indicated on the old map: "It's accurate within feet."[1]

For Viele, the quest to render Manhattan in its original state was a passion approaching obsession. During the decades he spent surveying and poring over colonial-era maps—he published a final, expanded version of his water map in 1874[2]—he also took every occasion to warn the public that to simply suppress the water coursing through this island city was not an option. "I know that it is generally supposed that when the city is entirely built upon, all that water will disappear," Viele noted tartly in an 1865 report for the city Council of Hygiene and Health, "but such is not the case."[3]

Drainage, drainage, drainage—this was Viele's almost talismanic defense against a truly terrorizing foe, the infectious fevers that stalked city life. The city's perimeter was racing northward during those years, its population growing faster than its public-health infrastructure; cholera, yellow fever, typhus, and smallpox struck with little warning. Viele perceived a relationship among these facts, but as the germ theory of disease was not yet in wide circulation, he blamed the "humid miasmatic state of the atmosphere," which in turn he attributed to building practices that thwarted the flow of waters back to the sea.[4] The neighborhood now called the East Village had sprung up in the 1830s as quickly as any latter-day suburban subdivision on "a very extensive area of low alluvial land, receiving the waters of numerous small streams."[5] But it was only one of Viele's trouble spots. "And while we are erecting our marble palaces of trade," he wrote, "rearing our domestic altars in gilded and frescoed halls, and seeking heaven with the spires of our gothic temples of religion, let us not forget that more than all this splendor surrounded the thrones of the Caesars, and yet Rome fell under the combined influences of a lawless democracy and the malaria of the Pontine marshes."[6]

More than a century later, people still predict a comeuppance from the marshes, but in the terms of modern environmentalism. Models of global climate change suggest that over the coming decades, the seas will rise while storms increase in frequency and ferocity, with obvious implications for the highly developed, low-lying shores of Manhattan and Brooklyn. In 2006, the city Office of Emergency Management sent around a flyer warning New Yorkers to gird themselves against the powerful storm surge that "could put some parts of New York City under more than 30 feet of water." According to the accompanying color-coded map, when faced with a hurricane of even moderate intensity, East Villagers will want to grab a "go bag" (to include photo ID, proof of address, and insurance cards in a waterproof container) and flee at least as far inland as 1st Avenue.[7]

"Mitigation" is what we hope for now. Take, for example, the U.S. Army Corps of Engineers' effort to put back the salt marsh lost to Jamaica Bay, the estuarine lagoon that borders Brooklyn and Queens. This was to offset the environmental effects of dredging New York Harbor, only fifteen to eighteen feet deep in its natural state, to accommodate a new generation of megaships with drafts of forty-six feet.[8] In the summer of 2006, as biologists sang the virtues of the marsh—nursery of a rich estuarine ecosystem! feeding ground of fish and fowl! bulwark against flood and filter for oily stormwater runoff!—workers assumed the posture of penitents and began plunking in, by hand, hundreds of thousands of marsh-grass seedlings specially propagated at a facility in Cape May, New Jersey.[9]

In short, there is a lusty, Roman kind of hubris in the way New Yorkers have transformed the shoreline, and they know it. For generations they have been expecting—getting, to some extent—a smackdown in the form of sinking foundations, pestilence, and flood.

All this is what you have to forget. It's the baggage you must set down to get back to the marsh, not as Viele depicted it, already overlaid by the grid that would be its undoing, but as it once truly was: just a mat of cordgrasses croaking with life, asking nothing, reproaching no one. When first mapped in the colonial era, it covered roughly seventy-five acres on the island's southeastern flank, a gently mounded terrain reaching from a girdle of wooded hills to the shore of the tidal strait we call the East River. In the sunken places near the river and edging the silty, eroding banks of the marsh's tidal creeks the salt-tolerant *Spartina alterniflora* grew in coarse deep-green spikes up to six feet tall. This was the low marsh, inundated twice daily by the tides. Behind this waterside fringe was a high marsh dominated by *Spartina patens*, a shorter grass whose fine, flexible blades swept back and forth with the tides, and, when dry, lay down in tufts like tousled hair. Perhaps there was some low, spiky black grass, of the genus *Juncus*, and the occasional seaside goldenrod or sea lavender with its cone-shaped purple blossoms in late summer. The high marsh was drowned in brackish water only during the high spring tides, but it was always spongy and wet underneath.

In winter, the glossy *alterniflora* died away, exposing the tidal creeks that flowed like black veins through a marsh frosted with snow or "brindled in color like a day that is as dark as evening."[10] The wind rushed unchecked over the land. Spring brought the tinkle of moving water, and the carpet of *patens* would turn a tender green almost electric in the sunshine. The marsh was forever making and remaking itself, the grasses one year catching sediment and throwing up new peat, and the next, swept away by storms or withered by drought. Slowly the soft-banked creeks carved new paths through the grasses.

This marsh that spread out from what is now the busy corner of 7th Street and Avenue C gave life to unnumbered creatures. American black ducks and Canada geese, the darting marsh wren, and the sharp-tailed sparrow might have nested in the thatch. Owls, terns, egrets, and ibis trawled for food where land met water. Mussels and clams and little fish like mummichog and striped killifish would have spent most or all of their short lives in the tidal creeks, while Atlantic silversides, alewife, striped bass, and perhaps menhaden and others swam into the fresher waters to spawn in spring or summer. Fiddler crabs and marsh snails clung to the muddy undersides of the marsh, shredding dead vegetation into the fine detritus the tides would carry out to feed the estuary. Biting greenhead flies, midges, and mosquitoes arose from their larval beginnings in the marsh sod or salty pools to search for a blood meal.[11]

Eventually—no one can say the day or the hour—people stepped into these grasses, their feet bare, or perhaps shod in soft deerskin moccasins. With a story about land and water, the Lenape ("common," "ordinary," or "real" people) explain how they came to be. In the beginning, they say, there was only water. Then a giant mud turtle emerged from the depths. Water ran off its back making dry land. There, a tree grew from which the first man and woman emerged.[12]

Scholars also tell a story of land and water: About 20,000 years ago there was nothing but ice. A vast glacier covered Canada, the upper Midwest, and New England, stretching more than a hundred miles east of New York's present shoreline. As the world warmed, this ice began to melt, unlocking huge volumes of freshwater that deluged beaches, river valleys, and inland depressions, making estuaries, bays, coastal salt marshes, and inland lakes and swamps. By about 4,000 years ago, the basic layout of New York City's six hundred miles of shoreline was in place. It was amid this intricate interplay of water and land that the Munsee-speaking Lenape, over many generations, increased and, treading their footpaths and plying their dugout canoes, developed a way of life that responded to its every bend and turn.[13]

Although evidence of human presence in the region dates back more than 10,000 years, archaeologists guess that the way of life Europeans found among the Lenape in the early seventeenth century had existed for perhaps six centuries—longer than the span of time between the birth in 1625 of the first European girl-child in the Dutch colonial outpost of New Netherland, reportedly a little Walloon named Sarah Rapelje, and today.[14] By the time Europeans arrived, perhaps 20,000 Lenape peopled a homeland stretching from northern Delaware through New Jersey and eastern Pennsylvania and as far north as the lower Hudson River valley. They lived in flexible, largely egalitarian family groups that in turn belonged to one of twenty or so tribes or villages. Individuals inherited from their mothers a phratry membership—turtle, wolf, and turkey are known examples—that linked them to all others so designated through a common mythical ancestor.[15] They believed in a benign creator and in a noxious spirit to be feared and placated. Indeed, to the Lenape, nothing in nature was inert; a spirit animated the deer, the burbling creek, even the stones.[16]

In human affairs the Lenape seem to have valued a kind of personal continence that required unstinting generosity, what appeared to Europeans as stoicism, and respectful comportment toward others. "When the savage has something," a German merchant remarked in 1765, "he divides it in equal parts with his family and friends; even an apple he will cut up in six or more portions if there be so many persons present."[17] This wasn't self-abnegating; the giver could expect to receive his due in return. And giving, not acquiring, was a way for the individual to establish his own worth. Lenape people did not contradict elders, whom they addressed as "grandmother" or "grandfather," and avoided open quarrels with peers. "They say that fighting is only for dogs and beasts," wrote the Moravian missionary John Heckewelder. "They are, however, fond of play, and passing a joke, yet very careful that they do not offend."[18] Children were warmly desired and "very much spoiled," in the words of the Dutchman Nicolaes Van Wassenaer. But infants also were dashed into cold water to "harden" them.[19] After giving birth, Indian women kept going. "They are obliged to cut wood, to travel three or four leagues with the child," the preacher Johannes Megapolensis noted with astonishment in 1644. "In short, they walk, they stand, they work, as if they had not lain in, and we cannot see that they suffer any injury by it."[20] The Lenape were unashamed about sex—"utterly unchaste and shamelessly promiscuous," according to the Dutch lawyer Adriaen Van der Donck—and divorced as it suited either partner. Yet men and women both carried love potions to secure the faithful affections of a partner, and when severely disappointed in love they were known to commit suicide by eating the poisonous root of the mayapple.[21] Indian men did not weep, but native women might vent a wild grief at the grave of a loved one.

The native people of New York were, by such standards as healthy skin, clear eyes, and a fit, upright bearing, a beautiful people. "The natives," wrote Van der Donck, "are generally well set in their limbs, slender round the waist, broad across the shoulders, and have black hair and dark eyes. They are very nimble and active."[22] The Dutch West India Company agent Isaack de Rasieres in 1628 admired native women's "black eyes set off with fine eyebrows."[23] Lenape men wore only a breechcloth in summer, women a wraparound deerskin skirt tied with a sash. In winter they covered themselves with leggings and warm fur cloaks. They painted and tattooed their bodies, rubbing their skin and hair with clarified bear fat for shine and protection against sunburn, chapping winds, and biting insects.[24]

Due to a scantiness of physical evidence, archaeologists are left to debate the extent to which early European accounts reflect how the Lenape of coastal New York lived before contact, or merely chronicle the Indians' response to the European incursion. An area of particular interest—and persistent mystery—is the question of when they began to grow crops and live in permanent settlements. It seems, though, that traditional Lenape villages were more like base camps they used again and again.[25] Their multifamily longhouses or smaller bowl-shaped dwellings of bowed saplings and bark were easily erected. While away from a base camp hunting or fishing, they might sleep under the sky. They generally limited possessions to what they could carry, and they organized their days, at least before they took up trading with Europeans as a mainstay, by a few broad patterns: a sexual division of labor, the round of the seasons, and movement among different kinds of terrain, each with its special function in the Indians' economy. A typical group might stay inland during the cold months, getting nuts and large game like bear and deer in the woods, as well as eating fish or meat they'd smoked the previous summer. This was the time for storytelling around the fire. In the spring and summer the women might plant crops of maize, squash, and beans on some rich alluvial soil or small patch of woods cleared by the slash-and-burn method, while boys and men would venture out to marsh or riverside to hunt birds and other small game and partake of the prodigious spring runs of fish.

And so perhaps lower Manhattan was a place to go when a temperate wind blew up from the south, "our grandmother where it is warm."[26] The east-side marsh would have been green, bursting with water and alive with fish and fowl. The hungry time was over. How the Indians came and where they stopped are suggested by the paths they'd worn into the landscape by the time Europeans settled there. A long artery stretched from the island's northwestern tip to its southern extremity. Just below the present-day 14th Street was what might be called the first crosstown path. It ran from an Indian planting field, *Sapokanikan*, by the shore of the Hudson River at what's now Greenwich Village, east across the north–south trail, and ending at a site known in latter days as Schepmoes.[27]

This site stood roughly at the northwestern edge of the marsh. Reginald Pelham Bolton, an early twentieth-century scholar of local Indian life, put the encampment at about Avenue C between 12th and 13th streets, on a little island of high ground bordering the wetland. Today that block has a ConEdison power plant on one side of Avenue C, and a high-rise public housing project, Campos Plaza, on the other. It's a place I visit frequently, since my children's school is on 12th Street between avenues C and B, and so is the little community garden where the kindergartners have a chance to see what strawberries and beans and sunflowers look like growing from the earth. Scholars differ on the exact location of Schepmoes, and perhaps Bolton went too far in interpreting the name as a native word meaning "the little brook into the river."[28] But he can't have been far wrong in envisioning the spot as bordering a "small fresh-water brooklet which . . . found its way into the East River in the midst of the wide-spreading salt-marshes."[29]

Maybe there was a native boy who delighted in the view from the little rise, in the verdant sweep of marsh he associated with the taste of fresh roasted alewife and the quiet company of brothers and uncles. Maybe he carried these things with him into the long nights of winter. If so, he didn't write it down. His way of incorporating the marsh was to move through it, revisit it, eat and drink from it, watch and know it, perhaps to dream of it or weave it into stories, but not to stay on it, or give it the name that was his alone and would die with him,[30] or make a fence around it, or build a permanent structure on it, or record his exclusive personal rights to it in a deed he could bequeath or sell down a line reaching, theoretically at least, to the end of time. It just wasn't how the natives thought. They undoubtedly understood themselves to have long-established rights to their homeland, but these were communal rights of use that did not necessarily exclude others. "My friend, it seems you lay claim to the grass my horses have eaten, because you had enclosed it with a fence," one Lenape Indian traveling in 1777 chided Heckewelder, the missionary, who had intended to mow his meadow for fodder. "Now tell me, who caused the grass to grow? Can *you* make the grass grow?"[31]

An old Lenape story describes the coming of the Dutchmen. In it the white people ask for land the size of a bull's hide. Then they cut the hide into a long cord and draw it around an unexpectedly large section of land. The newcomers bargain for more land—only enough to place a chair, they say. But the chair seat is made of cording, which they unwind, again encircling a substantial territory.[32]

The story evokes the surveyor's art, that method for measuring distances and angles—and for drawing boundaries—that must at first have seemed an inscrutable madness to the Lenape, but which had been in use among Europeans since at least Roman times and which, very early in the Dutch tenure, they applied to the marsh, slicing it into several shares. To read a colonial-era surveyor's description of the marsh parcel on which No. 239 was eventually built is to envision that cord being slipped for the first time around the drenched *Spartinas*, "beginning at the northeast corner of Minthorn's upland and running from thence south forty-six degrees east one chain and sixty-four links along the ditch; then south twenty-one degrees west two chains and forty links"—it goes on and on like this, seeming to double back on itself like a snowshoe hare—"then north seventy-eight degrees west twenty-three chains over the meadow to a Stake; then south thirty-three degrees west fifty links to the place of beginning."[33]

The Lenape could not have anticipated the momentum of this method, nor how the cord's grasp on the land would both expand and tighten, this particular piece of meadow eventually parceled out to the width of a thumb, the still-undeveloped plot from the site of No. 239 to the corner of Avenue C sold, in the mid-nineteenth century, "along with all and singular tenements, heritaments, appurtenances thereunto belonging or in any wise appertaining, reversions, remainders, rents, issues, profits thereof, estate, right, title, interest, dower and right of dower, property, possession, claim and demand whatsoever in law as in equity for the buyer's, his heirs' and assigns' proper use, benefit and behalf forever."[34] "Besides," the traveling Indian had argued with an aggrieved Heckewelder, "if you will but consider, you will find that my horses did not eat *all* your grass."[35]

The year 1625 was a turning point for the marsh, though the changes it set in motion were not immediate. That was the year engineer Crijn Fredericksz, in the employ of the Dutch West India Company, arrived on Manhattan's scalloped shore and got to work surveying off a town site and fort at the island's southern tip, along with the company's numbered farms spreading north along the Bowery Lane. In June, a small group of settlers, traveling cheek by jowl with the barnyard animals of every nursery rhyme, sailed into the harbor on ships called the *Horse*, the *Sheep*, and the *Cow*.

These offered a fitting contrast with the Lenape clan classifications turtle, turkey, and wolf. While the Indians found all their animal protein in nature (before contact with Europeans the dog was their only domesticate), the Dutch and the English who followed them had a tradition of animal husbandry reaching back thousands of years. When the new colonists saw the marsh spreading out along the tidal strait, they immediately thought of feeding livestock. "The country is in many places hilly," wrote Van der Donck, "with some high mountains, and very fine flats and mowing lands, together with large meadows, salt and fresh, all making very fine hay land."[36] The great advantage of *Spartina patens*—salt hay—was that it grew without cultivation. It required no laborious clearing of land but could be mown in late summer and stored, sustaining over the winter months animals that might otherwise have to be slaughtered in the fall. Even if the West India Company directors were interested primarily in trading New World furs—the silken, water-resistant beaver in particular—domesticated beasts, as sources of meat, milk, butter, cheese, leather, manure to fertilize crops, and power for all kinds of work and transportation, were the sine qua non of the settlers' daily economy.

The sturdy little cows that would here and there dot the New Netherland landscape would serve as a sign, symbolically and in fact, of European-style prosperity. Farmers leasing company lands were to pay in guilders and butter; the company owned the animals, but any increase the lessees could keep. When assessing the towns on Long Island in 1650, Van der Donck deemed Vlissengen (Flushing) "tolerably rich in cattle" but judged the little English settlement of Hempstead as "superior to the rest, for it is very rich in cattle."[37] Thirty years later, the minister of south Brooklyn communities at Flatbush and Amersfoort would offend the piety of Dutch traveler Jasper Danckaerts by gossiping with local farmers "without speaking a word about God or spiritual matters. It was all about houses, and cattle, and swine, and grain."[38]

Virtually at the outset of this colonial project, the marsh had its role to play. Dutch authorities surveyed it off in several horizontal strips each containing about ten acres and a little river frontage for easy transport by water, and designated each of these marsh parcels to provide salt hay for a particular company farm on Manhattan. The exception was a wedge that bordered the river near the present 9th Street, at a distinctive notch in the shoreline where two creeks let out. The future site of No. 239 lay just within this wedge; its lower perimeter was the stream that Richard had identified on Viele's map. This piece was given to a plantation that lay along the East River about a mile to the south. Sometime during the 1630s—in circumstances that must remain murky, since no patent survives—the plantation had come into the hands of a young Dutchman named Jacob Van Corlear. After hundreds, maybe thousands of years during which people ventured into or near our slash of meadow, one man called it his own.[39]

Van Corlear was only twenty-three when he voyaged across a frigid sea to the far-flung commercial outpost of New Amsterdam,* stepping off the warship *de Soutberg* (Salt Mountain) in the early spring of 1633. Slated to take up the job of commissary at a Dutch West India Company fort and trading post on the Connecticut River, during his long journey from the Netherlands Van Corlear had a companion in twenty-seven-year-old Wouter Van Twiller, who was to be installed as the fifth director-general of the colony.[40] Apparently friends and perhaps relatives, these two came from the same village, Nijkerk in northern Gelderland, and may indeed have spent many hours together there, learning the catechism and creed of an austere Reformation Christianity, studying

---

*This was the capital of New Netherland, on the tip of Manhattan.

reading and arithmetic, music, and manners in the local school, and walking and shooting in the wastes of the Veluwe (literally "bad-lands").[41] Soon, Jacob Van Corlear's eighteen-year-old cousin, Arendt Van Corlear, joined them in New Netherland, going up the Hudson to work for another cousin, Kiliaen Van Rensselaer, and eventually run-ning the older man's powerful Hudson Valley colony-within-a-colony, Rensselaerswyck. An uncle to the new director-general Van Twiller, Van Rensselaer was a prosperous jewelry merchant and major investor in the West India Company. It was Van Rensselaer who, without ever stepping foot in New Netherland, dominated the transatlantic network that in the custom of the time joined kinship with business and carried both advantage and obligation.

If Jacob Van Corlear sometimes went by the Dutch term of nobil-ity *Jonkheer*, this certainly did not imply lordship of a manorial estate. He'd gone to work for the company "in the trade of peltries" at around the age of sixteen, perhaps leaving his home in the Dutch countryside for the corporate offices and warehouses of Amsterdam. According to one source, his father, Joachim, had died without means.[42]

It must have seemed to the young Van Corlear that his people had been planted in the Gelderse Valley since time began (the name ap-pears in property records as early as 1313), their rootstock joined through generations of intermarriage with the Van Twillers and Van Rensselaers, whose family trees shared that sandy soil. A stained-glass window bearing all three names and coats of arms—Van Corlear, Van Twiller, Van Rensselaer—went up in the thirteenth-century church at Nijkerk in 1656, even as the three families' young representatives made their way in America.[43]

And so our land's first owner was the product of an old world—"Fatherland," they called it—whose image and insistent demands pur-sued him in the new. Among Van Corlear's first assigned tasks as the man in charge at Fort Good Hope (present-day Hartford, Connecti-cut) was to saber-rattle and remonstrate in vain against the British for sailing past the fledgling fort to plant a settlement on the Connecticut River, and, soon after, to hang several Indians accused of murdering a party of traders stopping in to do business there.[44] In the commotion of this new life, Van Corlear did not neglect to send ten of the precious beaver skins across the ocean to be placed as a gift in the hands of his grandfather, Goosen Van Corlear, onetime administrator and sheriff of Nijkerk.[45]

When I think of this first owner, I see him walking out of some oily Rembrandt into a rough, abundant, unfenced country, and can't help envying the sheer physicality of the encounter, how he must have felt this place in his sinew, going about by foot (Manhattan could be considered "about seven hours' distance in length" and "not a full hour broad," according to the Dutch traveler Danckaerts),[46] clopping along on horseback, and taking to water in small boats. Soon he would have known New Netherland's paths, forests, marshes, rivers, and bays; he would have known the rollers off Coney Island. He would have understood the area's ebb and flood tides and prevailing winds and become familiar with the sounds, "sweet and full of meaning," as one European called them, of the Lenape's Algonquian language (though its "difficult aspirates and many guttural letters" may have frustrated any attempt on his own part to master more than a crude pidgin).[47] Hunting was reportedly a favorite pastime. Van Corlear is said to have boasted of killing 170 blackbirds at a single shot.[48] "Good-tasted, and similar to the thrushes in Fatherland," blackbirds, along with snipe and geese, may well have drawn Van Corlear and his friend Van Twiller—who for his part became "so taken with the country" that it would be "hard for him to stay away"—into the east-side marsh with their fowl pieces.[49]

How natural for Van Corlear to experience, during these explorations, the ancient impulse of his people to annex to his personal estate some choice piece of what he saw. And by 1635, he found himself in an excellent position to do that—serving on Van Twiller's council at a time when it was granting land.[50]

The *Jonkheer* acquired three tracts of low, flat land along the shore, each accessible by water to the others and to the market of New Amsterdam. Van Corlear purchased from the natives a tract on the south shore of Long Island around the settlement named New Amersfoort (later Flatlands) after a town in Gelderland. In present-day Harlem along the East River around 108th Street, he acquired two hundred acres dubbed Otter-spoor (which means "otter-track," also a town in the Dutch province of Utrecht). Finally, Van Corlear obtained the lower Manhattan plantation of about seventy-six acres spread around a point that presses into the East River where it turns north between today's Manhattan and Williamsburg bridges. This point was a splendid landing place and lookout. Just below it was a rocky shoal that reached way out into the strait; there, it was narrow enough you could call across the water and be heard on the Brooklyn shore. The Indians had liked it, too; one of the trails they'd worn into the land led to this very place, called in their language *Nechtanc*, or "sandy point."

It was this lower Manhattan property—including the point known today as Corlear's Hook—that would carry the young Dutchman's name across the centuries and, for two hundred years, would come with the slash of marshland that lay outside its bounds, about a mile to the north.

Attuned to Viele's cautionary note about the unwholesomeness of wet-land, I was surprised to find colonial-era real-estate listings featuring such amenities as "a large quantity of salt marsh" or "a very good salt meadow." More than once Dutch settlers actually took to the courts to righteously dispute rights to the cordgrasses in our little marsh by the East River. In one case, the last Dutch governor himself, Petrus Stuyvesant, accused of appropriating a neighbor's meadow, argued that there had been an agreement whereby the neighbor was privileged to cut salt hay from Stuyvesant's sliver in exchange for an equal quantity of fresh hay from the neighbor's property.[51] It would appear that before salt marsh was bad, for a very long time, it was good.

In the way they first divided and used the land, the newcomers were creating an image of Manhattan after the images of their European home; they were laying the map of their old world over the land of the Lenape. For just as the Indians assigned different economic functions to different kinds of terrain, so had the Dutch and English for many centuries divided their environments into house sites, arable acreage for growing crops, commons in which to turn out animals to feed, and wastes in wood or marsh that might provide timber or turfs for fuel, or hay for fodder. Their way of life required access to all these types of land, the way modern life depends on the constellation of dwelling, workplace, shopping place, and transportation.

For centuries, the maps of Europe had reflected this necessity. As far back as Roman times, along the coasts of the Netherlands to the north of where the Van Corlears later settled, homesteaders built in the salt marshes themselves, raising their houses up on *terpen*, or mounds, to keep them from the tides. Their fields spread out from the *terp* like petals, with hay fields farther out in the marsh. In the great river valleys of the Rhine, Maas, and Waal to the south of Gelderland, houses were sited on natural levees, with low streamside meadows providing pasturage in summer and hay in winter for the cattle that were the center of the local economy. And in Gelderland itself, which would send so many young to America, beginning in the Middle Ages you had gridlike little villages girdled by an open *brink*, or green, beyond which lay the villagers' *enken*, large communal plots in which all were assigned strips in different areas so that each got a fair share of the richest soil. Each village sent its animals to pasture in lands it controlled, whether in the sandy hills of the Veluwe or in streamside meadows. Some communities enjoyed communal use, later ownership, of a prized oak forest; east of Putten, a village just up the road from Nijkerk, even up to the late nineteenth century the *Putterbosch* was divided into fifty-three shares, six of which were considered to belong to the forest itself.[52]

The English, neighbors to the Dutch across the North Sea as well as in New Netherland (they would take over the colony in 1664 and rename it New York), sailed from a countryside similarly studded with linear agricultural villages. Cottages pressed together along a main street punctuated at one end by a church and split around a village green. Beyond the village were the open fields in which villagers had their respective strips to till. Also close by were moist, streamside meadows—"ings," in the local parlance, or "saltings" in the case of tidal marshes—where they set their cattle to nibble the grasses, and which they mowed for hay. Farther out still were rough sheep walks and rabbit warrens, forested or marshy wastes where natives were permitted to gather what they may—turf, reeds, small game, mushrooms, timber. In the swampy English Fenland facing the Netherlands across the sea, parishes typically took on an elongated rectangular shape as villages perched on the silt banks reclaimed more salt marsh beyond their sea walls for pasturage, and, on the inland side, more boggy fen, a portion of which was reserved as meadow until each year's hay harvest.[53]

In all these communities, grass, today a kind of vestigial pleasure or merely ornamental status symbol, lay at the very center of human concern. Ordinary people made fine distinctions among different kinds of grass. In the English county of Kent, for example, five classifications of grassland, each with its own value for the purpose of ecclesiastical tithes, survived into the mid-nineteenth century: pasture, down-land, meadow, marsh, and saltings.[54] For a community to grow in population or expand its commerce in such products as cheese, butter, meat, or wool, it needed more animals, and to support more hungry herbivores it needed to control more grass. Both the local landscape and the balance of power were forever altered when townspeople decided to divvy up commons for private use or landlords enclosed large areas previously available to all—a process that had been under way in parts of Europe for many decades by the time the Nijkerkers sailed to America.

Grass. In America, this need for great swaths of verdure would also be the context for territorial expansion. The township of Brookhaven, for example, began in 1655 when a small group of farmers settled on the north shore of eastern Long Island beside a pretty creek in what's now Setauket. They pastured their beasts on a peninsula just west of town, remembered today in place names for the peninsula's West Meadow Beach and village of Old Field. By 1664 the need for more grazing land motivated the purchase of territory to the east, as well as a huge chunk stretching to the south shore and encompassing a string of necks, creeks, and marsh islands. This valuable tract the townspeople almost immediately cut up into shares.[55]

On western Long Island, the settlement of Hempstead that Van der Donck praised as so "rich in cattle" was inaugurated in 1643 when Puritans from Connecticut bartered with local Indians for a massive, vaguely defined piece of land that reached from the town just below the center of the island to the marsh islands of the south shore.

Shortly thereafter the town obtained a Dutch patent that extended its claims to the grassy necks of the north shore as well. So Hempstead-ers depastured their animals on the vast Hempstead Plains to the east and west of the town (memorialized in the place name East Meadow) but also fenced off peninsulas to the north (Cow Neck) and south-west (Rockaway) for this purpose. The marshes to the southeast of town they reserved for haying. To prevent greedy cutting, the town council decreed that no one could mow before September 1 and that each farmer might harvest only as much hay as he could remove in a single day. This set the stage for a boisterous communal event, with mowers staking out their positions days in advance. On the eve of cut-ting day, they'd sleep on the mist-shrouded marsh, sharpened scythes at the ready.[56]

All this made the land unusable to the Indians who had lived there, and they complained bitterly for years. In May 1660, seventeen years after Hempstead's founding, the Indian sachem Takapousha told the provincial council that Hempsteaders had fenced his people's plant-ing lands and threatened to burn their dwellings if they didn't leave within eight days. For their part, the order-loving Hempsteaders were exasperated with the natives' roving, predating dogs, and by their seem-ing refusal to recognize the finality of their land deal, however disad-vantageous it may have been. With both sides summoned before the New Netherland council, the Indians argued that they had not in-tended to sell the land at all, "but only the grass upon it." (The coun-cil told the Indians they might reap a final harvest, on the condition that they fence their gardens and kill their dogs.)[57]

These kinds of arguments were common during the decades when Indian and European ways of life actively overlapped. The natives' ex-ploitation of their territory required ready access to their planting fields and hunting grounds, fishing camps and nut forests; it depended on free movement among these various types of land according to the sea-son and fluctuations in natural supply. The Europeans' way of using different terrains was, on the other hand, to assemble them in a land-holding and control access to them—to put up fences. This difference was pervasive. When neighbors didn't get along, the Lenape were more likely to fission the group, while the Europeans were apt to divvy up

the land. The Lenape's small, slender-nosed dogs wandered freely between camp and woods. Europeans, meanwhile, expended a great deal
of energy accounting for their prized food animals (and preventing
them from trampling or eating crops). The European past was fixed
and stored in written documents, whereas even the stories of the
Lenape were a physical enactment, with the laying out in sequence of
pebbles, sticks, and other small objects both prompting and illustrating
the tale.[58]

Before his thirtieth birthday, Jacob Van Corlear had assembled and
cordoned off a fine collection of lands he never could have possessed
in Europe but that boasted the components of European-style mixed
farming: hundreds of acres of flat, arable ground (some of it previously
burn-cleared by the Lenape) for growing wheat, rye, barley, oats, or
the New World crops maize or tobacco; access by water to the town
and marketplace of New Amsterdam; and plenty of fodder for cattle.

But the map would not be complete until the land had been transformed in a particular way. Van Twiller, at least, took pains to import
not just the animals but also the people who might help him to repro-
duce the landscapes of his childhood. To cultivate his bowery number
one, which took up a good portion of what became the East Village, he
brought over people from home, including one from Putten itself, ex-
pressly contracting them to plant, plow, and mow the new land in the
Gelderse manner.[59] In a 1635 letter to Amsterdam, he likewise asked
for soldiers from around the River Ijsell that flows through Gelderland,
"as they understand farming and know how to use the land."[60]

Slowly the Europeans wore their ways into the marsh at the center
of our tale. First they dug ditches or dredged and straightened existing
creeks to establish property lines, facilitate navigation on the creeks,
and encourage the growth of valuable high-marsh *Spartina patens*—a
drainage system that, given the natural changeability of the marsh,
would have required continuing maintenance. Then, generation after
generation, mowers took to the marsh in late summer or early autumn
and "swept, scythe on scythe, their swaths along/The low green prairies
of the sea,"[61] in the words of the New England poet John Greenleaf
Whittier. They would cut the hard grass into windrows. Let it dry a little in the sun. Rake it into cocks. Then they'd load it onto a cart or into

a flat-bottomed meadow scow—*wey schuyt*, in Dutch[62]—and carry it along the creek that marked the southern perimeter of Van Corlear's meadow parcel, to the notch where it let out into the East River, and south along the shore of Manhattan to Corlear's Hook. There the salt hay would be stored for winter feed in a hay barrack, or *hooiberg*, which looked a little like a four-poster bed with a thatched roof. The very symbol of the Dutch farm, several of these *berghen* appear on one of the earliest maps of Manhattan, drawn in 1639 by Dutch cartographer Johannes Vingboons.[63]

Over the years, wherever they came from, the men whose backs accomplished all this heavy, fly-bitten work were not the same men who owned the wedge of marsh. They may have been farmers leasing rights to the salt hay for their own animals, or perhaps laborers hired by Van Corlear and subsequent owners of the plantation on the hook. Van Corlear hired as a superintendent Thomas Hall, an Englishman who had escaped his indenture on the Delaware River and become a freeman in New Netherland.[64] When Van Corlear leased out his Otterspoor property in 1638, he engaged an "active boy" to help the lessee's hired plowman.[65]

Until the nineteenth century the Dutch and English also used enslaved black people for just this type of agricultural work. The initial ditching likely fell to the company's slaves, who also cleared the land for the original farms and built their cattle barns, widened Indian trails, and put up wharves, mills, and fortifications.[66] For more than seventy years, beginning in 1668, Cornelis Steenwyck and his heirs owned the plantation and its marsh portion as part of a 260-acre Lower East Side land investment. This man, along with a partner, was the first New Netherlander to trade privately in African slaves, fitting up the *Witte Paert* in 1654 to fetch three hundred souls directly to the colony "in consideration of promotion of population and agriculture."[67] Some went to work building the famous defensive wall against the Indians that became Wall Street; other slaves, no doubt, could eventually be found plowing and mowing Steenwyck's own ground, swinging the scythe in the salt grasses that would become 7th Street. Perhaps they were among the thousands who went to their rest in the colonial-era African Burial Ground just north of present-day City Hall

Park. Remains unearthed there in 1991 during construction of a new office building bespeak an African homeland; some had distinctively filed teeth or wore beads traded at the time in Africa. The bones themselves, some with thickened muscle attachments or lesions indicating stress, reveal how in the New World they worked, as an anthropologist who studied the remains has put it, "at the very margins of human endurance and capacity."[68]

This was another way the newcomers differed from the Lenape: While the Indians were, in the words of one historian, "frugal with their own labor,"[69] Europeans believed deeply in "improving" the land, a job requiring enormous investments of human muscle. What made this possible were the institutions that allowed individuals to buy or compel the labor of others.

Today, my family and I live just a block from the East River where it sweeps around Corlear's Hook, the point between the Williamsburg and Manhattan bridges that still presses toward Brooklyn as it did when the people knew it by two syllables ending with swallowed mutes, that skipped stone of a word, *Nechtanc*. Here, between buildings, you can glimpse river in two directions, and there are cooling breezes not enjoyed elsewhere on the island. This is the place we moved to when finally we freed ourselves from No. 239. The territory between hook and marsh, marsh and hook, is one I've covered by several accustomed routes, walking, running, by bus, in the car, with bags, pushing a stroller, on a scooter, a child by the hand, in the morning and evening and all kinds of weather. This is my world. But it is of course just as intimately the world of countless others who walk their accustomed routes according to their own inner maps. All of us walk over the abandoned maps of generations past.

Historian John Kuo Wei (Jack) Tchen has observed that the story of how we live together has never been written. He was referring to New York's early "port culture," the everyday integration of the streets, something more rough-and-tumble than cosmopolitanism. But even today the intricacy of how we use this place together is as impressive as anything in nature, belying the stories we tell about a single class or ethnic group.[70]

How the earliest personal maps overlapped may have been mysterious even to those who observed the scene firsthand. Yes, Jacob Van
Corlear became the sole possessor of the plantation and hook and its
sliver of marsh in the 1630s, perhaps by some barter with local natives.
But what are we to make of the black man Anthony Fernando, his un-
named wife, and their children, who also lived on this land during Van
Corlear's proprietorship? We find in records of eviction proceedings
against this family that Van Corlear had verbally promised Fernando he
could "use and occupy" the spot—probably a modest portion of the
plantation—for his lifetime, in exchange for eight schepels (several
hefty sacks) of corn a year. In Fernando's next appearance in court—
the year is 1654—he produces written testimony from Van Corlear
himself that "the land was given to [Fernando's] children on payment
of the stated rent."[71] Another source puts Fernando on footing decid-
edly less firm, saying the place was promised to him "if no complaints
against him should be made by the neighbors."[72]

Whatever the nature of Van Corlear's relationship with Fernando,
their agreement did not stop the Dutchman from selling the plantation to William Beekman for a substantial sum in 1651. It was Beekman who lodged a complaint against the Fernando family, a complaint
that, along with Fernando's answers in court, give the impression of
people fiercely staking a claim to the land that was keeping them alive.
Fernando's wife had secreted corn, in sacks, from the premises. The
Fernandos had beaten trespassing hogs. Who knows what they suffered when, in October 1654, they were excused three years' back rent
but dispossessed, relinquishing to Beekman "all outbuildings, dwelling
house, fences, trees, timber, etc."

For many years, the map laid down by the Europeans failed to entirely occlude the old trails and stopping spots of the Lenape. Not permitted to stay overnight inside the fort at the island's tip, natives
passing through New Amsterdam camped by the sandy eastside point
they remembered as *Nechtanc*.[73] It was still very much an Indian place.
Was this by some understanding with the Dutch proprietor? Not clear.
But it was here that, one snowy February night in 1643, the overlap-
ping maps spiraled into incoherence and genocidal rage. A party of
Lenape, running from an attack by Mahicans to the north, had taken

refuge near the guns of the Europeans. After two revenge killings by Indians and assorted other confrontations, it was a time of heightened tension between the Dutch and native groups of the lower Hudson; Van Twiller's successor as director-general, William Kieft, took his opportunity to *"wipe the mouths* of the savages." Around midnight, Dutch soldiers attacked Indians encamped across the Hudson at the site of present-day Jersey City, while local burgomasters massacred the forty or so men, women, and children staying at *Nechtanc*. In the morning the snow was stained with their blood. The ensuing years saw the Lenape of the lower Hudson join together in unprecedented unity to resist and punish the Dutch: "They burned all the houses, farms, barns, grain, haystacks, and destroyed everything they could get hold of," wrote David Pietersz de Vries. "So there was an open destructive war begun."[74]

Now normally a lonesome place, on the Fourth of July this hook fills with people. They set up barbecues and boom boxes in Corlears Hook Park, the children waving pink and acid-green glow sticks in the darkness, and stream across the overpass to be near the water. The people carry within their Caribbean islands and burgeoning Chinese cities, their European towns emptied of Jews, and so does my little family, we four extracts of Germany, Ireland, and Russia via the American heartland, we Presbyterian, Catholic, Jewish, bring our lost tongues and lapsed faiths. The dead are with us, too. There is a carnival air, but also a feeling of restraint, of careful civility willfully but harmlessly violated by the occasional adolescent profanity. When the bursts of colored fire go up through the white lights of the bridges and of the subway cars pulling over them as if in slow motion, we all make the same utterance. *Aaaaah*. The story of how we live together has not been written.

The first owner, Van Corlear, left New York. He sailed away in 1669, on the *Duke of York*, at the age of sixty, not to return. As much as he had invested in New Netherland over most of his adult life—more than thirty years, a youthful marriage to Adreana and, after she died, to Lysbet, daughter of an Amsterdam basketmaker, in 1652, stints as a Manhattan schoolteacher and a Brooklyn magistrate, so many seasons of sowing and reaping—in the end it seems it was not his home.[75] He no doubt carried its image back to the old church where the light shone through colored glass bearing his name and that of Van Twiller and Van Rensselaer. Maybe he wanted to end his years in the bosom of his family. But he left behind a world bearing his imprint. He had founded a line of title, transferred the hook and its little sliver of marsh from one way of life to another, fundamentally different one. He had given it his Nijkerker name, so that it was almost as if a little piece of the *Jonkheer* himself were handed down through the generations, already thrice sold by the time of the American Revolution, also mortgaged, leased, enlarged, twice inherited.

And the moment when the soft moccasin of a Lenape stepped into the marsh for the last time? No one can say the day or the hour. By 1700 this "original people," as they thought of themselves, had been dramatically depopulated by repeated epidemics of European-borne diseases to which they lacked immunity. The ranks of the whites, meanwhile, had swelled from a few hundred to some 10,000. With as much as 40 percent of their ancestral land sold to Europeans, a few Lenape clung to unclaimed lots of Brooklyn, Staten Island, and the Bronx, but most were already forming the first grief-stricken and impoverished diaspora from the place called New York, the estuarine environment that had brought them into being.[76] They carried the memory of their homeland west across Pennsylvania, where they lived for a time among friends and in Moravian missions. Then north to Ontario, or farther west to Ohio, where war and broken promises propelled the Lenape to Indiana, then Missouri, Kansas, and finally, after the Civil War, to Indian Territory, later known as the state of Oklahoma. Today, some descendants of the Lenape people of coastal New York, known as Munsees, can be found in Ontario, Canada (at Six Nations, Moraviantown, and Muncy Town),[77] while their brethren of the Delaware River valley have a community in Oklahoma.

It was in Pennsylvania and Ohio that various contingents of the Lenape joined together under the name Delaware, learned the pitiless brutality of frontier warfare, and made a protracted, furious effort to beat back the swelling tide of "salty people" (as the Lenape had once called whites), whose desire for land seemed unquenchable. My own ancestors, the Scotch-Irish McClures, were typical of these pioneers in Indian country. They launched themselves from Ulster to make landfall in 1715 at the mouth of the Delaware and soon took up a fine, spring-fed acreage in eastern Pennsylvania known as Willow Grove.[78]

The land, who would use it, and how: This was the crux of it. When the American war for independence broke out in 1775, the main body of the Delaware had been settled in eastern Ohio for scarcely a generation. They continued their hunting and planting, but also lived in neat log-cabin villages where they raised cattle, chickens, and hogs.[79] After the colonial army failed repeatedly to protect or supply their hungry families, the Delaware threw in their lot with the redcoats, launching more raids against frontier settlements; the colonists retaliated by attacking their remaining villages along the Susquehanna and Allegheny rivers in Pennsylvania, later burning their Ohio towns, including the Delaware capital of Cochocton. In the wake of the Revolution, the Delaware joined a pan-tribal confederacy in a military campaign against the American settlers who with their cattle, horses, and sheep were now threatening to overrun the Ohio Country. This confederacy trounced two U.S. armies, finally going down to defeat in the 1794 Battle of Fallen Timbers in northern Ohio, which signaled an end to Indian claims on Ohio and the great westward-flowing Ohio River.

Those who chose pacifism did not always fare better. In 1782, a group of Christian Delaware was massacred by Pennsylvania militiamen while staging a temporary return to harvest their corn at Gnadenhütten ("Tents of Grace"), Ohio—the same Moravian village where the Indian traveler had asked his missionary host, "Can *you* make the grass grow?" After a night of singing and praying, nearly a hundred men, women, and children knelt and were executed, according to two survivors, with cooper's mallets.[80]

That very summer, back in New York, a certain Connecticut Loyalist by the name of Stephen Jarvis was working at the Royal Magazine at Corlear's Hook, dispensing fresh hay, oats, and salt hay—mostly salt hay—to the British and Hessian soldiers who occupied the city. In an earth-brown ledger flayed with use and mottled with bits of red wax, the twenty-six-year-old recorded in his spidery hand that he had issued forage to the King's Brewery and the King's Hospital, to an Admiral Digby and a General Bischhausen.[81]

The man who now claimed ownership of Corlear's Hook, and of the marsh that no doubt supplied salt hay dispensed from its Royal Magazine, could be found across the great waters, as natives sometimes called the Atlantic, awaiting the outcome of the war. A well-born, third-generation New Yorker, he, too, had had little choice but to take sides. He, too, was beginning to understand that he held his sweeping Manhattan property—this land that seemed to offer the truest, proudest reflection of himself—at the pleasure of the state.

That summer of 1782, the east-side marsh, our low green prairie of the sea, gave up its *Spartinas* for the horses of the city's occupiers, as it had fed the beasts of its European cultivators for 150 years, as before that, for hundreds and maybe thousands of years, it had fed the fish and the oysters, the ducks and the turtles that in turn nourished a dark-eyed native people. But it wouldn't be a marsh much longer. Its summers were running out.

Going and Staying

Tucked into one of my manila files I discover the twice-folded piece of printer paper on which, soon after our confused evacuation from No. 239, I wrote a list of instructions to myself.

Katharine's plan for emotional survival
1. *Take a deep breath.*
2. *Don't compare yourself to others. Their situation, whether "better" or "worse," does not pertain to yours.*
3. *Learn from the past but look to the future.*
4. *Remember: Nothing but death itself can deprive you of your family.*
5. *Remember: Nothing but death itself can prevent you from writing poems.*
6. *Try to act wisely + with full knowledge, but don't blame yourself or others for circumstances beyond your control.*
7. *Don't give up on your own happiness.*

The childlike quality of this note, its suggestion of a clutching at life's handrail, is much enhanced by its having been carefully printed out in purple Magic Marker. David recently confessed to me that around the time I was writing this note, he was having thoughts about taking his iron letter opener across town to meet with the developer who rehabbed No. 239 in the mid-1980s; it occurred to David that stabbing this person on the sidewalk might be the right thing to do as a father and husband. Of course it all seems disproportionate now, but there it is. We were unstrung.

The psychologist Stevan Hobfoll captures something essential about the truly scary life event in his Conservation of Resources theory, which says quite simply that people everywhere try their whole lives to build, retain, and protect what they value. They constantly use and re-plenish these resources, which consist of objects (the house, the car, the inherited watch), personal characteristics (your competence at work, your courage, your sense of fun), conditions (your happy family, your secure future), and enabling energies (money, time). You must invest resources to protect resources. Gain begets gain, and loss can accelerate into a spiral. Stress happens, according to this way of reck-oning, when resources are lost, threatened, or, despite the requisite investment, fail to accrue.[1]

A spatial metaphor pervades this idea of stress. Psychologists refer to a "resource reservoir" in which all good things, once gotten, are stashed and conserved. For me, No. 239 had become an embodied re-source reservoir. Its loss involved trouble of a financial, legal, emo-tional, and physical nature. I wasn't sick or dying or losing my family or my work, just caught up in a loss spiral that made it necessary for me to remind myself of that, itself a way of shoring up resources. We had come to No. 239 with the idea that we'd stay there, make and keep a family, invest, build, and through that investment weave ourselves into a particular place in the social world; that building had contained the very arc of our lives.

Was our predicament "better" or "worse" than that of others? In the big picture, it was pretty much the same. In staying and stowing so much in a single, fixed place, we were enacting a way of being in the world that goes back 12,000 years to the Neolithic Revolution that began in the Near East and, like a spore drifting on the wind, carried the first iterations of house, garden, lane, neighbor, and village.[2] In finding a promising spot and carefully marking it off as ours, we were renewing the prehistoric impulse that is the nucleus of that achingly meaningful word "home."

For all but a sliver of the human past, everyone everywhere was a hunter-gatherer, ranging over a territory of a couple hundred square miles or more to find food on the hoof and the branch.[3] What spurred foragers in the Near East, central China, Mesoamerica, and a few other locations to, at different times between about 12,000 and 4,000 years ago, independently "invent" food production has been a subject of fascination and debate for generations.[4] Perhaps environmental crisis or population pressure encouraged human groups to coax more food from every acre and stay put to claim their harvest. Or maybe it had more to do with some psychological shift internal to the cultures in question.[5] Some think it happened incrementally and more or less by accident.

Whatever the case, the transformation of humankind into settled agriculturalists unfolded over millennia, the components of this new way of life—plant cultivation and animal husbandry, year-round home sites, architecture, storage—often failing to arrive in lockstep or even in uniform sequence. Much depended on the local environments that provided raw material for both subsistence and culture. The Lenape of coastal New York, for example, were not mobile hunter-gatherers in any strict sense. Even before contact with Europeans, some stayed in their settlements long enough to require deep storage and trash pits.[6] And they knew how to cultivate maize. If they didn't make it a staple, it was perhaps not only because it was more difficult to increase yields of this New World crop than of the wheat and barley that grew wild in the so-called Fertile Crescent, but also because the Lenape didn't *need* to intensify food production.[7] Theirs was a world of relative amplitude supplied by woods and marsh, river and sea. For the Lenape, the critical environmental crisis came with the European incursion itself.

One of the first known villages anywhere was settled beside a spring on the West Bank of the Jordan River in a place called Jericho. The settlers were a typical band of the sedentary foragers known as Natufians, and the year was roughly 10,000 BC. By around 8500 BC, the Natufians' descendants had created a food-producing Neolithic village of rounded dwellings built of mud bricks that curved up at the ends. It was these "hog-back-brick people"[8] who, some 10,000 years ago, joined together to construct something astonishing and numinous at Jericho: a stone wall ringing the settlement, thick as a man is tall at the base, and higher than two men, along with a stout, round stone tower whose interior stairs gave access to its turret. Was it a defensive wall erected against raiders? Was it intended, as some archaeologists have argued, to keep out floodwaters?

It was a barrier, that much is clear, an emphatic communal statement about inner and outer and the need to control the boundary between. The wall says this was no loosely affiliated social grouping that might disperse for a season or move on to exploit some other part of the land. In the reconstructed prehistoric language whose speakers populated much of Eurasia and the Indian subcontinent thousands of years ago, there is a root word meaning "door."[9] This prehistoric door can be traced through the Latin for "toward out of doors" to the modern word "foreign," and through the Latin for "being out of doors" to the word "forfeit."[10] Beyond the wall is the stranger, and to join him on the outside is to give up belonging within. The wall—any wall—fixes and makes graphic *us* and *ours*.

But in Jericho as in Manhattan, the layers of the mound testify to its occupation and reoccupation by different peoples. At Jericho, albeit after more than a thousand years, the hogbacked-brick people yielded to the plastered-floor people. Their rooms were not round but rectangular, the interiors painted with a fine, hard lime plaster tinted red or cream and burnished until it glowed.[11] Home.

"How confusing and endless a large city seems to the new-comer, how cold and unfriendly!" the Russian-born radical Emma Goldman wrote of the day she arrived in New York, in the heat of August 1889. Her aunt and uncle, who lived on the Bowery, had made it clear they weren't pleased to see her, so she went door to door on the Lower East Side in search of a young acquaintance by the name of Solotaroff. Astoundingly, she found him. Solotaroff took Goldman to Sachs's, a café on Suffolk Street where Russian Jewish radicals and poets talked and nursed cups of hot, sweet tea late into the night. This was to be Goldman's world. But that night, it presented the exhausted seventeen-year-old with a hard, glittering surface. "I was almost overcome," she writes, "by this strange human medley."[12]

Goldman came to New York a foreigner, a young girl alone, possessing only $5 cash, a small handbag, and the sewing machine with which she intended to earn her keep. David and I were, by comparison, privileged Americans. We had spent our childhoods in and around Washington, D.C., and had met and fallen in love as college kids at Princeton. We were in our mid-twenties and newly married when we decided to shuck our jobs as reporters at a small-town daily in eastern Washington state and move back east. Even so, we were greenhorns. In at least one respect we were more typical of the class than Goldman. Like most of the people who passed through the environs of No. 239, we simply vanished into the "there" of the city.

We moved to New York on a raw spring day. The Holland Tunnel disgorged our tiny red Volkswagen into Canal Street's rush-hour melee with its McDonald's sign in Chinese, stalls piled with purses and watches, the darting of pedestrians and bicycles and long layings-on of the horn. My lips were chapped, and I licked them, and spoke brightly—too brightly—to David. As the sky dimmed, the city lights seemed to come up in a swarm.

My brother, Cameron, and his girlfriend (now wife), Lalou, lived on the Lower East Side—Goldman's Suffolk Street, as it happens—and were the first link in our particular chain migration. They were not at home. So we drove around for a while, then stopped for a beer at a hip, glass-sheathed watering hole called Spring Street Natural. This was early 1993. Young office workers were mingling at the bar. Like the newly arrived Russian or Italian peasant in her heavy skirts and homespun shawl, I became acutely aware of my rural Northwest getup: a multicolor, shoulder-padded cardigan in the pattern of a jigsaw puzzle over stirrup pants tucked into ankle-high, Gore-Tex-lined boots. The beer cost $6, another sign that the ramparts of this town would not be easily scaled.

Nor were we prepared for the ordeal of finding a place to live. Our erstwhile small-town home, a ground-floor apartment on a lot bordering the algae-rich Moses Lake in Washington state, had had its drawbacks, maybe chief among these that we shared it with a bold family of rats. But it was spacious, and at $300 a month was something you happened into casually. New York was another story.

Being freshly jobless did not enhance our profile as prospective tenants, a fact we understood, while stubbornly harboring—I did, anyway—

the fantasy that someone would see how nice we were and cut us a break. At one open house, a garden apartment in a graciously proportioned row house on the north side of Tompkins Square Park, the owner asked me what I did for a living. "I . . . I want to be a writer," I stammered, as if the woman were trying to plumb my soul. Lalou, worldly and protective at twenty-three, stepped forward, setting her blue swing coat with huge cloth-covered buttons slightly awhirl in her haste to impart more relevant information: "They've got $80,000 in an investment account!" This was David's inheritance from his grandmother, an embarrassment of riches that in fact had emboldened us to venture this cross-country move. We didn't get the apartment.

David and I both had formed our idea of a dwelling in pretty houses—freestanding buildings with sides and backs as well as fronts, paned windows, and lawns that sprouted daffodils in spring, dandelions in summer. Now we were touring spaces that spoke to us of the air-raid shelter, the monk's cell, the rabbit warren—or simply of the unknown, a life that had never been ours. It was enervating even to think of inhabiting all those places. At night David and I entrusted ourselves to a sour jug wine called Old Montecito and a futon on Cameron and Lalou's floor. Mornings they made *café con leche* with the good, strong, cheap Cuban coffee you can get in any bodega in New York. And the days turned into weeks.

Not long after the hogbacked-brick people ceded or perhaps abandoned Jericho, the settled farming way of life cropped up on the Konya Plain of what is now south-central Turkey, in a Neolithic town called Çatalhöyük. In the distinctive plan of this settlement, there were no streets. Houses were pressed together in honeycomb fashion amid piles of accumulated rubbish. To get home, you clambered across the tops of the neighbors' houses and entered through a hole in the roof, which led to a ladder against the south-facing wall. This wall held a clay oven. Nearby was an open hearth, and beneath the floor, a cache of obsidian, the black glass that spewed from nearby volcanoes and formed the basis of a lively trade across Anatolia and the Near East. This south side of the main room was the "dirty" living area, for making beads, working obsidian into implements, cooking, and extracting

grease from animal carcasses. The north side was defined by slightly elevated, white-plastered platforms. These were kept scrupulously clean
and may have been sleeping areas. Here, too, was a preponderance of
the artistic and symbolic work of Çatalhöyük—extraordinary wall
paintings of red ochre depicting headless bodies set upon by vultures
and wild cattle chased by huntsmen, as well as the horned bulls' skulls
that, by the time Çatalhöyük was settled around 7400 BC, had been
an important symbol of the Neolithic Near East for many centuries. It
was beneath these raised floors that the dead were laid to rest, the
body of one woman curled into a fetal position around the plastered,
painted skull of an older man.[13]

The people of Çatalhöyük had created a material enclosure that
both reflected and perpetuated their way of life, profoundly conditioning the existence of any person who would come into being within
its walls. "A child growing up in such a household would soon learn
how the space was organized—where to bury the dead and where to
make beads, where to find the obsidian cache and where to place offerings," writes Ian Hodder, the British archaeologist who has headed
excavations at Çatalhöyük since 1993. "Eventually, he or she would
learn how to rebuild the house itself. Thus the rules of society were
transferred not through some centralized control, but through the daily
practices of the household."[14]

Most houses, after about eighty years of occupation, were disman-
tled to their foundations and rebuilt in place.[15] But dwellings containing
heavy concentrations of burials tended to be re-created across more generations and with greater fidelity to the original. Hodder has posited that
inhabitants of these "ancestral houses" gained social power by forging
historical memory, linking their genealogies with rights and resources
centered in the house.[16] So, long before anyone wrote a syllable, it seems
people learned to "place" themselves by reference to a dense grid of man-
made stuff. Here, myth begins to cede to the fine reticulations of historical time, a different version of the truth in which people and places
can be objectified, particularized, literally brought indoors and kept track
of through time. The townspeople of Çatalhöyük polished pieces of their
precious obsidian to a reflective shine: the earliest known mirrors. Here
was a way to examine one's own strange and singular face.[17]

These images make me think of a moment with my son, Byron, on the verge of turning seven. I was napping on a Saturday afternoon and awoke to find him very close, gazing at my face with the most anguished expression. I asked him what the matter was, and, in a hedging way that made me understand he wasn't being entirely candid, he put his hands to his cheeks and said he felt he looked different, that he was getting older. I supposed he had been studying the lines in *my* face and been too kind to say so. But then it occurred to me that perhaps he was getting to a more complex truth: My changing face was a map of his lost babyhood, and held an omen about the impermanence of childhood, too. The fixed and settled home can be like that—an instruction, a mirror, a map, like your own mother's face—telling you more than seasons or stars ever could about who you are, where you fit in, and what comes next.

East 7th Street begins at the historic edifice of Cooper Union, runs east along the southern perimeter of Tompkins Square Park, and dips slightly as it nears the river, coming to rest in a sweet, tree-lined block of old row houses and tenements. The first time David and I came to this easternmost block of 7th Street, I had the sensation of dropping into place. It was markedly different from the surrounding blocks, as if we'd gone through an invisible portal into another world. The trees were thick enough to give a sheltered feeling to the sidewalk and street, and there were little runs of Greek revival row houses—houses like the ones we drew in kindergarten—in a neighborhood given over mostly to five- and six-story tenements. A few lots on the block remained unbuilt, instead planted with fruit trees or a jumble of flowerpots and old cars.

The far East Village was like that in those days, casual and blowsy, with that half-abandoned feeling left over, I suppose, from the '70s, when the neighborhood was so drastically devalued that cars (and buildings) were regularly torched. In the early 1990s it had the improvised, various, and colorful air of a place where for many years poor people had hammered together a life outside the bland attentions of officialdom. Chickens pecked in the yards, and there were little *casitas* where people listened to salsa music and drank beer of an evening. If

you wanted proximity to the subway or clean-finished walls with a reasonable number of functioning electrical outlets—if you insisted on
"amenities" as such—you went elsewhere.

David and I had an appointment with a drummer friend of my
brother's, who was also the super at No. 258, a redbrick three-story
row house on the south side of the street. This building was not the
kind on which you'd bestow the honorific "in original condition"—it
was just old, with a sagging wooden stair, the parquet floors broken
and dirty. Glass-paned pocket doors separating the front room from
the rear of the apartment had been sprayed with canned frost to allow
for privacy among roommates. I don't think Mark, the drummer, vetted
us in any way—the second floor was ours if we wanted it, and we did.
Our chain migration had a brand-new link.

The first thing David and I did on that block was scrub away, with
the tiniest frisson of foreboding, the evidence of former inhabitants.
Young Italians, they'd gone in some kind of hurry, leaving behind not
only a lot of top-shelf liquor, the bottles furred with grease and dust
and set out on a table littered with butts stubbed out in bottle caps, but
also some film-editing equipment and, in a drawer, an inescapably bad
film script. On the fridge was a clipped cartoon of a hapless-looking
fellow above the caption, "Waiting for an idea." We cleaned, received
the truckload of our stuff from out west, and bought a few mismatched
lamps on the Bowery. Every day I'd sit at the huge square wooden desk
the Italians had left and work on story ideas and pitch letters.

In October came the evening that stands out in my memory: David
and I had eaten well and were making our way east, arm in arm, along
St. Marks Place. Walking in the crowd on the lighted street was like
being held up in warm, moving water. We looked up and noticed the
moon—a full moon, as the *Farmers' Almanac* later confirmed, a blue,
harvest moon. We made that little drop into place and were home. It
seemed to me that blue moons were what one could expect here, an inexhaustible excitement like a parasol opening and opening. And we
had a safe place from which to watch it all unfold.

We began to publish in magazines and get various kinds of itinerant
editorial work. Within a year or so the work was steady, though never re-
munerative enough to amount to more than a slim living. David received

another influx of family money, this one substantially larger than the first, and began to rack up gains in a riotously booming stock market. This made it possible for us to purchase, in 1996, "a piece of the rock," as David used to say: a majority share in a co-op across the street, No. 239 East 7th Street Inc. We bought the middle and top floors from two separate owners, investing the requisite amount—that is, somewhat more than we could afford, nearly $400,000.

From the Konya Plain, the Neolithic spore drifted westward across Europe. About 5,000 years ago, it touched down on an island in the North Atlantic, in the tiny village of Skara Brae. The prehistoric stone dwellings of this Orkney farming and fishing people are so well preserved as to be almost ludicrously familiar. Looking into these rooms, you'd have no trouble identifying where things go. In the center of the floor is an open rectangular hearth—a container for the keeping and sustaining of that primordial energy source, fire. There are clay-sealed vats to hold life-giving water, as well as drains to draw away wastewater or perhaps human waste. Food goes in upright storage bins; for tools, dishes, and such, niches are cut into the walls and a stone "dresser" made of two slab shelves sits on stone feet. And there are places, at Skara Brae, for people to put themselves: a stone bench by the fire, and against the walls, box beds defined by three stone slabs set on their edges and likely made soft and warm, those millennia ago, with bracken and skins.[18]

This is the "resource reservoir" that when emptied causes such distress. It represents storage in the broadest sense, an interruption of process, a pushing- and fixing-together of things that might otherwise flow or fall apart—things like fire, like water. Like families. The earliest villages typically consisted of round huts large enough to shelter only one or two individuals, with communal food-storage bins. This settlement type eventually gave way to structures like those built by the plastered-floor people at Jericho, with rectangular rooms big enough for a small family and storage within or next to each dwelling. The nuclear family was now the basic economic unit.[19]

The settled home is and always has been both a keeper of dead ancestors and a receptacle for the to-be-born. A hunter-gatherer mother carried her infant over many miles in her daily treks; her physical exertions, coupled with the prolonged and frequent nursing of the infant at her hip, tended to suppress ovulation, producing birth intervals of several years. (Lenape women apparently supplemented this natural birth control with abstinence from sex while breastfeeding.)[20] When populations settled down, a baby boom invariably followed. Indeed, the corpulent, heavy-breasted figurines found in Neolithic sites have often been interpreted as evidence for the celebration and even deification of this womanly fertility. Others have described the effect of settled life on actual women in less appealing terms. "Woman the forager adjusted to the more sedentary routine of woman the grinder," writes the anthropologist Sarah Hrdy. "Multiple dependents became the 'facts on the ground' that mothers had to adjust to and eventually even adapt to."[21]

A potent association between home and mother as the nested laps into which many children are gathered also became a fact on the ground. During the nineteenth and early twentieth centuries, the married women of 7th Street were invariably listed in the census as "keeping house," a term that might conceal a good deal of paid labors (and certainly implies a variety of unpaid ones), but that suggests a container as coolly impassive as a butter dish, a "keeper" of house and home. When I lived there a century later, my days, typically split between hours spent working in our apartment and ventures around town with the children, qualified me (if imperfectly) as a "stay-at-home mom," a locution that neatly links up the ideas of stasis, house, and mother.

As for the dead, the burial of human remains under house floors at Çatalhöyük was in no way an exotic practice during the Neolithic period. At Jericho, the plastered-floor people stashed headless skeletons under the floors. The skulls they carefully filled in with clay and sculpted with plaster, sometimes with shells at the eyes, giving each such "a strongly marked individual character" that archaeologists have been tempted to describe them as portraits.[22] The skulls of Neolithic dead have sometimes been discovered in poses that seem to suggest an emotional tie—the head-cradling woman at Çatalhöyük, for example, or another pair of skulls, one of a woman in her twenties, the other a boy perhaps twelve years old, found touching at the forehead.[23] The bodies' placement under house floors of course also linked them closely with those who ate, worked, and slept only inches above them. This connection, like the connections among the living members of the household, would have been both emotional and, as the literal foundation for ownership claims, economic. The presence of dead forebears was a potent reminder that living residents belonged to this place—and that the place belonged to them.[24]

So home stored the most material of things—food, fire, water, babies, the bones of the dead—and highly abstract things—memory, expectation, rights, economic value. Beneath all these is time. To keep grain against future hunger and seed for planting in another season is to harness time to human advantage. To link the newly born with the very old bridges time. And ownership secures with past use the right to future use, fixing the status quo against the erosions of time. If the hunter-gatherer discovers the seasons and their places in concert with movement—a fish run in spring, a sheltered place in winter—the homesteader seems to want time to converge on the place where he, too, stands still.

Our building was three and a half stories over a basement, six lots from Avenue C on the north side of 7th Street. Painted a creamy white, it was devoid of external ornament save an ornate iron stoop railing that ended in two spirals and, over the front door, a green plastic awning more suggestive of a suburban dental suite than a nineteenth-century townhouse. Inside the second and third stories, two steps divided the back and front of the apartment into separate levels. With its raised floor, our third-story living area was low ceilinged to a degree that might have been oppressive were it not flooded with southern light. At the north end of this space, an open staircase of blond wood led up to a small aluminum-sided sunroom that gave onto a wooden deck. The bones of No. 239 presented an odd, fun-house collage of an aesthetic, with a whiff, I thought, of the '70s beach house.

Anyway, I was uncurious about the building's provenance. I remember the engineer we hired to inspect the building saying it was in remarkably good shape *considering how old it is*. Just how old I didn't ask. I remember how, after walking through the place with a broker, I stood on the roof deck in the sunshine idly prodding a waterlogged blue tarp with my foot. This time I did ask: Why the tarp? But I can't recall the answer. All I could think of then was settling in, getting paint up and the cups put away. Our new home was the usual set of empty rooms painted white, full of loss and promise. Willfully, perhaps, I sensed only promise. I was focused on the baby drumming in my belly. Our first pregnancy had, at eleven weeks, "gone south," as David put it (a phrase he would later apply to the building, and to things in general).

This daughter, though, Lucy, we'd keep. Once she was sure on her feet, I'd take her walking around the neighborhood. *Que linda, God bless huh*, neighbors would say as we passed along the dark, rain-slicked ribbon of Avenue C, a benediction on the little girl in the purple raincoat with flowers for pockets, a plastic barrette pinning a wisp of hair from her serious face. We stopped for everything. The chickens. The woman bent over her work beyond the half-open door of the stained-glass shop. Or the ramp that led to the spinning machines and white light of the Laundromat at C and 8th. *A child soon learns how the space is organized—where to bury the dead and where to make beads, where to find the obsidian cache and where to place offerings.*

Lucy was nearly three when she and I planted daffodil bulbs in the yard next door. *When the yellow trumpets appear*, I told her, *that's when your brother or sister will be born*—just as, the winter I was four, my own mother had promised that when the daffodils bloomed my father would come home from his months-long work trip, an echo of her own father's homecoming from a Europe at war to Iowa, his pretty, formidable wife, and their child of corn-silk hair. When Lucy was born, my parents had come up on the train from Washington; what they'd thought to bring was a fistful of sweet, vegetal daffodils from the yard. So when I planted bulbs, I was putting us down there. Without thinking much about it I was planting a simple but flexible symbol that encompassed ancestral memories, return of the beloved, and a song sung across the generations, a wordless petition that our home should be a garden, that our daughter and our son might flourish here. *Eventually, the child will learn how to rebuild this place.*

People matter more than things. That's what we tell the kids, and they have learned to throw it back at us when we least expect it. The trouble is, it's not always so easy to tell the difference. Somehow, a long time ago, brick and mortar, wattle and daub, stone—this *stuff*—became suffused with life. In the inferred prehistoric language that gave rise to all the Indo-European tongues, the word for "house" implied the structure, but also the people inside. The word for an extended family or social unit of settlement was the same word used to indicate the cluster of buildings they inhabited.[25] This, of course, is precisely how censuses traditionally count up people—by *household*, individuals held together by sets of walls like so many utensils in a drawer. It's a handy unit of measurement because walls help tell us what people are to each other economically (breadwinner, dependent, boarder); by extension they also describe emotional ties (wife, son, mother-in-law). To "live together"— that is, to store ourselves in the same box, put ourselves to bed under a single roof—is one of the deepest expressions of human connection.

Somewhere in the rooms of prehistory the notion was hatched that to remain in place, to abide at a particular location, is a prerequisite to being fully human. Indeed the proto-Indo-European root "to dwell" leads to various derivatives meaning simply "to be."[26] I dwell therefore I am. And the *dwelling* becomes a representation of this being. This perspective sees the self not as process and movement—something that, after the fashion of some Native Americans, might in due course take on a different name—but as a fixed thing with an inside and an outside, a soul or mind sealed in the container of the body. It's a conception of self, one Buddhist psychotherapist observes, that focuses attention on the spatial experience of hunger—the need to fill, refill, and defend the grain bin, as it were—as opposed to the temporal experience of breathing. One of the most striking features of Skara Brae is the heavy stone doors each family could shut against its few neighbors, and how the hearth and bench were oriented to this door.[27]

Now, of course, the revolution is nearly complete. All the earth except frozen Antarctica is parceled out to nation-state proprietors; hunting and gathering peoples in isolated pockets around the world are often seen not as practicing an alternative contemporary lifestyle, but as deeply anachronistic, their claim on land through habitual use and movement long since plowed under by the ownership society of settled farmers.

In this world, to find oneself homeless—without defensible claim to some specific place—is to be radically alienated from the environment. The temporariness of the refugee's UN-issued shelter is not that of the hunter's campsite or the seasonal fishing village. It signals not a freedom to move about in an intimately familiar landscape ("I am too heavy to rise at this present time!" the Lenape would say when too much property burdened these movements),[28] but a paralyzing separation from place, one that locks a person away from life and seems to suspend him in a time out of time. Here in New York, it's okay to sit on a park bench but not to sleep there. A homeless person is permitted to read books in the library, but let him use the toilet and people wrinkle their noses in disgust. His bodily functions thus proscribed, it's as though his very existence were banned. Lacking access to a place of his own means he cannot control access to his own person. There is no street he can walk down to find his reflection standing silently among the other edifices. No wonder he slumps there, a scarcely human figure. There is no place in this world for him to *be*.

And yet none of us has relinquished the possibility of migration, a feature of human existence since some of our kind first made their way out of Africa. On the contrary, it has been argued that it's agriculture-based societies with their bumper crops of offspring that are more apt to be restless, to quit ancestral lands in search of new territory, sometimes crossing oceans, like the "salty" folk who first colonized New York, a people whose own origin myth recalls an expulsion from the garden where you could live forever.[29] New York City itself is indeed an elaborate and sublime expression of staying, but also of going, a massive heaping up of material culture in the ultimate container on the one hand, and on the other, a threshold to the country and an unending process, its population and wealth dependent to this very hour on immigration and trade from afar.[30]

Populations across history, families over their generations, individuals in the course of a lifespan—all enact this oscillation between settlement and migration. Beginning in the 1700s, my McClure ancestors remained in Pennsylvania's Monongahela Valley for some six generations, acquiring and defending, investing and building, sowing and reaping, then tore themselves loose, my own father carrying his anguished, infuriated grandmother bodily from the premises of the old farm in the year 1958. Emerging from our settled childhoods, David and I moved from Washington, D.C., to Princeton, New Jersey, to Chicago, to Moses Lake, Washington, in a quick series of migrations that seemed perfectly natural to that time of life, until the same deep current told us it was time to go and stay, bearing us to the place we would learn to recognize as home.

You might almost say we heirs of the Neolithic have two modes. In the first mode, we bind ourselves to a single place and become almost one with it. In the second, we range over the earth sampling its variety or seeking new opportunity. If space is the wide-openness across which we travel, then place, writes the geographer Yi-Fu Tuan, "is pause; each pause in movement makes it possible for location to be transformed into place."[31] Seventh Street was one such pause, a stopping place whose very shape and meaning derive from the journeying of those who dwelled there. Embedded in its identity are the circumstances that propelled the native Lenape out across the American frontier, and those that drew a certain Hungarian Jewish couple named Simon and Gizella Wieder from their ancient town at the edge of the Carpathian Mountains. In staying and going there is a corresponding vastness, one deep, the other broad. When we are putting down roots, we still can consider or dream of movement, of breaching distant shores; when roaming, we carry an image or an idea of home. And so each of us contains these immensities always, in an inner space that, like the city, touches infinity.

The Landed

IN THE YEAR 1732, in an upstairs room of the stout brick house built by her father-in-law, Anne Heathcote DeLancey gave birth to her first child, a son. James DeLancey Jr. came into the world a hundred paces from the salted waters around Manhattan's tip, and no one seemed better poised than he to reap the harvest of this prosperous little town at the edge of the British Empire.

That house still keeps quiet vigil over the corner of Pearl and Broad streets, nearly hidden among the towers of the modern financial district. It is a house of memory. Manhattan's oldest surviving dwelling, it plays host to flocks of schoolchildren who stand behind a rope to peer at the strange clay pipes and tricornered hats, the punch bowls and foot warmers placed to give the appearance that our colonial forebears might at any moment return for a draught of that era's fiery Madeira. But the house is not remembered for James DeLancey Jr., nor for the milk-white, ample-bosomed heiress who bore him. The lock of hair kept in a glass case conjures a noble old head; it is not that of James DeLancey's grandfather, the swashbuckling Frenchman who built this house.

It was for love of another man that New Yorkers spared No. 54 Pearl Street[1] and, at the turn of the twentieth century, carefully restored it. Then as now, they revered its very timbers for having held up the father of our nation, George Washington, in his hour of utmost triumph and pathos. In this house (it had long since been converted to a tavern), New York's governor feted General Washington and his officers on the November day in 1783 when, after a long, destructive occupation of the city, the redcoats at last took to their boats and left the new republic to its future. The toast went up, "May the remembrance of this day be a lesson to princes!"[2] About a week later, in a room said to have been the drawing room of James's grandmother,[3] Washington gathered his officers for a final good-bye. Men wept, overcome with the emotion of events they knew had bound them together, and changed them—changed the world.

The same crisis that displaced James DeLancey Jr. from American memory banished him forever from the place of his birth. The Revolution parted him from family and friends, from the society that had acknowledged his "rank," and, not least, from the source of his sumptuous living, the lower Manhattan estate that covered a mile of East River shoreline and of which our separate patch of salt meadow formed a part—a small part, to be sure, but one always carefully accounted for. And who, without these things, *was* James DeLancey Jr.? In severing the umbilicus that tethered him to this home, the Revolution parted him from himself.

The DeLanceys began their sojourn in America as "capitalistic adventurers" in search of booty,[4] thrusting, restless, loosed upon the world like the Lenape's "salty people." The family's founder on the continent, builder of the brick house on Pearl Street, was James DeLancey Jr.'s paternal grandfather, Etienne DeLancey. A Huguenot who escaped his native France in 1685 when Louis XIV outlawed Protestantism there, Etienne DeLancey became a British subject, changed his name to Stephen, and settled in New York. He quickly became a major player in the shipping that brought skins and other commodities from the colony's hinterland to the port and sent them out over the ocean to England and the Netherlands, while fetching sugar and cotton from the Caribbean and clothing and other dry goods from Europe. His enormous success depended upon energetic adaptation to changing market conditions and a certain lack of moral fastidiousness. Stephen DeLancey supplied American pirates haunting the distant African island of Madagascar, where pipes of Madeira bought for £19 could be sold at £300,[5] and on at least one occasion he helped receive pirated goods (ivory, opium) in America.[6] He smuggled goods around British ports of call to avoid paying duties[7] and was known to carry slaves.[8] Later, as the Crown beat back French claims to America in the French and Indian War, the DeLanceys won plum contracts to provision the military.[9]

The DeLanceys were socially entrepreneurial as well, making friends in high places among the English despite their foreign background. James's father, James DeLancey Sr., had chosen as his tutor at Cambridge one Dr. Thomas Herring, who remained a friend and later became Archbishop of Canterbury, head of the Church of England.[10] And the year before James was born, his aunt Susannah had accomplished perhaps the family's most impressive social coup in wedding Peter Warren, later Admiral Sir Peter Warren, whose capture of various French and Spanish vessels during the colonial wars of the 1740s (and the policy that allowed him to profit from the sale of their loot) brought cachet to the DeLancey name and treasure into DeLancey hands.

But early on, American land—the harvest that comes with staying put, investing, securing the earth underfoot—was also an important source of family wealth. Strategic marriages once again furthered the cause. (As James's aunt Elizabeth once quipped in a letter to his aunt Anne, "Love and a Cottage is your Maxim, [but] *give me indifference & a Coach & six*, When Poverty comes in at the door love flies out at the window.")[11] Through his marriage, Stephen the patriarch had linked DeLanceys to Schuylers and Van Cortlandts, old Dutch–New York families that controlled vast acreages north of the city. And the younger James's mother, Anne, was the eldest daughter of the merchant Caleb Heathcote, first Lord of Scarsdale Manor, a self-service nobility in which you bought land from the Indians and other locals, got the imprimatur of the king, and began to settle the hands—free, indentured, and slave—who eventually would fill your barns with produce.[12]

So young Jemmy, firstborn son of the eldest surviving son of one of New York's most prominent families, found many "connections and relations" among the city's 11,000 or so inhabitants. He probably knew every house and store from Dock Street on the east side to Broadway on the west. And he, in turn, would have been widely recognized as the son of the chief justice, for these were the years of his father's early ascent to political stardom.

James the elder was appointed chief justice, a position he would hold for life, the year after his first child's birth; when the son was fifteen, the father attained the top colonial office of lieutenant governor (though he wouldn't serve for a few more years because of a dispute with the governor). In a youthful portrait, James Sr. wears a long, curled wig and lace tie, his right hand resting inside an unbuttoned waistcoat. His large almond eyes gaze at a careful angle from under long, arching brows. While his colleague and brother-in-law John Watts credited the chief justice with "uncommon abilities, in every view, from the law to Agriculture,"[13] a contemporary of a less friendly political stripe, William Smith Jr., suggested De-Lancey was too glib to be a substantial leader: "Confined to the narrow sphere of a small colony," wrote Smith, he "was satisfied with the pre-eminence of his parts, and hence sacrificed to pleasure and power."[14] The elder DeLancey was intelligent but not intellectual; he was a confident, active man of large appetites (despite the family motto, *certum voto pete finem*, "Set a definite limit to your desire"). Even Smith conceded his social talents. DeLancey, he wrote, "was all his days addicted to company and knew mankind well from the highest to the lowest orders."[15] What we know about Jemmy's mother, Anne, meanwhile, is that she filled the stately DeLancey apartments with children—first James, then Stephen in 1734, followed by Heathcote, Susannah, Maria, Anne, Martha, and finally, in 1753, John Peter.[16]

Not long after James Jr. was born, the family moved from Pearl Street to the mansion his grandfather had built farther west on lower Broadway.[17] This house, with its encircling balconies, passed to the chief justice on Stephen DeLancey's death in 1741, when Jemmy was nine.[18] It had a large ballroom for the formal dinner parties and dances that defined the social calendar, and with the Hudson on one side and elegant, tree-lined Broadway on the other, was excellently situated for visiting and promenading. Around the time of Stephen's death, James also purchased for himself a country seat, the estate in the "Out ward"

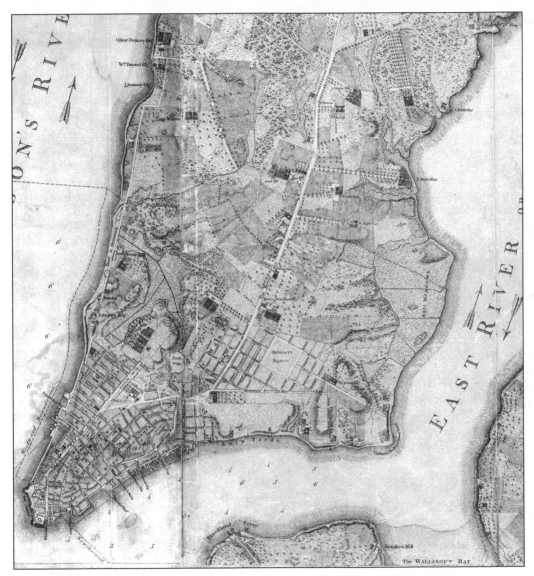

"Plan of the City of New York in North America: Surveyed in the Years 1766 & 1767."
This detail of the map, by military engineer Bernard Ratzer, depicts Manhattan before
the Revolution. James DeLancey's estate stretches from his mansion on the Bowery Lane,
south across his neatly arranged blocks to Division Street, and includes Corlear's Hook.
Farther north, in the east-side salt meadows, DeLancey's sixteen-acre portion can be
found within the wedge with the word "meadows" across it. This piece of property, first
surveyed off early in the Dutch era, includes the future site of No. 239. (Courtesy of the
Lionel Pincus and Princess Firyal Map Division, New York Public Library, Astor, Lenox,
and Tilden Foundations.)

that would be most closely associated with the family name in years to come. This was an irregularly shaped holding of some three hundred acres stretching from the East River to the Bowery Lane. (The gray, multi-lane Delancey Street plows east to west through this acreage today.) Its mansion house, fronting on Bowery Lane, was about a twenty-minute carriage ride from the town at the island's tip. Still, farther north along the East River lay the sixteen-acre strip of salt meadow first measured off by the Dutch; it came with the farm property, the only piece lying outside its bounds.

James and Anne Heathcote DeLancey kept, in their houses, beautifully made and carefully maintained objects of silver and mahogany, silk and porcelain. Every hinge and lock and drawer pull received timely attention.[19] For transportation to their relations in Westchester, across the ferries to Long Island, and from townhouse to country seat, there would have been an assortment of conveyances—the coach, the chaise, the snow-worthy sleigh. And tucked away at night in the townhouse attic or perhaps above the kitchen at Bowery Lane were the enslaved people who cooked, drove, cleaned, worked the fields, cared for the animals, and very likely fed and bathed the De-Lancey babies.

Slave names come barreling down the centuries with precisely the weight they were not intended to carry. Tom. Jupiter. Othello. The first two, valued together at just over £117, came as part of James Sr.'s inheritance.[20] Othello was the chief justice's personal manservant, his shadow, if you will, and the memory of how he died indeed must have stayed with the DeLanceys. Pompey, a slave in the Westchester household of James's brother, Peter, accused Othello of conspiring in a putative plot by blacks and poor whites to burn down the little island city and kill prominent whites; Othello was said to have pledged his assistance in murdering the chief justice and his family. At work on a political matter in Rhode Island with Othello in tow, DeLancey Sr. had his slave shackled and sent home to face justice. To what extent the "negro plot" of 1741 was the product of a terrified, guilty white imagination was not illuminated by the trials that ensued. In hope of obtaining mercy, Othello, one of the "head negroes in town," confessed, according to a judge in the case, "with an air of sincerity which very much affected, for from the intimacy I had the honor of with his master, I had frequent opportunities of seeing this negro at his house." Nevertheless, Othello was hanged just beyond the city gates in a gruesome public spectacle in which the accused ringleaders had been gibbeted, their bodies left to bloat and split in the summer heat.[21]

James DeLancey Jr. was not permitted to linger long in this "small colony," but in his early teens was shipped to Eton and, later, Corpus Christi, Cambridge, where his father had been known as "the handsome American." Here, amid Gothic spires, the ruddy-cheeked young James partook of a "liberal" education, a term that hearkened to its Latin meaning, "free." This was not the apprenticeship by which ordinary boys were put to a trade, but the general education befitting an English gentleman—hour upon hour of Greek and Latin, oratory, ancient history. Classical tales of heroism in war were a strong wind that filled young hearts like bright white sails with patriotism for the British Empire. Students learned cricket, fencing, music, and dancing, all necessary for manly refinement.[22] And no doubt various youthful rehearsals also reinforced in James the elaborate pecking order of the British upper crust.

Then there was English law to master—James studied at the ancient and venerable Lincoln's Inn, London—and, finally, the art of warfare. In 1757 James DeLancey was commissioned a captain in the Royal American Regiment and called to arms against the French in his native America. He was an aide to General James Abercrombie in the summer of 1758, when Mr. Nambycrombie, as his soldiers derisively dubbed him, led a disastrous frontal attack on Fort Carillon, well garrisoned and perched on the spit of land between Lake George and Lake Champlain in today's upstate New York; here, James DeLancey Jr. beheld the butchery of 1,600 compatriots. But the next year brought victory in the capture of Fort Niagara. James himself had the honor of relaying the news to colonial officials in a breathless blow-by-blow featuring "their Indians"—an alliance that, one may recall, included the Delaware or Lenape—and "our Indians."[23]

The army was marching east toward another fight when shocking news reached the column: The chief justice was dead. James's youngest sister had found their father gasping in his chair and sent word to their kinsman, John Watts, who had mounted hastily and ridden to Bowery Lane. There he found DeLancey Sr. reclining in his chair, one leg extended, the other drawn in, his arms folded as if in sleep. [24]

He had died unexpectedly and without a will. Everything would go to James Jr., who finally, gratefully as I imagine, came home. When he rode up the long drive under an allée of shade trees to the house on Bowery Lane, reversing the path his father's body had taken to its final rest under the center aisle of Trinity Church, James, at twenty-eight, was master of it all—of the large, double brick house and manicured parterres, the acres of valuable pasture, an orchard, a sandy hook along the East River, and, about a mile to the north, a strip of good salt meadow.

During the next fifteen years, DeLancey's American land would absorb his most passionate energies. He was not a merchant but a landlord who knew every corner of his ground and just what it fetched in pounds and shillings per annum; he devoted himself to maximizing this income. He carved the fields below his country house into a grid of city blocks and lots surrounding a fine square that would bear his name, in the canny calculation that the little city at the tip of the island must spread north. These lots DeLancey let mostly on long-term ground leases that permitted the tenant to build a house and remove it at the expiration of the lease, in the meantime increasing the attractiveness of the neighborhood. Later, when the hour came to defend his right to the land's value, the point DeLancey seemed most intent on making was that he had made it yield more—far more—than his father ever had.[25] His marriage in 1771 to the propertied Margaret Allen, daughter of the chief justice of Pennsylvania, also expanded the family holdings.

Just below his house in Bowery Lane, James DeLancey kept a racing stable, and beside it a paddock, to which he added the rarified extravagance of a private track for training.[26] On this track some of the founding horses of American thoroughbred racing stretched their powerful legs—horses like DeLancey's English Cub mare, progenetrix of three Kentucky Derby winners, five winners at Belmont, and three top finishers in the Preakness Stakes.[27] "The turf" seems a natural pastime for this man, a form of high-stakes gambling in which a belief in pedigree, in inherited blood, could be tested, vindicated perhaps, in a spectacle of flying mud and lather. In 1757, one New York newspaper tellingly used the thoroughbred as a political metaphor: "If you should see . . . a noted Race Horse yield the Plate to a common Hack," wrote the commentator, "would you not, Sir, suspect a Cheat?"[28] Well known along the East Coast as an importer, breeder, and owner, DeLancey brought home many a silver plate.

Politics, of course, was the other game DeLancey played, his father's game, and his grandfather's and uncles', for that matter. At first it seemed it would be the familiar partisan contest between the De-Lanceys and their friends—an Anglican, mercantile elite—and, on the other hand, the Hudson Valley Livingstons and their company—a landed elite of Protestant "dissenters." The DeLancey party stumbled after James Sr.'s unexpected death and lost dominance in the provincial assembly, not to regain the majority until 1768, when James Jr. took his seat there. By this time, the playing field had changed. Most New Yorkers, DeLancey included, were focused with bitter consternation on the government in England, which had embarked on a unilateral program to cut costs and raise revenue in the colonies: determined enforcement of the tax on molasses and new taxes on certain other foreign goods, a ban on the issuance of colonial currency, a tax on all sorts of documents from newspapers to deeds, a requirement to quarter British soldiers. Trade suffered, prices rose, and everyone smoldered in frustration. But something else was happening too. The city's mechanics—the printers and smiths and saddlemakers on whom New York's political elite had always depended for votes—had begun to form a vanguard that spoke in a more independent and radical voice.

For years DeLancey managed these shifting currents, trading on all the DeLancey easiness with people "from the highest to the lowest orders," and winning the approbation of the Sons of Liberty for his vocal opposition to the Stamp Act. But as the parties drew further apart he was stretched to the breaking point.

This internal struggle reached its apogee in January 1775, when De-Lancey and his party defeated by one vote a measure in the New York assembly to approve the proceedings of the First Continental Congress. Instead the assembly sent DeLancey's own more deferential "remonstrance" to the imperial government, where, incidentally, it was rejected. Meanwhile, New Yorkers determined to give succor to the patriot cause met in their own extra-legal body and picked out delegates for the Second Continental Congress. It was as if they all had grown weary of DeLancey's voice droning on in the traditional terms of Whig politics—"We claim but a Restoration of those Rights which we enjoyed by general Consent. . . . We desire no more than a Continuation of that ancient Government to which we are entitled"—and switched off his mike.[29] Now came the midnight ride we learned about as children: *The British are coming, the British are coming*, beaten out in the rhythm of galloping hooves, and first blood shed at Lexington and Concord.

In the end what was required was to make a choice, but DeLancey didn't so much take a firm direction as slip away, traveling north to Canada and across the salt spray to a gray and bustling London.

He left behind a wife, Margaret, and three very young children, his mother, Anne, indeed all his connections and relations, and the house on Bowery Lane with everything it held, the wigs and wig stands, the looking glasses, the sheets and spoons. On the April day when he turned onto Bowery Lane for the last time, James DeLancey cannot have imagined he would never come home again.

Shortly after DeLancey's disappearance, the colonial army arrived in New York City and briefly held sway there. But in early July 1776, the king's navy landed a menacingly large fleet on Staten Island. Nervous Yankee officers gave the order that no one leave the city on the ferries without written permission from the commandant. It happens that on July 4, 1776, a certain New York lady "of the first rank, character and family"—James's younger sister, Anne Jones—wished to return from Manhattan to her family on Long Island and didn't know who the commandant was. She sent a polite note to General George Washington through a male relative. He found the general conferring with Alexander McDougall, the radical New Yorker who would help devise a plan for the rebel soldiers to escape the city and live to fight another day. As the lady's husband recounts it, "Washington read the note, whispered to McDougall, turned round, tossed the paper towards the gentleman, and insultingly said, 'Carry the note back to your Tory relation, I have nothing to do with it, and if I had . . .'" And here he turned back to McDougall, letting those words hang in the air.[30]

September 1785. Went with Coll Morgan Lewis showed him the 16 Acre Meadow lot went over the whole and made a plan of the Same for him.

So wrote an industrious surveyor by the name of Evert Bancker Jr. in his daily work journal.[31] Morgan Lewis, the man whose boots sunk along with Bancker's into the mud of the ancient salt marsh, was its new owner, the first to possess this ground under the authority of the independent State of New York. In October 1779 the New York legislature had passed a law banishing from the state on pain of death a list of British Loyalists including James DeLancey, his uncles, Oliver DeLancey and John Watts, and brother-in-law, Thomas Jones; it also seized their property. So when the "political bands" that had connected Great Britain to America gave way, certain New York landholdings it had taken more than a century to assemble also flew apart. The meadow parcel first attached to the hook by the city's Dutch founders came free of it. When he bought the sixteen-acre parcel, Colonel Morgan Lewis was living in another newly purchased piece of the former DeLancey estate, a pretty, tree-ringed house at the highest point of Grand Street, the erstwhile home, in fact, of the above-named Tory lady and her husband.

Lewis was a rising star with money to burn. In many ways his background was similar to DeLancey's. His father, Francis Lewis, a Scottish immigrant, became a prominent merchant whose country seat was in Whitestone, Long Island, on land given him by the Crown. He kept a townhouse near the Battery. Lewis remembered fishing as a child from the upstairs room of a building nearby and getting lost in the woods that became Greenwich Street. There was a little slave girl named

Aminta who used to stand behind his mother's chair at dinner as the others ate their pie, awaiting the ritual in which Mrs. Lewis offered her a morsel from her plate. (One night the mistress forgot, and the little girl bolted from the room crying, "Nothing for Minty! Nothing for Minty!")[32]

But rather than sail for England, Morgan Lewis went to school close to home at the Presbyterian College of New Jersey (later called Princeton). Here young men like James Madison were hatching republican ideas as members of the American Whig Society. On the very day when DeLancey's sister was being so rudely snubbed by George Washington, Morgan Lewis's father was in Philadelphia putting his name to the Declaration of Independence, that flaming arrow aimed at the heart of empire.

Having graduated college with high honors in 1773 and begun a local law study, at the outbreak of war Morgan Lewis joined a patriot rifle company near Boston and later was chosen captain of a New York company. In those anxious days when city residents awaited a likely conquest by British warships hovering offshore, Lewis helped to empty the contents of the arsenal near the Battery. Not long after, the British sacked the family house at Whitestone and took revenge on his mother, Elizabeth Annesley Lewis, by tossing her into prison in New York, where she remained for months.

Like DeLancey, Morgan Lewis carried a musket into the upper reaches of the Hudson River valley, and like him, saw his hopes dashed there, then rewarded. He served in the northern campaign of 1777 as British General John Burgoyne bore down from Canada with plans to meet detachments moving north from New York City. Lewis was at Ticonderoga (formerly Carillon) when it fell to Burgoyne's superior force. The next year, though, he was chief of staff to General Horatio Gates as his men clashed with Burgoyne's at Saratoga, finally encircling them in a jujitsu that changed the war's momentum. Morgan Lewis turned twenty-three on October 16, 1777. The next day he helped receive Burgoyne's surrender. He would never forget it. "My Dear Love," he would write his wife more than thirty years later to advise her that some military men had accepted their social invitation, "You can look out for us on Saturday, the 17th, the day of Burgoyne's surrender and the succeeding one to my birthday. Have a light on the wharf. I hope we shall be in time for a dance."[33] As the redcoats lay down their arms that day by the banks of the Fishkill, there rose, from the American camp, the smart rattle and crack of the snare drum, and the sweet, high, melancholy whistle of the fife. *Yankee Doodle, keep it up. Yankee Doodle dandy.*

If the Declaration of Independence was the flaming arrow, Saratoga proved that its aim was true. The Loyalist refugees in England had never expected the rebellion to survive this long, let alone to succeed. And the blows kept falling. In the autumn of 1779 came the shocking news of New York's law for banishment and confiscation, "awful thunderbolts of vengeance," as one Loyalist wrote to his father-in-law.[34] Two years later General Washington and his aristocratic French protégé Lafayette marched to victory at Yorktown. Two years after that came a peace most unsatisfactory to the homeless Loyalists.

DeLancey had since 1779 been receiving a pension from the Crown of £200 a year, about the annual salary of a college professor or court official in America, and not enough to prevent a painful and, to him, humiliating reduction in circumstances.[35] Cut off from the fixed resources accumulated over three generations in America—a roof over his head, servants maintained at little expense, a farm yielding produce—James DeLancey's situation worsened as upheaval in New York pinched off the flow of rents from his land. "Tyrannical law! made to take a man's life for the express purpose of getting his estate," wrote one Loyalist, a distant relative of DeLancey's, railing against the seizure of Loyalist property. "The law," he went on in stubborn disbelief, "is too severe to be continued."[36]

When James DeLancey departed New York he apparently left behind not only his legal wife and their children, but three older "natural" children born before his marriage, their mother an accomplished woman of "slightly lower social rank" who had died in 1770, according to DeLancey genealogist D. A. Story.[37] By Story's account, these three offspring, John, James, and Mary, never were taken in by DeLancey's wife, Margaret, but were embraced by others in the family. DeLancey at least acknowledged them; perhaps while still in New York he had discreetly managed their support himself but his correspondence hints that in exile he was obliged to rely on the discretion of others.

Margaret Allen DeLancey, meanwhile, who had brought 1,500 Pennsylvania acres and £1,000 Pennsylvania currency to her marriage,[38] was raising her own three children, the oldest a boy of eight, amid grim wartime conditions in British-occupied New York. By the passage of the confiscation act, five years had gone by since her husband's abrupt departure. The troops had taken the mansion house on Bowery Lane for a hospital to Hessian soldiers, torn up the pasture for sod to build a fort, and, for fuel, felled ninety-three locust trees—perhaps the very ones whose fragrant, lacy canopies had once made it so pleasant to approach the DeLancey threshold.[39] Jamaica was a place of safety, little more. The village served as headquarters for James's uncle, Brigadier General Oliver DeLancey, a staunch Loyalist entrusted with command of Long Island whose own northern Manhattan estate called Bloomingdale had been torched one night by a band of rebels, his wife and daughters driven into a neighboring swamp. On the outskirts of Jamaica were mile-long rows of soldiers' barracks, thatch huts with sod floors and rough stone hearths in which the king's men burned the wooded hillsides bare.[40]

This chill at the heart of James DeLancey's family, whatever its source, would endure long after his death. Around 1821, a niece in the countryside near London would receive a visit from a very elderly and senile Margaret, accompanied by their British-born youngest daughter, Susan. "I fear they are a very divided family," this niece would observe, "but what can be expected from such a Set of conditions."[41]

During and for some months after the war, though, DeLancey hoped to regain his former place in the world. He seemed to reach for his American property as if struggling to wake from a dream. He kept his New York agents very busy.

August 28, 1780, George Stanton to James DeLancey. *Shall be glad you will give me a particular account in your next how matters is likely to turn out on your side the watter between Governments and the opposite party,—and if any likeleyhood the Latter is likely to get the better Let me know in time, with orders in what manner I am to Transact with your Estate here—in regard to our affairs here with the Rebels we stand much upon the same foundation when I wrote you last—*[42]

January 16, 1782, George Stanton to James DeLancey. *I have made it my Business to acquaint your Tenants, I have Received your orders— and have given them timely notice to Purchace or Lease—they answer me in general Let's know how the war will end—*

May 20, 1783, George Stanton to James DeLancey. *The present Critical situation of affairs which seems to increase daily, rather deems it almost impracticable to Collect any Rents. . . .*

October 24, 1783, George Stanton to James DeLancey. *I am Sorey it is not in my power to Remit you Sum moneys. . . . I have lett your Dother have £23 by Mr. Rivington orders. . . . I have paid her board up to 31 August £17.6.8.*

December 20, 1783, James Rivington, printer and agent, to James DeLancey. *As the matter stands, we cannot, by any sort of interference of us your representatives prevent this coercive manner of levying your rents and properties. . . . This must prove most inconvenient and highly mortifying to you for the present, but I flatter myself you will still be able to recover the whole by either an exception from the prosecution act, or the fair construction of the Treaty.**

December 12, 178(4?), John Watts Jr. to James DeLancey. *The State, you must have heard . . . has proceeded in the Sales of your Estate, which is very nearly completed. I mention this circumstance to you, as the knowledge of it ought to accellerate Government to make you Restitution. We have no Reason here to think it will be in any wise adequate to Peoples Losses. . . .*

---

*The Treaty of Paris had recommended that Loyalists' rights and properties be restored to them.

Indeed, DeLancey already had turned his attention to the tortuous process of extracting from his so-called real property in New York whatever liquid assets he could. His landed interest had once promised a more reliable living than the trade so subject to swings in the market, the legal environment, even the weather; it had signaled his attachment to place. But now he found out how difficult it was to pick up that wealth and walk away with it.

In particular DeLancey began a protracted and pained correspondence with the commission established by Britain in 1783 to analyze the value of Loyalists' individual losses in America and make cash restitution. He served as the representative of all New York Loyalists to this commission. In his own case, he had the galling task of assembling proofs to support his title to and valuation of the land, which under the circumstances was like being asked to climb a scaffold that lay in a heap of rubble at his feet. By mid-1786, DeLancey apparently had received an initial disbursement from the commission, which gave him an inkling that the final payment would fall short of his expectations. A pleading tone entered his communications.

> July 28, 1786, James DeLancey to the Office of American Claims.
> *I am confident, none of the Loyalists, who professed the Fortune and Consequence, which I did in America, have been reduced to live in the manner I have done for these two years past, in Lodgings, and without a Made Servant, with an Increasing Family of young children now consisting of four . . . and my little Son, who, before the loss of my Estate, would in Point of Family Consequence and Fortune, have been on an Equality with the first Persons in America, will now have scarcely sufficient to afford him a liberal Education. . . .*
>
> *Every gentleman from New York acquainted with the value of Property in that Country, with whom I have converred on the subject, have expressed their Surprise at the Smallness of the Sum which I have received. . . .*

On this question of value he waxed on at length, poignantly invoking the testimony of those still free to enjoy America, including that of Morgan Lewis himself. The Oz-like Office of American Claims, however, proved a more impenetrable echo chamber than any voice-mail system ever devised.

> February 3, 1786, John Forster, for the Commissioners for American Claims, to James DeLancey. *I have received and laid before the Commissioners your letter of the 28th of last Month, & am directed to inform you in answer thereto, that tho' they would be very glad to give you all the satisfaction in their Power consistent with their Duty, they do not consider themselves justified in the present Stage of the Inquiry in saying any thing further in Answer to your Questions. . . .*

> February 1, 1787, Forster. *I am instructed to acquaint you generally that the Commissioners do not enter into such minute communications with any claimants. . . .*

> March 11, 1788, Forster. *I am directed to acquaint you that the Commissioners cannot consistently with their Rules give you any other Information than they have already done. . . .*

What a dull, eked-out, ironic education for DeLancey, to be treated with so little distinction, to discover that his Consequence and Fortune did not abide at such a distance from American soil. In the end his restitution, though little more than half of what he'd claimed in losses, was sufficient to restore his financial condition to that of a moderately rich man: £29,848 sterling.[43] But his life—that was something else. As the commission wound up its business, DeLancey and the other Loyalist agents composed a memorial to the king in which they "humbly beg[ged] leave to approach [his] Throne, to pour forth the ardent effusions of their grateful hearts." On the occasion of this memorial's presentation by the Lord of his Majesty's Bedchamber in waiting, after years, *decades*, spent first in enervating remonstrations against the mother country, then in vainly banking the fires of revolution, finally in a sour assay of that rupture's extensive damage to himself, James DeLancey Jr., at fifty-eight, was permitted to lay a kiss on the hand of His Majesty, King George III.[44]

Now he would be the one to receive carefully crafted entreaties for assistance. His firstborn child, his "natural" son, John, a lieutenant in the British army stationed on the Caribbean island of Montserrat, wrote to his younger brother, James, in a tone full of longing and resentment for the father he referred to variously as the Old Man, the Old Buck, and the Old Genl. "I begin to think my conversations with him ~~has revived~~ accindled some sparks of Paternal affection for us which may in time be more substantiated," wrote John. "I know perfectly he has a large family perhaps an encreasing one independent of *us three* & the character he has to support," he went on. Even so, John reasoned, with their father newly compensated for his American property, and the three of them old enough "to be entrusted with a secret of that nature," now might be the time to press for financial help.[45] Just over a year later, James DeLancey's youngest brother, John Peter, addressed a tender, intimate letter to his nephew advising him just how to approach the Old Man; he should tell him "in a very delicate handsome manner" that John Peter found himself incapable of helping, that he, John, would pay back his father with interest, that he would never again bother him with a similar request. And the letter should be impeccable of form, "not a word mispelt or a stop wanting."[46]

DeLancey did advance John £400 to purchase a captaincy in the army. "I have it in my power to leave you something in my will," he wrote to the latter in 1792, "if you continued to behave as well as you have hitherto done." When John was denied the command, his father scratched out another two paragraphs to him. "I am very much grieved at your disappointment in not getting the Company," he wrote. "You must however reconcile yourself to the Misfortune and bear it like a Man."[47]

James DeLancey lived out the decade at Bath, a place where, in the estimation of his contemporary Jane Austen, a gentleman might "be important at comparatively little expense," a place, she wrote, of dashing carriages, carts, and drays, of bawling newsboys, muffin peddlers, milkmen, of "extensive buildings, smoking in rain."[48]

Not long after Saratoga, Morgan Lewis was married in the parlor at Clermont, a beautiful house on a bluff overlooking the Hudson. The DeLancey homestead some one hundred miles to the south was already falling to ruin, Bloomingdale burned, the Lewis property at Whitestone plundered. Clermont, the bride's childhood home, also had been ravaged during the Revolution, but her stalwart Yankee mother had soon returned to supervise its rebuilding. Neither did the young couple await the peace to wed, he, with his long, mild face, auburn hair, and protruding chin, already a hero, she, not beautiful but highly cultured—no one was a bigger fan of Molière—and the beloved daughter of a very large, compelling, close-knit family.

They "both looked charming," reported the bride's mother, but "Col. Lewis appeared to great advantage—his deportment suited to the solemn occasion, and to my girl tender and soothing beyond expression. Immediately after the ceremony he took her with one arm round the waist, and led her up to me, and jointly had my blessing, and next to his father, who catched him in his arms with transport and kissed him twice."[49] As well he might. The bride was Gertrude Livingston.

Francis Lewis had seen his eldest son, Francis Jr., marry into the Tory Ludlow family, and his daughter, Anne, wed a British naval captain and move to England. Both offspring would have money trouble after the war, and Francis Lewis, who had not attended much to his own fortune these last years, would be in no position to help.[50] But Morgan, on that May day in 1779, had joined a family so squarely in the patriot camp that years later, his wife could demonstrate for their grandchildren just how General Washington had danced, keeping time by waving his arms before him until his hands almost crossed.[51] And they were very rich. Gertrude alone would have 20,000 acres. Her kin commanded hundreds of thousands more, both in the Catskill Mountains across the river from Clermont, and on this eastern shore of the Hudson where their estates dominated a landscape of dramatic vistas and strange, honeyed light.

Archrivals to the DeLanceys for decades before the war, the Livingstons had chosen sides in the end, and chosen wisely, bravely even. Morgan Lewis now threw in his lot with theirs. Winter evenings the couple joined the "elegant salon" maintained by Gertrude's mother at her city house on Pearl Street.[52] In spring the families engaged the cabin of a sloop fitted out with every comfort and sailed up the Hudson to spend the summer in the country.

The removal of Indians had produced opportunities for the earliest European settlers of New York, and now the banishment of the Loyalists gave new openings to those who remained. The young attorney Morgan Lewis could earn a robust living from "frequent litigations occasioned by the late war concerning Property,"[53] and he put his surplus funds into city property formerly belonging to DeLancey and a handful of other Loyalists. He "believed in the value of real estate in the island of Manhattan," his granddaughter would write, and "early invested in town lots." Lewis put up several rows of houses in Church Street and West Broadway, whole blocks "in the eastern part of the city," stores in Maiden Lane.[54] In 1823 he successfully petitioned the city government to alter the as-yet unexecuted street plan for his meadow parcel, narrowing Avenues A, B, C, and D, and thus augmenting the parcel's buildable area.[55] The next year, he sold the sixteen-acre meadow to a syndicate for the enormous sum of $44,000.[56] Just as DeLancey had predicted, the city was growing, and this property, however low and wet, now lay directly in the path of urban advance.

The nearly four decades Lewis held the meadow spanned all the years of his public life and beyond. He had, in part through a series of lucky accidents, served as New York's attorney general, as justice of its Supreme Court, and finally, between 1804 and 1807, as governor. After a somewhat embarrassing turn as general in the War of 1812, he retired to his estate called Staatsburgh, whose lawns tumbled like bolts of silk to the riverbank some fifteen miles south of Clermont's wharf.[57] He and Gertrude shared this home with their only child, Margaret Lewis Livingston, her husband, and their passel of offspring. During this time, Morgan Lewis told Margaret that his agent would now pay the proceeds of his city property directly into her hands. "What the country property produces will be enough for me to play with," he said.[58]

"We were a merry family of young people in those days," remembered one of his granddaughters, Julia. "I often wonder at the General's patience in allowing his house to be filled as it was, year after year, with tutors, governesses, drawing and dancing-masters—all that the tastes and wants of a dozen children of all ages made desirable.

Carriages and horses of every description were at our disposal; perhaps I owe the health which enables me at this moment to write the life of my grandfather to a fleet and beautiful mare which always stood ready in the stable to carry me over the country."[59]

And so it may be that our spongy, creek-watered salt meadow, this Manhattan ground pulled out from under James DeLancey's feet, helped to produce, in a new generation, an American childhood as fortunate as his own—more so.

When Morgan Lewis sold the meadow that would become 7th Street, the change was afoot; Manhattan already had fallen upon itself with the strange fury of an autoimmune reaction. Between 1807 and 1811, a three-man commission sketched out the simplest grid—twelve avenues running the length of the island, 155 streets slicing it crosswise, all quite sensibly labeled with numbers and, in a few cases, letters, and creating more than 2,000 rectangular blocks. Then people began the work of making it so. They bought up lots and sold them. They fought in court over who owned what, and traded gores of land to square their property lines with the new city plan. They paid taxes and penned letters arguing for this or that public-works project. They blasted Manhattan schist and plugged up creeks, cutting down hills and raising sunken "vallies." They "opened," "regulated," and "macadamized" new roads through a once pastoral and wooded terrain of commons and country seats. It was, on one level, a highly participatory process, involving gentlemen and lawyers, but also surveyors, cartmen, laborers, and builders. In what the Dutch architect Rem Koolhaas has called Manhattan's "freakish history," this was the primal scene.[60]

It's not that gridiron planning was new. To the contrary, as the principal form used by Greco-Roman colonizers to plant new settlements, the grid was altogether familiar across Europe as well as America. But here, it was as if New York were *recolonizing* itself, showing little regard not only for native topography, but also for 150 years of *its own* land-use history. The commissioners self-consciously chose building density and unrelieved regularity, rejecting, in their report, the comely "circles, ovals and stars" of the new capital city designed by Pierre

L'Enfant in favor of something more closely resembling the pragmatic rectilinear plan Thomas Jefferson had first proposed for Washington, and which his 1785 Land Ordinance had set up as the repeating settlement pattern of the American West.[61]

"Who shall write the history of the American Revolution?" wrote John Adams to Jefferson, his old friend and rival, in 1815. "Who will ever be able to write it?" "Nobody," came Jefferson's crisp reply, "except merely its external facts; all its councils, designs and discussions having been conducted by Congress with closed doors, and no members, as far as I know, having even made notes of them. These, which are the life and soul of history, must forever be unknown." Jefferson went on to inform his fellow former president that their active correspondence had been noticed at the post office, and a printer had proposed publishing it. "These people think they have a right to everything," he wrote, "however secret or sacred." [62]

So the Revolution, by Jefferson's reckoning, was a kind of *secret*, a sacred and inviolable mystery. But I walk the streets of the former meadow—up Avenue D to 7th Street and west to 1st Avenue, which tunnels north to the edge of the world—and begin to think that the soul of our history is written right here. And if it is written here, then that secret must also be inscribed on our bodies and in our minds. The grid, after all, is both an act of city planning and an image older than geometry, a piece of art, a radical scarification that emerged from the imagination of the revolutionary generation. And we live in it.

The commissioners insisted that certain "plain and simple reflections" had carried the day: The city was to be "composed principally of the habitations of men" and "straight-sided and right-angled houses are the most cheap to build and the most convenient to live in."[63] Indeed the grid is the very symbol of rationality, of Cartesian order. But what is orderly about tearing up the known world and replacing it with an imagined one?

Instead of mapping the city, in the early years of the republic, New Yorkers citied a map. They settled, in a stroke, all the fractious disputes that had taken place over how to build Manhattan. Here is another contradiction: This furious change they undertook reflects, I think, a weariness of change, a need to finally contain the unknown, to "capture," in blocks and lots, the "conjectural," the "nonexistent," indeed "all future activity on the island," to quote Koolhaas.[64]

And so, where a meadow once dipped and gurgled, we turn corners.

The external facts are as follows. Calling themselves the Lewis Association, nine men—a few merchants, a shipbuilder, a lawyer—bought the sixteen-acre parcel from Morgan Lewis in 1824.[65] They drew up a contract in which each agreed to pay his share for improvements, the nature of which almost beggars belief. By 1826 they had lotted the parcel and were ready to divide it into eight equal holdings (two men held a share together). "The average quantity of Earth above the level of the meadow is 5360 loads," reads the partition deed. These are *horse-drawn cartloads*. "Those shares having more than the average are to pay for the surplus at the rate of 10 cents per load—shares having less than the average are to receive for the deficiency the same ratio—shares having creeks running through them have been allowed earth sufficient to fill the same to the level of the meadow."[66] Very simple, no?

That same year, 6th and 7th streets from the Bowery to the East River were "opened"—the land taken for the municipality, its former owners compensated.[67] Here, you might say, was a new kind of commons, these streets that would roar with the play of city children.

Meanwhile, a loud fracas was taking place among property owners and city officials over how best to pitch streets throughout this low, swampy area—*Spartina patens* was of precisely zero interest now—in such a way as to encourage the runoff of its all too plentiful waters. Proprietors didn't want their cellars to flood with every rain, but they also had to pay for sections of road fronting on their lots, and the more dirt required, the bigger the bill. In July 1827, the common council adopted what was later referred to as the high filling plan: "Resolved that all the streets between First Street and Fourteenth Street including the latter and between the Bowery and the East river be regulated with an ascent of *Seven and one half inches to One hundred feet*."[68] The water would, by force of gravity, pour down all the cross streets from a high point at the Bowery into the river. Property owners were sharply divided on this plan. In 1832 more than three hundred signed a petition calling it "at least too expensive to be attempted by the proprietors, if not utterly impracticable."[69] The city's street commissioner agreed. To fill a lot and its proportionate length of street on 7th Street between Avenues C and D would, according to his calculations, cost about $1,156.75, a multiple of what the lots were worth. Then there was the question of *"where all this immense quantity of earth can be obtained at a reasonable expense,"* nearby hills having already been eliminated.[70] He supported another plan: to make Avenue C the low point of an inverted arch. Water from as far west as the Bowery and as far east as Avenue D would drop into Avenue C and flow north along this avenue until it reached the river around 14th Street. The aldermen and mayor approved this plan in 1832.[71]

Avenue C would thus, in the words of the aldermen's street committee, "unite all the waters of a very large section" nearly three hundred acres in extent. This now required the re-widening of the avenue, which though originally laid out at one hundred feet had been narrowed to sixty at the request of Morgan Lewis and others about a decade since. It would also require the construction of a sewer, a controversial facility at the time, as sewers tended to trap decaying offal and other horrible-smelling stuff, a problem, the committee suggested, that would be addressed by covering openings with improved receptacles or "stench traps." All of which was brought into effect by the council on June 9, 1834, and all of which I felt, more than 150 years later, in that dip, that dropping into place as I approached home on 7th Street just east of Avenue C, and in the dank odor emanating on hot days from the basement of No. 239.[72] (This street design, by the way, also can be seen quite clearly in the pooling of water along Avenue C on one hundred–year flood maps created by the Federal Emergency Management Agency.)

Driving all this movement of earth and water was an equally strenuous movement of money. In 1827 the Lewis Association faced an imminent foreclosure sale of the marsh property, having failed to pay a mortgage held by the children of merchant Henry A. Coster, deceased, and transferred the whole to two Lewis Association members, Henry Brevoort Jr. and John Flack, both merchants who apparently were best able to handle the debt.[73] In 1833 Flack's executors advertised an auction at Merchants Exchange offering 150 lots out of his estate; these constituted most of the three blocks between 6th and 9th streets and Avenues C and D. The executors later deeded these lots, some under lease and others in fee, to a gentleman, James B. Murray. It so happened that Murray, who bought the lots with a large mortgage to Flack's heirs, was himself on the upswing from a trying period in which he'd narrowly escaped debtor's prison. In the autumn of 1828, he'd written to his wife, Maria, that he was "unable *as yet even to lay in our winters fuel.* . . . As for a wet nurse, I am afraid poor little Washington will have to forego the luxury." Murray was elected city alderman in the spring of 1832 and helped to pass the street plan for the east-side area in which he subsequently invested. Real estate here and in the West helped springboard his financial recovery.[74] Murray soon sold a two-thirds share in his east-side lots to a business associate, Thomas Davis,[75] and they sold off these lots to various parties in smaller parcels until just a few lots, including the one that would be No. 239, vested in a lawyer by the name of Gilbert M. Speir. Upon his election to a local judgeship some years hence, Speir would appear in *Harper's Weekly* looking rather Whitmanesque, with a sweep of white hair across the brow and heavy weathering at the eyes.[76]

I think he is the one who built No. 239, or rather, hired people to build it. There are no records of its construction, nor were any such records required. No architect or builder claims it. But what's clear is that Speir bought the lot in early 1845, and that same year the property's valuation jumped from $600 to $1,900.[77] It was a speculation on Speir's part. He lived at a swanker address in Greenwich Village and in all likelihood hired an agent to collect rents.[78] So the house that would hold so many of us in its mute embrace was nothing like Morgan Lewis's Staatsburgh or DeLancey's Bowery mansion, and I don't mean merely that it was less luxurious. It began life not as a home but as "housing"—a blank, unbranded product, a place where someone else's family might live.[79]

Maybe the entire trajectory, from Jemmy's birth in 1732 to the building of No. 239 in 1845, comes down to money. Sometimes I think that's the obvious and only conclusion, DeLancey's painful loss merely another rich man's gain, the half-crazed lotting and building of Manhattan in the aftermath of the nation's founding resembling nothing so much as the hasty butchering of a poached carcass. We must remember to thank those republicans for the crowding and bad smells.

And yet. And yet. Walk the old streets with their runs of row houses. See how they stand, shoulder to shoulder, showing one decent face to passersby. Consider that anyone—anyone at all—can find the corner of, say, 2nd Avenue and 10th Street. We keep no secrets here; Manhattan is a map laid out to the world. And think of No. 239, erected in mediocrity, not one thing special about it, so that in fifty years' time its ownership, free and clear, might be left to someone of such negligible Rank and Consequence as Clara Phillips, an old woman, an immigrant no less, a widow, a Jew.

"Legislators cannot invent too many devices for subdividing property," wrote Jefferson in 1785. "The small landholders are the most precious part of a state"[80]—a few lines plucked from a published correspondence that now fills many volumes, and that, like any sacred text, can point you just about any direction you want to go. Which of our dreams should we call American? Jefferson, that American Sphinx, as historian Joseph Ellis calls him, was right about one thing.[81] Ours is not to solve the riddle but to walk these streets, which every morning receive anew their portion of daylight. We walk the streets of our revolution.

The House

BEHOLD THE NEW HOUSE, ringing with emptiness. It is the first building ever to rise on this piece of ground. It looks south. Timber joists set into masonry bearing walls support three stories, capped by a flat roof. A basement floor rests in the earth, with below-grade entrances onto the street and rear yard. Inside the house are hearths for burning wood and coal, and along its western wall a narrow stair climbs to a hatch in the roof. In the yard a cistern collects rainwater. At the rear lot line is a privy. There are windows in front and back, none on the sides. A stone stoop flanked by the building's single ornament—that gracefully coiling railing—forms a dais from which the front door seems almost ready to speak. But it does not speak. There is nothing, yet, to tell.

One hundred fifty-seven years later, I am a small figure awake in the night. I sit up in bed, a thumping in my chest, and look out my window at this very same house, rinsed in neon streetlight. I can see that it is not only empty, but *vacant*. I can see now, from this startling new vantage, that its face is cracked, its posture out of plumb, its windows black and curtainless. The sight of it fills me with sorrow and dread.

After long, patient service as a home, the house is now fated to pass a season in purgatory. There hangs about it not the incipience of the newborn, but the eeriness of the undead. Those windows with their dilated pupils suggest a materiality from which life flees, pausing at the threshold. Or a rudderless insanity. The Germans have a word for it: *unheimlich*, translated as uncanny, but meaning literally unhome-like. The *unheimlich* is more than frightening, it's disturbing, an effect that occurs in the presence of doubt as to whether an apparently living being is actually inanimate or, conversely, sentience hides within a seemingly lifeless object.[1] Freud points out that the word *heimlich* can mean both the easeful familiarity of home, and something secret, concealed from view. What we experience as uncanny, he says, is actually something quite intimately familiar—infantile superstitions long since surmounted, wishes repressed—that returns unbidden.[2] Thrust upon us in a new guise from without, the old internal image upsets, is a kind of haunting. It is home, but unhomelike. And it raises the possibility that, finally, there is no home.

The unhomelike, whatever its exact nature, attaches with some regularity to houses themselves. Sooner or later, doesn't everyone meet a haunted house? Someone dies. There is a divorce, or a child leaves home. And the rooms left behind are filled with that singular presence and baffling disappearance. I'm thinking of how, after my grandfather died, my grandmother stacked clean laundry on his side of the bed, his heavy watch dangling always from her wrist. Or say the childhood home must go on the block, its ancient keepers no longer able to clean the gutters and mow the lawn. How strange to see the place divested of its long-accustomed family life, that indescribable flavor boiled away; how much stranger, how appalling, really, to watch it fill promiscuously with the life of some other family. They chop down the gnarled old crab apple tree. They gut the kitchen. Their bicycles clutter the driveway. How do we bear it?

Not long ago my father's brother died unexpectedly and too soon; the two were close companions as boys and shared a room at the top of the beautiful stone house their parents built during the Depression outside Cincinnati, Ohio. After the funeral, we went by to see the old house; its kindly owner let us in to look around, but he kept apologizing, saying, *You can't go upstairs, the children are sleeping.* This is how it has to be. We must defend our houses against the claims of past occupants. We don't want to know that another child slept here once. And when we move into a new house, we disinfect; a single hair curled on the tub is the most disgusting thing imaginable. The woolly cardi-

gan left behind, draping a chair, is not remotely to be tolerated. *Out,*
we say. *Out!*

On 7th Street, in the middle of a February night, I sit up in bed, my
husband and children warm beside me, and look out at a house whose
image within me is alive, moving in the stream of time, but out there
is palsied, stopped. I am afraid of myself, and of the house, I've been
told by men of science that *a soaking rain could bring it down,* that
*continuing rot of the first floor joists could trigger motion in the already-
weakened masonry bearing walls resulting in a catastrophic collapse,* I
want to smother it with a pillow, drive a stake through its heart. I can
hardly stand to look at it. On the few occasions when I must enter the
house again—to retrieve some item or record the serial number on the
boiler, say—my blood rebels at its icy chill, at the dust settled on everyday objects left behind in haste.

I decide, at a certain point, that I won't go back. I'll do the paperwork and make the phone calls, I decide. So David is the one who,
over the course of nearly two years, regularly returns to No. 239 to
shovel the sidewalk or show contractors around. I tell myself the house
doesn't trouble him the way it does me. But much later, the whole ordeal safely over, David and I will walk onto the block to have dinner
with friends, and he will astound me by reporting that in nearly 2,000
days of living quite nearby, during which I've passed by the old place
countless times, he has managed to avoid doing so even once.

It hardly needs saying that the house is a figure for the human body. To
build is to part the elements and create a world. Naturally we build in
our own image. Americans overwhelmingly prefer houses, ideally freestanding single-family houses, to apartments. This obviously has to do
with light, air, space, and privacy, but I think it also reflects the fact that
a house, unlike a flat, is available as an image of the body—and by extension of the self—in its dignity and independence. An apartment may
be oriented toward, say, a western and southern exposure, but the house
is oriented like the two-sided body, with right and left, front and back. It
has the body's verticality. It has an energy source that generates heat, a
kitchen and plumbing (or simple basins) for gut and bowel, the upper
floors for sleep and talk. Apartments give onto a hallway or landing. But

the front door of the house opens and closes like a mouth, letting in sustenance and sending people into the street where like words they represent the life inside. None of this is a coincidence, of course, because the house is meant to serve the body, a sanctuary for its private functions, for the awkward, vulnerable postures of sleep, defecation, sex, and, to some degree, eating, washing, crying, cuddling; it is, as the French philosopher Gaston Bachelard puts it, "the non-I that protects the I."[3] The crucial fiction of the house is its permanence. It seems—only seems—to harden the corporeal into something that can last forever.

During the three months we lived across the street from No. 239, in dreams, my own vital structure was falling apart, the way it *does*, because the body is an object, too, that becomes unhomelike in its failure. I dreamed of teeth gone loose in my head. I dreamed of incontinence.

These hallucinations only complicated the process of dealing with the house itself, whose problems were real and required attention, though their precise nature was maddeningly elusive. We consulted, in all, three or four engineers, two architects, ten contractors. There were soil tests and plumb-line measurements. We studied digital photos taken in the crawl space beneath the basement floor, in which two-by-fours and little brick piles appeared to prop up blackened, partially mashed structural beams. Disagreement among the professional men (they were all men) left a great deal of room for doubt. The most harrowing ambiguity had to do with whether the building was in imminent danger of falling down, posing a deadly threat to anyone who might venture inside or even near it. Some described the foundation as being already in a "collapsed" condition, but the city never sealed the building, only issued costly tickets, one after the other, some labeled with the disheartening and inscrutable words "Chief's special." The house, we learned, was leaning significantly to the west; its interior floors had been leveled up to conceal this tilt, which explained the fun-house aesthetic. Possibly as a result of this sinking, both its western and eastern walls were buckling outward at the middle; some thought one or both walls needed to be replaced entirely. One engineer told us that theoretically—and this was sometimes "appropriate," he said—a whole building could be replaced, piece by piece, until it was altogether new, like the body after seven years' cell turnover. But first we'd have to stabilize No. 239, a procedure that could set us back more than a hundred grand. On the other hand, one or two contractors threw up their hands and said no, demolish it. Which would mean paying someone hundreds of thousands of dollars to crush No. 239 and cart it away. Much of this was explained to me over the phone, as two-year-old Byron screamed for my attention.

The structural engineer we settled on, Richard, bless his soul, waded into this muck with a matter-of-factness that called up a response in kind. He made a drawing calling for "shotcrete" to reinforce the walls, joist "tiebacks" on every floor, "new made beams" in a foundation that would rest on thirty-five-foot-deep screw piles. "Installation into the soil," according to one of several articles Richard included in his report, "is accomplished by five to 10 rpm, high-torque continuous-rotation hydraulic motors that can be mounted to just about any type of machine (e.g., bed-mounted drill rigs, rubber-tired backhoes, skid-steer loaders, mini-excavators, and track-hoe excavators)."[4] Maybe because its particulars lay so wholly outside our field of knowledge, the drawing became a kind of article of faith with us. Sublime as it was, the drawing didn't make it so.

As it happened, a rubber-tired backhoe *had* turned up in the lot next to No. 239—in the garden where Lucy and I had planted daffodils—the very week we moved out. At an auction of city-owned property, a developer had bought the middle of three garden lots, outbidding a group of neighbors that included me and David. Now he was building an impossibly narrow structure there. So nights when I looked across 7th Street at the shell of No. 239, I also looked down on a construction site. I often thought of the words the developer's representative had used to convince me the man couldn't be stopped: "He has more money than God," he said. And that, I thought, is what it would take to save No. 239. More money than God.

Once upon a time, goes the beloved children's story, *there was a Little House way out in the country. She was a pretty Little House and she was strong and well built. The man who built her so well said, "This house shall never be sold for gold or silver and she will live to see our great-great-grandchildren's great-great-grandchildren living in her."*[5]

Our children were just shy of their second and fifth birthdays when we decamped from No. 239. While we lived there (and for some time after), David or I used to take them nearly every day to Tompkins Square Park. On the way, I'd point out the squirrels chittering in the elms and lilacs soaked with spring rain. Once inside the fenced playground, I would sit on a bench and talk with friends while the children climbed ladders or slid down ramps on their bellies. My job was to stay more or less in one place, and theirs was to remember that place and return there. Once in a while I'd lose track of a child. A few moments of fruitless searching and my mouth would go dry, the city transmogrifying into an endless, sickening welter. I'd stalk the playground crying out the name of the lost child, until I found him sitting cross-legged under a jungle gym tending a pile of plucked leaves and bottle caps. Or sometimes I was the lost one, it was the child's mouth that went dry, and when she found me she'd exclaim searchingly, "Where *were* you? Where did you *go?*"

It was my job to mark their place in the world. It was my job to hold them until sleep came, to take them into my lap even when they railed against me as the representative of everything beyond their control. And the house marked my place. It held me, held us all, together. It mothered me as the surrogate mother to our children, the cradle into which we laid them and could rock with one toe while reading a magazine and nibbling a Twizzler.

"As for woman," writes the French intellectual Luce Irigaray, "she is place. . . . If she is to be able to contain, to envelop, she must have her own envelope. Not only her clothing and ornaments of seduction, but her skin. And her skin must contain a receptacle. She must lack

—neither body,
—nor extension within,
—nor extension without,

or she will plummet down and take the other with her."[6] Failure of the maternal body is a dire circumstance for all. I swear I could not, cannot, shake a quite disgusting association between looking at those digital photos of the crawl space below No. 239 and at the ultrasound image of my miscarriage. The doctor shook his head. "There's no good news in there," he said.

Mothers and houses are mythical but they are also real. No child longs for the comfort of "the" mother; it's her own mother she wants, and her own father. My mother had long, cool hands; my father whistled as he came up the front walk. It's not "the house" you internalize, it's *the* house. These "places" attain mythical significance only because they come into every life as something highly, exquisitely, personal.

In most cases, the environment in which a new baby develops into an individual is specially attuned to her unique innate tendencies. The bathwater is not too warm. The towel is made ready. There is chatter and song when she is lively, and quiet when she needs rest. Psychoanalysts call it the "holding environment."[7] Being responded to in this personal way, a baby comes to live in her own body and to feel, like the storybook Velveteen Rabbit, *real*.

Independence doesn't mean giving up the holding environment so much as finding it, re-creating it, in your own person and in the world. The home you make in adulthood is perhaps the paramount example. At home you can be real. You can let it all hang out. The place and your behavior inside it reflect your own inner life. Subjectivity reigns. So, on the inside, each house is unique. Steeped as a child in the indescribably personal atmosphere of my own household, I remember being startled by what felt like an abrupt change in temperature when entering other people's houses. I remember the stillness, dark, and extreme tidiness of one corner house, the mother's insulin vials illuminated as if by stage lights in the fridge. I remember a house with an entire wall sealed in tinfoil, the stairs to the basement so jammed with dirty laundry as to utterly prevent passage. I remember white carpeting and a shuddering china cabinet as you stepped ever so lightly around the sleeping tiger in one house. Another was a pinball machine of titillation, from the six flavors of Pop-Tarts lined up in the cupboard to the mom who sat around wearing nothing but a lace bra and panties, to the *Playboys* in the magazine rack in the den. And there was a house with miles of attic space like open fields given up to young legs, and light, and a feeling that was raw, unfinished.

When you grow up, you make a home that reflects you in ways you may not consciously choose; you live in your dream house. To you it is *heimlich*—cozy, intimately familiar, also secret, hidden from view. It must be defended. Your home is your castle, according to English common law, meaning it's your fortress, the place from which there is no duty to retreat in case of confrontation. In many American states, the so-called Castle Doctrine is encoded in laws that say if someone threatens you in your own home, if some outsider breaches that protective wall, you are within your rights to literally slay him.[8]

The dream house of adulthood differs from the holding environment of infancy in the important respect that often you share it with a cocreator, another adult who also dreams, who also insists upon feeling real and being acknowledged as such. The question of what kind of home David and I made at No. 239 for ourselves and our children does not belong safely to the past; to a large extent, we re-create that home wherever we go. I have this notion that inside that house, our subjectivities—David's and mine—should have risen to meet each other in some delicate pas de deux that could demonstrate to our children the beauty of reciprocity. But often he and I have made inhabitation a competitive contact sport, home the arena where we grapple under a fine sheen of sweat, muscles bulging cartoonishly out of our singlets.

First there's the relentless struggle to gain ground for one's personal aesthetic. My taste when we moved to No. 239 ran to a sort of farmhouse plainness, reflected in the pine sideboard and heavy tavern table I had from my grandparents and the sweet botanical prints I'd acquired here and there. I liked muted colors. I liked to fill small pots with pink and white Sweet William or tulips. I could not abide the appearance of everyday technologies—cords, the backs of televisions, the black artificial materials of stereo speakers. David, on the other hand, really wanted the technology and couldn't fathom my vendetta against cords. He liked very bright colors and angular contemporary design. He also had a thing about oriental rugs, feeling, in the tradition of his own family, that they should be generously dimensioned and very fine but used without undue reverence. When Lucy started crawling, we chose, with much stress and rancor, an enormous, expensive wool rug that she regularly peed on. David craved massively solid objects. Thus at No. 239 we traded in a headboard that had always rattled for a cherry sleigh bed and a ridiculously weighty mattress we nicknamed Gibraltar. I eventually turned on the sleigh bed because I battered my shins to a pulp maneuvering around it in our small bedroom. David, meanwhile, never stopped being disgusted, year upon marital year, by the flimsiness of the butcher block I purchased online. He could tolerate the farmhouse stuff but harbored a deep and intransigent loathing of any sofa that could be described as overstuffed or chintzy. We "compromised" on a beige sofa with very high, straight arms and floral back pillows; I must have mentally erased it a thousand times. That and the rug, another ill-advised concession on my part, so bright I felt my nose would bleed.

The differences that emerged as we tried to set up a permanent home together were not just aesthetic, they were functional. I need surfaces—kitchen counter, coffee table, bookshelf edges, dressers, and especially windowsills—to be clear, like runways. That way you can use them, and you can see the few objects you've placed there precisely to be seen in a particular way. It is my aspiration that other things be stowed, and I don't mind if they are somewhat jumbled inside the closet, under the sink, in a basket or cupboard. I am constantly picking up objects and tucking them away. David, on the other hand, requires use objects of all kinds to be arrayed before him in operational readiness. He likes to keep a card table set up in the bedroom for a puzzle that never gets finished, and he likes to empty his pockets and satchels of change, receipts, his wallet, keys, books, manuscripts, nail clippers, sunglasses, etc., on the nearest surface as soon as he crosses our threshold. At No. 239 he always wanted the yoga mat to lie at the ready against the wall. I wanted it in the closet. I stacked dishes in the sink. He would say, "The sink is the engine of cleanliness," and "Don't stuff the sink," as if these were dictums handed down by the ancients. It annoys him when I put things away, and it annoys me when he dumps things out. It is not uncommon for him to come after me with the accusation, "Did you *do* something with my . . . ?" It is not uncommon for me to deliver a censorious remark at the crashing sound of him upending the plastic tub that keeps our hardware, or the little

French cachepot where I stash combs, paper clips, our EZ pass, super balls, and plastic rings the kids pick up at the grocery store. He'll wash and dry a staggering amount of laundry and dump it out on the floor, always with the satisfied expression of a man whose offering cannot fail to please the gods. I follow, ritually, with my weekly fume-and-fold session. David likes to fill our rooms with rollicking sounds; I feel he is driving out the quiet I love. He enjoys applying strong-smelling tinctures—spicy oils, colognes, fruity lotions—but sometimes finds he cannot, around me, enjoy them with impunity. He has always enjoyed rearranging furniture often and with a vigorous, happy impulsivity: *Ta da! What do you think?* I think he's a vandal.

Inhabitation, for us, is a process in which we impinge upon each other, often without resort to whatever stores of maturity each might possess. Until he hollers, "You're trying to erase me!" or I yell, "You're burying me alive!" These are things we've actually said to each other while discussing the proper handling of spare change or the location of the armoire, at which point, nobody's laughing. At which point, we stop short. We do not destroy each other, nor permit ourselves to be destroyed. And then I see him. I notice, after all these years, that this serial drama isn't just me, blenching from a split-off self. Shipwrecked, I glimpse in the distance the light of a fire. I am not alone here.

In order to find each other, says Irigaray, both woman *and* man must constitute a place "appropriate to and for the other."[9] She suggests that woman's physiology all but fits her out as place, even exposes her to displacement by the man who seeks a home in her. Which I allow. But maybe man's physiology, his primordial homelessness, subjects *him* to an early lesson in relinquishing the beloved to the place she is and makes for herself. Isn't that what he's asking for, when he gestures ruefully at the denim slipcovers? To be, not implaced, not housed, but released unto himself? Just as sometimes I ask, on the contrary, to be situated, made comfortable, in him, to be seated beside the improvised, stone-circle hearth of him. Years go by when we don't understand each other.

I suppose what we keep out with our house walls is what we all have in common—the storm, the wolf, the people with clubs. But what in the world goes on behind the facade? What do you make a place for, in that clearing called home? My parents did not allow me and my brother to say "shut up" to each other, something I think about every time I overhear one of our children say to the other, "Shut *the fuck* up." Ah, home. Does everyone live like this? I have the impression of two figures lying in the sleigh bed nose to nose, believing no one *out there* could possibly experience such a ridiculous plenty of private delight. Home entailed a lifting of moratoria, a suspension of rules of order. We laughed at each other's rude or antic jokes. We ate candy and cookies in bed and dropped the packages sleepily over the side like Colette finishing another page. Does every couple wake to find their baby standing in her Onesie at the bedside, her face covered in chocolate?

So much blossomed in that clearing. Even I did. It was a marvel how the children came forward, and we started writing, and we began to study the world and ourselves. Lucy sat up and spoke. Byron sat up and spoke. Like any parents we wanted a child of ours to live in a good strong house with windows and doors and we knew we hadn't built it yet. That was an advantage, we thought; ours would be an unfinished house. *Come as you are*, we used to say. Also: I have the impression of terrible words David spoke to me, for days the taste of ash on his mouth, and coals that would not go out, that lay in the corners candescent with harm. And of things I would not say, my implacable inwardness whose method was to leave no trace, a stinginess that, I know, could strip paint from the walls.

Together we made space for the impulses, and then, in our different ways, in spite of ourselves, we doubled that space, to make room for shame about the impulses. How we bulged at the seams.

But I see I have exaggerated. Then overcorrected. What goes on inside any house is so subjective it resembles madness.

Every house harbors secrets. But the domestic life of New Yorkers has for a long time been set apart as faintly abashing in a particular way. The space we occupied at No. 239—about 1,100 square feet, with another 900 square feet of work space below—was very large by New York standards. The apartment across the street was significantly shy of 900 square feet, and later, the four of us lived in an apartment on 8th Street that was fewer than 600 square feet. Our home today, on Grand Street, is 1,000 square feet, about average for a Manhattan co-op. On the other hand, single-family houses haven't been built that small in America since the 1950s. Today, the average new single-family house is more than 2,400 square feet. That's the norm; it's the house people live in on television. For many New Yorkers, it's the house our relatives live in, and we go to them on Thanksgiving for the same reason Rockwell did not serve up his golden-brown bird in an "eat-in kitchen."[10]

The typical Manhattan abode simply lacks the square footage necessary to organize interior space according to expectations. What you get instead is a commingling of functions that are normally segregated and an intimacy some find inappropriate or uncomfortable. Children share a bedroom, or even sleep in their parents' room. Often there's only one bathroom. In a few of the oldest tenements, the bathtub is still in the kitchen. People often eat in their living rooms. Entertaining in these circumstances is almost unavoidably casual. If a couple who live in a tiny walk-up invite you to dinner, you will witness the ferocious labor required to prepare a hot meal in a galley kitchen, to drag out a folding table while kicking toys out of the way, and then to tidy up the blitzkrieg that results. It is all very unlovely and close; acquire the taste, and nothing could be nicer.

No. 239 was pressed into this nonconformity from the start, in an era when New York was only beginning its lingering, reluctant abandonment of the single-family house. Not far from No. 239, on 4th Street, another house began its more conventional career about a decade earlier. Known today as the Merchant's House Museum, it was occupied for decades by the family of well-to-do hardware importer Seabury Tredwell. On the basement floor was a busy kitchen and family eating and living area, with a back entrance for deliveries and one fronting the street for the family itself. Above was the neoclassical front parlor where the Tredwells received guests; visitors first entered the vestibule, then waited in the hall to be announced. Sliding pocket doors opened from this parlor onto a formal dining room. On the second floor, Seabury and Eliza Tredwell each had a large, airy bedroom joined by a dressing area, and above that was the nursery, and finally the servants' garret.[11] No. 239 was a modest version of this same house. But before 1850, more than one family divided its interior space in ways that remain obscure—did they share a kitchen?—and that were not sanctioned as socially appropriate. As late as 1872, an opinion in the *New York Times* reiterated the persistent idea that increasing numbers of New Yorkers were actually rejecting the single-family house, and not out of economic necessity but because of something like moral turpitude. "They are debasing their mental and physical energies," the article complained, "losing their self-respect and taste for improving entertainments, and placing themselves gradually but surely, and *of their own free will*, upon a level with those abroad who are born to degradation."[12]

One house, one family. That's the basic requirement for respectability. To be more specific, the house is seen as properly containing and representing the generativity of a single traditional marriage: one man, the head of the house, one woman, who represents the body, and the children who are its fruits and its ornaments. Couples who can't afford to maintain an independent household are considered not quite equal to the institution of marriage, and those who maintain a fully functioning household but aren't traditional nuclear families—gay couples, unmarried women— are accused of somehow misrepresenting themselves in the house, which maintains them in the same safety, dignity, and independence their neighbors enjoy. So powerful is the house as a symbol of the idealized nuclear family that for some of us, the house seems at once to represent and to fictionalize what we are; it tells a convenient half-truth.

For others, it is a mask that fully obscures identity. Father, mother, daughter, son, boarder, servant, slave, cousin, caretaker, mother-in-law. All breathe within the same walls. But the house, even as it holds up an image of some, erases the others. To lie down at night in the attic of the Tredwell house as an Irish servant girl—"bridgets" or "biddies," they were called—must have been to experience the slow and almost painful return of self-awareness, like blood to the frostbitten extremity. Inside this house, the defining fact is that you are not a Tredwell, and so your thoughts fly away to the places where you, too, were a daughter and sister, or where you will be, one day, a woman, teacher, wife, mother. In the most extreme cases—let's say you're Aminta, born in slavery—there may be no place to fly but heaven. Your lot on earth is to stand behind the mistress's chair, watching and wishing for a bite of pie. You do not dwell within the estate of the Francis Lewis family, you are *part of that estate*. You are a not-there, incorporated like a lintel piece or doorpost into the non-I that protects the I.

But you *are* there, aren't you? Living together in an arrangement that marks off some as being-there, others as there-only-through-the-other, barely-there, or not-there, one lives among shadows. And monsters.

Lord knows, our neighbors at No. 239 taught me this: The figure of the house links people one to another, like it or not. From the point of view of the outside, it *implicates* them in each other.

When we moved into No. 239 in 1997, having purchased the third floor with its roof deck (the next year we would acquire the second floor, too), we joined two other parties in the house. Gary owned and occupied the basement. Oren owned the parlor floor, which he rented to recent college grads.* We hardly noticed them. David and I were in the very act of producing our first child; I remember my seven months' belly tightening into a fist as I hauled our books and dishes from their boxes. We were preoccupied with a fruitfulness—biological, material, and, what, spiritual?—that seemed fragile, requiring exquisite care. While becoming mother and father, we also were taking up the top half of No. 239 and assuming the majority of shares in its corporate structure. We claimed the most space, the most light, and, in any decision the co-op might make, the most powerful vote. Finally, we took over the "books," such as they were, from the guy who sold us the second floor, a gay man of boyish good looks whose scrupulous tending to co-op affairs had (I would learn much later) nearly wrung the life from him.

Gary and Oren, however, had history in the house. They'd both bought their units immediately after No. 239 was renovated and offered as a co-op in the mid-'80s, when crack cocaine sales were descending like a plague-cloud on Alphabet City. To the best of my

---

*These are pseudonyms, as is the name for Gary's companion, Joanne.

understanding, the two men had come, in fact, as a package. Both
were married, Gary to Oren's sister. Or was it Oren who was married
to Gary's sister? In any event, Oren and his wife were raising a baby
daughter. The two couples shared the rear yard. For a number of years
they all lived together in what must have been a family, indeed a growing family. It came apart. Both couples divorced, apparently not without bitterness. Gary stayed on in the basement apartment his former
brother-in-law had, we gathered, helped him to acquire. Oren, though
he moved at some point to Queens, also kept title to the scene of his
early family life; in co-op files was the single page on which his ex had
signed over proprietorship, a document he consulted more than once.
On the day we moved into No. 239, Gary and Oren already had invested twelve years in a house that, for them, brimmed with meaning.
On that day, wholly naive to the fact, we took up residence in their
dream house.

And it isn't hard to see how we became, as Gary used to say—and
we would squirm and grimace—"one big dysfunctional family." It isn't
hard to see how David and I became house mother and father. "You
two are always *double-teaming me*," Gary sputtered in one phone call.
"Just because you're married doesn't mean . . ." I don't remember the
rest, but I do recall that David and I had indeed struck a deal to take
turns answering his calls. It isn't hard to see how David became the
Callow Manor Lord, with Gary soliciting cash for small jobs like shov-
eling the walk, or how I became Head Bitch, penning officious letters
explaining that subletting was a *privilege* and not a right, in response to
which Oren hissed, "How *dare* you send me certified mail? Do you
think you're a *lawyer*?" His young tenants understood the family differently; one night, after knocking and asking them in what I thought
was a friendly way to discontinue their band practice, I overheard them
speculating that I was Oren's daughter, that their rent was, in fact, my
living. "They're *always* here," one said, laughing. "I mean, what do they
do all day?"

Gary was always there, too, in his earth cave. He had the misfortune
to occupy that part of the building that was inarguably its netherpart.
It was from somewhere beneath Gary's floor that, due to mysterious
fluctuations of a geologic nature, there sometimes arose a mustiness

that reached the first-floor stairs; on one or two occasions the odor was downright fecal. Certain friends and neighbors claimed never to have laid eyes on Gary. He was bearish in shape, chesty and a little plump, with pleasant brown eyes looking out from under a moppish haircut. He wore baggy T-shirts and sweatpants exclusively, which contributed to an air of vulnerability. Gary was ingratiating. He wanted you in on the joke, to partake of and endorse his boisterous enthusiasms and extravagant fantasies. *I got a lotta friends, okay?* he once told us. *All I gotta do is ask, they show up tomorrow with a bag a money.* When he felt threatened, and he was sensitive to threat, he would erupt loudly and furiously. He was into Ultimate Fighting and kept hairless cats. He worked at times in construction, other times, so he said, as a bodyguard or bouncer. What I noticed the first time I entered his apartment was how, amid an abundance of stuff, the walls were white and generally bare, save for a large poster of Yoda, the troll-like Jedi master from *Star Wars*.

Gary's neediness and, yes, considerable charm, recruited to his side a handful of ferociously loyal helpmates, among them a freckled cable installer whom David and I sometimes referred to as "Gary's butler," and, far more important, Joanne, a new girlfriend. She was quite a bit older than he, wore long T-shirts over skinny black leggings and a puff of bleached-blond hair drawn into a low ponytail for which we privately (but still to our shame) called her Coonskin Cap. When Joanne first moved in with Gary, she had a broken front tooth, but she soon inherited a sweet yellow dog and, she hinted, substantial assets, some of which she put toward dentistry. On a beautiful spring morning, Joanne would sit on the stoop beside her sweet yellow dog to enjoy a cigarette and light coffee from the corner bodega, and in those moments I felt happiness coming off her in waves, sensed her tensile strength. Joanne was nobody's fool; even if she slept on an inflatable mattress in a basement, she was determined to set things straight, to raise Gary's stock in the world, and along with it, her own. I never knew exactly what their story was. But I had no trouble recognizing it as a love story.

Gary's connection to the building itself was a vigorously active one. He had, at one point, plans to pave the garden next door (notwithstanding we didn't own it) for a driveway, which would lead to the martial-arts studio he planned to build in the backyard; not to worry, he said, there's a roof terrace in it for you guys. Or he wanted to enclose the building's front setback area in glass for a kind of solarium effect. And he actually completed any number of more modest jobs. In the vestibule, he put up mirrors and a security camera by which he (and he alone) could monitor any who might appeal for admittance there. Gary was both adept at home maintenance and repair—a trait we lacked, and that held us somewhat in his thrall—and, at times, seemingly quite unrealistic about what sorts of projects were advisable or even practicable. I felt toward him an unstable mixture of distrust and allegiance.

Oren was another matter. His presence was characterized by absence and repeated offense by his proxies. A taciturn, moody Israeli with an appealing accent and quite handsome features dominated by dark eyes, he, too, could erupt, but otherwise affected a very high disdain for all proceedings having to do with the building. It was with some effort we convinced him it was not our job to collect his rent from the tenants who, at the end of their leases, were apt to leave great mountains of refuse in front of the building for us to sort and bag. Oren for the most part scoffed at even attending co-op meetings; indeed their agendas were increasingly dominated by discussion of how to establish and enforce rules that might somehow bring him to heel. Once, without even informing anyone much less asking permission, he sent a crew of construction workers to punch a big hole in our bearing wall and install central air conditioning in his apartment. The ductwork required a slight lowering of the ceiling in the first-floor hallway. This particularly upset Gary, who needed the clearance for his martial-arts lances.

Oren had handily and at times cruelly dominated Gary, but with sharp-tongued Joanne in the latter's corner, things were changing. (The way Oren talked about her—"that *woman*"—you'd think she was a Gorgon.) Gradually, the family discord converged like an anguished somatization on one part of the building: the membrane between Gary's and Oren's places. There were leaks, Gary said, and did we know there was no insulation, and did we realize that Oren's tenants came home at all hours, scraping chairs, clomping around *boom boom boom* in their enormous boots? This was why we were getting phone calls from Gary. This was why I was asking Oren's tenants to turn down the amp, for Christ's sake. As board members and majority shareholders (aka Mom and Dad), it was our job to referee. Per Oren, Gary and *that woman* were nuts, end of story. Gary's countermove: He'd sue us if we didn't throw the book at Oren. The summer of 2001, while we were at my folks' place in Vermont, we got word the police had been summoned to No. 239 to defuse what seems to have been a gladiatorial clash between Oren and Joanne that left trauma and outrage in its wake.

We made an excellent start at fixing all this. At the same time we were engaging professionals to do a top-to-bottom assay of whatever structural problems we might have, we also solicited the assistance of our sage co-op attorney, Stanley, to broker a tentative peace among us. Oren, it was agreed, would carpet and pad; the rest of us would approve his tenants before they moved in; Gary could go into Oren's place and apply Liquid Nails until he achieved satisfaction. We even agreed the co-op would share the cost of adding soundproofing to Gary's ceiling, provided he submit, in advance, a reasonable professional bid.

But it soon became clear from the comings and goings in Gary's apartment that he and Joanne were embarked upon a major nesting operation, an all-out renovation that, though perhaps overdue, was ill-timed considering our structural problems. Gary sent us a note: "Joanne and I are very appreciative of you both sticking with us to produce a civil and somewhat fair game plan to cut down on the noise that is created by the tenants upstairs," it began, but warned the job was turning out to be "a lot tougher than we originally thought, only because I have to move the stuff around in my apartment and really don't have any place to put it." Also because "two layers [of insulation] are called for" and because of another "problem that no one knew about until now," to wit, "When we were taking down the ceiling I thought it was like a miniature Twin Towers. I am going to have to replace my air conditioner due to the extreme amount of dust, dirt, and debris created by this job." I jotted off a quick and, I hoped, preemptive reply: "We just want to remind you that if you have additional expenses . . . you should bring this to a co-op meeting for *pre-approval*," I emphasized. "Normally we wouldn't want to be sticklers about this but we really must watch out for mission creep as we have other big expenses coming and will have to *prioritize.*" Soon thereafter, Gary submitted an invoice for nearly $16,000, much of which, notwithstanding my obnoxious use of italics, had not been submitted for *pre-approval*, and to which he affixed a single receipt for $1,400.

It was around this time that David, reading in bed, suddenly sat up eager to share with me a quote from Thucydides that he felt sure offered a bolt of insight on how best to handle Gary and Oren. It had to do with the Peloponnesian War: "Sincerity (whereof there is much in a generous nature) was laughed down; and it was far the best course to stand diffidently against each other with their thoughts in battle array. . . . And for the most part, such as had the least wit had the best success; for both their own defect and the subtlety of their adversaries putting them into a great fear to be overcome in words . . . they therefore went roundly to work with them with deeds. Whereas the other . . . thinking they needed not to take by force what they might do by plot, were thereby unprovided and so the more easily slain." I had to read it a few times before I grasped what David was urging, namely, that when it came to our co-owners, we should quit cajoling, quit assembling evidence in our just and proper cause, and instead, when we got the chance, run them through.

And so we had arrived at the neighborly maxim *kill or be killed* even before that fateful night when the call came and we all were tipped from our ship of fools into an ice-cold swell.

Over the next few months our contact with the "others" came in desperate, rageful blurts. A few days after we moved, there was the meeting at our lawyer Stanley's office down the block. Snappishly I announced my feeling that there was little hope we could manage a major rebuilding together. I wanted a *divorce*, I said, and I used that word, Gary rearing out of his chair to scream his protest over our failure to remit his invoice. He'd brought along his tassel-loafered personal attorney, who looked alarmed. Then there was the meeting in Oren's unit at No. 239, all of us sitting on our knees on the floor. Oren insisted we hire (and we did) an architect acquaintance who would not, he said, submit to our insulting request for a résumé; indeed Oren, an air-conditioning contractor, planned to effect the repair himself without delay; all *we* knew how to do, he sneered, was to sign checks. More screaming all around. Finally, we gathered at our little place across the street, a meeting we'd called in order to serve Gary and Joanne with a notice of default for un-permitted and very likely illegal alterations in their apartment, our way of saying there was no way in hell we were paying for them. Joanne, in her formidably aggressive way, rushed the arena; David barked that Gary was the shareholder, not she; whereupon Joanne, to our astonishment and dismay, let loose a croaking sob. "That's it," said Gary, pushing back his chair with a clatter. "That's it. You made Joanne cry. We're lawyering up."

After three months, we got away—from them, from financial burdens that were all but crushing, and from the sagging visage of our former home—by taking Lucy out of pre-kindergarten and heading down to Virginia to live for a time at David's parents' house. We had officially slipped from the status of householders, of mother and father maintaining our young in safety and self-sufficiency. Even at this distance the house in its diseased, undead condition swam always in my head. It had failed to secure our family but bound us more tightly than ever to the people we most longed to escape. We couldn't make a move, couldn't sell, couldn't fix, without the support of at least one other shareholder. "Stuck w/ these people," I scribbled dejectedly in my little notebook. "Too difficult to solve."

In mid-summer, Gary graciously suspended his maintenance-fee strike—Oren never did—and met a few times with professionals working on the building, for which he submitted an invoice that included tolls, cab fare, lost pay, and lunch, with a cc to Tassel Loafers. On one occasion, when he was dunning me for payment thereon, I told him that I was sorry for the situation, but we all were suffering, to which he replied, bellowing down the phone, "I don't want you to say you're sorry for the situation, I want you to *take care of me!*" I heard him. I saw him. I knew he was *there*. But he wasn't mine to take care of. And that's when I knew we'd have to play out this game that had started in the house, in which I hadn't seen and didn't take care, in which I played, in short, one evil mama.

Moving Day

*G*ET UP EARLY. *Select a good-natured carman with a stout iron-gray horse. Eat a hearty breakfast.*[1] This, in the opinion of one newspaper columnist, was how best to fortify oneself against the most wearying occasion of the year in mid-nineteenth century New York, Moving Day. In a custom particular to the city that had embraced the nickname "Gotham" (after a village in English folklore whose residents evaded the king's will by feigning insanity), rental leases expired on May 1, and intensely mobile New Yorkers switched houses, en masse, that very morning. Doors on every street flung open to disgorge their occupants into a thronging kaleidoscope of people and things. On that day of noisy social encounter and sweaty, exasperated striving, New Yorkers, as if caught up in some abstract dance, *performed* the new urban lifestyle in their dirty streets. It was, fittingly enough, an enormous hassle.

In the spring of 1849, Elisha Wolcott Barnard and his wife, Frances (Dodd) Barnard, were set to enter this crush, moving from the crowded, time-worn quarter just north of Jacob Van Corlear's hook to a new rental house in a developing neighborhood on the outskirts of town. They were to be among the very first tenants of No. 239 E. 7th St.[2]

And as they were long-married, middle-age folk, as both hailed from hearty old Yankee families—his people from Hartford, Connecticut, hers from the vicinity of Newark, New Jersey[3]—let us assume they *did* get up early that May morning in 1849. Let's give them a good breakfast with a cup of strong tea. On a spring morning more than 150 years ago, a horse drew up before the Barnards' Broome Street address pulling a simple two-wheeled wagon. It would be naive to imagine the cartman charged only the legally prescribed fee for carrying the Barnards' things uptown; this was his harvest day, after all. But let's say the bargain went off well, with a minimum of the requisite cursing and fuming.

Even under ideal circumstances, the day was sure to enervate all concerned. *Let your wife direct the cartman*, our columnist advised the paterfamilias. *She* will *do it, and you may as well let her first as last*. Indeed, Frances Barnard had every reason to cast a concerned eye over the wrapping of table legs and looking glasses, the packing up of bedsteads and chairs, crockery and cutlery, hatboxes, trunks, carpets, curtains, washtubs and oil lamps, for their rough journey over the cobbled streets. The respectability and comfort of the Barnard home were hers to defend, and Moving Day, with its inevitable damage to family objects, was a hazard to both; occasionally an overloaded cart simply capsized in the public way, smashing the lot and bringing traffic to a clattering halt. "Three movings are as bad as a fire," or so the saying went.[4]

Keep cool, our reporter urged. *Don't scold the servants and don't worry the children*, the servant in this case a girl of eighteen named Theresa, born in New York but probably of Irish extraction, and evidently poor; the Barnards themselves were hardly rich. It is likely that Mrs. Barnard wore an old dress and dirty gloves and issued orders to Theresa but worked alongside her. As for children, such was the strain of Moving Day that a contemporary newspaper reckoned by sundown any number of mothers would have "flogged their primary offspring and declared they did not care 'if they cried their nasty little eyes out.'"[5] But the three grown children of Elisha and Frances Barnard were more likely to lend a hand than whimper and get underfoot. Frances, at twenty-two, would soon marry a Williamsburg pharmacist.[6] Levi, named for his father's older brother (who died young), was now twenty; once ensconced at No. 239, he would find work in a tea shop just around the corner on Avenue C. Sixteen-year-old Elisha, the baby of the family, was already at work in a pianoforte manufactory.

Get one or two rooms in order at the new house, as soon as you can.
Sage advice that in all likelihood would have to wait until morning. If
they were like other New Yorkers, that night the Barnards fell exhausted onto featherbeds thrown down in the parlor, having eaten a
cold supper rather than take the trouble to light the stove. On May 2,
they would wake to a day on which, as one local observed, "every man
feels himself a stranger in his own house. . . . Coffee pots refuse to
boil until they have 'got the hang of the kitchen.' The maid has discovered that the Croton in the new hydrant has a peculiar flavor—not
half so pleasant as the old, and the mistress is sure that *that* Mr. Smith
has got her into a most odious neighborhood. The sugar at the new
grocery is at least half sand, and the Graham bread of the new baker
has a great deal too much molasses. . . . In short, every thing is wrong
and must be for a month to come, at least."[7] Theresa would set to
scrubbing away the filth of former tenants—not so terrible a job as it
might be, since No. 239 was only a few years old. The Barnards would
tack down their carpets and reassemble furniture in their new rooms.
Very soon, they would begin getting to know the other families with
whom they'd share the house and the block.

The street so recently imposed on marshland must have had the
undifferentiated feeling of any new housing block, a canvas of washed
mud and new brick, dotted here and there by a lithe-waisted sapling.
It had all the necessities. The three- and four-story houses were not as
generously proportioned as the new dwellings on St. Marks Place or
along Washington Square on the west side. But neither were they the
wooden hovels of the Five Points farther south. From their new home,
the Barnards looked down on a large coal yard across the street. For a
beefsteak or sausage, they could choose the butcher on the southeast
corner of Avenue C, or another on the northwest corner of Avenue D.
Grocers, which probably doubled as grogshops, also could be found at
both ends of the block. Baker Caspar Trumpy (whose Graham bread,
one hopes, was not overcharged with molasses) bore his hot loaves
from the oven just around the corner on Avenue D.[8]

What really made the location attractive, though, were the places of
work that lined the river. If you took a walk one day in the 1850s, beginning at Houston Street, where the ferry left for Williamsburg, and

strolling north along the riverfront, you'd come across the large ship-yard of Westervelt & Mackey's that reached up to 3rd Street, then Smith & Dimon's shipbuilding establishment, William H. Webb's sprawling, brick-gated shipyard between 5th and 7th streets, the Neptune Iron Works, Morgan Iron Works, the Dry Dock Company's bank and ironworks, John Englis's shipyard, Secor Iron Works at Avenue D and 11th Street, the Steers brothers' shipyard at the foot of 11th, and, at 12th Street, the massive Novelty Iron Works, taking up two city blocks with adjoining waterfront slips—and you'd have passed, in addition, a number of small joineries and yards that fashioned ships' spars and planks.[9] Though their locations changed a little over the years, most of these businesses had been established for years, together employing thousands of men. Throughout the 1830s, only two lonesome houses, belonging to shipbuilder Francis Fickett, stood at the eastern end of our block;* but already the riverfront echoed with the clatter of the caulking iron and the hiss of the blast furnace.

The decade leading up to the birth of No. 239 and its neighbors was one of wild, booming expansion, punctuated by a series of chastening blows that hardened class divisions among New Yorkers and stunned them—temporarily, of course—into wondering whether their "go-ahead" lifestyle was the object of some awful divine judgment. During the summer of 1832, cholera came on emigrant ships to North America, an infectious affliction so fast-acting and violent it shredded the intestines in an effusion of "rice-water" diarrhea. The well-to-do beat a quick path to the countryside; in town, thousands perished. Then, in 1835, a terrifying two-day blaze left the grandiose new Merchant's Exchange and, indeed, much of lower Manhattan's "golden toe" a soot-black, smoking pile. These setbacks quickly overcome, growth raced forward on the newly greased skids of capitalist exchange: railroads, canals, and plenty of credit for manufacturers, merchants, and farmers settling the frontier. "Every body was becoming suddenly rich,"

---

*Fickett had been a member of the Lewis Association that bought the meadow slice from Morgan Lewis, set it off in lots, and filled them. During this same early part of the nineteenth century, proprietors filled "water lots," extending the shoreline by a block or more beyond its original location around the present-day Avenue D.

as *Niles' National Register* put it. "Houses and lots became more profitable than fine gold."[10] But when European investors began calling in debts, and the federal government decided to take only gold or silver for public lands, coin—hard money—became the order of the day. On May 8, 1837, the Dry Dock Savings Bank, at 10th Street and Avenue D in the heart of Manhattan's shipbuilding industry, was the first to withhold specie from depositors, and to fold. There followed a general collapse of banking, widespread business failures, and a long, grinding depression; mothers went door to door begging a crust of bread.

It was upon this scorched earth that our block of row houses finally sprang into the light. Like the marshy terrain that physically underlay it, the events leading up to the development of our block would deeply mark its character. Lots on 7th Street between Avenues C and D had been valued as high as $1,200 during the inflationary spiral of the '30s. By the early '40s, the city assessor marked them worth half that. Agonizing as it was, the bottoming-out of the economy created an opening, a window of opportunity. It wasn't just wealthy men like merchants J. G. Coster and David Codwise, or even the prosperous lawyer Gilbert Speir, who bought lots and built houses on them. So did the Irish-born cartman John Turner and his wife, Eliza, who became the first proprietors of No. 258, my own first home in New York. As the Barnards moved into their rental house at No. 239, across the street, the Sparrows—James, a shoe salesman from Delaware, and his wife, Jane—were resident owners at No. 242. The Barnards' neighbors to the east were Abby and John Hedden, both born in Westchester; he was a cartman who later became an agent, tending affairs of the more well-to-do. At No. 245 were the Littles: James, a painter, his wife, Harriet, and their four young children. The year before the Barnards moved to 7th Street, a skilled ship carpenter named Christian Metzgar had been able to buy the new house at No. 247 from his boss, shipbuilder William H. Webb, "in consideration of services rendered and $1787.04."[11] There, Christian and Adaline Metzgar would raise their large family and be among the very few resident proprietors able to make ends meet without renting out a floor or two to other families.

The neighborhood's first householders negotiated a world in which the constant challenge of working families was to find affordable apartments near work on the one hand, and work that would pay the rent on the other. In this generation, a journeyman no longer slept under his master's roof and ate at his table; he was his own man. But he might spend his whole life seeking new markets for a day's labor. When orders slackened, wages fell and workforces shrunk at the establishments along the river. The new city rental market was similarly volatile. Neighborhoods changed quickly with the uptown march of the fashion-conscious, and demand for shelter intensified with the years' massive immigration from Old World ports. Landlords constantly tested the market to see just how much rent they could get; tenants who found their rates unreasonable were free to do the same. At the age of forty-five, Elisha Barnard was himself adrift on these currents. The year 1849 found him not only moving house, but abandoning his trade for a new job as house agent. He had been a bookbinder, a handicraft traditionally involving a few artisans working in a small shop, but increasingly systematized in factories where paper folders, sewers, and pressers stood at long tables performing their single function.[12] Maybe Barnard couldn't establish himself as a manufacturer but aspired to more than a place on the factory line. Instead, he would handle leases and collect rents for propertied folk.

In this new environment of mobility and risk, people like the Barnards, the Metzgars, and the Turners, when they moved to 7th Street, were throwing down their chips. They were laying bets that the new neighborhood's houses and jobs would keep them secure as one season turned into the next. These families had seen plague, fire, and the black years of a severe depression. They had known the exhilaration of change, and they surely understood its destructive power. As they took up residence on this new block at the edge of town, they made their homes along the great, hinged jaw of an industrializing New World metropolis; they settled in the very teeth of their untamed age.

All this made for a vexed relationship to place. Every May Day the papers and journals lamented a bygone time when the first of May meant children prancing around the maypole on the village green, and maids, like their grandmothers before them, washing their faces in the dew of the new grass, thought to impart a lovely complexion. "The household gods, the Lares and Penates, are scattered like rats by a badger," one commentator fretted in 1856. "Boys before they pass from tunies into pantaloons forget where they were born, and their fathers almost forget."[13] "Somehow," another quipped, "the idea obtrudes that some vestige of *monarchy* has lurked unperceived in our political system to cause so large a portion of our people who have no *home* to be turned out of *house* every May Day."[14]

For many, this relentless mobility did amount to homelessness. Some families stayed one step ahead of the rent collector by staying on the move. For another group, it reflected a kind of fevered acquisitiveness stimulated by scarcity. Even the comfortable attorney George Templeton Strong was not above ogling other people's digs, a not uncommon pastime in latter-day New York. "Brooklyn has advantages, too . . . ," he mused in 1865. "The situations on the Heights overlooking the bay can hardly be matched in any great city of Christendom. How often have I wished I could exchange this house for one of them, and that I could see from my library windows that noble prospect and that wide open expanse of sky."[15] Moving Day gave New Yorkers a chance to exchange this house for that one, even if that meant abandoning a tiresome walk-up for a smoking stovepipe, running, to quote the *Times*, "from the evils which they had to others that they knew not of."[16]

In the process they got to know their surroundings. Of necessity they foreswore the privacy associated with home and exposed themselves to one another. Once the notices, "to let," were posted on a building in February or March, current tenants might be repeatedly "surprised at their prayers, their meals, or social conversations" by a knock at the door and a request to inspect the premises.[17] Meanwhile, apartment seekers walked the streets, sometimes for days, checking out closet space and braving the grillings they'd receive from landlords or their agents.

House hunters, inquisitive landlords, and "to let" signs made regular appearances on our block during the middle decades of the nineteenth century. In 1850, John and Ann Ogden, an English couple in their early thirties, lived near the corner of Avenue C in No. 233, another rental property owned by Gilbert Speir. The next year they moved in with the Barnards at No. 239, where, in a back bedroom no doubt, Ann gave birth to their second child, John Jr.—something to remember the place by. After two years at No. 239, the Ogdens moved farther down the block into the home of gas dealer James Mangin, No. 255. Finally they crossed the East River to Greenpoint, probably following John's work as a machinist, and set up a household with his brother, William, and his young family. In 1855, young Charles and Hester Kelsey and their three little ones, as well as Charles's father, John, and an English boarder named Agnes, all lived on one floor of No. 269. Between them, Charles and John Kelsey, both ship carpenters, had already sampled the living at Nos. 221, 223, 253, 275, 277, and 289 E. 7th St.

The sheer frequency of these short migrations bespeaks a certain tension in the annual bargaining between landlord and tenant. But unlike in those poor areas where rents flowed mostly out of the neighborhood, this was an intimate tension in which propertied and tenant classes lived together, worked in the same trades, and, like it or not, needed each other's participation to bring down that big game, a house in Manhattan. Renters helped landlords defray the substantial cost of proprietorship; landlords anchored the neighborhood and made it accessible to working-class tenants. "Part of a house wanted: in a good locality, not above Twenty-eighth street, consisting of four or five rooms; lower part preferred; rent moderate."[18] "Board—A Family Having more room than required; would dispose of excellent Accommodations to a small genteel family; on second floor, for the ensuing winter; location desirable, accessible by cars and stages."[19] This is how it was done. In some cases, the women of the house may have cooked for tenants in exchange for more rent, one of a very few ways a married woman could bring in cash. In other cases families may have shared a basement kitchen. Sometimes tenants took just a room or two—a back parlor and bedroom, say.[20] While they lived together at No. 239, the Barnards, Ogdens, and a young married couple named Cooper would have shared a single outhouse in the backyard, drawn rainwater from the same household cistern, and pumped Croton, the potable city water, from a common street hydrant. In this way, together, they picked the carcass clean.

This nomadism, this domestic mingling among strangers, was deemed irregular—"socially promiscuous, nonselective, and immediately vulnerable to market determinations of personal worth," as historian Elizabeth Blackmar puts it—by the society at large and perhaps by the block's inhabitants themselves.[21] In papers like the *Charleston Mercury* or *Southern Literary Messenger*, residents of distant cities and towns could read about New York's Moving Day and shake their heads at this extreme version of modern American life.[22] But, increasingly, it was the only way to get along in this town. Over time, the epic hassle of Moving Day became part of New Yorkers' sense of their own exceptionalism. They came to see the untidy spectacle as a kind of urban festival that brought them together and set them apart. Amid the lamentations for a village paradise lost, you find, creeping into contemporary descriptions of Moving Day, that perverse sensibility that sees sublimity in the very wretchedness of city living. "The zest of the enjoyment," as one reporter explained it, "is in the discomfort, and topsiturviness . . . in the general antagonism and won't-come-to-rights obstinacy of everything."[23] The night of May 1, as New Yorkers lay their spent bodies down in a strange room, outside, the dimly gas-lit streets would be littered with debris in such a way as "can only be appreciated," wrote another, "by those who have indulged in such migrative campaigns."[24] Even the scribblers acknowledged that something was lost in the telling; you really had to be there.

They rise at first light. At the shipyards, work starts at six. At No. 274, on the south side of 7th Street near Avenue D, Frances Steers feeds the stove and puts the kettle on. Her husband, James Rich Steers, is a ship carpenter born the son of a ship carpenter in Plymouth, England. In the '40s he worked as foreman of the Smith & Dimon yard below 5th Street, but today—three years since the Barnards moved in down the block—he and his brother, George, have their own yard a few blocks to the north. George recently designed, and James helped to build, a yacht called *America*, a schooner of great beauty and renown, whose razor-sharp bow cut so swiftly around the Isle of Wight they renamed the regatta *America's Cup*.[25] Everyone knows James R. Steers; men hail him as he heads north on Avenue D. Across the street and

William H. Webb's shipyard as it appeared in 1863. From *Harper's Weekly*, November 14, 1863. The men were at work on *Dunderberg*, a massive ironclad ram of heavy wood construction ordered by the U.S. Navy the previous year. By the time she was launched in July 1865—some 20,000 people are said to have gathered for the event—the Civil War was over and the government had little need for the ship. Eventually Webb sold her to the French government. (Courtesy of HarpWeek.)

closer to Avenue C, Jabez Williams is up at No. 265. "Honest old Jabez Williams,"[26] they call the Connecticut-born shipwright, now in his sixties. He has moved his yard from the foot of 8th Street across the river to Greenpoint. He, too, heads north, to catch the ferry at 10th Street that runs every twenty minutes, starting at four a.m. His eighteen-year-old son goes with him. They are at work on a full-rigged, two hundred–foot ship to be christened the *Sirocco*.[27]

At No. 247, maybe Adaline Metzgar is still in bed, the youngest Metzgar, Cornelia, asleep in a small cot nearby. The Irish girl—her name is Bridget, Bridget Mooney—can see to the stove and chamber pots. But Christian Metzgar is foreman of the Webb yard, the most prolific and most famous in the city, if not the country; he must keep mechanics' hours. And though Christian's employer lives among fine things in a more capacious dwelling off Tompkins Square Park, he, too, will be at the yard bright and early. A fair, balding man with a pronounced brow ridge, William H. Webb's prodigious energies have been focused on designing and building seagoing vessels since he was a boy of ten and, during a break from school, built a small skiff entirely with his own hands. Webb places confidence in Christian Metzgar, but his nature is exacting. "As to his building a wooden cover above the hurricane deck instead of using a canvas awning," he writes Metzgar from a business trip abroad, referring to an associate working for him under contract, "I positively forbid his doing so. . . . I wish and expect my instructions to be literally obeyed, unless impossible."[28]

One by one, the ship workers come shuffling down the stoops into the gray dawn: Jonathan Ryder, No. 237, a ship caulker; William Tracey Jr., No. 241, Richard Morgan, across the street at No. 240, Robert Bowie at No. 254, and B. G. Conkling, no. 276, ship joiners; and more than a dozen ship carpenters—names of Van Benschoten, Lewis, Niles, Kelsey. One carpenter, Francis Ferry, comes out of the house near Avenue D he shares with Mary Fickett, widow of the shipbuilder Francis Fickett. Jonathan Jarvis, a joiner, emerges from No. 251 with four apprentice boys, who, anachronistically, bunk with him and his family. These men are by today's standards small and lean, an army of shirtsleeves and work trousers that makes its way east to the riverfront six days a week in all kinds of weather.

They build the bluff-bowed, wide-bellied sailing packets that keep regular time bearing large cargoes, mail, and immigrants between the trading ports of Europe—Le Havre, Liverpool, London—and New York. They build oceangoing steamships, and others that ply the coastal waters between New York and Savannah or New Orleans. They raise, on their riverside stocks, the clipper ships whose light, sharp bodies fly under a vast expanse of snow-white sail around the Horn of South America, up to California, across the Pacific to China and the East Indies. The clippers' job is to get there fast, carrying hopeful miners and scarce supplies to the newly discovered gold fields of a wild California, and rushing silks and fresh teas from Asian to North American and European markets.

So in earning their $15 or more a week—good money for a mechanic[29]—the men are building the city, and the country, and the world. It begins in the mold loft, where they chalk out on the floor the dimensions of the various pieces to be hewn from raw timber: the majestic New England oak, white pine, and chestnut; live oak from Florida; locust from Long Island. From the chalk marks they make a lightweight template used to guide sawyers and pliers of the adze in shaping the wood. One man stands in the saw pit, the other above; as they heave the two-man saw across a large timber, the man below eats sawdust. Inside a shack in a corner of the yard, junior workers feed a fire to ferocious temperatures; here, wooden parts that need to be curved are steamed into submission. Other carpenters ascend a ramp to stand high on the scaffolding and attach planking to the ribs of the hull, pounding in treenails until evening comes. Caulkers, sometimes lying on their backs, jam oakum in the seams with sharp metal caulking irons, then seal them with hot pitch. Joiners fashion ship cabins, doors, stairs, and furniture, including the oak and rosewood wainscoting, panels, pilasters, and carved cornices that embellish grand staterooms.[30]

Breakfast is at nine. Dinner at one.[31] Sometimes the children come with baskets on their arms and watch the goings-on. The work of their fathers' hands is everywhere on the seas and bays and rivers. Across the world, a clipper launched a year ago by the Webb yard, after a disastrous maiden voyage that included a shipboard murder, is running from Hong Kong to San Francisco at a speed that will not be bested by her kind. "Her sides are smooth as cabinet work and every line and moulding is graduated to correspond with her sheer," wrote a Boston reporter as she lay in her natal port, her bowsprit reaching above the shop roofs of South Street. "End or broadside on, her appearance is truly beautiful; if cast in a mould she could not have been more perfect to the eye."[32] And everywhere she goes she announces in gilt letters what she is and where she came from: *Challenge, New York.*

Along the riverfront, the block's ironworkers will pass the day shaping metal to human use, tending their furnaces, drying rooms, molding pits, and forges, wielding their planers, lathes, punching machines, and enormous iron-cutting shears.[33] Smoke rises from the stacks of the E-shaped Morgan Iron Works compound at the foot of 9th Street, "Iron Founders & Manufacturers of Land & Marine Engines," says an advertisement. "Vertical or Horizontal, High or Low Pressure Engines of All Descriptions. Saw Mills, Sugar Mills, Grist Mills. Cotton Presses, Pipes, Screws. Geering of all Kinds & c. Ship Engines, Boilers & Machinery Repaired at the Shortest Notice & With Dispatch. Castings of Iron or Brass. Including Bells of Every Size. High & Low Pressure Boilers. Smithing, Turning & Finishing in All Their Branches with All Kinds of Iron, Brass and Copper Machinery."[34] As afternoon wears on, pity the strongest men, five of whom are assigned to carry the ladle of molten iron for pouring into its mold at the Novelty Works, foot of 12th. John Ogden of No. 239, and from just across the street, John A. Secor, proprietor of the Secor works at Avenue D and 11th Street, William Wade next door to Secor, and Ames and Throckmorton and Edmondson and a host of others— they, too, are building the city and the world. Their machinery drives the steamers that carry staples and manufactured goods all over the globe, whose steerage brings strivers and seekers by the tens of thousands to Manhattan's shore. They are molding and polishing the ingenious tools that mechanize an industry like sugar refining, and in a decade's time their labor will bear fruit in massive production capacity— city plants will process 200 million pounds of crude sugar in a year— and its attendant cornucopia for consumers. *Rock candy, gum drops, jujube paste!* the confectioners will cry. *Pastilles de Paris, sugar plums, candy lozenges!*[35]

As much as it is a ship- and ironworkers' block, ours is a block of cartmen. They tend to settle together, and so it is here: the Heddens at No. 241; the Drakes at No. 253, who have seven children to feed; the Turners, on the south side at No. 258, whose glass-paned pocket doors separating front and back parlors may be the very ones from which David and I will scrape artificial frost one day in a distant future; the Powers family at No. 257; and the Brandts at No. 275—all have ridden a cart and horse to home ownership on 7th Street.[36] Irishmen Morris Powers and John Turner had to be naturalized as U.S. citizens before they could attain the requisite license from the city (in keeping with an 1826 law intended to exclude the Irish that only promoted their massive enfranchisement by the Democratic Party). Carting opened the way to something bigger for another Irishman, John Sudlow, at No. 266. He now operates a line of thirty-one horse-drawn stages running on a schedule from the corner of 13th Street, down Avenue C, and across town to the shore of the Hudson at Courtlandt Street, where passengers can catch the ferry to Jersey City. Sudlow hires other men to drive. As for the carters, they are manual laborers—"truly the sons of toil," as mustachioed Mayor Fernando Wood will put it a few years hence in an ingratiating speech to the Cartmen's Protective Association.[37] They are also petty entrepreneurs with a reputation for independence, reckless driving, and a steely determination to wring their pay from whoever hires them.[38]

John Hedden and Charles Drake and Morris Powers and Isaac Brandt get up early to fetch their horses from wherever they drowse—in the stable behind No. 251, perhaps. They harness the beasts to their carts, each with a license number painted in white on its side. "Imagine this City suddenly deprived of carts and modes of conveyance," the mayor will tell the cartmen. "The injury would extend to the whole Continent of America, because every State, every city, every village and every hamlet is connected with and interested in the continued and uninterrupted commerce of New-York." The horses will earn their oats today. It's hard work bearing the uninterrupted commerce of New York. When they can no longer pull, they will fall in the street and be carried to Barren Island in Dead Horse Bay, a place off the south shore of Brooklyn where their bones will be rendered for further use. Picking through the piles there in 1855, an inspector will find 150 dead horses, 4,000 barrels of bones, 6,000 jaws, four tons of horseshoes, and five tons of the hooves whose ceaseless ringing against the cobbles once had meant another nickel earned.[39]

Among these shipwrights, machinists, and carters is a smattering of men who, like Elisha Barnard, work as agents or clerks (even if, like Melville's Bartleby the scrivener, they would prefer not to). There are a few storekeepers. Leonard L. Johnson, No. 243, sells candles and lamp oils. Daniel D. Wright, No. 267, is in hardware, and his next-door neighbor, Gilbert Pine, has a feed store on Avenue D. Ichabod Burgess, No. 247, is a sea captain. At the end of the block, the resident owner of No. 273, Gould Selleck, makes capstans, the handled drums used for cranking up ship anchors.

If only one or two households on our block makes do without a male breadwinner—widows find shelter with wage-earning kin—the household without an adult woman is just as rare, and equally impoverished. Indeed it is heavy, unrelenting female labor that constitutes the household. Frances Barnard, Martha Selleck, Maria Burgess, Addie Metzgar, Ann Ogden, Nancy Sudlow, Sophia Drake, Eliza Turner, Hester Kelsey, and other women of our block form a working regiment of their own. Alongside them are the Irish women whose hunger and abundance make their labor cheap, whose own marriage and birthrates are held in check as they lend their young arms to the care of other women's families.[40] Sarah Jarvis, the ship joiner's wife, has help cooking for the children and apprentice boys in the person of young and illiterate Margaret McGee. In her forties, Martha Selleck oversees a household that includes her spouse (the capstan maker) and six offspring ages five to twenty-five; Bridget Murphy passes her early twenties at Martha's right hand.

They meet at the corner hydrant, their petite bodices and full skirts, perhaps covered by a bib apron, swaying over button-up boots. Everything that takes water—cooking, washing dishes, laundry, bathing—requires hauling it in buckets from hydrant and cistern into basement kitchen, or, for those without access to that amenity, up the narrow stairs. They go on foot for provisions, visiting the corner butcher, baker, grocer, perhaps heading south to Union Market, or west to Tompkins Market, where they can procure the produce of the countryside, a chicken, a slab of butter, a small basket of strawberries. To prepare the midday repast, the day's main meal, they clear the stove of yesterday's ashes, feed it with coal, light it, and adjust the dampers. The women pluck, chop, whisk, all the while tending the stove, which pours out a merciless heat on a summer's day. Husbands duck in, eat their dinner, and soon are back to work. The women boil water for the washing up. They scrub the heavy cast-iron pot with sand and haul the slop water to yard or gutter.

Still, everything is dirty. The children are sticky. The men perspire. They all track in the dust and muck of the streets, "composed of house-slops, refuse vegetables, decayed fruit, store and shop sweepings, ashes, dead animals and even human excrements."[41] The stovepipes leak soot, and the oil lamps give off a greasy smoke. Bath time for a half-dozen children can be managed once a week at best; ditto laundry, that much dreaded round of soaking, boiling, scrubbing, rinsing, bluing, wringing, starching, and heaving of sodden clothing to the back-yard line. A white collar is what they get for their effort.[42]

All this the women do in various stages of pregnancy, parturiency, nursing, and weaning. Ship carpenter's wife Hester Kelsey, at No. 253, has three-year-old Charles and one-year-old Mary; she will soon be pregnant again. At forty-two, Webb yard foreman Christian Metzgar's wife, Adaline, will soon give birth to their last child; with seven siblings in the house to look after her, tiny Christianna will no doubt enjoy a certain freedom from parental oversight. But at No. 239, machinist's wife Ann Ogden worries as she pulls baby John into her lap. The gap between this child and eleven-year-old Julia hints at a terrible loss. The hot months, when milk and other weaning foods teem with germs, are most dangerous. An infant is liable to grow glassy-eyed and limp with fever. Give no milk, says the kind young doctor from the dispensary. Cut the gums to complete the pernicious teething process, advises an international authority. Purge the baby with castor oil, rhubarb, jalap, insists a third expert. Maybe Ann Ogden goes to the corner druggist, Samuel H. Brown, and comes home with a pretty bottle. "MOTH-ERS!" scolds an advertisement for one opiate-laced elixir said to cure diseases incident to teething. "Do not let your own prejudices, or the prejudices of others, stand in the way of the relief that will be sure—

yes, absolutely sure—to follow the use of Mrs. Winslow's Soothing Syrup."[43] The feeble crying must be hard to bear.

Ann will no doubt rejoice when her boy pulls clears of his fifth birthday. Then he can join the older boys shooting marbles on the sidewalk. He can fly to the schoolhouse on 9th Street, where the primary department, under the direction of Miss Euretta M. Nicholson, strains at the seams with 650 pupils but has a spacious playground and a new piano.[44] That year, 1855, in the few blocks surrounding No. 239 more than fifty children ages five and under will not be saved.[45] In January, Mary Eliphant of Avenue D, at four years, one month, twenty-one days, will die from pneumonia. In May, five-month-old Michael Foesh will succumb to pertussis on 5th Street. Henry Francis of Avenue B will die of scarlet fever in September, three months shy of his second birthday. On October 15, five-year-old Ichabod Burgess Jr. will meet a different calamity; he and his two sisters will lose their mother, Maria. And it will fall not to their father, the sea captain, who for all we know is lashed to his post on the raging seas off Cape Horn, but to the women of No. 247—a grown adoptive daughter and perhaps the two dressmakers who board there—to close the blinds and sit with Maria as she threads the shoals of a painful gastrointestinal ailment and makes for the wide open. The vigil keepers' work is not heavy, but it is hard.[46]

At six the mechanics' bell tolls the close of the workday. The houses once again fill with the people Walt Whitman likes to walk among, whom he admires, emulates in his rough gear and easy posture, speaks to across any distance. "The hourly routine of your own or any man's life," the poet exclaims in his long, ambling line, "the shop, yard, store, or factory,/These shows all near you by day and night—workman! whoever you are, your daily life!"[47] Everyone is tired as evening falls.

After a grueling, sleepless night of travel from Paris, it was with considerable relief that Mr. James B. Murray greeted the dawn in the French port of Le Havre. This was the morning of April 29, 1841, Murray the New York gentleman who traded in lots on our block during its predevelopment years. That morning, as on many occasions during their long marriage when business parted him from his wife, Maria, Murray took up his pen to write her. The stage, he reported, had accommodated himself and all of *eight* Germans bound to the sea-port for emigration to America. "The children were from three to seven years old," he wrote, "and when I complained against this invasion of Goths, the only answer was a shrug of the shoulders and the 'Monsier, vous ne seres pas incommode—Il faut que les parens apportent les in-fans aux genoux.' [*sic*] This promise of keeping them on the knees was soon 'broken to the sense'—for as soon as night drew on, the children were squeezed in to the seats, and thus we sweltered away until 5 o'clock this morning. My cravat is almost literally melted, and the color of the green silk lining is distributed all over the shirt and [coat] lining, besides which smothered with dust."[48]

The Murrays, with their wide-ranging investments and Connecticut country seat,[49] represented a past already eclipsed on our block. Those Germans making the journey of their lives represented its future. The German tailor who in time would become the first person to both own and occupy No. 239 sailed for New York in 1839. He might have been one of those anonymous "Goths" sweating the night away with a rather ef-fete American in a green silk tie—except that Abraham Weinstein, in-stead of traveling overland to France, headed north from somewhere in Hesse or Bavaria to the German port of Bremen.[50] Nor did he have weary children to carry on his knees, and this may have been a motivation for leaving home. With his twenties drawing to a close, it was well time We-instein settled down and had a family. Perhaps he was a journeyman whose *Wanderjahre*, that mobile period of life in which a young man searched for an opportunity to establish himself as master and proprietor, stretched on and on until waiting began to seem like a loser's game. Men who could turn fabric into a suit of clothes were being turned into per-petual wage workers even faster in the erstwhile artisan strongholds of the German Confederation than in the far-off United States of America. As a Jew, his options would have been further curtailed by communities that had the right, by custom and by law, to suppress the establishment of new Jewish households, barring a young man like Weinstein from res-idency, from the practice of traditional Jewish occupations, and even from marriage itself. For him, it wasn't just time to move. It was time to leap.[51]

As he climbed the gangway of a square-rigged sailing vessel called the *Republic*, his future hidden beyond the horizon, I suspect that his mind's eye was keenly focused on a near-term plan. Maybe he was like me, my first child on the way, absently foot-tapping the tarp on the roof of No. 239, willfully believing only in the day's promise. At any rate, through circumstances that must remain obscure—perhaps the pair had met under the wedding canopy before sailing, although they don't appear to have traveled together—Abraham had a wife, Regina, and a baby son, Samuel, more or less immediately upon arriving in New York.[52] The little threesome probably would not have been out of place amid the working-class immigrants who enjoyed the green grass of the Battery on a Sunday afternoon, leaning over the railing to gaze at the sea. "They are the newly arrived," wrote editor Nathaniel Parker Willis, "the artisans, the German toymakers and French boot-makers—people who still wear the spacious-hipped trowsers and scant coats, the gold rings in the ears, and the ruffled shirts of the lands of undandyfied poverty."[53] But Saturday, not Sunday, was the Weinsteins' Sabbath, and it seems certain they tried to keep it. In 1842, three years after immigrating, Abraham joined with neighbors in signing the founding document of Rodeph Sholom, a congregation that cleaved to Orthodox traditions in those years, and whose first humble meeting place was the very building in which the Weinsteins lived, on Attorney Street just south of Houston.[54] The synagogue was a kind of be-all in-stitution, a center of mutual aid and charity for the needy, celebrations for Purim and the Fourth of July, study for children and adults, Jewish burial, and, of course, Sabbath and holiday observances. In these serv-ices, which lasted for hours, the Weinsteins could meet their friends and take in the words of Rabbi Max Lilienthal, reputed as the best German-Jewish preacher in the country.[55] If the demands of tailoring permitted them this one day of rest, they certainly did not permit two.

Abraham Weinstein had landed in New York during the swift and tumultuous rise of the ready-to-wear industry, which was utterly transforming the terms of his chosen work. Custom tailoring, espe-cially in the Broadway shops, still paid well but was increasingly a fusty preserve of the elite. In the ready-made business, wholesale clothiers divided the *craft* of making garments into tasks—measuring and cutting, basting, sewing, pressing, making buttonholes—which they contracted out to tailors of different skill levels while they focused on the clothing *business*. This meant finding fabric and labor as cheaply as possible, stepping up the speed of production, competing fiercely on price, catering to the latest tastes, and, most important, connecting with an enormous market in the burgeoning West, in the slave shacks and along the Main Streets of the South, or indeed among style-conscious urbanites themselves. This transformation made a good-looking broadcloth suit available even to the average mechanic; in Gotham, only the most indigent wretch need give the appearance of "undandyfied poverty."

What the transformation probably meant for Abraham and Regina Weinstein was very long days bent over needle and board in their home on Attorney Street. "One apartment frequently serves as bedchamber, kitchen and workshop," noted the *Times*. "The German settlements in this City and Williamsburg are alive with knights of the needle who work cross-legged in doorways and windows all the fair days of Summer time."[56] The "knight" usually did the measuring and cutting, but in order to make ends meet he typically required the constant participation of his wife, a circumstance that must have taxed Regina to exhaustion; she had, by 1845, three small children to look after—Samuel, Moses, and little Caroline—plus all the usual domestic duties.[57]

Caught on a wave of change, the Weinsteins could sink under it, or try to ride it. They did the latter. In the mid-'40s, Abraham was listed in the city directory as a tailor, his residence the only address given, implying waged or piecework for someone else. By the early 1850s the family had moved a few blocks to Houston Street, where they occupied an entire building, their business, listed as "dry goods," perhaps taking up a first-floor storefront. This seems to suggest that, even if they still sewed, they also may have hired others to perform the various tasks of clothesmaking; Abraham was now in retail. By 1855, the couple and their five children (as well as a German servant girl) were living and working on Avenue C at 6th Street; to the state census taker, Abraham gave his occupation not as tailor, but as merchant. Finally, in January 1860, the Weinsteins bought the three-story house around the corner, No. 239 E. 7th St., and established a separate warehouse way downtown in a marble-front building on Murray Street, a block west of City Hall (and not far from a sixth ward chockablock with immigrant stitchers). His oldest son, Samuel, now a young man of twenty, would serve as clerk in the wholesale clothier's business they called A. Weinstein & Co.[58]

By turning the corner of Avenue C onto 7th Street, the Weinsteins were venturing just beyond the borders of the German community to integrate our block; they were one of the first German families to settle there, and were among a tiny minority as Jews. As landlords, they would bring other Germans (including German Jews) to the block. At the same time, Abraham Weinstein, it would seem, had become a boss, perhaps hiring outworkers to fill bulk orders for coats or vests he received from a distant hinterland. As they skipped up the stoop of No. 239 for the first time, holding onto its ornately curved iron railing, the three younger Weinsteins—Caroline, fifteen, Clara, twelve, and Aaron, ten—must have felt proud of their papa and mama and all they had accomplished. Even as they brought a new wave of change to 7th Street, for them, this was the crest. No. 239 was their place of arrival.

And then the wave they had ridden broke, mysteriously, into a kind of stuttering chop. It had to do, I imagine, with Abe Lincoln, the wolfish-looking Illinois lawyer elected president the year the Weinsteins moved to No. 239, and with the dispatch the newsboys cried on the streets of New York about midnight on April 13 of the following year. Walt Whitman, out late after seeing Verdi's *A Masked Ball*, was among the pedestrians who gathered under the lamplight on Broadway to hear the news read aloud: As the residents of Charleston looked on, the South had attacked Fort Sumter, firing until defenders of the United States of America were ousted along with their flag.[59] Within days the man in the White House was calling up tens of thousands of soldiers and commissioning ships to blockade the South's major ports.

Both these actions may have occasioned anxiety in the Weinstein household. Before and during the war, the city assessor scribbled the word "infantry" or "military" next to the Weinstein name, a designation that earned the family a tax abatement and that surely signified military service of some kind.[60] Since the teenage Moses was not at home during these years, it's possible the Weinsteins (like the Barnards, whose son Levi would soon be encamped near Alexandria, Virginia, with a New Jersey Cavalry regiment) gave flesh and blood to their country's cause. If so, Moses apparently did not serve from New

York. Perhaps one of the Weinsteins was in a volunteer militia regiment responsible for drilling, parading at ceremonial events, and quelling local riots (which were rather common), whose members gave their time and money "from a thousand motives other than a desire to don the insignia of command," according to an official report that seems to protest too much.[61] At any rate, in a city where Douglas, not Lincoln, had won 62 percent of the vote, New York's Germans were, as a rule, and the Weinsteins were, almost assuredly, both pro-Union and antislavery.[62] At the same time, if Abraham Weinstein's new clothing house depended on Southern markets, he had to be worried. At the rather abrupt loss of this trade, the wholesale clothiers had stumbled into a trough from which many of the smaller firms would never emerge.[63]

This much is certain: After eleven on the night of September 9, 1861, a fire broke out in Weinstein's warehouse on the fourth floor of No. 45 Murray St. All the heroism of the city's volunteer firemen was brought to bear; in fact the struggle is captured in a romantic Currier & Ives lithograph, "The Life of a Fireman: The New Era: Steam and Muscle," that shows red and yellow flames roaring from the windows of a corner building, the smoke almost blotting out the moon above the cupola of City Hall. No. 45 fell in upon itself, and the buildings on either side and behind it were heavily damaged or destroyed. The *Times*, the *Tribune*, and the *Herald* all had the story the next day. "The light from the conflagration," reported the *Tribune*, "completely illuminated the lower part of the city." By September 11, the fire marshal had announced that he "strongly suspected" arson. All the buildings' occupants, clothing wholesalers and importers mostly, had been fully insured. Weinstein, whose own loss was estimated at $5,000, was insured in the amount of $8,000, with benefits going to an assignee, Isaac Bernard, a creditor perhaps. All these facts seemed to imply that someone, maybe even someone connected to Abraham Weinstein, set the fire to make good on fall merchandise that otherwise would have to be chalked up to a loss.[64] In 1861, that implication was simply left to hang in the air; the case apparently was not pursued, a course of events that, like arson and unproven accusations of arson, was not at all unusual. In 1865, for example, the *Times* complained that during the six months ending in May of that year, 90 of

195 fires had been considered "of incendiary origin," but led to only seven prosecutions and two indictments.[65]

Whatever happened that September night suggests a personal crisis for Abraham Weinstein. In city directories, he never again listed an occupation next to his name. When the census taker came in 1870, he called himself a retired tailor. It was also during his seven or eight years at No. 239 (precisely when, I cannot say) that Regina, Abraham's wife and helpmate for more than thirty years in America, vanished—died, I assume, since divorce was exceedingly rare in their community. It would be understandable if he came to associate this house of arrival with the agonies of a country he surely loved, and bound these up, in turn, with his own midlife losses.

When the war was finally over, it was a new day on our block. Work dried up in the manufactories lining the river. Blame the federal government's high tariffs on imported materials like iron, hemp, and Canadian timber, or its failure to subsidize steamship lines as the Europeans did. Blame the war, during which American ships had been pressed into service and the Brits were able to divert trade to their own vessels. Blame the high cost of real estate and labor in Manhattan, or the island's relative lack of access, in the new age of iron ships, to the coal and iron ores that fed the developing iron furnaces of western Pennsylvania.[66] Whatever the causes, the decline of shipbuilding and related industry in Manhattan was astonishingly precipitous. "The Novelty Iron Works has sold off most of its machinery and tools," the *Tribune* would report in 1870. "W.H. Webb's shipyard is to let. Henry Steers' yard is empty. The Continental Iron Works is almost deserted and green grass is growing in nearly all of the shipyards which, five years ago, were alive with workmen."[67]

It had not been all work. When a ship was launched from one of those yards, thousands of people would converge at water's edge to take part in that proud, cathartic drama. The builder, in frock coat and silk top hat, greeted the crowd. A girl on the edge of womanhood broke a bottle of wine over the vessel's bow. Finally the workmen pulled out the chocks; their enormous creation would glide from her ways into the East River as a brass band struck up a patriotic tune. Here was a chance for the workers to show off their handsome families, and for everyone to get well drunk. The young woman chosen to christen the ship, enjoying a moment of neighborhood celebrity, selected her wardrobe with care. When she launched the sloop-of-war *Brooklyn* in 1858, Eliza Westervelt, daughter of shipbuilder Jacob Westervelt, wore a green silk dress with three silk flounces of highland plaid, a lace berthé at the shoulders, and "a jaunty little hat of the most tasty pattern."[68] In 1869 came sixteen-year-old Chrissie Metzgar's turn. Last child of Christian and Adaline, Christianna had been born and raised on the block. She knew the Webb yard her father had supervised all these years, and she knew many of the people gathered there that May morning; and they knew her. "I christen thee 'Charles H. Marshall,'" she chimed. "May'st thou be as successful as thy predecessors on the Black Ball Line to whatever part of the world thou may'st go." Chrissie cracked the bottle over her bow, and off sailed the very last square-rigged vessel ever built in New York.[69]

It was again time to move. By 1870, a few original residents remained on the block. There was the painter James Little, retired now, and his wife, Harriet, and Sophia Drake, widow of Charles, the cartman. Morris Powers, also a cartman once, was now in liquor. But almost all of the ship carpenters and machinists had gone, off to seek the work without which there could be no home. The Ogdens and Ficketts were in Brooklyn. The Barnards had gone back to Newark, Frances's hometown. The Metzgars were free now to move to a more fashionable neighborhood in the east sixties, with Christian, always a man of influence, enjoying a soft landing as vice president of the Dry Dock Bank, now located on the Bowery. Abraham Weinstein, at fifty-four, also made a new start. He married a woman two doors down, a recent widow named Caroline Steinberg. She owned No. 243, so he sold No. 239 and, along with his son Aaron, moved in with her.[70] There, he would watch the block fill up with his countrymen.

Those early residents could not have imagined what would survive into this millennium none of them would live to see. Of 135 ships launched from Webb's yard, all except a single cabin are gone— burned, rotted, flogged to splinters by the waves.[71] Instead of great works or monuments, we have, salvaged by archaeologists from an abandoned cistern at 8th and C before the 1990s construction of a housing-police station, the simple evidence that they lived—the leavings of a festive meal, pig's jaw, goose sternum, the spines of fish, pipe, and flask. Oyster shells long ago dredged from the bosom of the bay. Pits of cherry, peach, and plum. Buttons, bottles, and coins. These objects are tucked away in some dark place at a museum in Albany. Marbles. Dolls.[72]

The block itself, of course, survives, including a dozen or more of the houses that long-ago generation lived in and passed by morning, noon, and night, whose faces, to a sixteen-year-old Chrissie Metzgar, must have seemed anything but blank. "All architecture," sang Whitman, "is what you do to it when you look upon it,/(Did you think it was in the white or gray stone? or the lines of the arches and cornices?)"[73]

Small Worlds

SIX

A FEW YEARS AFTER the conclusion of our family's housing debacle, Lucy's fourth-grade teacher gave her class an assignment to write a short essay on a significant moment. Lucy chose to write about the first night of our abrupt displacement, shortly before her fifth birthday, from the only home she'd ever known. On the essay's cover page is the title, "Moving," above a drawing of—what else?—a fast-food drink, burger, and fries, their packaging rendered in loving and accurate detail. She remembered her Aunt Lalou and little cousin Clara had been there, and that we all sat on the bare floor as we ate. "The snow white walls were almost hurting my eyes," she wrote. "Us, our clothes, our chocolate shake, burgers, and French fries were the only color in the room." And this had all been rather pleasant. "The Burger King," in particular, had "tasted warm and salty."

"Moving" reminded me that, given an empty room painted white, each of us will wash it in her own affective tint, inhabit it with her own body, and take away a correspondingly singular image of the place. To Lucy, the sudden change of perspective had given the new place a kind of holiday excitement. She was, after all, still a small child, her world full of vivid objects in a loosely structured physical environment oriented around her mother and father.[1]

My cosmology had placed the house at the center. Looking back at it from across the street, the tools of our daily existence rearranged in a seemingly random pattern, I was literally turned around. It was a time of frantic outward action coupled with a strange inner paralysis. I found it difficult to focus. Despite my nagging worry for them, I found it hard to pay attention to the children. My own worried mother sent me some Klonopin taped inside a wildflower seed packet. Each evening the swallowed blue pill, hardly larger than a seed itself, shrunk the world to the shape of a small oval frame, in which I read a storybook to Lucy and Byron.

But in the morning the world in all its terrifying scope reasserted itself. Shifting our center by only a few yards had torn us from some silken web, utterly changing our relationship to the neighborhood around us. For the first time it seemed like a mean, scary place that intruded unpredictably on our domestic sphere. A few weeks into our tenure in the new building, its management agent, exuding a preppy sangfroid, tossed out a shockingly lowball offer to buy No. 239; when we stammered a demurral, he advised us to be in touch when we got desperate. The *ssserpent*, we called him after that. Then there was the guy with more money than God. He drove up in an SUV to watch his excavator clawing up a couple of the smaller fruit trees and the daffodils Lucy and I had planted. I tried to assume a philosophical attitude, clapping a hand over my mouth for good measure.

Finally, there was the fact of our dwindling resources. How many beloved venues had opened to us, I belatedly understood, only because we'd possessed the magic passkey: money. You can't get an *ice cream* around here without a fistful of dollars, I thought in wonderment. That this could squeeze you out of a neighborhood you called home was old news to many longtime residents, of course. Defiantly, bitterly, I thought, *I'll sit in the park and breathe*. The air itself seemed thinner.

We were running out of room to maneuver when David's parents, on a reconnaissance mission to the city to find out what in the world was up with us, threw us a line. They offered "the farm" as a refuge. This was not a working farm, although it had been for many years, its Jersey cows producing milk for the markets of Georgetown, Washington, and Alexandria; it was the place where David and his five siblings had grown up, a large house surrounded by glittering lawn, pasture, and woods in the prosperous Washington, D.C., suburb of McLean, Virginia. His parents were in the process of selling it—they now lived full-time in the city—but would take it off the market for the summer, they said. It seemed a drastic move to absent ourselves from lives in apparent mid-collapse, to yank our kid from the pre-kindergarten class where she was learning to read and move back to Mom and Dad's place in another state. And yet, we figured, maybe a little time out of time, a little space out of space, were just what we needed to interrupt certain dire trends—chiefly that of our expenses-to-income ratio. So we stuffed the last of our furniture and toys into another storage unit, threw our clothes into the Dodge Neon, and headed for the Jersey Turnpike.

The car ride ended in the familiar crackle of tires on a gravel drive, a sound that meant you were entering another world. What a relief those first weeks at the farm were. At dusk we'd sit in the hammock under the heavy boughs of old trees and luxuriate in the deep, deep privacy of the place. "Buffered" is the word that comes to mind. We were wrapped in the concern of our families—my parents, David's, and two of his sisters lived not far away—and swaddled in a material amplitude that felt unearned, provisional, but for the moment, blessedly safe. We set up Lucy in her aunt Molly's old bedroom, a yellow corner room with twin four-poster beds, and Byron in his father's old room with its mirror shaped like a ship's wheel. My head began to clear. I completed the paper I'd been working on as part of my third semester in a master's program in poetry (a program that, by the way, I never finished, nor have I since composed a *single* poem despite having asserted, under number five in my list of self-instructions, that only death itself could prevent me from doing so). I sent out some résumés and soon got a freelance job writing a long piece for the union group AFL-CIO explaining the machinations of the U.S. pharmaceuticals market, a thicket I began to beat my way through in an attic room appointed with the stray artifacts of David's brothers' adolescence. David, who had always managed to work mostly from home as a freelancer, began a serious bid for a full-time office job. Our guiding principle: earn something, spend nothing. Except of course for the funds we sent north to people like Richard, the worthy, the *noble* structural engineer we'd engaged before fleeing, who assured us he was on the scene, he had the key, he would enter that banshee-haunt of a house and make it safe again.

Do the next thing is a favorite maxim I got from my brother, Cameron, who used it mainly while he was quitting cigarettes, to get past the moment when he really wanted one. I've found it to have broad practical application. You know: Make the next sandwich. Pick up the next sock. Open your eyes, put your feet on the floor, and stumble down the hall to the bathroom. Before you can do the next thing, though, whatever it is, there's one thing you need to know. You need to know where you are. It's important of course to locate yourself in time—is it Christmas morning? Are you late for first period?—but orientation in space is a prerequisite for even the simplest action. If you can't accurately plot your own body in relation to certain other points of interest, you end up peeing in a wastebasket.

This sort of thing happens to some people more than others. I've always had to work at spatial orientation. When I was a young child, I visited an amusement park fun house with my mother's family in northwest Iowa. One of its features was a long rotating tube painted with a spiral you were supposed to walk through. I watched the others make their way easily enough. Then I stepped in, and lost my feet without an instant of delay, as if I'd walked off a plank. My pretty young aunt wore a quizzical expression as she urged me on from the far end of the barrel. At both openings, a gaggle gathered to observe. A few times I struggled to my hands and knees, that spiral rearing and sinking away beneath me, but I soon pancaked again. That was one of the first times I remember coming to that inner cul-de-sac, that giving-up feeling I would meet again in windowless department stores and at cloverleaf off-ramps. Eventually, fun house authorities were persuaded to take what they assured us was a most extraordinary measure; they stopped the spiral turning so I could crawl to safety.

I suppose this is the kind of inborn trait that pushes you to pursue some experiences and avoid others, thereby reinforcing itself. Drop any handful of people into a new place, and there's always one who right away sizes up the territory, finds out where the train depot is, where to buy groceries and stamps. This person quickly develops a fervent opinion about whether the interstate or the toll road is faster at rush hour, and, if prevented from taking the helm in any wayfinding that might be required, seems to find this almost physically painful. I'm the one discreetly hitching myself to that person. This strategy will tend to further retard my own learning about the place, sometimes forcing me into such uncomfortable positions as having to insist, after, say, fifteen years of living in New York, that *bien sur* I know how to get to La-Guardia Airport, I mean, *really*. I'll MapQuest the trip (in both directions, because reversing steps can be surprisingly tricky), and mark out each leg on the odometer as I go. With enough repetitions I'll learn the route, but I may never get to what psychologists say is the next stage of place awareness, when trips from A to B to C become embedded in an overall picture of the area.[2] In my head, the road to La-Guardia might as well be a flying carpet for all it relates to the rest of the world.

I think this issue with "spatial cognition" may be why I'm such a reluctant traveler. It's not that I'm uncurious about people and places. I like the idea of Kerala in the rainy season. I think of certain rivers—the Nile, the blue Danube—with longing. But I don't like not knowing where I am. When I'm jogging on a deserted beach far from home, every footfall feels tentative, every breath improvised. I'd have to jog that beach fifty times before it would start to feel as good, as right, as jogging up Avenue D ripe with garbage after a holiday weekend. I know this is a limitation. Poor David is forever planning compassionate interventions, trying to persuade me that while it's true the geriatric social work community has amassed convincing empirical support for the benefits of "aging in place," this model is not meant to apply to people in their early forties.

But maybe there's also something affirmative in a well nigh pathological attachment to the local, to neighborhood. For a certain kind of person, the *there* in being there is a small, particular piece of the world that seems to hold all its variety. I'm kind of like the farmwoman Dorothy Hammer, who in 1961 traveled to California on a honeymoon with her new husband, Bill, but quickly returned to Scales Mound, Illinois, because, as Dorothy explained, "It's so unreal to be gone."[3]

For me and Dorothy, the place to be is the place you can truly inhabit. It's the place you can walk to from home, or the idiosyncratically shaped ground of your daily rounds. No one, however worldly, truly inhabits a large city, much less the world. Say every morning you take the subway from Kingston Avenue in Brooklyn all the way up to 125th Street in Harlem. You don't experience Brooklyn, the East River with its plunging cormorants, Manhattan island; you experience a rattling car on the A train. Telephones, computers, TVs, cars, airplanes—these connect the planet in an abstract sense, but it's an "abolition of distances" that fails to bring nearness.[4] Thousands of years of culture and technology have not appreciably lengthened the human stride. And walking, getting around on body power, is still, according to research, the surest way to incorporate a place, to establish a working inner model of it.[5] The small worlds mark us most deeply. Indeed they literally shape us, with some studies even suggesting that the more your neighborhood places shops, schools, and other routine destinations within reach by foot, the lower your body mass index is likely to be.[6] Standing between the dwelling and some chartless beyond, the small worlds are the social and physical precincts into which we first emerge as toddlers, and to which we may withdraw in advanced old age.

My first world was a white brick house with a stone front porch. Sitting on the porch, you looked down across a sizeable lawn to Utah Avenue, a fairly busy street in what was generally a quiet residential neighborhood. My first world beyond the house was the strip of sidewalk in front of it, which I knew with a kind of psychedelic clarity, down to the worms drowning in the drainage pipe and the anthills that materialized here and there from cracks in the cement. There we ran barefoot and rode our tricycles, regularly encountering a small assortment of other children. It was, actually, an enormously complex world, with distinct boundaries we spooked ourselves by testing but not breaching. The day I ran away from home, I lay my sleeping bag in front of the McConnell house at one end of the block. When I dared Cameron to streak naked down the sidewalk in a rainstorm clutching a bar of soap (this was the '70s, recall), I didn't dream of urging him past the mailbox at the other corner. The wide street itself was also a boundary, one our parents patrolled rather actively. We once spent the better part of an afternoon inanely tossing Magic Markers into this road and, even more inanely, darting out to retrieve them, as if determined to find out whether the curb really was the far edge of the universe. Eventually there was the morning trek up the hill to Lafayette Elementary School, and the afternoon descent home, a repetition that enhanced the vividness of seasonal displays—winter's gunmetal skies, or the candy-pink azaleas that every spring spilled out over the lawns.

I had no particular desire ever to leave that place. It was full of sensation, social interest, and meaning. Besides which, I knew where the hell I was. I think if I weren't so attached to David and our children and the city we live in, I'd be quite content to go back there and walk up and down that hill every day again. I did leave, obviously, at eighteen, for college. But it felt, for longer than I like to admit, *unreal to be gone*.

It was nine springs after the last spring I lived in my parents' white brick house that David and I first approached the easternmost block of 7th Street. And we gently dropped into place. I don't know that my attraction to the place wasn't a form of recognition, a kinesthetic awareness of descent to a home-place lined at least in part with houses rather than tall buildings and sheltered, in the month of May, by pink-blossoming trees. "One of the most photogenic blocks in New York City," a Realtor's website calls it.

To say "photogenic" is emphatically superficial, of course, but the point is, I was hardly the first person, or the last, to "recognize" this small world even as a newcomer. My personal experience and wiring primed me to respond to certain qualities in a place, but places, too, seem to differ in their degree of what urban planner Kevin Lynch calls "imageability."[7] Some places are more available than others to be taken up by the individual and made into a strong internal image that, in turn, readies the person to operate there with comfort and pleasure. Such a place is readily perceived *as* a place.

Evidence that for generations this has been so of our block can be found in the fact that so many have seen fit to give it a name. In the nineteenth century, this part of East 7th Street was known as the 5th Avenue of the eleventh ward for its handsome, well-kept row houses. From very early on, people also called it Political Row. This identity apparently took root with the settlement of people like James R. Steers and Jabez Williams, respected shipbuilders who also served as ward alderman; by some mysterious alchemy, the theme cropped up again and again. In the early twentieth century, the block hosted a lively political rivalry, with both Democratic and Republican district clubhouses located there. In the 1960s and '70s, it was home to an assembly district leader, among other local pols, and had perhaps the most fervent block association in the area. The community life of this single block has inspired two award-winning documentaries and a 1975 social science graduate thesis that described the block as being in much better physical condition than the surrounding neighborhood, as well as markedly more middle-class, more heterogeneous (including blacks and whites as well as Puerto Ricans), and more contentious. "Many people on the street are directly or indirectly involved [in block conflicts] simply because this block is so 'close' and self contained," writes the author, Stephen Barto. "The block in some ways genuinely resembles a small town with the sort of intense in-fighting and high degree of personal interactions that go on in such a place."[8] For perhaps a hundred years the block has been recognized as especially rich in trees and other plantings, even if successive generations of residents believed they had inaugurated the trend.

This tiny snippet of city life has all along held a special position within a larger place that also claimed, from the beginning, a distinct identity people recognized and named. The eastern part of Stuyvesant's Meadow became the Dry Dock District in the shipbuilding era. Then Germans resettled the area as part of what they called Kleindeutschland, the city's first large ethnic enclave. In the late nineteenth and early twentieth centuries, Eastern European Jews called it the East Side, eventually including it in the Lower East Side to the south, the core of their first settlement. In the 1960s, hippies and other bohemians spreading east from an increasingly pricey west side brought the new handle East Village, semantically connecting the neighborhood to Greenwich Village. The blocks east of Avenue A (formerly the Dry

Dock District) became *Loisaida*—Spanglish for Lower East Side—in
the 1970s after postwar Puerto Rican migration made them a center of
New York–Puerto Rican life. Nuyorican poet Bittman "Bimbo" Rivas,
said to have coined the term, anthropomorphized the place as a lover:
"I dig the way you talk/I dig the way you look/ . . . siempre,/En mi
mente, mi amada,/yo te llamo Loisaida."[9] Alphabet City was the term
used by white "urban pioneers" who rediscovered the area east of Avenue A in the '80s, a locale at once celebrated and lamented as the
wild edge of the city.

You could never unravel all the factors, economic, historical, cultural, social, that draw people to any small world and give it identity.
But is there something about the *shape* of a place that makes it livable? "We must have found or built, long ago, something other than
trees and grasses, rivers and lakes," muses architecture scholar Grant
Hildebrand. "In whatever version of nature we found ourselves, we
must have sought some more particular circumstances. What would
they have been?"[10] The answer, according to Hildebrand and others,
is that we looked for places that felt safe, that secured us against the
elements and other threats, but that also held signs of abundance
and opportunity, the promise of something tasty to eat (and more
where that came from). "It becomes clear," according to psychologist Stephen Kaplan, "that neither being out in the open nor being in
the woods is favored. These opposing vectors would tend to place
the individual right at the edge of the forest. Ecologists point out that
such an area is the richest in terms of life forms; it is likely to be the
safest as well."[11]

Scholars have described the complementary elements of this livable place in various terms—as legibility versus mystery, order versus
complexity, "making sense" versus "involvement," "prospect"—a vantage from which to survey our world—versus "refuge"—a zone of protection from it.[12] We need our immediate environments to hold us,
but also to let us go. We need them to tell us clearly where we are, but
not to lay themselves bare, leaving nothing to discover or imagine.
Order permits exploration. Intrigue *invites* it. And exploration, in time,
leads to the deep familiarity that gives people a special ease in their
surroundings.

The first requirement for exploration is a system of orientation. Think of the winding, unrepeating, and often unsigned streets of certain ancient villages (or New York's old financial district, for that matter); they embrace the native, training him from the cradle to their idiosyncratic requirements, but seem to resist the newcomer, or ensnarl him, mark him out as an interloper. The Manhattan grid, on the other hand, for all its supposed coldness, defies anyone to get lost, with signs at every intersection that say *you are here* in a sequence based on universally understood numbers and cardinal points.

What's more, the district known today as the East Village has from its beginnings been set off by clear boundaries, *edges* as Lynch calls them. There's the wide commercial strip of 14th Street to the north and, to the south, Houston Street, which like a seam stitches the district to the related neighborhood around the hook, the old Lower East Side. To the east is the river. To the west the boundary is softer; it could be Avenue A (the far edge of Tompkins Square Park) or it could be the Bowery, that early trail joining the Dutch farms, in Whitman's day, an exciting nighttime promenade and locus of working-class entertainment. This was a place that could *hold* something; it could even hold, for one brief historical moment, before it dispersed like a clod of soil thrown into the sea, the shape of the place you left behind.

Streets are not only boundaries, though; they are paths—paths that penetrate Manhattan's every nook. (The Hudson and East rivers once were heavily trafficked paths, too, with ferries leaving from various points.) This is a landscape that promotes individual access, mobility, and choice, potent forms of personal freedom You can press your nose against just about anything that might interest you, and you can choose among a variety of routes to get there. Better yet, keep your options open; reconsider every two minutes, when you come to an intersection.

How to describe the easefulness in the legs, walking the East Side streets? I have a recurring dream in which I stand on the edge of a swimming pool. There's a problem. The lanes are clogged with slow swimmers, or dominated by fast ones, or my goggles are fogged, or the lifeguard is gesturing inscrutably about the rules. Only occasionally do I find an opening, dive, and move swiftly, cleanly, through an element that's buoyant, soft, and ripples away like satin. Sex, to be sure. But more broadly: the freedom to move at will. In those streets, I was never in fear of getting lost, so there was no hesitation. I could explore endlessly, and the more I explored, the more I found interesting things to see. The fruit stacked under awnings along the sidewalk. The tiny lights wrapped around tree branches. Or the young Hare Krishnas clinking their hand cymbals and tossing saffron-colored flowers under a giant elm in Tompkins Square Park. I never knew what the treat would be but it would be something. The tree man, for example. He was a person who wore a fairly large, apparently fresh-cut sapling down the back of his shirt. Its crown rode around above his head, giving the appearance of a walking tree. He had a strange, laughing demeanor.

I could have told anyone exactly where I was: in the heart of a neighborhood that hinted at inexhaustible possibility. Along the banks of a port city that opened out to the world. At the very threshold of the country whose purple mountains and amber waves of grain I sang about in kindergarten. By itself, it's not enough. But this was my edge of the forest.

The longer we lived at the farm, the more we noticed that we were having trouble inhabiting the place. For starters, the house. It was suited to a family with six kids and a taste for the company of friends old and new. With just the four of us there, and the kids pretty little at that, there were rooms we never got to. We were always caterwauling through doorways, trying to find each other. Lucy developed an inability to endure being alone, and when David or I left the room would run after us or call out frantically. For the first time in our adult lives we had at our disposal several perfectly lovely bedrooms, a full kitchen, outdoor gas grill, and screened-in porch. But we ended up dragging mattresses into the upstairs TV room, where most nights we would huddle together munching junk food in the glow of the screen. We watched Hitchcock's *The Birds* and *Strangers on a Train*. Also a lot of the British home decorating show *Changing Rooms*. Maybe we were just too depleted to do the physical and emotional work of inhabitation, of filling up a place. Or maybe it was because, in the arc of our lives, the farm was a place without a future, but so brimmed with the spirit of the past.

The whole property, really, was the surviving fragment of a defunct landscape. There were two fine old barns. A black oak, massive and ponderous with age, stood sentry by the drive. For all its having been retrofitted for late twentieth-century suburban life, this acreage still held the basic shape of the nineteenth century farmstead that for more than a hundred years had taken its place among other farms and horse-friendly country lanes. Now the farm was cut off in an almost brutal way from its surroundings. Inside the perimeter, human presence at an ebb, the natural world worked its heart out to reclaim the turf, the columns of ants marching, marching, a line of golden kits trailing their mother across the far pasture. But outside, a different world was in full swing, a world of luxury houses, immaculate cul-de-sacs, shopping malls, and ferocious snarls of traffic, in no particular order that I, at least, could discern. You could turn cartwheels all day long at the farm, but try venturing onto the fast, shoulderless, blind-cornered road beyond the driveway and you took your life in your hands. It was not possible to breach this perimeter on foot. You had to take the wheel. Whereupon, for me, the threat of getting lost all too quickly became a reality. The houses all seemed to be on quiet roads that ended in stubs or curled back on themselves, roads that took you somewhere you understood you weren't meant to be. There were very few sidewalks. Most of the time, the yards were deserted. Sweltering in the Neon with no AC, I'd turn around with two violent jolts to the transmission, only to spill into a main drag bristling with high-speed lane changers.

Sometimes the stubs dropped you into other self-contained worlds. David once made a wrong turn off the highway and drove a carload of kids smack into the checkpoint that guards the CIA's sprawling Langley compound, where he was briefly detained, vetted, then briskly sent away. This was nary more than a stone's throw from the turnoff that gives access to the adjacent Claude Moore Colonial Farm; here visitors are invited to tour an accurately re-created hardscrabble ("low-income," as the website calls it) tenant farm of the sort that once studded the area. We took the kids one Saturday. I remember the teenage staff dressed in coarse homespun, and the tiny one-room cabin with whitewashed interior where they all (not in real life, of course) slept together in an open loft. *Like us!* I thought. *So*, I thought, trying for connections, *you've got the spymasters hatching Lord knows what behind a screen of trees, and, maybe a half-mile away as the crow flies, a hog drowses in the sun.* It was too hard. We had no friends nearby, no favorite spots besides the 7-Eleven and the little luncheonette right near the house. Aside from the longer journeys we made into Washington and Alexandria to see our families, we came to feel we had no place to go.

Mostly we stayed at the farm and went slowly crazy. David took to lighting inappropriate fires, sometimes in more than one hearth simultaneously. One night, he plunged into the woods shirtless and barefoot, having, he thought, spotted a human figure hiding in the tree line. After quite a long time, he reemerged bramble-torn and wild; he'd gone down the ravine and up again, where he'd been stunned to discover a cluster of new houses, their decks built to overlook the terrain he'd wandered in the seemingly endless hours of childhood. He joked about Ishi coming out of the woods, the last of his kind, but my heart ached for him that night. *Come to bed, Ishi*, I said. More often I was brittle and unforgiving. I reamed him out about the fires, which smoked. I stiffened if, on descending from my attic lair, I found him in some posture other than bent over his computer mining the job sites, never mind that the children were fed and at least partially clothed.

The real trouble, of course, lay two hundred miles to the north, and we never really got away from it. The farm and No. 239 were always connected that summer, as if by a gleaming wire. A fuse, perhaps. In early summer, Richard sent us his report on the condition of the building, along with a drawing calling for screw-piles and tiebacks. Somewhat later Gary, after the long "rent" strike based on his suspicion that we were misappropriating co-op money, went downtown to pay the building's latest ticket. (He and Joanne had initially moved to 9th Street but by now were living in New Jersey with his mother.) Nearly every day, I'd take a midday break from work to telephone, once again, each in turn, the contractors who for reasons I did not understand seemed reluctant to end our communications, but equally loath to finally show up and make a bid on the job. Or I'd call the ssserpent to complain about his having kept $1,500 of our security deposit as penalty for Byron's wall doodle. Or I'd call the guy who was supposed to be boring holes in the ground near No. 239 to determine just how deep the piles should go. Then, a thirty-five-year-old woman, I would call my mother and cry.

If you had to capture Manhattan's East Side, past and present, in a single word, that word might be *density*. Multitudes dancing on the head of a pin. After density you might get words like "poverty," "foreignness," and "counterculture." These associations come partly from the fact that to occupy large spaces is the age-old prerogative of power and wealth, and partly from demographic realities that reached their sharpest expression around 1910. At that time, 40 percent of New York City residents were foreign born, the East Side wards were home to a disproportionate number of these immigrants, and the neighborhood achieved the astounding population density of some 400,000 souls per square mile. In the early twenty-first century, Manhattan is a great deal richer and, in most ways, less diverse than it was a hundred years ago; when it comes to immigrant life, Flushing, Queens, is the new Lower East Side. But with 66,940 people per square mile, versus 22,403 per square mile across the five boroughs and only 79.6 per square mile in the country as a whole, Manhattan remains the single most densely peopled place in America. The East Village still contains some of the country's most jam-packed census tracts.[13]

This density represents a way of life that really is different from how most Americans live. It means there are always people near. You see each other. You hear each other. You brush against each other. This constant nearness makes us negotiate the boundary between public and private space in a different way. There is not room in our dwellings to accommodate the living that typically goes on in two-story houses with yards. So this intimate life spills, day and night, into the streets.

Nowhere has this been truer than on Manhattan's East Side. Its built environment of close, low-rise buildings and narrow, pedestrian-friendly streets has always encouraged street life, and so have the more informal, expressive social traditions of its working-class immigrants, whether Russian or Puerto Rican, not to mention of freethinkers and free lovers, Beats, hippies, and squatter punks. "The East Side is especially convenient for the observation of people because there are such shoals of them always in sight and because their habits of life and manners are frank, and favorable to a certain degree of intimacy at sight," as one observer wrote in 1898. "Where each family has a whole house to itself and lives inside of it, and the members never sally out except in full street dress—hats, gloves, and manners—it is hopeless to become intimately acquainted with them as you pass on the sidewalk. You may walk up and down Fifth Avenue for ten years and never see a Fifth Avenue mother nursing her latest born on the doorstep."[14]

A century later, I too found the hatless, unself-conscious life of the streets beguiling. People sit on their stoops. They play music from their windows. They run to the bodega for coffee despite a spectacular case of bed-head, or walk the dog in togs that look suspiciously like pajamas. They eat in sidewalk restaurants, and in the park, they throw their children birthday parties or lie in the grass and neck. They argue. More than once I have seen a couple reel through the streets in desperate combat, one stalking away with a fixed expression, the other scrambling to catch up, or the man screaming, "Well, I'll just go home and be your little *bitch* then. Is that what you want?" to which the woman grimly responds, "Oh, *please*, Martin." Sometimes they shake out their brilliant plumage in an obvious display. I once saw a young woman on Avenue A wearing a crisp white shirt open to the waist, her fully exposed breasts as wholesome and lovely as two scoops of grain. Men on a nearby construction crew eyed her nervously but kept their peace. There are limits, of course. Some things you don't do in public, even here. It's not hard to tell the difference between a free-spirited line crossing and the kind in which the person seems to have lost track of perimeters altogether. One of the more disturbing cases I've come across was a woman sitting on a bench in Tompkins Square Park, her pants down below her knees, a wad of toilet paper in her hand. She wept helplessly. *Emergency*, was the wordless and unanimous interpretation of onlookers. People whipped out their phones to call 911.

Mostly, it seems to me, people take their privacy with them into the streets. They wear it around their shoulders like Harry Potter's invisibility cloak. Only they're not invisible; on the contrary, they are eminently observable. They put up no more resistance to being seen than a pool of clear water. Look at them if you like. Look right *into* them. Because to them, *you* are scarcely there, or rather, you are there only as part of the great, oceanic swell of the city. You are folded into this urban *there*, not personal, but the element in which they move. This differs from the not-there status of a servant in the master's house in that it happens by tacit mutual agreement, and enhances everyone's freedom, allowing us to be very near each other, even to savor the mammalian warmth of this nearness, without sacrificing a sense of space. When you live in a city apartment, it may in fact be the street that offers escape from the pressure of being observed. The Wieder family lived at No. 239 in 1910. Inside, in a space of perhaps nine hundred square feet with a hallway toilet were a middle-age mother and father, their five sons—smart young men ranging in age from sixteen to twenty-nine—and a servant woman. I imagine the Wieder boys sometimes flung themselves into that mass of population, that "swarm," as it was often described, and felt the same way country boys feel deep among the tasseled cornrows—deliciously at liberty.

To experience teeming streets as spacious like the sea or the woods is a special adaptation to urban life. In general, psychologists worry about high-density environments because they can lead to the psychological phenomenon known as crowding, with its attendant stress, aggression (at least in men), and social withdrawal. But density, they're careful to add, doesn't always lead to crowding. It partly depends on the person; "affiliative" types, for example, seem to be more tolerant of human density. More important, perhaps, it depends on the precise circumstances of human plenty—on whether all those people threaten to impede your movements, constrain your choices, or gobble up scarce resources, leaving you to scramble for crumbs. Among the research findings: Commuters who board a train at its origin and can choose a seat feel less stressed-out than those who board later, even though their ride is longer. Children cope better with large numbers when there are enough playthings to go around. In one 1978 study, people standing in a crowded elevator felt better and saw the elevator as more spacious when allowed to stand beside the control panel. In other words, lots of people are fine and dandy as long as you can be the one to press the buttons.[15]

And so it makes perfect sense that the same East Side crowd that delighted the casual stroller in 1898 appalled someone like Bella Spewack. A Russian Jewish immigrant girl growing up there during its years of peak density, very poor, the lonely daughter of a beleaguered single mother, Spewack burned with ambition to better her lot. It makes sense that she would remember Cannon Street for its "sour . . . smell of crowded human flesh" and Lewis Street as merely "a badly painted backdrop against which the people of my books, school and settlement played the most important roles." When the mean, rheumy-eyed crowd of her backdrop loomed into focus, Spewack "drew back and hid." Pressed into a thronging ghetto surrounded by "very definite high walls on all sides of us," she longed, so to speak, for a crack at the control panel.[16]

I began to see how the crowd could seem to turn against you when, firked from No. 239, our zone of safety and control, we were thrown upon the tender mercies of people like the ssserpent. I came to sympathize with the perspective expressed by the friend of my father who, on hearing we lived on 7th Street between C and D, remarked, "Oh yeah, I know the place. My grandparents got out of there the minute they could rub two nickels together." But after a few months of exile, I also could understand how Bella Spewack, the wildly successful writer for stage and screen, having long since burst free of the ghetto, might feel a bit lost in her spacious uptown apartment. "Too big," she used to say, "too big."[17]

It takes time for a personal world, a small world, to lay itself down in the city. After two or three years on 7th Street, it began to happen for me. The swarm was still there, moving through all the time, but pieces of it reappeared again and again and became distinguishable. I began to recognize how the everyday routines of individuals, funneled through the fixed structures of street and buildings, gently but insistently place certain people in each other's way.

Sometimes the contact is purely visual. When I lived at the cartman's old house, No. 258, I could look down slantwise through a rear window into another apartment, where every evening an old Puerto

Rican woman combed out her long, wet hair before a mirrored dresser. She wore a white nightgown. I don't think she ever noticed me, and I'm sure she's dead and buried now, but I keep her somewhere, enacting, with her deliberate, womanly gestures, some value I cannot name. Sometimes the contact is acoustical. One night in our sleigh bed at No. 239, David and I heard the most harrowing cry; it sounded, we thought, like the cry of someone in the initial moments of a piercing grief it would take years to heal, and we quietly wished her strength to get through the night. But when the cry recurred most nights for weeks, we finally understood it to represent the climax of some neighbor's lovemaking. Whether accurately or not I don't know, but we put this soundtrack together with the carpenter next door, who, coming home one day with a mop and detergent, had told us with undisguised delight that he had a girlfriend and was scrubbing the place for her; the mournful soundtrack of her cries played in our heads again when we heard she'd left, and he had hanged himself.

Every little piece of human settlement affords its tiny perceptual knotholes, and circulates people according to its peculiar logic. Our block was a narrow chute that pressed people into encounter as they entered the stream from a few dozen separate thresholds. Though in the decades of the working waterfront the pedestrian stream probably flowed east, in our time it mostly flowed west, into the heart of the city. The block you experienced could be altogether different depending on your exact location and the hours you kept. Generally speaking, people who lived across the street were people you watched, while people who lived on your side were ones you ran into. After we moved from No. 258, on the south side of the street, to No. 239, on the north side, we entered the orbit of a young drug dealer we'd known only by sight. He took to ringing our buzzer to warn us of an impending parking ticket with such touching regularity that later, when we saw him with his arms cuffed behind his back, we only wished there was some way to return the favor. After the move we hardly ever ran into people we'd seen every day while at No. 258. The long, peroxide-haired, bandanna- and muscle-tee-wearing type who'd occupied the parlor floor, for instance; I missed his metamorphosis into a glasses- and pleated-dress-slacks-wearing substance abuse counselor.

I had a few good friends on the block, people whose life stories I knew and who knew mine, people I called on the phone or had dinner with. Ruth, a college roommate, had a son, Andrew, around the same time Lucy was born; we saw a lot of each other. But mostly the people I came across were some variation on what psychologist Stanley Milgram called the familiar stranger. In 1972, Milgram's students at the City University of New York took photographs of people waiting on a suburban train platform to commute into the city, then returned another day at the same hour and asked commuters if they recognized anyone pictured. On average, people identified four individuals they recognized, saw routinely, but didn't interact with—familiar strangers. They often admitted to wondering about their familiar strangers, even developing fantasy lives for them. In Milgram's study, familiar strangers rarely acknowledged each other. But in the far more intimate context of a residential block, a nod or hello is apt to enter the protocol. Sometimes familiar strangers become friendly acquaintances.[18] The point is, they are neither associates nor utter strangers, and you encounter them routinely but *incidentally*, in a way that "implies no private commitments," as the urban anthropologist Jane Jacobs put it.[19] Like human signposts, they help mark out the dimensions of your small, everyday world. Indeed, the only time Milgram's subjects were moved to greet a familiar stranger was during an emergency, or if they encountered one outside the accustomed meeting place. If, in 1855, Harriet Little happened upon Sarah Jarvis, the joiner's wife, at the street pump or the corner market or even the ferry launch, she'd have thought little of it. But if she ran into her at Bowling Green? That's when Harriet would have recognized Sarah as a little piece of home.

Milgram also identified a number of sociometric "stars" on the train platform, individuals who stood out and were disproportionately tagged as familiar. Eighty percent of commuters, for example, recognized the woman who wore miniskirts even in winter.[20] It's as though some individuals lend an especially strong personal tint to the urban mix, acting as a kind of binding agent, and so it was on 7th Street. Felicia was an older woman with melancholy eyes and an abdomen greatly swollen with fluid, the result of a developing cancer. Every day she went around dropping pans of food in designated spots for the block's stray cats, each a unique being requiring her watchful care. Felicia also made the rounds of certain cat ladies (I was one of them), who gave her money or food for the cats. And she gave sermons at a nearby Hispanic Baptist church.

Felicia was a star in part because she circulated constantly in the immediate neighborhood, and in part because she worked at knitting her incidental contacts into a web of mutual acknowledgment and even commitment. Other people became stars in a quieter way, by reappearing, again and again, in a characteristic posture at a particular place.[21] Lonnie, for example, longtime super of one of the big tenements on the south side of the street, could often be seen out front taking the air. I never exchanged more than a nod with Lonnie, but I did remark the beneficent shade he seemed to drop across your forehead as you passed by, a feeling so missed when he died that residents of the block put a plaque at his old spot. And Cathy, a self-effacing aesthete and intellectual with a short wedge of white hair, was—is—the keeper of the garden where Lucy and I planted our daffodils. There, she could be seen to water, prune, sweep, and rake, laboring tirelessly against blown trash. When I asked Lucy to draw a map of our old block—this was more than five years after we lived there—she drew the south side of the block as a row of blank boxes with one labeled "Andrew's house"; on the north side, "our house" was a box stacked atop "Gary's house." Next door to us she drew a box labeled "the garden," and beside that, "Cathy."

Children themselves are not stars exactly, but they are a cementing agent for the small world. Children provoke comments and hellos, and some will toddle up to strangers of any age. They bring their elders into contact. They also colonize the small world in a very visible way; we'd always see the same local child-parent duos at the library, the park, and the pizza shop, carrying family life into the public sphere. And once children become independent, the extent of their wandering defines the far edges of the near world. Lucy, eleven as I write this, can go unaccompanied just as far as the invisible tether that connects her to home allows, and neither she nor I knows how far it reaches until it's tested; recently we discovered it's okay if she takes the fifteen-minute walk to Tompkins Square Park to meet a friend. It's the unveiling of something we've been building together since she was a baby; with a surprising joy, I now bequeath her our world.

In past generations, unaccompanied children thronged East Side streets, were *identified* with these streets, and claimed them in increments as proprietary turf, to an extent that is all but unimaginable today.[22] The little ones would tag along after older girls. "We would toss them our bean bags, little cloth containers filled with cherry pits, [and tell them] 'Now see that you play here on the stoop or you won't get any ice cream when the hokeypokey man comes along,'" recalls Sophie Ruskay of her early twentieth-century childhood. Siblings thus subdued, the older girls would proceed to their game of potsy or hopscotch. Sophie's mother didn't like her chalking up the sidewalk or scuffing her shoes, a sentiment the child acknowledged "by playing farther down the street and marking up someone else's sidewalk."[23] Bella Spewack, when living near Corlear's Hook, walked with her toddler brother mornings to the busy 3rd Street pier on the river. When Herschey fell asleep in his carriage after his noon egg and glass of milk, Bella would run the several blocks home to fetch their infant sibling, then race back to the pier, *where she'd left the toddler alone*. (As late as the 1930s, a mother who could not pry her baby from the swings could leave her in the local park with a playground worker employed by the city.)[24] Boys shot marbles or spun tops on the sidewalk and played stickball smack in the middle of "our child-impeded streets," as one playground advocate lamented in 1913.[25] Other games, variations on hide-and-seek, cops-and-robbers, or kick-the-can, had their home base in Tompkins Square Park and gave players a territory of a few blocks in which to chase or hide.

Sometimes the children's games were brutal or antisocial, a phenomenon adults greeted with a certain amount of hand-wringing, but also with the kind of winking amusement that makes you suspect they were loath to banish this wildness from their midst. Around the turn of the twentieth century, a gang of boys might waylay the teacher's pet on his way home from school and coax him into a game of horseshoe-the-mare, for instance. Their adventure would culminate in tying little Georgie's reins to the bell knob of a cranky neighbor—some "carpet-slippered old fossil"—and lashing him forward. "Grown-ups . . . have been known to laugh as they passed and saw the prank in swing," writes a contemporary. More than one group children's game has involved beatings with a knotted handkerchief.[26]

Though this particular way of marking out a habitual world is more firmly circumscribed today, I suspect the deepest patterns have held across time. Alfred Wieder and his cousin E. Walter Snyder both used to visit their grandparents on the block in the 1930s. Both quite vividly recall a figure they knew as Ike the Wood Robber. This was a hobo who wrapped himself in a great burly coat he tied with a length of rope. He would sleep in entryways and pinch wood, perhaps to burn for warmth, maybe to sell. Alfred's grandmother, Gizella, gave him alms. A star. If Ike could send some of his Ikeness to California with Alfred, and to Florida with Walter, might he not have left some right there, on the doorsteps he haunted? Is it possible for such color to pass, not only among contemporaries as they cross paths, but hand to hand to hand across time, as people move away from the block and others move in? Maybe all that treading, treading, treading, and mixing, mixing, mixing, have created a singular tone that, if only you could see it, would map the core of the little world itself, shaded darkest on the block but also flaring into Tompkins Square Park and along Avenue A, then fading out to the west.

In 1952, the French urban sociologist Paul-Henry Chombart de Lauwe published a detailed study of Paris that included a diagram representing the daily movements, over a year, of a student in the 16th *arondissement*. Its principal feature was a tight, heavily retraced triangle connecting three locations: the student's home, her piano teacher, and the School of Political Sciences where she studied. Secondary outings included soirées with friends, shopping in the city center, trips to see family. The diagram, wrote Chombart de Lauwe, illustrated "the narrowness of the real Paris in which each individual lives."[27] To this practical point one avant-garde thinker, the Situationist Guy Debord, responded with a wail of protest "that anyone's life can be so pathetically limited." I understand. Surely there is a time to "drift," as the Situationists urged, to let the city's currents carry us into the urban wild without regard to the plodding purposes of daily life.[28] There is a time to advocate, like the Situationists did, for dim, flickering lights in the subways of Paris, or that all the world's equestrian statues be arrayed across a single desert in a mock cavalry charge.[29]

But there is also a time to once again tread the close, beaten path. Basic facts pertaining to the lives of former 7th Street residents show me that often they didn't go far for the things they needed.[30] I can see that the triangle points for the ship carpenter were the family hearth, the hull building on the river, and wherever he went to pray or drink on Sundays. I notice that Abraham Weinstein found a second wife, a witness to the marriage, and, much later, a doctor to tend his final hour, all within two house numbers of his own. And the Wieders—they had their synagogue and political club on the block, their Torah school a block over, their shop a few blocks south on Avenue C. All these people found their little way stations of novelty and reward, their treats, whether Graham bread or strudels, goulashes or *cubanos*, on the same near corners. Each created a unique map of that place whose blank spots and foci of exaggerated detail reflected his own daily movements. It takes a lot of repetition to make such a map.[31] It takes a lot of people walking their close, crossed paths to create the very ambience the Situationists so admire in an urban environment. This is how, together, people hold their small worlds in place. By being there.

I miss the chickens pecking in the yards! I miss that casual, come-as-you-are feeling. I miss Felicia dropping her pans of food while there was breath in her old body, never mind the contingent that was always fretting about rats. This chapter has been hard to write. As David gently points out, I've *chosen* to go back there—back to the worst year of our lives, and back to a small world we no longer inhabit. I walk that way every day, even while I tap on a keyboard a mile away. David's choice is to take, in our actual walks about town, 6th Street or 8th Street—any street but the one we lived on with our little girl and our baby boy at a certain time in our lives. Neither strategy can change the fact that the neighborhood goes on, and we go on, but separately. The small world in which the two were knitted together is no more. It's not possible to pay it even an hour's visit.

Likewise, when we left the cocoon of the farm, we understood it was for the last time. We knew it wouldn't hold its shape much longer.

Once the Neon was packed, David drove the rest of us to my parents' house in D.C. and returned, alone, to smoke a cigarette in the late-summer pasture. Then it was done. We were quiet on the turnpike, thinking about the summer, and starting over again. Byron had given up diapers. Lucy would be starting kindergarten. I had gotten a contract to turn my pharmaceutical-industry reportage into a book and David had a promising lead on a job at a small publishing house. Like the first time we moved to New York, we'd be sleeping at Cameron and Lalou's on Suffolk Street, hunting for an apartment by day and returning, by night, to the welcome of their kitchen table. Rents had risen sharply since the first time, and we were, if anything, even less desirable as tenants. But we'd find a little piece of luck on 8th Street, nearly six hundred square feet of strictly neutral modern space, which we'd outfit with plastic furniture rather than plumb the storage units.

Crossing into Manhattan through the Holland Tunnel, that long tube of white tiles glinting in sour light, we really didn't know what world we were entering. When we emerged, the night was warm. We rolled down the windows. We'd gotten as far as the Village when we spotted a young couple, college kids probably, standing on a corner, mouths locked in a kiss. Then it was as if the kiss suddenly struck them funny, and one of them palmed the other's butt cheeks, and they chucked each other on the shoulder, giggling. We could drive forever and never get back to the beginning where they stood. We knew that. But the color they gave off was golden. And that night, we wore it in our hair and lashes.

The Tenement Class

SEVEN

JULY 4, 1865, dawned fair and calm, the waters of New York Bay a mirror for the fleecy clouds that here and there slipped across the sky. But the children of New York could not be kept for long from their rockets and Chinese crackers. Before the sun was high, doorsteps across town exploded with their racket and with the sulfurous smell of punk. Everyone took to the streets. Thousands poured in from the countryside wearing straw hats and ribbons, picnic baskets on their arms; they thronged the streetcars and ferries, festooned for the occasion with bunting. A few elderly veterans of '76 came out wearing their waist-belts and swords, far outnumbered by the returned boys of '61, whom the last years had made old before their time. The men treated each other to rounds of cooling beer in neighborhood saloons. It was a day of music and marching and pistols shot off in exultation. When night came, the crowds gathered in the parks, where simultaneous fireworks displays lit the upturned faces of a new-made, expectant people.[1]

But in a poor East Side tenement far from the sights of Broadway, twenty-one-year-old Rachel Hart was full of a quieter and more private sense of incipience. Though she surely heard the din beyond her window, a woman so near the ordeal of birth would not have ventured out. On the 7th Rachel pushed her child into the world.[2]

Attending her was a physician named Maurice Michaelis. A German immigrant and probably Jewish (he went by both Maurice and

139

Moritz, common variants of Moses), Michaelis may have treated Rachel as a charity patient. He was an original member of the Society of German Physicians of the City of New York, founded in 1847 on a tradition of both scientific learning and liberal-minded philanthropy; doctors could sign up through the society to provide free care at the bedsides of the poor. But by 1865 the German Dispensary on 3rd Street had largely taken over the doctoring of indigent Germans. And upon the celebration of this dispensary's twenty-fifth anniversary, its most eminent founder, Dr. Abraham Jacobi, would recognize Michaelis and several other German Society members not for their philanthropic contributions but for their role in "the intellectual life of this city."[3] Michaelis's obituary many years later would credit him with "building up a large and profitable business in his profession."[4] It seems likely that Rachel's German Jewish family marshaled the funds to pay the good doctor. In any case they had seen to it that Rachel's accouchement was attended by no less than a graduate, with high honors, of the University of Berlin. Michaelis would have kept abreast of medical literature, known how to turn the fetus or resuscitate the newborn if necessary. He would likely have ligated the cord in two places, snipped it, tied the infant's side loosely with a piece of linen.[5] *Eine tochter*. A daughter.

I think that in naming her Clara, Rachel meant to confer importance on her child. It was her mother's name. This formidable woman lived just the other side of Delancey Street from Rachel and stood, no doubt, right there in the room with her, ready to aid and instruct her own eldest in the arts of new motherhood. Clara (née Dittenheimer) Phillips had spent her own childhood in a Bavaria dotted with rural villages. Now she had a grandchild: this tiny American, a second generation sown in the city she and her husband, Levy, had adopted nearly thirty years before.

Rachel's husband also was a German immigrant, thirty-year-old Joseph Hart. When their daughter was born he'd been in America eight years, only two in New York. The couple's courtship (no doubt conducted under the pragmatic supervision of Rachel's parents) evidently had been brief. Joseph worked as a peddler, the means by which Jewish families had subsisted on the fringes of European economies for generations. To countless Jewish men in America, peddling offered a first toe-hold, a bottom rung on the economic ladder they hoped would lead to something better. Initiation varied little over the years. A young man bought, on credit, a small assortment of goods—tin cups and spoons, glassware, fabric, thread and other dress goods, candy—slung these goods in a bundle on his back, and tried like hell to sell them. He might journey on foot into the countryside to hawk his wares among villages and farmsteads; or perhaps he plied them through the city streets.[6] "When I reached the blocks of private houses, I was to walk up the stoops, pull the bell, and when the door opened, to say, 'Buy tinware,'" recalled one New York immigrant, Samuel Cohen, of his introduction to peddling in the 1880s. At the first door, a burly young redhead appeared, wordlessly laid his hand on the large washtub Cohen wore strapped to his chest, and pushed him backward down the stairs. "I could not pull another bell if I tried," Cohen wrote. But then he came upon an open door, and a woman standing beside it; she bought a cup, his first sale. For a peddler with mouths to feed, pride was a costly impediment; it was physical energy he needed, persistence, and a thick skin.[7]

And for Joseph Hart, there was to be no other life. A year after small Clara entered the world, Joseph and Rachel had a son they called William, who in turn was scarcely a year old when Dr. Michaelis returned to the Harts on a grim errand. Joseph had fallen abruptly, gravely ill. Indeed when Michaelis arrived at his bedside in May 1867, he likely recognized the direst stage of diphtheria—the pallor and perspiration, but especially the slow, whistling breaths, and the sudden, blue-faced paroxysms as the patient fought to pull air past the false membrane thickening at the back of his throat. In 1860, Michaelis's colleague, Jacobi, had published the first American paper on diphtheria, based largely on cases seen through the German Dispensary[8]—there had been 122 that year alone. Many physicians engaged in a more "fashionable practice" had not seen a single case, a fact, remarked the president of the New York Academy of Medicine, that "forcibly sustained" the widely held view of the disease as one "bred by poverty out of uncleanliness." (The doctor was careful to point out as an obvious *exception* to this rule the unfortunate case of the child of the academy's secretary.)[9]

Protecting the children from Joseph Hart's affliction—diphtheria was largely a pediatric disease—would have been a chief concern. There was little Michaelis could do for their young papa. Perhaps he cauterized the membrane with nitrate of silver; maybe he gave an astringent gargle or prescribed steam inhalation of some common antiseptic like carbolic acid.[10] In a last-ditch effort to save the suffocating patient, he might perform a tracheotomy, opening the windpipe through a small incision in the throat.[11] Kindness, in a case like this, was all. "I found it easy to imagine myself in the place of a patient and to spare his feelings if I could not preserve his life," Jacobi told a group of admiring colleagues in 1900, looking back on the early days of the dispensary. "Where you cannot save you can still comfort. I never told a patient he had to die of his illness, and I hope I shall never be so careless or so indolent as to do so in future. . . . Another lesson I learned early was this, that my patient had to be treated, and not the name of his disease."[12] According to Joseph Hart's death certificate, the disease ran its course in just four days.[13]

Rachel's married life—her tenure as mistress of her own household, however humble—was over almost before it began. Not yet twenty-five years old, she was now a peddler's widow with two babies. Assuming she knew how to sew, she could stitch shirts all day and night and still never hope to keep her children from hunger and cold. Such a circumstance raised the specter of almshouse and orphanage. But Rachel was not without recourse. Not for nothing had Clara and Levy Phillips given the force of their early years to America. Not for nothing had Levy trawled the streets of New York with his glazier's diamond and basket of delicate glass panes, crying the glazier's distinctive, doleful-sounding cry. *Glass! Glass put in!* This was another typical occupation for Jewish men. Having no doubt repaired his share of windows, Levy had risen to the status of "merchant," perhaps made alliances in the building trades.[14] Levy and Clara had worked, saved, and brought four children out of infancy on Delancey Street—Rachel, the eldest by six years, then Moses, Samuel, and Isabella. By their early fifties, the Phillipses had accumulated the very large sum of $7,000. And with that money, plus a mortgage in the amount of $2,000, they bought No. 239 E. 7th St. from Abraham Weinstein, the retired tailor who would be their neighbor. The purchase took place in April 1867, one month before Joseph Hart died.[15]

Rachel and her children would return to her parents and the younger siblings she herself had likely mothered as a teenager. Not since James DeLancey's time had a family been so closely identified with the property as the Phillipses would be with No. 239. They would fill it from stem to stern with Strausses, Seligs, Schupards, and Wollsteins, whose rents would help support them. By far their most significant asset, the house would serve as a nest egg and a shelter for three generations. It would keep them, body and soul.

Here we come to the image that first drew me into the building's past: another mother and her children on the front steps of our old home. How many times have I watched her grasp the railing and mount those stairs, lifting a cumbersome skirt, her face turned to the child beside her. The door shuts behind them. Her thoughts are her own. But I always think of a line from a favorite poem, Ellen Bryant Voigt's "Year's End"; a husband and wife, after a harrowing night in which one child has died but theirs has lived, listen to him breathe, "like refugees who listen to the sea/unable to fully rejoice, or fully grieve."[16]

The Phillipses would live thirty years at No. 239, people who never would know life in a "private" (single-family) house, immigrants and children of immigrants, a working-class family in whose midst infectious disease had struck and would strike again. They were both tenement dwellers and tenement landlords. These were critical facts in a New York City fast becoming a major metropolis.

From the opening of the Civil War to the close of the nineteenth century, Manhattan's population more than doubled. Massive immigration brought a multiplication of ethnic groups to the urban scene; to the Irish and Germans were added Russian and Polish Jews, Italians, and a sprinkling of Greeks, Hungarians, Romanians, Bohemians, Swedes, Chinese, and others. This fresh supply of humanity powered the combustion engine of the city to an unprecedented heat. It produced more of everything. More opulence and sophistication found expression in things to buy, ideas to dabble in, entertainments to enjoy.

More wretched poverty took the shape of homeless and barefoot children sleeping in entryways, of abject alcoholics begging change from passersby. It was a time of escalating extremes.

The rich threw off a blinding glitter. Morgan Lewis's early nineteenth-century life of comfort and ease on his Hudson River estate called Staatsburgh seemed quaintly countrified compared with what his flame-haired great-granddaughter, Ruth Livingston Mills, was doing with the place. His wife having supplied the highly acceptable Livingston name to her marriage, the groom, Ogden Mills, brought the enormous new fortune his father had made in banking and trade in gold-rich California. Mrs. Mills's annual winter balls at their mansion on 69th Street and 5th Avenue, each a shot across the bows of rival society hostesses, featured seated suppers and late-night dancing for hundreds, with towers of elaborate French tchotchkes to be given out as favors. The Millses and their two daughters summered at their seaside "cottage" at Newport and, near the end of the century, fitted out a place for fall by entombing the old house at Staatsburgh within an outlandishly gargantuan eighty-room Greek revival manse. "Ionic, Doric, and Corinthian are combined," the *Times* remarked obsequiously, "with surprisingly harmonious results."[17]

In the iconography of the Gilded Age, the outsized accommodations of the super-rich were tied to the abodes of the poor—the downtown tenements—as to a bitter, stunted twin. While the refurbished Staatsburgh had more than a dozen bathrooms with toilets and hot and cold running water, by the late nineteenth century the law for tenements called for one water closet for every fifteen occupants. An 1894 inspection of 3,984 tenements considered among the worst found that 3,392 still had their privies in the yard, 240 had them in the basement, 301 in the hall, and only 51 had toilets in the apartments themselves.[18] This, too, was a new lifestyle you could read about in newspapers and journals, how families were stacked atop one another like so much cord wood, packed into six-story dwellings invariably described as *dens, barracks, hives, rookeries*. It was common for a large family to live in 350 square feet warmed by a coal stove and lighted by one or two smoking lamps; in the front a few windows might face a street heaped with manure or a sooty yard, and in the rear were the notorious windowless sleeping closets, also the places of birth and death.

Today, you can visit the Mills mansion, count for yourself the several seconds it takes just to walk the length of its gleaming dining table. And you can tour a typical tenement apartment at the Lower East Side Tenement Museum on Orchard Street and feel the walls close in, see where for years a child slept by the kitchen stove on two wooden chairs pulled together. Both places leave the visitor more or less agog, the former provoking questions about the limits of appetite, the latter raising doubts about the extent of endurance. In the Mills mansion, it's nearly impossible not to take the suggestion, so palpable in the surroundings, that its occupants must have been inwardly "bigger" than the rest of us—royal or divine—to fill so much space with their subjectivity. In the cramped tenement, on the contrary, one wonders how identity ever could assert itself here; where could the self find a place to stand? And where would the body with its needs find sanctuary? It's little wonder that nineteenth-century writers bent these jarring extremes into metaphors that joined and organized them in one image of the city. Uptown and downtown. American and foreign. Clean and dirty. The high, wide stoops of the rich, and the low cellars of the poor. The sunshine of reform would scour out the darkest inner bedrooms of the East Side.

Most famously, reporter and reformer Jacob Riis wrote of the city's poor as a kind of underworld, the "other half" that had been hidden from view. A familiar, sympathetic presence among the working class, Riis aimed to bestir the more fortunate to undertake major social changes. It wasn't just terrible housing he attacked but the starvation wages of working women, the subcontracting production system that created the tenement sweatshop, and even unethical milk sellers whose adulterated product deprived poor babies of wholesome food. His rhetoric, though, emphatically reinforced the notion that what defined this nether half were the buildings they lived in, the tenements. "The boundary line lies there," he wrote, "because . . . in the tenements all the influences make for evil; because they are the hot-beds of the epidemics that carry death to rich and poor alike; the nurseries of pauperism and crime that fill our jails and police courts; that throw off a scum of forty thousand human wrecks to the island asylums and work-houses year by year; that turned out in the last eight years a round half million beggars to prey upon our charities; that maintain a standing army of ten thousand tramps with all that that implies; because, above all, they touch the family life with deadly moral contagion."[19]

Dwellings always have stood for the human beings they shelter, and the poor in every age carry the social and the physical stigmata of their impoverished surroundings. Never was this truer than in the tenement districts of Rachel Hart's New York, where "decay," as one reporter put it, seemed to "[reign] supreme over habitation and inhabitant alike." A very broad brush indeed, this negative designation covered a huge swath of population, not *half* of New Yorkers by the time Riis was writing in 1890, but a substantial majority. As he himself pointed out, "The tenements to-day are New York."[20] Though outwardly re-sembling a private house, since at least the early 1850s No. 239 had met the strict definition of a tenement—a dwelling occupied by at least three separate households. Indeed, during the 1870s and '80s the building's occupancy swelled to a new high as tenants for the first time moved into the chronically damp basement and some families took on boarders. But the definition was rather muddled by the emergence in the same period of multiple dwellings for the affluent, which were carefully distinguished as "apartments" or "French flats."[21] By Riis's time the tenement was a kind of know-it-when-you-see-it phenomenon that defined a set of people, body and soul. Like the term "inner city" a hundred years later, it implied a host of pathologies that threatened to pollute the culture. There was a tenement *class*. "Tenement" be-came the name of its disease.

Disease itself was at the center of this evolution. The theory so pas-sionately espoused by Egbert Viele, the sanitary engineer who'd mapped Manhattan's swamps, held that contagion was carried on an atmospheric "miasma," the gaseous emanations of sewers and privies, damp soil, and decaying matter. This theory increasingly ceded ground to the notion that sickness passed from person to person on droplets of sputum, bowel discharges, oozing rashes, and, with the rise of the germ theory during the 1880s, the tiny invisible organisms they contained. Meanwhile, in the decades after Darwin, hereditarianism in various forms—the belief that crazy, sickly, drunken, criminal, or, indeed, destitute people would beget more of the same—was deeply influential. Could tenement buildings make any occupant sick from lack of ventilation, plumbing, and space? Or did poor immigrants with their dirty ways create "infected houses," their very walls "saturated with the bodily emanations" of their occupants?[22] Sorting out the causes of illnesses like diphtheria, cholera, typhus, and tuberculosis was as complicated a project as defining the causes of, say, cancer or autism today. Real relief—the plummeting of deaths from infectious disease that came with a better standard of living, effective prevention, and cures—would await the twentieth century. Only then did it become possible to live in an enormous, densely settled city like New York without substantially shortening your life expectancy.[23]

In the meantime, among commentators less sensitive than Riis, an entirely necessary emphasis on sanitation slid into shuddering revulsion for the bodies of tenement dwellers—*filth* was a constant theme—often mixed with a deterministic racial parsing that seemed to cast doubt on the reformist agenda itself. Italians living in rear tenements were "a grade lower" than those whose apartments faced the street, reported one tenement inspector in the 1890s, but he adjudged the Italian ragpickers "the lowest of all"—they lived in cellars or basements.[24] "Education in the sanitary laws is not attainable among a large proportion of the immigrants who occupy our tenements," asserted a member of the Ladies' Health Protective Association in 1892. "We have had experience in the matter and know whereof we talk. Bathtubs have often been placed in these houses, and upon our next visit we would find them serving as receptacles for potato barrels, coal scuttles, and the like. We must recognize that there is a law of evolution, and these immigrants will have to remain in the country many years before they will be entitled to be called a clean race."[25] Or maybe these tenement dwellers would learn to fill their tubs when the single most important requisite for bathing—water—could be had at the turn of a spigot, rather than at the end of a groping journey down a dark hall with pail in hand.[26]

The tenement was not only a disease. It was a sin, a way of explaining the fates of human beings, and giving the universe moral order.

First of all, the tenement was the sin of the rich against the poor; it "bore the mark of Cain from its birth," as Riis wrote, "the child of our own wrong."[27] But in this morality tale, punishment for the monstrous greed of landlords in penning their brethren like so many sheep would be visited on the society at large when a morally and physically deformed generation came wailing out of the tenements. Again and again commentators on the tenements remarked that these hovels could not be considered *homes*. "They have habitations, but not homes," wrote James D. McCabe. "Within the same walls are gathered the virtuous and the depraved, the honest laborer and the thief. There can be no such thing as shielding the young from improper outside influences."[28] Men and women, girls and boys, washing, eating, sleeping, and working in a single space? This was a life, wrote another contemporary, "as promiscuous as that of brutes."[29]

Having even a wretched home depends on being able to shut the door behind you. The irony is, New York's "better half" often helped deprive the tenements of this status. A parade of reformers, nurses, and journalists freely trampled across the thresholds of tenement dwellers, many bringing nothing but a determination to be useful, others waving sticks of camphor to ward off the stench and clucking over the women's bare legs or the refuse collecting in the sink. It was not in well-to-do neighborhoods but in the tenement districts that sanitary police conducted house-to-house inspections for infectious-disease victims "secreted" by family and friends, hauling off the sick to public hospitals that were roundly dreaded as merely a lonesome place to die.[30] Only the tenement class was admonished, for the sake of cleanliness, to whitewash their walls and leave the floors of their hallways bare, forgoing the wallpapers and carpets all New Yorkers favored as a stylish, personalizing touch.[31] In exchange for assistance, one charity required families to post in their own homes a placard with sixteen rules: "The furniture, clothing, and bedding must be kept free from all filth and vermin. . . . Stale food of every description must be strictly avoided. . . . When cooking avoid creating a mess and allowing it to accumulate."[32]

Even in their need, tenement dwellers often responded as anyone might: They burned with indignation.[33] In one East Side home, on an afternoon in the waning years of the nineteenth century, a girl of about eight stood in a washtub by the stove while her mother ironed and her ten-year-old brother and his friend played checkers across the room. A visiting reformer later recalled,

> There was no consciousness of embarrassment shown by the children. The mother was ashamed, not at the exposure, but at being found out in permitting such an exposure. She was a member of a club where the training of children was a constant theme. The necessity of physical cleanliness, its relation to health, she had grasped, and her children profited by it. The relation between privacy and morals she had not grasped. It was as though a veil had fallen from her eyes as she looked at her daughter of eight standing naked before the two boys.[34]

This mother, who "never forgave the caller for finding her out," cannot have missed the specter of a whore the visitor invoked, and which now hung over her girl, washing by the warmth of the stove in the only room in the apartment large enough to accommodate a tub. And whose filth, after all, was this? Who had brought this vileness into her home?

When the Phillipses came to No. 239, they had edged uptown. They fled the notoriously ramshackle, disease-ridden tenements of Columbia and Delancey streets to settle on a frontier, a place where, in the eyes of some contemporary observers, the hale, decent, *private*, and *American* row house made a last stand against the tenement and its engulfing alien hordes. "Since the tenements grew up around it the people have called it the Village," wrote a reporter for the *New York Sun* in 1895 of the area east of Avenue C on 6th and 7th streets. "In walking along Avenue C one comes upon the Village sharply. On either side of it stand the big tenements which might be flats but for the bed clothing put out to air on the front fire escapes. In these tenements live people who have known Castle Garden and Ellis Island. Not so the inhabitants of the Village. Irish-Americans and German-Americans are they with the accent on the American. And not a foreign accent at that."[35] In 1902 the *Times* reported on plans to

demolish a few more of the block's comely houses for new construction. "New Tenement Invasion in the Famous East Seventh Street,"
announced the headline. Looking back forty years to the 1860s, this
reporter waxed nostalgic over the fact that "any foreigners who found
their way into the ward [had been] promptly made to feel so uncomfortable that they moved out. "[36]

So it seems the Phillipses came to the block as aspirants to the
respectable middle-class American life it held out. And yet the tenement, and all that it stood for, cast a long shadow even, and perhaps especially, here. No. 239 *was* a tenement, by law and in spirit if
not outward appearance. Around the time little Clara Hart was eight
years old, the early 1870s, she shared a flat of perhaps nine hundred
square feet with her mother, Rachel, and little brother, William; her
grandparents, Levy and Clara; and her uncles and aunt, Moses,
Samuel, and Isabella, all in their twenties. Moses engaged pretty
steadily in the liquor business during these years, as did Samuel, when
he wasn't working as a clerk. Their business addresses, including one
on Avenue D and another on the next block of 7th Street, changed
frequently; probably they ran one of the neighborhood's ubiquitous
small dramshops, selling whiskey, gin, and schnapps, or perhaps *lager-
bier* by the pail to be drunk on stoops and around kitchen tables. When
Isabella and Samuel married and moved out, the family took in a Canadian cigarmaker to board with them. Levy and Clara Phillips gradually
paid down their mortgage, in 1875 spending $1,500 to build a rear ex-
tension on their dilapidated building (the record of which would ig-
nite my interest in the Phillipses more than a century later).[37] This
seems to have been a sort of retirement plan, as Levy was no longer
working. "Keeping house," the census designation given to both Clara
Phillips and her daughter Rachel, may have entailed cooking for the
cigarmaker and acting as building janitresses. By 1880 the family
shared No. 239 with three other households. Tenants included six
children nine and under, four teenage or young adult offspring, one
fifteen-year-old servant girl from Wurtenberg named Mary Zimmerman (who no doubt helped Bertha Hahn, from Damstadt, with her
newborn), and another boarder, the nineteen-year-old Bavarian-born
Leopold Adler, a bookkeeper. Since some buildings department

records are missing, it's hard to tell whether the twenty-plus occupants of No. 239 shared water closets in basement or yard, or already had access to toilets on the landings of each floor (as they did shortly after the turn of the twentieth century). Separate rooms for bathing weren't added until 1904. Also at that time, airshaft windows were cut in the sidewall to at least dimly illumine what apparently had been dark inner bedrooms.[38]

When Levy, the Jewish glazier from Hamburg, signed the official application for a permit to alter No. 239, he signed himself John; better safe than sorry. And perhaps it was ever thus on this block, its sturdy brick houses shaded by ailanthus trees whispering an appealing tale about "Village society."[39] Behind those facades the rooms always had held multiple families, with a generous smattering of the foreign-born.

The existence of this tiny "village" was a fine point that probably was lost on most uptowners, who regarded the lower wards as wholly a tenement district, the scene of "strange foreign life."[40] During the years Clara and William were growing up in their grandparents' house, in fact, the names on their block and for many blocks around were mostly German. Kleindeutschland or Deutschländle, New York's first ethnic enclave substantial enough to give the impression of a vital, self-sufficient city within the city, boasted a larger concentration of German people than any city apart from Vienna and Berlin.[41] Like the dwelling itself, the neighborhood of No. 239 helped shape the identities of the American-born Rachel and her children. It maintained their connection to immigrant life; it made them more German.

"The Germans like to live together; this permits them to speak their own language and live according to their own customs," wrote a long-term visitor to New York, Karl Theodor Griesinger, in 1863, some twenty years after the German settlement began to take shape farther downtown just east of the Bowery. "Life in Kleindeutschland is almost the same as in the Old Country," he continued. "Bakers, butchers, druggists—all are Germans. There is not a single business which is not run by Germans."[42] By the 1870s this German universe had extended north and spread out around Tompkins Square, prefiguring a similar migration of Eastern European Jews. The residents of No. 239 could stroll down Avenue B admiring goods arrayed beneath the awnings of the "German Broadway," or dip into the characteristically German saloons, oyster bars, and groceries along Avenue A.[43] Rachel didn't have to go far with her stout woven basket to procure the ingredients for German-style dishes, some of which found their way into the American diet well ahead of the Italians' spaghetti: cakes sprinkled with cinnamon sugar or currants and washed down with good strong coffee, pretzels and cheese with beer, hearty potato soups and salads, dense loaves of rye and pumpernickel, frankfurters, and seasonings at once sweet and vinegary. In the German dwellings, wrote Griesinger, there was "a penetrating odor of sauerkraut."[44]

News, politics, and intellectual and social life all could be taken in the German way, too. Among several German-language newspapers, the *New Yorker Staats-Zeitung* or "Staats" became, in the 1880s, the city's third-largest daily. New York's first public reading room was housed in a decorative terra-cotta building on 2nd Avenue (now the Ottendorfer branch of the New York Public Library) and offered books in German and English. German assembly halls like the Concordia on Avenue A and the Germania on the Bowery "grew into large conglomerations of meeting halls, bars, ballrooms, billiard rooms, and bowling alleys."[45] These halls and saloons gave Germans places to affiliate in trade unions, emergent political movements, and clubs of every description. Singing, shooting, and gymnastics were especially popular, but there was even a German Bald-headed Men's Verein.[46] Moses Phillips would join the Masons, as well as a boxing club, and his wife, Sarah (née Oldenberg) Phillips would take part in the Ceres Frauen Verein, a charitable society, and be the first president of the similarly inclined Ceres Sewing Circle.[47]

Perhaps Levy took his family, on a Sunday, to one of the neighborhood's German beer gardens, large open halls with long picnic-style tables and sanded floors. An orchestra played at one end, and pretty women served beer, light wines, and simple German fare. "The German capacity for holding beer is immense," remarked one author. "An amount sufficient to burst an American makes him only comfortable and good humored. . . . [The Germans] come here with their families, spend a social, pleasant evening, meet their friends, hear the news, enjoy the music and the beer, and go home refreshed and happy."[48] Notwithstanding a growing temperance movement, contemporaries tended to share this admiration for the cheery *Gemütlichkeit* of German Sundays. Journalist Hutchins Hapgood, for example, hailed the "spirit of gentle loafing and amusement" in which families conversed and sipped for hours as a welcome contrast to "the fearful Anglo-Saxon habit of standing at a bar and draining off whiskey."[49]

Although Kleindeutschland may have struck startled outsiders as monolithically "Teutonic," internal diversity was part of its energy. People from different regions of the German Empire formed in 1871 not only harbored distinct and powerful cultural affiliations, but spoke different dialects, the High German Bavarian tongue, for example, being unintelligible to Prussians from the northeast. Rachel Hart and her younger siblings and children certainly spoke English, in fact may have stumbled in German; the German community lobbied for German-language instruction in the public schools precisely to combat this loss of fluency.[50] The neighborhood also was a place of diverse beliefs. The gray spire of the "always overcrowded" Church of the Most Holy Redeemer, which even today rises high above 3rd Street, represented the most numerous group, the German Catholics.[51] The sober Lutherans, a much smaller group, had a church on Avenue B opposite Tompkins Square. Jews like the Phillipses and Harts constituted a still smaller but distinct group. In Kleindeutschland, though, religions were perhaps less in competition with one another than with the community's cosmopolitan secularism and, in some quarters, staunch atheism. The argument over the value of religion itself, the *Times* commented in 1882, was a "wordy warfare conducted almost exclusively in the German language."[52]

As for the Phillipses, they stayed within the basic parameters of the Jewish community—married other Jews, buried their dead quickly and in Jewish cemeteries. But there's nothing to suggest they were devout. Clara Phillips's will named no Jewish charities or schools. When Isabella married in 1877, the rite was performed by Rabbi Henry Wasserman, said to have married a hundred couples a month; he was affiliated with a congregation of mostly French Jews on 6th Street, apparently that of Isabella's French-born groom, a paper-box maker, Alfred Salomon.[53]

The most curious and most direct testimony as to the Phillipses' faith came almost a decade later, when Moses L. Phillips allegedly "denied belief in God" in the big public school building on 7th Street a block west of No. 239. This supposed utterance of "improper language" on school property was the basis for charges by a local machinist, George B. Riggins, to remove Moses as the ward's representative on an advisory body to the board of education. Riggins's secondary complaint was that Moses had run a gambling house in the same block as the schoolhouse (a not uncommon adjunct to liquor sales). The schools' adjudicator let Moses keep his seat but remarked that if he'd known "as much about Trustee Phillips as the latter himself admitted at the investigation," he would not have supported him for the office in the first place.[54] What Moses's mother, Clara, made of his apparently unapologetic and self-governing ways, no one can say. But when it came time to write a will bequeathing mainly the value of her house, she did leave Moses's share in the name of his wife, Sarah. In a codicil she records having lent her daughter-in-law a large sum of money—$1,000—and directs that any debt still outstanding at her death be taken out of Sarah's inheritance "together with interest thereon at the rate of four and one-half (4 1/2) per cent, per annum, compounded semi-annually."[55]

Clara Hart, the little girl born in an East Side tenement, came of age in a lively and intimate world. And it was not so much the latest operetta playing on the Bowery or the pronouncements of tenement reformers but this even smaller world of daily connections that surely held her interest. She would have had a few things to call her own—a woolen cloak, a few dresses, petticoats, stockings, hankies, ribbons, button-up shoes, perhaps a cigar box of mementos—and otherwise partaken mostly of what was available to all.[56] "It must not be forgotten that much that satisfies the extra-physical wants can be had free of cost," noted a study of working-class New Yorkers' budgets from that era. "Public schools provide education for the children, the parks and playgrounds give opportunity for fresh air and recreation, the intercourse with kindred and neighbors gives social satisfaction, and the varying pattern of street-life, sordid though it often is, gives constant novelty and diversion."[57] One family in the study reported as its principal fun that "in the evening they sit in front of the house."[58]

When No. 239 held and augmented the summer's heat until it seemed one would cook, everyone went outdoors. Girls almost universally loved to dance and would strike it up right there on the sidewalk, stepping to the boisterous oompahs of roving German brass bands. Maybe Clara walked with her mother to the free, floating bath that lay on the East River at 5th Street. Women's days were Monday, Wednesday, and Friday. You could plunge into the sixty-five-by-eighty-five-foot receptacle of dark, brackish currents as the sun rose in a steamy haze over the river—the bath opened at five—or by gaslight in the evenings. An 1876 drawing from *Leslie's Monthly* shows women flipping and diving from the railing in their sleeveless tunics and swimming knickers.[59] Or maybe Clara and William went past the riverside lumberyards (the builders of sharp-bowed ships gone if not forgotten) and out onto the wharf where breezes stirred their hair and they could watch the steamboats pass. By night the busier wharves became "the ballrooms of the poor," some local boy accompanying on the mouth organ. "Polkas, waltzes, and even quadrille compositions are wheezed out of the little instruments that they all but enclose in one hand," wrote a *Harper's* correspondent. "And as they play, the couples whirl and balance and trip and spin with a vim and an enthusiasm that more than offsets their lack of other merely ornamental qualities that prouder folks may boast."[60]

And in the other direction, there was always the park. Not long after its founding, Tompkins Square had become the place for working-class political outcry. In the depression year of 1857, for example, Germans held a mass meeting there to protest the police killing of countryman John Muller during an altercation on Avenue A.[61] A few months later, thousands gathered in the park in a series of demonstrations to agitate for relief from a long, famished stretch of unemployment; their banners read "Work—Arbeit," and "Work We Want—or Bread."[62] Not coincidentally, after the war the city leveled the scantily planted park and turned it into drill ground for militia. This did not prevent thousands from once again marching into the square on a January morning in 1874 in what labor organizer Samuel Gompers called a "folk-movement

"Tompkins Square, New York—Out for a Breath of Fresh Air." *Harper's Weekly*,
September 13, 1873. Clara Hart, who lived at No. 239, just a block away, with her
mother, brother, and grandparents, was eight years old. (Courtesy of HarpWeek.)

born of primitive need"—the business cycle had once again made it
impossible to exchange work for bread. Mounted police charged into
the park and down 8th Street, clubbing heads in "an orgy of brutality."[63]

But the September Clara was fourteen, 1879, thanks to the growing
clout of the German community, the renovated park was ready for a
dazzling unveiling. And I wouldn't doubt that she was there among the
10,000 pressing in to see hundreds of new trees, newly planted grass,
and 160 gas lamps ringing a band pavilion and spraying fountains.[64]
During Clara's teen years, the park was mainly a place to while away
the hours, the older people smoking their clay pipes on the benches
and listening to the music, the young circling one another. The girls
would dress up in a style "either gay or neat" and parade before the
boys with a formality that, in the estimation of one contemporary,
"would be comical if it were not so praiseworthy and well meant. These
girls are nearly all good dancers, and therefore are not ungraceful; but

in their opinion it is the eminently proper thing, when 'passing in review' of the other sex, to stiffen their bodies, hold themselves rigidly erect, and to walk on their heels, seeing everything and everybody, but seldom turning their heads in order to aid their vision."[65]

These are the sorts of things that would have interested Clara—the boys she passed, among other little pleasures, as well as the highly local tales of intrigue that certainly reached her ear. Weddings, funerals, illnesses, and scandals were the talk of the street. What affected her most deeply had to be the movements inside her home, and No. 239, during her teen years, was emptying of her kin. In 1877, when she was twelve, Clara's young aunt Isabella wed her Frenchman, moved uptown to the German neighborhood of Yorkville, and soon bore the first of many babies, Lily.[66] A couple of years later, Samuel married a girl named Fannie, born in New York of German extraction; they moved to 10th Street and had a first child, Carl. And in 1882, Dr. M. Michaelis, the physician who had delivered Clara and presided over her father's last days, came to perform a similar office for her Grandpa Levy, who was suffering from asthma; the glazier from Hamburg closed his eyes at No. 239 on April 16, at the age of sixty-four.[67] Then Moses left; already in his thirties, he wed Sarah, who was born in London but probably also of German descent. The couple stayed nearby for a while but after a few years moved uptown to 50th Street. They had no children. William, Clara's little brother, made a somewhat more mysterious and unhappy disappearance after 1880, when the census records him at thirteen, living at No. 239 and going to school. The likeliest explanation for his absence from subsequent directories, censuses, and his grandmother's will is that he died in adolescence. Samuel also died in this decade, leaving at least two children.

Amid all this leave-taking, the relationship of various family members to the house—the mother ship, as it were—shifted. Shortly after Isabella married in 1877, the Phillipses conveyed No. 239's title to Rachel, their eldest, perhaps assuming she would be the one to tend their old age, or perhaps as a kind of consolation prize, since the marriage of her younger sister would have tended to imply no wedding was expected in her case.[68] Several years later, not long after Levy expired, Rachel transferred the house *back* to her mother. Clara, a widow now herself, would continue as the family matriarch; she would hold title to No. 239 until her death.

By about 1884, then, only the three women remained: Clara Hart, nearly twenty now; her long-widowed mother, Rachel; and the elderly Clara Phillips. Notwithstanding all the talk about the evils of tenement-house "packing"—notwithstanding its real discomforts—it's hard not to see sadness in their diminished numbers. And perhaps a touch of fear, or at least a heightened sense of urgency about making ends meet. They had the house and its income, thank goodness, but that came with expenses, too. To live reasonably well, a working-class family typically depended on a few incomes, including at least one living (i.e., male) wage. Clara Phillips and her daughter Rachel had always been *hausfrauen*. Rachel's daughter, Clara Hart, would be a working girl. And she may well have welcomed the role. "The boys and girls in the family of the workingman anticipate from early childhood the day when they can earn money," wrote one reformist author. "Far more frequently than the reverse, this is wholly unselfish. It comes from the desire to lessen the family burdens or increase the family comforts and pleasures. The test of the goodness of a son or daughter in a working-man's family is that he or she give to the mother the envelope in which the week's wages is received, unopened. . . . What is given in exchange, or taken without consent? Liberty."[69] I imagine that when Clara came home on a Saturday night with her pay, she brought the fresh air into that house, too. She belonged to a wider world.

Clara went to work, but she entered a trade that, like the block where she lived, offered the prospect of genteel status. She became a milliner. A cut above factory work, millinery was the province of mostly native-born, upwardly mobile daughters of working-class families, "a female aristocracy of labor," according to one historian.[70] This was in part because it was still largely a custom trade. The streets of Gilded Age New York were a sea, not of bare heads, but of hats. Women might wear fur-trimmed toques or satin-lined velvets and felts in winter; they might favor the jaunty straw sailor hat one summer, and the next, a wide-brimmed horn of plenty heaped with an enormous tulle bow, soft "cameo-tinted" roses, and grapes in shades of purple and pale green.[71]

As the Inuit are said to distinguish qualities of snow and ice, stylish women could readily discern in the shape of a crown or width of a ribbon the spirit of a bygone season, one that time had rendered "*outré*, if not ridiculous."[72] Most bought one or two new hats each spring and fall, or had old ones or ready-made "pressed" forms prettified with a bit of new fabric or trim; though less exacting in their requirements than wealthier ladies, even servant girls called on a milliner.

In the midst of the Industrial Revolution, hatmaking was still something women did with their hands, drawing on skills acquired only with experience. Certain workers even arose to the status of artists. Milliners themselves were careful to insist that "millinery sense"—the ability to strike a mood, produce a singular aesthetic impression, with a piece of headwear—was a gift that didn't come along every day and could not be taught; it was "born, not made."[73] Millinery work also opened a slender path to independent proprietorship. A woman who acquired the requisite skills, a reputation for gentility and flair—and access to credit—could open a shop of her own. Millinery's special status probably also derived from its situation at the heart of a fashion world that itself was intensely aspirational.[74] New York, after Paris, was a fashion mecca, with milliners on working-class streets like Grand, Division, or 3rd Avenue flipping through magazines or peering into shop windows on "the Avenue"— 5th—for inspiration and guidance. "We may picture Fifth Avenue as the goal of all retail milliners," observed the author of an early twentieth-century study on the trade. "It is probable that with the traditional American spirit even the owner of the small shop on Avenue A or First Avenue is not without hope that some day she, too, may work in the blaze of light which is supposed to illumine the center of fashion."[75]

We do not know what proximity to 5th Avenue (or distance from Avenue A) Clara achieved by nimble hands and wit. She didn't list her name in business or house directories, and so apparently was a millinery worker, not the owner of her own concern. Her place (or places) of work can't have looked much different from the typical millinery workrooms Lewis Hine documented in a series of lovely early twentieth-century photographs: A handful of girls and young women sit around a large table covered in brown paper, each with a hat resting in her lap or on the table before her, perhaps a few ribbons laid over an arm. The room is close, and full of hatboxes and finished hats. The girls wear their hair in braids down the back, the older women in the airy rolls and twists of the fashionable pompadour. Their dresses are slightly rumpled. All fasten their eyes on the work in their hands.[76] This table is a little unit of production consisting of young apprentices, "makers," and a "trimmer." The apprentice is a girl just out of school— fifteen or sixteen—who works without pay for a couple of seasons learning the trade. She runs errands and stitches bands; then she begins handling millinery wire and buckram, materials that are bent or blocked and stiffened into "shapes," the hat's foundation; she learns to make folds and facings, shirr materials, and sew on braids. The maker not only creates the hat shape, but must stretch velvet or other materials over it smoothly, avoiding a "handled" appearance. Finally the hat comes to the trimmer, who both garnishes it, and plans and supervises the others' work. She is the artist, sits at the head of the table, and, particularly if the shop is a chic one, takes home one of the fattest pay envelopes of any female worker in the city.[77]

In becoming a milliner, a girl deferred income she might make immediately on the factory floor and coped with frequent layoffs as each year the busy spring and fall seasons gave way to summer and winter slumps, all in the hope of attaining greater status and security in the long run. By her middle twenties, surely Clara had gained some measure of these rewards. Having failed to pursue the almost universal ambition of working girls, marriage and motherhood, she was approaching the age of spinsterhood. Perhaps there was a "fellow" she talked with on the stoop after work, in whose arms she waltzed on a Saturday night. Or maybe her mother's example—for years Rachel appeared in directories as "Hart, Rachel, wid. Joseph"—taught Clara not to put all her eggs in that basket. "Should a successful milliner marry?" asked a correspondent to the *Illustrated Milliner*. "Marriage is truly a leap in the dark," one reader replied. "If success has attended a milliner before marriage, by no means should she hazard a risk." Better to invest in wax figures, wrote another, "than in a man without means."[78]

It is also possible that Clara didn't marry because no young man wanted to invest in *her*—because she was dying, and everyone knew it.

Dying was something young people did then, and it could take time. Maybe Clara was like the haunting figure of Henny Gaddis, Francie Nolan's neighbor in *A Tree Grows in Brooklyn*, who cried in the hallway of their tenement, his mother forever pleading with him to go sit on the roof for the fresh air. *Francie had been told that Henny Gaddis was dying but she didn't believe it. He didn't look it. In fact, he looked wonderful. He had clear skin with a beautiful pink color in his cheeks. His eyes were large and dark and burned steadily like a lamp protected from the wind. But he knew it. He was nineteen and avid for life and he couldn't understand why he was doomed.*[79]

It began with a loss of flesh, and the night fevers that brought color to the cheeks but spoiled one's sleep, cresting and breaking in a profuse sweat. A deep lassitude must have swept through Clara during the long days bent over hat shapes. Eventually she must have developed the illness's signature symptom, a harassing cough that produced thick, yellowish expectoration. The stigmata of the tenements were catching up to Clara, stricken with what the Eastern European Jewish immigrants, tongue in cheek, would call "Jewish asthma," and Lillian Wald would dub the "tailors' disease." In fact, the heavily Jewish wards had low rates of death from tuberculosis, perhaps because Jewish dietary laws required inspection of meats, or maybe because of Jewish families' early attention to worrying symptoms—one more indication that the perception of tenement districts as seedbeds of disease was not strictly objective.[80]

In 1882, a medical textbook published in New York listed eleven different causes for tuberculosis. The first was heredity or family disposition, followed by such factors as a "feeble and delicate" constitution, work in an indoor occupation that exposed one to "irritant inhalations," sedentary habits, unfavorable hygiene, moist climates, intemperance, masturbation, and inadequate nutrition. "It has been imagined," the author acknowledged as cause number eleven, "that consumption is capable of transmission by infection through the breath, or by eating the flesh of animals who have been subjects of phthisis [tuberculosis], but the evidence in support of either of these modes of origin is extremely unsatisfactory."[81] Death was seen as the all but inevitable outcome.

By the early 1890s, doctors and even the general public were beginning to understand the communicable, bacterial nature of the disease—

an awareness that, with no reliable cure in sight, tended to cast the stricken patient as an object of fear. In 1892 Dr. Lawrence F. Flick charted a quarter century of TB cases in the fifth ward of Philadelphia and declared that fully half were due to living in "infected houses," rooms where a consumptive had been nursed and died.[82] Philadelphia started requiring reporting of consumption cases, and New York followed suit a few years later, both moves meeting with strenuous objection by doctors convinced that reporting would only add to patients' burdens, "stamping them as the outcasts of society."[83] In 1893, Wald began to seek out patients among the East Side poor to dispense sputum cups and disinfectant and instruct families how to prevent transmission. That same winter, a rider of the elevated trains wrote to the *Times* complaining that the cars' filthy jute flooring was a "fruitful source of tuberculosis." "Something ought to be done with the expectorator," he wrote. "There are so many."[84]

One suspects that all this hocking on the way to work—not to mention the ads in women's magazines for Maakfat Pills to "give you a good appetite" and Fat-Ten-U Food Tablets, thought to "quickly build up wasting tissues and flesh and add fat to bony ladies"[85]—reflected a population that was chronically unwell, and, in fact, widely tubercular. Toward the end of the century, a quarter of deaths among New Yorkers ages fifteen to sixty-five were attributed to the disease.[86] In the meantime, people continued as best they could, some cases "running on for years and still permitting the victim to make himself useful at some easy occupation."[87] The treatment: Throw open the windows, day and night. Take walks in the sunshine and sleep out of doors. One of Riis's photographs, captioned "Fighting tuberculosis on the roof," shows a slightly hollow-eyed young woman smiling out from under a tent on a snow-covered roof. Under the tent is a cot, and just beside it, a sling-back chair. The woman is wrapped in a fur-collared coat. The look of the surrounding tenement roofs is almost exactly the view from the roof of No. 239.[88] And the patient must eat! Surely plenty of eggs, milk, beefsteak, and cod liver oil would restore her. I feel certain it was a worried mother, Rachel, who fed and cajoled the patient at No. 239, calling in the doctor as her firstborn's twenty-eighth summer turned to fall.[89]

What everyone dreaded was the spot of blood in cup or rag. "Haemoptysis, or the Spitting of Blood, May Be a Symptom of Different Diseases," ran a contemporary headline in the *Herald*, and the physician must treat this symptom, said the paper, "before anything else, as it is that which terrifies the patient and the persons about him." For the consumptive variety, the *Herald*'s consulting physician advised applying dry cups, ice, or chloroform-soaked flannel to the chest, and feeding the patient a syrup laced with ergotine, used to stanch bleeding, or a spoonful of ordinary table salt. Typically, the doctor observed, the patient would cough up a little blood, frothy and cherry red, over the period of a few minutes or half an hour, after which it would vanish, only to reappear hours or days later. Finally one day there would come a serious hemorrhage, the stuff brought up "in quantities through the nose and mouth," the last of it darker and thicker than the first.[90] It was a bitterly cold winter. January brought the heaviest snows in years, the drifts piling up in the streets below Clara's sickroom. "The east side is suffering," said the daily *World*, its families shivering for lack of fuel, but they "bore up bravely and pinned their hope to the coming of spring."[91]

Soon, indeed, the streets would blossom with the lush garnitures of spring millinery, and the papers would gush, "Such roses! Great pink ones in fullest bloom of most delicious hue, a pink that has the loveliness of Summer days, June days."[92] But Clara wouldn't see another June day, or another June evening under the lamplight of Tompkins Square. She died late on a January afternoon in 1893, in the home on 7th Street she shared with her mother and grandmother. In the blank on her death certificate next to "class of dwelling," the doctor wrote *tenement*, and, next to "sanitary observations," he jotted the word, *fair*. Within forty-eight hours, Clara was in the ground.

Rachel would have ridden the ferry with the horse-drawn hearse that held her daughter's body, left her there at Mount Hope Cemetery on the border of Brooklyn and Queens, then returned the way she came, childless. And I imagine it was then, as she grasped the iron railing of No. 239, that the dwelling filled with a woe terrible to contemplate, black and fathomless as the river at night. It was past bearing. Nothing could keep it or hold it, certainly not the masonry walls of an old house on 7th Street.

I found Clara Hart's death certificate by accident, while looking for her mother's. I thought Rachel might have died around 1894 because it was then she dropped out of sight. The entry "Hart, Rachel, wid. Joseph, h. 239 7th," after showing up in city directories nearly every year for a decade, appeared no more. Instead, Alfred Salomon—he'd become a tinsmith—was listed at that address, along with his mother-in-law, Clara Phillips (wid. Levy). Alfred and Isabella had moved into No. 239 with five (they had lost four) children: Lily, a lace maker at twenty; Joseph, a clerk in a lawyer's office; fourteen-year-old twins Oscar and Leon; and the youngest, twelve-year-old Clara.

Rachel Hart had named her first child after her mother; Isabella, her last. And it seemed that family relations had indeed come full circle. Clara Phillips's will, written the year after her first grandchild died of consumption, made it clear that Rachel remained alive, but seemed to imply dire illness or incapacity. Clara bequeathed Rachel's share in trust, directing the executors to pay her expenses from it, and adding that "should the said Rachel Hart not then be alive"—a circumstance contemplated in her case alone—the money would go to a grandson of Samuel's living with his aunt in Denver. Only Isabella, meanwhile, was embraced with the endearment "my beloved daughter"; she was to receive all Clara's clothes, jewelry, furniture, and other household items, and the right to stay at No. 239 rent-free until it could be sold and the proceeds divided.

Where did Rachel go? Year by year, as Riis had written, the tenements "[threw] off a scum of forty thousand human wrecks to the island asylums and workhouses."[93] It was apparently in the period of her bereavement that Rachel Hart joined this tide of human wreckage. She went to an island that sits in the turbulent waters known as Hell Gate, where the northernmost portion of the East River splits, branching westward into the Harlem River, and eastward toward Long Island Sound. There, she became an inmate of the New York City Asylum for the Insane. Her diagnosis was melancholia.[94]

Unless Rachel caused some public disorder such as might attract police attention—and that seems improbable—someone in her life had to request her commitment. Her closest family members are by far the likeliest candidates. "Most often families took that step only after long struggles to confine [the] madness within familial rather than asylum walls," writes the author of a history on two nineteenth-century public insane asylums in upstate New York. "In general, the greater a family's (or community's) social resources, the longer it tended to postpone seeking institutional assistance."[95] Or, as the *Times* put it, lunatics were often "concealed in the families of the poor as long as circumstances [would] permit" and "only reported when the persons afflicted [became] violent or when their relatives and friends [were] no longer able to take care of them."[96] Maybe Rachel's despond had become frightening, more than her family could manage. Clara, her mother, signed her will in a tremulous hand that suggested the frailty of advancing age. And Isabella, who'd endured tremendous losses herself, had her mother and a large family to look after. Then there was the matter of the pay envelope a certain milliner would never again place in Rachel's hand. *I can carry no dead weights. There must be no invalid bees in my hive.* This was the austere calculus poor families faced when deciding to commit a mentally ill member, according to an 1894 *Herald* exposé on the Ward's Island insane asylum where Rachel was incarcerated. "Where a woman is old or sickly, and, therefore, useless in the hard struggle for existence which constantly confronts the city's poor, their families soon become reconciled to their absence, as it serves to lighten somewhat the burden upon the breadwinners."[97]

Rachel's family may well have held out hope that she would find on Ward's Island the isolation, exercise, and mental rest considered beneficial for her condition. A rich person similarly afflicted could withdraw to an upstairs room at home or take an extended vacation abroad; the middle-class sufferer could check into a small private asylum. But learned opinion held that "our large public institutions" were fitting destinations for the mentally ill without means.[98] There can be no mistaking this: When they sent Rachel away from her home of twenty-five years, they sent her to a place that carried the stain of both poverty and mental illness, a notorious place that had been the subject of damning official reports and lurid journalistic exposés, the *Herald*'s being only the latest. On assignment in 1887 from the *New York*

World, the intrepid Nelly Bly herself had feigned insanity to enter the women's asylum, then on Blackwell's Island just to the south of Ward's, and emerged to pronounce the place "a human rat-trap."[99] The moment Rachel left No. 239 for the last time must have been a desperately unhappy one.

As a practical matter, though, the thing was rather easily accomplished. The paperwork could be assembled at home, or the commitment could take place through the Insane Pavilion at Bellevue Hospital on East 26th Street. Two medical examiners specially credentialed for the purpose would interview and examine the patient and take information from accompanying witnesses. "Was the present attack gradual or rapid in its onset? Is the patient cleanly or uncleanly in personal habits? Is the patient violent, dangerous, destructive, excited or depressed, homicidal or suicidal? Has the patient insane relatives?"[100] The doctors recorded their findings in a signed legal document known as a certificate of lunacy. Then the papers went to a judge for assent; for some time during the early 1890s, an old man collected Bellevue's daily batch of certificates of lunacy in the evening and simply couriered them to the house of a jurist who lived nearby.[101] Once certified insane, the patient was carried to the dock, where she climbed aboard a steamer for the ride upriver.

Poor Rachel. It was an enormous, dreary institution. The men's branch, on the island's east side, was housed in a dourly handsome edifice flanked by two enormous wings, with a mansard roof, windows shaped like gothic arches, and ivy climbing the fancy brickwork; it was fronted by a privet hedge, beyond which spread a great lawn. On the west side of the island, by contrast, the women inhabited a scattering of decrepit buildings formerly occupied as the Emigrant Hospital and Refuge, where generations of destitute or sick arrivers had been detained for treatment. The old Verplank Hospital, a colossal, many-turreted heap, served as the main building. It had ten open wards, each adjoined by a corridor used for dining. In each ward, according to the *Herald*, the iron cots were lined up so close together that the women had to climb up over the foot of the bed to get into them at night. By day, they sat on benches in the same room. The attendants, mostly very young women newly emigrated from Ireland, each held a key that unlocked all the building's many iron doors. A similar setup prevailed in single-story satellite pavilions A, B, C, D, E, and F.

The 1900 census counts Rachel here, one name in a monotonous list of 2,000, nearly all identified, somewhat ironically, as housewives like her, or housekeepers, or domestics. They were expected to continue their domestic labors in the asylum. The *Herald* charged that many had developed "housemaid's knee" from being made to scrub on all fours, a claim a follow-up report by the state Commissioners in Lunacy didn't exactly refute, except to point out that the condition could occur for no apparent reason, or as a result of a woman's being "much addicted to the kneeling posture."[102] Many of Rachel's fellows at Ward's Island were of German and Irish descent. More than a few, according to the census, were illiterate.

Twice a day the patients walked the grounds for an hour, in double file. Twice a day they performed a fire drill. They were bathed in groups, each waiting her turn, plunging into the tub, then dressing once again in the coarse muslin underthings and shabby, ill-fitting blue gingham dress that were the standard issue. Even the outdoor band concert pictured in an annual report looks hopelessly forlorn; portly men in white pants and dark military-style coats play to an audience of inmates seated, at some distance, in rows.[103] The tenements, No. 239, whatever anyone said, could be the intensely meaningful locus of a personal world. It could be home. But this—this supposed annex to the tenements—what reflection of herself could Rachel find here, what reason to lift her eyes from the ground?

She did not get well. Rachel apparently was among the five hundred or so women transferred in November 1901 from the West Branch of the asylum, which now included both the women on the western side of Ward's Island and a large contingent on Blackwell's Island, to the East Branch theretofore occupied solely by men.* In his

---

*In 1890 the state Commission in Lunacy had taken over from county governments the management of public insane asylums in New York state. New York City, however, had been an exception; it maintained control of its own asylums until 1896, when the Commission in Lunacy also took charge of the New York City Asylum for the Insane, changing its name to the Manhattan State Hospital, with the East Branch housing men and the West Branch women.

monthly reports to the Commissioners in Lunacy, men's asylum superintendent A. E. MacDonald[104] seethed at the bureaucratic shaft-
ing he perceived in the transfer, complaining that the furniture should
have been moved with the women, that the East Branch was, by comparison with the West, short on medical staff, and, most emphatically,
that the women sent there were of an "unsatisfactory character."
"These women are old chronic cases, of the least desirable type, of
which the transferring hospital took the opportunity to rid itself," he
pointedly observed. "There were among them several cases of phthisis,
many uncleanly dements, and many more who were paralysed, or crip-
pled, or too feeble to walk."[105] Before long, however, the women were
performing a number of useful duties for the men's branch, laundering
its dirty linens, making mattresses, and sewing and mending uniforms
and other clothing.[106]

That June, the superintendent opened an outdoor tent ward for some
of the old and sickly women, after a model used to treat men with tuberculosis. A picture of these women shows large, open-sided white
tents surrounded by trees, and beside the tents, a row of benches where
white-haired, aproned women sit slightly apart from one another and
look at nothing in particular, their arms hanging at their sides or folded
in their laps. It's a surreal photograph; amid leafy, light-dappled environs, the women seem placed like furniture. They are extraordinarily
inert. The asylum's annual report for 1902 captions the photograph,
"Manhattan State Hospital—East—Exterior Camp C—Demented and
Uncleanly Patients."[107] The West Branch, MacDonald wrote, had agreed
to make "partial amends" for sending these women by taking back those
still showing evidence of active TB when Camp C closed in the fall.[108]

Rachel was one of the consumptives, but she died the morning of
June 3, 1902, a few weeks before Camp C was opened. She may have
been wasted and coughing all along, a memento of her last months at
No. 239. On the other hand it would not be surprising if she contracted tuberculosis in the asylum's open wards. The high prevalence
of tuberculosis in insane asylums could be explained by their crowding
and failure to isolate infected patients, a charge made by the *Herald* in
Ward's Island's specific case, and affirmed by the subsequent official
investigation.[109] When a twenty-five-year-old junior physician of the

East Branch prepared Rachel's death certificate, he gave pulmonary tuberculosis as the direct cause of her death, chronic melancholia as the indirect cause. In blanks for the names of her mother and father, Dr. C. Floyd Haviland scribbled simply "unknown." Her last address he did supply. It was No. 239 E. 7th St.[110] It had been nearly ten unthinkably long years.

I want to believe Rachel knew, at the end, that it was her brother, the dauntless Moses, who would bring her home. After her burial, he placed a dignified death notice in the *Times* implying she had been with him all along: "HART—June 3, Rachel, relict of Joseph Hart, residence of her brother, Moses L. Phillips, 359 East Fiftieth Street."[111] He apparently selected the uptown undertaker, too. And even if he wasn't religious, I like to think that Moses followed the basic tenets of Jewish burial, so that Rachel understood she would be relieved, finally, of the blue gingham dress and clumsy brogans, her body washed from head to toe in pure water and wrapped in a clean white shroud. Finally, finally, she would get what she must have wanted day after bleak and lonesome day: to lie down beside a young milliner, the child she'd raised, and sleep.

It seems telling that Rachel's husband and father slept through their starless night in another cemetery altogether, though it wasn't far away. Within the year, her mother would join the two men. Clara Phillips died in the house she had inhabited more than a third of her ninety-one years.[112] Her executors put No. 239 on the block, where it brought $12,100.[113] After paying taxes and debts, they divided the cash according to Clara's wishes. Rachel's $1,250 went to the great-grandson in Denver. A daughter of Samuel's received the same share, and so did Moses's wife, Sarah—although Moses himself signed for it. The youngest of Clara's children, Isabella, came away with $2,250 (the extra $1,000 awarded in a codicil signed in 1898, possibly to compensate her for the $1,000 previously lent to Sarah) and her mother's personal and household effects.

Isabella stayed on for a number of years in the neighborhood that had been Kleindeutschland. By 1910 the German city within a city had faded into memory, the burgeoning Jewish East Side having spread up from its origin below Houston Street to encompass all the streets below 14th, the names along these streets now "end[ing] in the telltale 'vitch' or 'owski,'" as the *Sun* put it.[114] That year finds Isabella renting with five other families in a house just a block north of No. 239 on 8th Street—still standing, in other words, a survivor of the attrition that had punished her clan as if with some cruel and persistent purpose. No. 239 also had proved to be the last home of her husband, the French tinsmith Alfred Salomon. He died of lung cancer—it was always the lungs with this family—in building 9D of the Montefiore Home for Chronic Invalids, a Jewish charity set high on a bluff overlooking the Hudson at 138th Street. His doctor, T. Abrahamson, gave exhaustion as a contributing cause of death.[115] And Isabella reported to the 1910 census taker that only three of her children still drew breath. Clara, twenty-one, and twenty-four-year-old twins Oscar and Leon, both working as salesmen, all lived with their mother. The years since 1900 apparently had taken from Isabella her firstborn, Lily, and her second-eldest, Joseph. I could not find their death certificates; maybe they, too, went away somewhere, perhaps to a sanitarium in hopes of a cure. And what could Isabella make of this fate? What order, moral or scientific, could explain why the house of Phillips and Salomon was stricken, but next door the Biebers had twelve children, all spared, ten of them living right there in the house they owned? And their oldest son a doctor.

I wonder, too, what she thought when she walked past No. 239, that ship of ghosts, wearing her mother's favorite brooch, perhaps, or a dress taken in at the waist. "Do you want to pay doctors' and undertakers' bills OR Do you want to keep well?" a pamphlet from the city's Tenement House Department fairly taunted. "Don't Rent Dark Rooms," it warned. "A dark room is a Consumption Factory. . . . It will pay you to move where the children can have sunshine and fresh air in which to grow strong."[116] If a house can kill, this one had taken its share of victims, and maybe Isabella hated it for that. But it also held the memory of their words and gestures. *My beloved daughter*, her mother had written. Anything they could save they'd saved in that house. And it had carried survivors into a new century.

Real Property

ONE BRIGHT, COLD January morning about a year after the architect's call set new terms for our lives, David and I took the F train to downtown Brooklyn. There, around a large oval table in a windowless conference room of the bank that held the debt attached to No. 239, we gathered at the appointed time with Gary and Joanne, and with two loan officers. Sandra, a faintly maternal woman of ginger-tinted hair, had always taken a sympathetic, almost conspiratorial tone when urging us not to be late with the mortgage payment. Gina was Sandra's rather more hard-edged boss; on hearing the news about No. 239's structural flaws, she'd come to inspect the bank's collateral wearing a full-length fur and a string of pearls. Our errand that winter day was to determine the status of the application I had prepared to extend the co-op's mortgage debt with a new construction loan in the amount of $250,000, the estimated cost to make the building habitable. In more general terms, it was an occasion for the interested parties to hash out whether we would stay or go. We could hold our ground, retain our rights in the fixed resource that was No. 239, doubling down on the house in order to restore some of its lost value. Or we could literally cash it in as the Phillipses had done on their matriarch's death, perhaps locking in the loss of value, but stemming further losses and freeing us to invest what remained in some other, possibly more productive, resource.

The job, for each party, was to carefully weigh the value of No. 239. This meant implicitly to weigh it against the value of all other things.

It meant, for me and David, restraining the mental habits that might compromise our ability to objectively perceive its place in the realm of things. This was not about daffodils sprouting in the yard. It was not about our secrets or our hopes. It was not even about what we'd paid for No. 239, or how we got that money, or what we'd thought the building was worth eighteen months ago. The past with its reams of content only distorted the lens through which we squinted at an obscure future. To stay or to go? Which lever would yield the bigger pile of pellets? Did door number one conceal the brand-new bedroom set, a late-model sedan, or some belittling joke, a toaster oven, perhaps, or an absurdly oversized T-shirt?

It was about money, that bridge to every other thing, that last train out of Dodge. Around the conference table this particular January morning in 2003, nerves were tuned to a high pitch. The bankers had the discomfited air of ones charged with managing a scene that promised to expose something distasteful and raw. The four of us holding a more complete stake in the building sat rigid in our seats, coiled, no less avid than hungry beasts.

It may seem obvious that things are important, money (as the wild card representing any and all things) especially so. But I've always had a hard time looking squarely at money. It's not a question of indifference. My pulse literally quickens when the ATM asks, *Would you like to view your balance for this account?* I look away out of insecurity. Money comes and goes according to no particular schedule that I control or understand. For me, the whole subject engenders this rush of horrible feelings: a sense of inadequacy at being such a pitifully low earner, and therefore of disgraceful dependency, and therefore of desperate risk—a sense that I will never, ever feel safe.

David and I had been given every advantage in life. As a young man David had come into a large chunk of money. This happened to be in the mid-1990s. We put most of it in the NASDAQ. Oracle, Sun Microsystems, Nokia. David was well informed, knew the ticker symbols and price-to-earnings ratios, understood all the up-and-coming technologies. And we got rich. It was easy and quick, money coming in like the fog on little cat feet.[1] It was exciting. We bought a place on 7th

Street. We had a child, dressed her dimpled chubbiness in nostalgic sun suits and excellent shoes, took her to England, and chased her down the grassy garden paths at Sissinghurst. We paid off our mortgage. It was like pruning a shrub: The money grew back. We routinely spent $300 at a shot in the Astor Place Barnes & Noble; anything that remotely interested us we took home. The money was there. The tectonic shifts of new parenthood having brought one or two shattering marital confrontations, we each embarked upon a psychoanalysis—a project we found far more vital and contemporary than college readings on Freud's analysis of the "Rat Man" might have forecast, and, incidentally, kind of pricey. We hired a woman to clean our apartment once a week, a Latina named Berthe whose loveliness and personal vigor I associated with the lemony smell of Murphy's oil soap. David always made her a cappuccino.

Before long we were accruing and spending sums that made our earnings from work seem not just meager but trivial, and since this work frankly had been a little disappointing—I was writing mainly short pieces for women's magazines, David was editing and vetting copy for *Spy*—we began to neglect it for other things. It's not that we didn't talk about this, we did, ad nauseam. I spent a lot of time feeling bad about it. And probably no one was more against our living off the NASDAQ than certain members of our own families, who thought it risky, if not dishonorable. But since the money was there, I reasoned, since it had come to us, shouldn't I take the opportunity it afforded to do something that really mattered to me? Over Greek salad and veggie burgers at a little café off Tompkins Square, we'd debate the question of whether the money was sapping our motivation to tackle difficult challenges, but at the time, reading my poems aloud in graduate workshops didn't seem easy, it seemed pee-your-pants scary. Would it not in fact be *cowardly* to do otherwise? Didn't I want my little girl to see that I was, I don't know, *involved*, in my own life as well as hers?

It was in this slow, insidious, inexorable way that the so-called tech bubble recruited us to its inane purposes, like a tumor building new capillaries, diverting a blood supply to feed its own anomalous growth. At no time was I unaware that some might regard *us* as the tumor. That was a fact you could hardly miss, living in the East Village. I remember reading an article on real estate that quoted some fellow saying he wished the stock market would crash and all the trust fund kids would jump off their roofs, leaving the neighborhood to the locals. *He means us*, I thought, with an awful jolt. And there was no sense in wheedling. It was no use braying about how we supported public schools and community gardens, gave away X many thousands to environmental groups, friends of farm animals, advocates for the poor. We were latte drinkers, *Wall Street Journal* subscribers—plastered-floor people to his hog-backed-brick people—and it's true, we were destroying his world.

Or *were* we latte drinkers? The market, as many will recall, did crash. I'm a big believer in the idea that, assuming your basic needs are met, you're going to be roughly as contented living on ten ducats a year as you were living on forty. I often think about this as the difference between the family that Lucy knew as an infant and toddler, and the one Byron knew. Born in May 2000, a couple of months after the market peaked, Byron never learned to call the restaurant delivery guy "dinner man." He's taken aback at the idea of a maid, and he's rarely seen the inside of a taxicab. What's the big deal? But this describes two stable planes; it's getting from one to the other that's hard. It can't be accomplished overnight. As the NASDAQ pitched itself into the red, we saw the iceberg, we turned the wheel, but our lifestyle was a supertanker that wouldn't turn on a dime. We cut out the easy things, retail goods, entertainments, restaurant meals. We apologized, and said good-bye, to Berthe. Then we both quit analysis; that was awkward, not to say painful. In the apartment on 8th Street, I wrote a letter to the poetry program saying I would not be returning for my final semester.

Looking at the stocks-index chart today, the spire-tip at March 2000 followed by a precipitous decline that lasted through our evacuation from No. 239, the summer we spent at the farm, and the months leading up to that January morning bank meeting, it's clear we didn't have a chance. The old life was never coming back. You see the full shape of such things only in retrospect. But even if we could have seen the chart line "going forward" (to quote the financial analysts' euphemism for an unknowable future)—even if we could have plotted the points yet to come, we could not have admitted that a door was closing, for the simple reason that we didn't yet imagine what other door would open. Should we move out of town? Could I get a shift at Starbucks? It is a testimony to our state of denial that David, rather than sidelining money we could no longer afford to risk, embarked on the disastrous course of trying to time the market's bottom. I say David did this because I was frozen with fear and as much as begged him to throw a burlap sack over my head and lead me through the burning timbers. He began buying stock derivatives, little "boats" or "baskets" of options, he called them, that he was confident would give our holdings a propulsive "bounce." (*Cat! Please!*) Each time one of these was set to mature, I would avert my eyes from CNBC, as if the news there could be any worse than what I read in my husband's face and body, racked with agitation. Our account was sinking fast in the market and, eventually, also hemorrhaging cash as a result of our expensive real estate problem. Not long before the bank meeting, we'd reached the place we hadn't dared to imagine. The money, well over a million bucks at one point, was gone. Like, your-ATM-card-doesn't-work gone. And as our earnings, though augmented, were nowhere near equal to present requirements, we'd begun to, essentially, panhandle among our family members. I *would* laugh about this one day, joke that our money-management strategy had been *flush twice*. That day was a long way off.

And the house? Well, before the fateful phone call, we'd thought the house just might save us—preserve us and our things in the constellation we'd long enjoyed, save all the value, economic and otherwise, real and otherwise, it had held in holding us. At the time, even as the stock market tumbled, all the disappointed hope of investors was spilling into real estate. Remember? Prices were going through the roof, nowhere more than in an East Village under conquest by the sippers of expensive coffees. There was a happy chitter-chatter on 7th Street about this, at least among apartment owners, and often punctuated by a kind of mock dismay at what the rising tide brought in. *Can you believe the swank place that opened on Avenue C? Oh my God! I remember when that was a beeper store!* The conversation I had with the graphic-designer neighbor out walking his shaggy little dog evidently held a certain satisfaction for us both, because we had it more than once: Yes, the place was now worth an enormous amount, so much so that one had to consider selling, but then again the resulting geyser of liquidity could be exploited only by moving to a less high-flying economy, some cheap, pretty little town, where the plan would be to ensconce oneself in a modest abode, squirrel away the cash, and . . . and what—ah, here was the problem—what would one do there and with whom?

David and I did develop a plan to "tap" our real estate, as we liked to say. As part of our retrenchment, we moved out of the second-floor apartment, had it gussied up as cheaply as possible, and rented it to a very nice young couple with a large, docile seal of a dog that, as we met with them for the first time, chewed one of Lucy's sturdy wooden blocks to a slobbery mash. Their rent would cover our co-op maintenance charges. We liked them, and I think they liked us, and I suppose this is the reason why neither one of them uttered a single word of reproach the night I knocked on their door—she was in her robe, up late drinking tea—to announce they could consider themselves homeless. They later broke up, and I'd see her once in a while, looking thin, tossing a stick to that big dog in Tompkins Square Park. Obviously our retrenchment plan—not a bad one in principle—aborted.

As soon as the building was vacant, as soon as it entered into uncanny ambiguity as to its aliveness or deadness as a home, it also entered a period of wild uncertainty as to its economic value. This was a madness that had many participants, a game of bluster and sham in which nobody knew what was real about the house, or about the guy sitting across the table, sucking his teeth and holding his cards to his chest. You had on the one hand a lack of clarity about just how irremediably wrecked the building would turn out to be, and on the other, a near feeding frenzy on East Village real estate. Everybody was afraid of getting tricked.

Without our having advertised No. 239 or even listed it for sale, a surprising number of people came sniffing after a piece of the deal. There were opportunists like the ssserpent, who baldly tried to pick up the building for a song. But there were also serious people who at least temporarily stoked a fantasy that we were on the verge of a grand redevelopment scheme in which No. 239 would be expanded vertically, the extra square footage sold at a profit, after which we would retake the citadel, all of us emerging miraculously "whole." Gary was

especially attracted to this possibility. But the two or three development teams we talked with nibbled, crunched the numbers, and finally shook their heads or simply disappeared. Then there were the
offers to purchase No. 239 at a price that even we, in our wishful condition, recognized as outlandishly high; naturally we pounced. One was
from an Englishwoman who met with David late one night at a local
watering hole and explained that she rather *preferred* to acquire failing
structures as long as the neighborhood was chic, a meeting from which
he returned to me breathless with hope. Later there came a call from
a mysterious Greek gazillionaire who claimed he would pay well over a
million dollars for the whole building. When we tried to bite down on
that, he abruptly halved the offering price. Members of the co-op next
door to No. 239 told us they, too, were considering making an offer to
forestall undesirable development on the lot. Even some friends of
ours, frustrated at the seeming impossibility of ever owning a place in
New York, asked if perhaps there was a way to put in a little money, get
in on the ground floor? Incredulous, we beat them off with a stick. Nor
did we take either of two discreetly tendered suggestions that we accept a lowish price for the building in exchange for a finder's fee that
David and I would pocket on the down-low, thereby screwing our co-
owners out of their rightful proportion.

Individual shares in the co-op—our apartments—were, of course,
essentially worthless by now, the ultimate pig in a poke. That didn't
stop Oren from enlisting one broker, and then a second, in an attempt
to sell off his place. He actually held open houses in the cracked and
vacant building. "Very quiet" was one of the selling points listed on a
flyer, which offered his parlor-floor space for $475,000. "Owner must
sell," it said. "Make an offer today!" David laid out to Oren the apparent obstacle that any buyer would have to come to the co-op—us—
for a stock certificate, at which point we would fully inform this person
of present circumstances. Eventually, he started talking about buying
us out at an unlikely but, in our present state, incredibly enticing
$600,000. He didn't know exactly when he'd have the money lined up.

To stay. Or to go. By the time we met at the bank offices in Brooklyn,
I felt like I'd been sitting for days at the poker table, drunk, unkept,

staring with fatigue, and *losing*. I knew we could not afford any more hallucinations. It was time to snap out of it, time to get real. But where was the real value—real, in the sense that it wouldn't vanish into thin air? The house was a physical thing, something you could see and touch; it was as particular and material a support to life as the body itself. Here, the power would come from long dwelling in place like the nobility of old, or for that matter, the peasants whose rights to till their respective furrows vested in them by virtue of long-established ties to place. Early on in our debacle, I had phoned the state attorney general's office for advice. An assistant AG listened patiently to my tale of woe, then responded with a world-weariness that gave weight to his words. Typically, he said, in a case like ours, owners who managed to effect a repair themselves reaped the reward; if, on the other hand, the owner surrendered the property in a distress sale, he'd lose out and someone else would make money off the deal. Well, the place was ours, and we had sown our row. Why the hell should we go anywhere? Why should we forfeit?

On the other hand, as the German sociologist Georg Simmel pointed out in 1900, ownership is nothing but the sum of the uses and enjoyments of a given thing, and the thing itself can place rather firm limits on these.[2] That No. 239 was a real, physical thing only made it, like the body, like anything you can see and touch, perishable. In our real estate, we were bound to a fixed resource that was drawing near to the end of its productive life—that was dying.

So maybe money was the way to go—life-stuff slipped free of the organism—like excrement, as Freud famously observed, or blood, or seed, in itself inert, immaculately abstract. Deathless. Money would unbind us! It was "the purest example of the tool," "an absolute means," as Simmel puts it, infinite possibility.[3] Can *you* make the grass grow? the Indian asked. Why, yes, I can—with money. If for the Lenape a spirit animated everything in nature, for us the spirit that lives in objects is abstract economic value. Money. It breathes in people, too, because we are at once beings and, like it or not, exchangeable tools—instruments of production and containers for "net worth." Money is the magical shape-shifter that can turn itself from an hour's pencil-pushing to a pair of pants, from a truckload of oranges to an acre of grass. It finds its identity in movement, this ceaseless pouring from cup to cup. Maybe money was the real thing, a hard truth that outlasts us all. Why else would people say *money makes the world go round* and *everyone has his price*? Maybe the abstract exchange value that hides in every single thing—people, too—is the Oneness that holds the world together.

But the unbounded potential of money also represented its pitfall; we could not join the realm of deathless abstraction, but would have to exchange the money for something material if it was to be of any real use. And would it stretch far enough? How long could it last? As soon as money's potential was realized, you ran smack into the limits of its power. This habit I'd had of mentally spending the same money twice—so that the grand I'd made on a short article had in the manner of loaves and fishes paid for the month's health insurance as well as co-op carrying charges—well, that was just the mind playing tricks on itself. It was time to get real.

The meeting began in what I thought was an auspicious manner. Sandra praised our application as admirably complete. At this I cast a bitter look at Gary and Joanne, who despite my solicitations had been no help with this chore. David had, thank goodness, landed the job at the small publisher and was now working full-time. So it had fallen mostly to me to find a contractor, go back to him three times for changes, locate an expeditor to navigate the permitting process, negotiate with the city for permission to work on No. 239 from the city-owned lot next door, and procure new insurance on the building, all while finishing up my manuscript on the pharmaceutical industry and trying to provide a modicum of motherly care to Lucy and Byron. *Unfortunately*, one of the bankers now ventured, it didn't look like there was enough detail in the proposed scope of work, and it seemed unlikely the contractor I'd found (the lowest bidder) could meet the bank's standards. We could vet the project ourselves, she said, in which case we'd each need to sign personal guarantees on the entire amount of the loan. Or the bank could use its own professionals to do so, which would add something like $100,000 to the price tag. Also—and this came as a decisive blow—there would be no suspension of debt payments during construction. Work like this, they further offered, invariably dragged on much longer than anyone anticipated; we should bear in mind we'd be expected to make payments even if construction hit a terrible snag.

All this, rather than disheartening Gary and Joanne, seemed to whip up their confidence and ire; Joanne kept snapping that this or that would be a "deal breaker," as if the bankers had shown any eagerness whatever to make a deal with us. Our co-owners insisted, with enormous indignation, that the bankers and perhaps David and I were, for whatever reason, grossly underestimating the value of what we had in No. 239. They clearly suspected a trick. The moment Sandra and Gina began signaling an end to the meeting, Gary and Joanne broke for the elevator. I ran after them. "I think we should talk," I said. "We need to talk." But they made off with an ostentatious display of haste, Joanne piping over her shoulder that they had an important meeting scheduled, by which we clearly were meant to infer, *Tassel Loafers*.

I was deflated. We'd moved three times in a year. I'd thought the bank meeting would be like the finish line in a cross-country race—you fall across it in a puddle of your own vomit, whereupon nothing further is required of you. But it had turned into another starting line. It had become clear that we didn't really *own* No. 239—the sum of its uses and enjoyments being nil—but would have to repurchase it. The economic value of a thing, says Simmel, is measured in the act of exchange, by what's sacrificed for it. We had to ask ourselves just how little we'd accept to finally let go of No. 239, but also, just as important, how much more we would sacrifice to get it back.

As we waited on the subway platform, I told David that I could see quite clearly the next months and even years of my life, the paperwork and the fighting with Gary and Joanne and the fear and striving for gain, and I didn't want them. You could have them, I said, *take* them. By the time we were on the F train, hurtling beneath the East River toward Manhattan, I was openly, messily crying, and, given my usual abhorrence of a public scene, it was probably this as much as anything I'd said that made David's eyes widen in alarm. He put both his arms around me. And he said with a strange, quiet certainty, "We're done. It's finished. We're getting out."

It had been such a lonely time in our marriage. A lean time, in which we both were forced to understand we'd better bring some value to the table, in which I had to know that no one was put on this earth to carry me, not my parents, not my analyst or my friends, certainly not my children, and not my husband. It was sink or swim. But that afternoon, David made himself a place for me. That place was a simple wooden skiff. He laid me in its sun-bleached bottom, where I closed my eyes. Before long there came a knocking in the oarlocks. In a moment he brought us back around. People matter more than things.

This was early 2003, the aforementioned real estate bubble still vigorously inflating. Nobody was reassessing the logic behind the run-up in prices. Talking about downsizing as if it might be a good thing was about as fashionable as coughing up a hairball.

With the historic foreclosure crisis that began in '07, I've had the sensation of belatedly finding lots of company in the experience we went through with No. 239. Suddenly their images are everywhere— men and women standing on a patch of lawn or in an emptied-out room, wearing an expression of helpless apology as they try to explain just what happened here. One couple talks to the camera from the deck of a swimming pool, their children rolling like otters in the blue water. They took out the home equity loan to build it, they explain, figuring the boys were going to be around only so long, and this was their thing; the pool was the center of their family life. I'm thinking, the money was there, right? And now the house and pool keep jacking you up for more, this cursing, stamping Rumplestiltskin? "You can't afford to leave," as President Barack Obama described the predicament, "and you can't afford to stay."[4]

There's this pervasive feeling of having been *suckered*—not, generally speaking, by the fine print in a mortgage contract, but by something much broader and more nebulous, a smudge on the lens through which we'd viewed our lives. What most of us wanted from our real property was a sense of permanence and control. We wanted to know that we could paint the walls the colors we like. We wanted to make sure nobody could ever dispossess us. We wanted the thing to pour its value like a shower of coins into our laps, to work for us and not the other way around. The mistake was to assume that holding title to a place accomplishes this. Very often there's a Rumplestiltskin ready to spring from hiding and claim his due, the guarantees implied by the word "homeownership" sharply limited by the claims of a bank or other mortgagee, by the state, which can tax the property and exert control over how it's built and maintained, by neighbors who can eliminate your shade with the felling of a single tree, and even by the property itself, which, as in our case, may exact ever-increasing investments just to redeem the value you thought you'd already bought. A few unlucky twists of fate, and suddenly, the homeownership that was supposed to bring freedom and control seems like some kind of indenture or snare.

Such turns can come as a particular shock to those of us who urged ourselves across the threshold of homeownership as a more or less unquestioned rite of passage, something you naturally strived for if you were thirty and married and pregnant. "Americans of all ages, incomes, and ethnic backgrounds believe deeply in homeownership," wrote Franklin D. Raines, chairman of Fannie Mae, the nation's largest purchaser of home mortgages, in 2003. "They will go to great efforts, if necessary, to realize their American Dream of owning a home."[5] But isn't the very universality of this dream suspect? Maybe the dream is the smudge. Maybe it keeps us from examining the complex relations underlying our own ownership of property, or indeed thinking about our freedom and independence in more ultimate terms.

Since before the Great Depression we've been listening to this steady stream of rhetoric that denigrates renters (including more than two-thirds of New Yorkers today) and offers ownership as the panacea for all manner of personal, social, and economic ills. A 1920s homeownership campaign by the federal Department of Labor even included a letter submitted to newspapers addressing America's children. "When your father and mother pay rent they are paying someone else for the use of the place they live in," the copy said. "It is not a good thing to do that. It is like wearing someone else's clothes." Or, it said, think of renters as being like the cuckoo, so "lazy" it lays its eggs in other birds' nests: "Birds hate the cuckoo, and will drive it away."[6]

"You want to reinforce family values in America, encourage two-parent households, get people to stay home?" President Bill Clinton asked in 1995. "Make it easy for people to own their own homes and enjoy the rewards of family life and see their work rewarded."[7] Several years later, President George W. Bush did not court controversy in telling a White House conference, "We want everybody in America to own their own home. . . . An ownership society is a compassionate society. . . . Owning something is freedom. . . . And ownership of a home helps bring stability to neighborhoods. . . . It brings pride to people."[8]

As every homeowner figures out sooner or later, these are appealing but false assurances. Even the most straightforward financial benefits are far from certain. Savings are a reliable benefit of homeownership *if* you stay for more than a few years, *if* you pay the mortgage, and *if* you refrain from borrowing against equity. You get a return on those saved dollars if you can afford the insurance, taxes, and (ahem) maintenance required to protect your investment—and if you happen to buy and sell in the right place at the right time. Though it's often said that Manhattan real estate in particular is a fail-safe investment, the sales history of No. 239, at least, suggests otherwise. Abraham Weinstein, the first owner-occupier, bought it in 1860 for $4,300.[9] In 1973, an owner who'd held it more than thirty years sold for $12,250.[10] Over more than a century during which the city developed into an ass-kicking center of fashion and finance, this little piece of the dream lost nearly half its value in real dollars.[11] As an investment for individuals, buying No. 239 was a crapshoot whose outcome depended as much on accidents of history as sage planning. Weinstein, for instance, did rather well. The period of his tenure brought massive inflation as the government printed money to finance the Civil War; on the other hand, much of this money found its way into the city's thriving war economy. Weinstein sold in 1867 for $9,000, getting about 17 percent more buying power than he paid.[12] Whether ownership had promoted the tailor's contentment in his work or family life I wouldn't venture to judge. The question of his freedom is perhaps even more complicated. Weinstein was in charge of No. 239 while he owned it, but unlike his tenants, who could move on at will, he was bound to keep paying the mortgage, and dependent on those tenants to do so.

In the end the calculation of costs and benefits is highly individual. On the F train that January day, I finally felt it in my gut, finally choked on the cost of reclaiming No. 239. Meanwhile, the very last item on my purple Magic Markered list, number seven, *Don't give up on your own happiness*, so long submerged, kicked and pulled for the surface. By the time I got off the train in Manhattan I knew: I wasn't going to jump off any goddamn roof. My days! I wanted them back.

For most people, "the question of 'How much?'" as Simmel puts it, mediates the satisfaction of every desire. Only the super-rich, he says, can go about their business without a care for the money value of things, a way of life that in his view possesses "an extraordinary aesthetic charm."[13] But can any of us name the person who actually lives that charmed life, whose heaping portion liberates him from even the consideration of economic value? The idea that some amplitude of supply can finally free one from money seems to me just as much a dream as the notion that a piece of property can establish ultimate security and independence. Even Gandhi, who took the opposite tack of voluntary poverty and *non*-possession, was not free from the everlasting work of renouncing things, a project that presupposes the question *how much?* (or how little?) and that involved the renunciation of his own body as a "cage."[14] Pull it close or push it away, the very stuff that's supposed to offer itself in mute service has a sneaky way of gaining the whip hand.

God knows David and I, when we parted on the platform in Manhattan, were not through with *how much*, nor with scratching and clawing after wants and needs. But we each had undergone one of those internal adjustments that colors subsequent experience. The new priority we'd set was simply to notice what it felt like on any given day to be alive. No. 239 and what it would yield—the thing jumped at, as Thoreau put it—were important. But so was the jump.[15] What this meant in concrete terms was that we'd decided, for our part, not to double down on the house, but to liquidate it. We'd go with the money and, in the interest of bringing the episode to a close with some efficiency, intended to be smart but realistic in our expectations as to how much.

Recall, though, that No. 239 also figured prominently in the personal narratives of Oren and Gary. Our ownership was limited by theirs, by the bank's, and by the interests of the party to whom Oren had mortgaged his individual unit. Getting out would not be easy.

The bankers had made clear that to get the construction loan, all the shareholders would have to sign on. Nothing could induce us to do so; on that point we were decided. Neither of our co-owners was in a position to buy us out, and to sell our apartment to an outsider, if that could be accomplished at all, would entail a near-total loss. But neither could we unilaterally decide to dissolve the corporation and sell the building. Paragraph 4c of the co-op's proprietary lease, a sort of corporate charter, held that, in the event the building was severely damaged by a condition not covered by its insurance, only a vote representing two-thirds of shares could authorize a dissolution and sale. Gary and Oren together constituted fewer than half the shares; we held 58.5 percent. Failure to agree, in other words, would put us on a path to mutual destruction.

At this point, a party who'd long stood in the background of our debacle stepped to the fore. Oren's private mortgage holder was a Florida widow whose dapper, worldly wise brother, Frank, had gotten her into the investment. In the year since we'd all left the building, Oren, having paid not a cent of what he owed to the co-op, evidently also defaulted on payments to this creditor. Now, feeling awful, Frank wanted to get his sister's money back. Taking possession of shares in a co-op of yahoos about to embark on a leveraged, iffy construction project would hardly have served Frank's purposes. Now that he understood David and I would vote to sell, he moved with alacrity to foreclose on Oren.

David and I, meanwhile, had come a long way from being the young couple who thought it would be charming to raise a family amid the broken floorboards and water-damaged walls of an old tenement. *Hell* no, it was all about risk management now. We announced, in writing, the requisite meetings. We asked Robert, the co-op litigator, to talk with Frank's lawyer and draw up conditions for the transfer of shares to him. We took notes on conversations and dated them. Now that we'd pronounced it dead, the house was a thing of unmixed aversion, the pitch-dark horror-movie house; you slide along its walls with your eye on the front door and every muscle quivering to bolt, but you must go slowly, slowly, and not make a sound, because there's someone else creeping around in there and he's got a knife.

Oren, who'd been so aggressive, quickly folded. He was into Frank for a pretty good chunk of change, and I guess he knew the gig was up. Still, on March 6, 2003, fearing an ambush, I went down to the New York

County Courthouse to observe the public auction of his shares. The broker/developer who would ultimately handle the sale of No. 239 came with me, mainly for sport. This was Bob, handsome and full of himself in a not altogether unappealing way; he had the high thrill threshold necessary for this kind of roller derby. He also understood East Village property. (Early on, when I'd called him for advice, he'd told me that if we should decide to sell, we'd need to do two things first: get an engineer's assessment of the building's condition, and sort out our corporate mess.) It was midmorning when Frank's lawyer stepped into the courthouse rotunda, an august space ringed with pillars beneath an elaborately decorated dome. With a minimum of fanfare he announced the sale, which summoned, like iron filings to a magnet, a motley assortment of maybe a half dozen men. Bob explained with unmistakable relish that these were the bottom-feeders, hoping to get something for nothing. I was aghast, but the sheepish bids they tossed out never came close to the upset price, and in no time Frank, that blessedly known quantity, was our new cooperator. I heard from Oren exactly once after that. He left a message instructing me to make him a new set of keys.

So far, so good! Now that we had three functioning shareholders, we called a meeting to vote on whether to pursue the loan for repair, or dissolve the co-op and sell the building. If Gary voted against the sale, well, we had the shares to overrule him. The days were full of a tightly wound anticipation. We had rounded the first year since ejection from No. 239, and now the cold rains of early spring were coming on again, buds readying in the trees. We were going to be free. Two nights before the meeting date, David and I sat in our clear plastic chairs in the tiny apartment on 8th Street, talking and swilling our usual surfeit of cheap wine after dinner. The kids were asleep in the bedroom. The buzzer rang. *Delivery,* came the voice on the intercom, *can you come down?* Hmm, how unusual. A late birthday present for Lucy, perhaps? Had someone sent flowers? When David came back through the door, though, his color was all wrong. He flopped the papers on the table like a fish. After more than two years of harrying us with threats, Gary had gone and done it. He was suing us.

Today I can read the documents one sentence at a time and understand that his suit rested on three separate causes of action: breach

of fiduciary duty (itself explicated in thirty-nine paragraphs of allega-
tions), waste and mismanagement, and breach of the "warrant of hab-
itability" we, as co-op board members, supposedly owed him in respect
to his apartment at No. 239. At the time, though, my mind toppled
about like a cabbage butterfly in a field of asters, lost in the shock of
the details. The papers accused us of "failing to correct the hazards in
the building; failing to obtain the construction loan; failing to deal with
the city agencies or pay the fines; failing to pay professionals; orches-
trating a sale of the building on less favorable terms than if repaired;
flooding the building and failing to fix it; placing an illegal roof deck
and air conditioner on the building; failing to keep proper records and
give access to records; failing to reimburse plaintiff for expenses; failing to comply with the requirements of the proprietary lease; and, generally placing [Gary's] home in danger of destruction."[16] In other words,
even though Gary had been a shareholder, officer, and director of this
boondoggle long before we ever showed up, and even though we'd
spent the better part of two years doing our utmost to untangle the
very issues he mentioned, literally *everything* that had happened here
was the result of our malfeasance. And he was going to make us pay.
One big dysfunctional family, indeed.

Oh, and there was this detail: Gary was seeking an emergency injunction against our holding a co-op meeting to vote on whether to fix
or sell, stay or go. He asked that authority over all the co-op's affairs instead be placed in the hands of a receiver. Namely, himself. Good
news, though: "He has sworn that he will serve without salary."

Within a few days, we all appeared in court for action on this last
bit. Gary and Joanne came in flanked by two wide-tied, wing-tipped
attorneys—*not* Tassel Loafers, but more so. Their solicitous attentions
to Gary and Joanne suggested a strong, principled alliance, something
out of *Erin Brockovich*. Gary himself, spit-combed and wearing a dark
suit and tie, swept in without a glance in our direction. I'd come ready
with the same cardboard box of files I dragged out to begin this story,
but it remained tucked under my chair. The hearing was quickly over.
The judge—Saralee was her name—declined to appoint Gary our lord
and master, but she did bar the meeting to vote on the final disposition
of the building, pending a further hearing.

Gary was trying to block our exit. He was trying to take from my family the last of our resources. And he was claiming to do so by right, calling us liars and cheaters in a court of law. This produced in me a potent stew of fear, shame, and, mostly, rage—a sleepless, hair-on-fire rage such as I never felt before or since. If I'd had horns, I would have gored Gary. If I'd had hooves I would have stomped him into prostration and silence, until he made not the tiniest squeak. Instead I wrote a thirteen-page, single-spaced chronology and point-by-point rebuttal for Robert, the attorney. It had lively subtitles like "Paying ahead, getting behind" and "Our right to meet/vote blocked by malicious suit, endangering equity and building." It included documentary attachments A through Z and 1 through 15 (plus E1, E2, M1 through M3, and a few others stuck in upon later consideration). Robert was very good, but it seemed to me he had an air of manning up to the unpleasantness of litigation. Such tasks as extracting a timely retainer for his work he performed with evident distaste, as if swabbing out a toilet. I had the impression that what drove him forward were thoughts of his family's comfort; he spoke of them often and a little wistfully. Stanley, meanwhile, the other co-op attorney and for some time a friend, had never made any pretense of bloodlust. He was manifestly a man of peace; his gift was to work through conflicts quietly and deliberately. And I wanted killers! Into the ears of both men I poured a steady stream of invective about Gary and Joanne, a battle song I hoped would inspire them to whatever clench-jawed animus might be required for victory. It seems incredible to me that I actually gave Robert a copy of my book inscribed, "Knock 'em out cold!" but so it was; I can only plead a litigation-induced spleen that, thankfully, proved temporary.

The second court date, in preparation for which we had provided Saralee with a legal document strung with phone records, canceled checks, spreadsheets, and Kinko's and postal receipts, came on April 16. David and I sat in the front row, cotton-mouthed, holding hands. This time Saralee put some tough questions to both legal teams. But the onus was on Gary's side. Exactly what eventual remedy did he and his lawyers contemplate? How much would the construction cost and where would the money come from? Since Gary had accused us of "commingling" the co-op's funds with our own, she wanted to know where, exactly, we had put co-op money to personal use. Had it paid for work in our apartment, what? With a hail-Mary exuberance, Gary's lawyer pointed at me and David and urged Saralee not to "reward" us for our misconduct. "Let me put my guy in front of a jury!" he exclaimed, gesturing to the judge's left at these imagined good folk. At one point, he reiterated an argument made in the papers—that we lost nothing by the granting of an injunction, whereas Gary could lose his home, and that was irreplaceable. At this, Saralee took off her stylish tortoiseshell glasses, stuck them into her wavy brown hair, and took a good look at the lawyer. "Children are irreplaceable," she said mildly.

Here was another surprise: Gary himself had opened the door. By suing us, he finally had let us out of the dark, airless world of the house, in which subjectivity was all, passions reigned, and no one could say for sure what was real. In court, we could find out. Here, Gary's fury to pursue us to the ends of the earth for payment on any expenditure he chose abruptly lost its power. In the house we'd shared, he had made us mother and father, the arbiters of reality itself and thus the objects of wild protest. To quote his motion, "All these problems exist because Andrews and Greider have mismanaged the Corporation and breached their fiduciary duties to me and to the Corporation." But in court, it didn't make sense that we should be held responsible for the building's demise, compelled to assume and guarantee debt, or deprived of rights specifically laid out in the lease that governed our cohabitation. "Andrews and Greider have made their own interests paramount and have breached a duty of loyalty to the plaintiff," Gary bleated in his papers. Had he expected us to put *his* interests before our own, like a loving mother would, or like the Buddha, perhaps, who fed the starving lioness on his own flesh? Gary, Robert wrote in his response, "demonstrates by this action that he wants someone to 'save him,' a course and option that, I believe, the law does not permit." This time Saralee permitted us to vote—which we did, in Stanley's office, with Gary abstaining while we and Frank voted to sell—but not to carry out cancellation of the leases until Gary had one more chance to substantiate some misbehavior on our part. We should bring witnesses to testify on this question at the next hearing, she said. Around midday on the eve of the scheduled hearing, I got a call from

Robert. Gary was withdrawing his motion for an injunction. When we showed up in court the next day (along with a potential witness, Richard, the engineer, wearing a tweed jacket and smelling faintly of soap), Gary and Joanne were nowhere in sight. Gary's lawyers insisted on his right to withdraw the motion, conveniently excusing themselves from at last bringing evidence, while refusing to drop the lawsuit itself. Saralee, not amused, permitted this but sternly warned the lawyers that they'd better not come back without a clear demonstration of fraud. And she gave us the green light to cancel the leases and proceed with a sale.

It was a qualified victory, further muted by the fact that the most important reality test still lay ahead. What *was* the building's real value? That would now be measured very precisely by what somebody was willing to pay for it. And we truly understood by this time that all the talk in the world wasn't worth a gob of spit until you had a signed contract and money down. Fortunately, we now had in our corner Bob, the intrepid real estate agent, whose job was to prevent any number of bullshitters and con artists from playing with our heads, and to do justice to everyone with skin in the game: us, Frank's sister, Gary, the bank. And now, of course, himself. May, June, July, we lived with our fingers crossed, our stomachs knotted, money tight, the bank breathing down our necks. "I don't know that we're not going to sue you," was Gina's confounding locution when I explained to her that we'd dissolved the co-op and, thus, its right to collect shareholder dues. On August 1, Bob brought us the coveted quarry: a signed, cash-sealed contract of sale. You simply can't imagine the relief.

One million, one hundred ten thousand dollars and no cents. That was how much.

October 1, 2003, the day possession of that place passed out of our hands into those of a local restaurateur was, for me, a bitter one, but not because we were losing a home. That was old news. While David went to the closing, I was at my painted plywood desk in the apartment on 8th Street, facing up to the limits of money, twisting in one final paroxysm of regret. Specifically, I was sizing up the hit we would take from the federal tax on capital gains. Gains? I sputtered. *Gains?*

The usual exemption on the sale of a primary residence did not apply to this sale, because the property was held by a corporation established in the 1980s. So the treasury got its take. So did the bank, not a penny less than $195,633.57 (including of course a penalty for early payment). The broker and lawyers and title companies all got their due. The rest we divided according to shares. When the dust settled, we—David and I—came out nearly even in real dollars. It was all in the timing. The surge in East Village real estate prices had been enough to balance the sagging condition of the building itself.

This still-spiraling market also meant that what we'd paid six years earlier wouldn't be enough to replace our home on 7th Street. The act of exchanging the building for money had identified its precise value in relation to all other things, and the verdict was this: A failing structure in the East Village of 2003 was worth roughly the same as an apparently sound one in 1997. Well, we were living in 2004 now. We had bought into a tumbledown neighborhood with chickens pecking in the yards. That place had slipped away. In selling, we had indeed forfeited our little niche in the world.

On the other hand, we had changed, too. Rather than representing a piece of our wealth, the sale proceeds represented the whole, making each dollar less powerful—it would not, for example, be rising like a loaf in the stock market—but also more precious. Our earnings no longer seemed in the least bit trivial. I'd spent a lot of time feeling bad about having money, then feeling bad about not having it, and now I was going to try to stop feeling bad. Our lives would be different. And it was all good. We'd almost found our stable plane, our solid ground.

Before we could get there, though, we'd have to snip the last thread tying us to No. 239. Gary. I kept thinking the sale was some horror-movie false ending, that any minute Gary would leap from the bushes swinging a hatchet. But the last time I laid eyes on him he was wearing that dark suit. In the months after the closing, Robert held in escrow $50,000 in proceeds from the sale, which, by requirement of the company providing title insurance to the buyers, couldn't be distributed to the shareholders until Gary's lawsuit resolved. Gary's share of the overall proceeds sat in another segregated account. We sent Gary accounting for all these funds, and Robert made occasional calls to his attorneys. Still no word. Then, in late November, Gary's lawyers filed papers asking to be relieved as his counsel.

For them but especially for Gary himself (who after all *did* face something awful in the loss of No. 239), the lawsuit had been a terrible miscalculation. The attorneys told the court that their client—their "guy"—not only had declined to direct them how he wished to proceed, but had failed to pay invoices in the amount of more than $27,000. This mess they now dumped in our laps. Gary failed to appear at the hearing on his attorneys' withdrawal, nor did he comply with the court's order to appoint a substitute. He would not or could not finish what he had started. And Joanne, who'd once spoken so forcefully for Gary, made not a peep. Finally, in early 2004, we submitted a request for summary judgment, quickly granted. We had Gary's checks prepared and mailed them to an address in New Jersey along with a letter explaining that cashing the checks would constitute a final release of liability.

So it was the disappearance of funds—the zeros where Gary's money had been—that let us know we were at long last free of him, and free, in the same moment, of the building on 7th Street. The house that had been home to us all, our intensely personal dream house, was now finally and wholly converted to money, a thing representing precisely the exchangeability of things.

Money mercifully permitted us to save what we could, leave the sinking hulk of No. 239, and go our separate ways. But even now the house exerts a centrifugal tug. I think of Gary often. And, knowing nothing of his present circumstances, I tend to picture him against an abstract ground of sea and sky, sitting in an inflatable lifeboat—an imagining that keeps a safe distance, but is not, after all, without some small measure of the care and loyalty he felt were his due.

A Crossroads

NINE

ALFRED WIEDER remembers No. 239 E. 7th St. through the perspective of a child and across a distance of more than sixty years.[1] He remembers the dauntingly steep wooden stairs, dark and rickety, that led to his grandparents' second-floor apartment. Since a fall down a flight of stairs was said to have precipitated his mother's early labor, Al associates this staircase with his own premature birth in June 1923. His parents, who were living in the Bronx at the time, wrapped their tiny second child in a cotton blanket and placed him in a box on a radiator. (Al likes to joke that that's how he got his start in the heating and cooling business.)

Louis and Laura Wieder would soon move to Washington Heights, the uppermost extension of Manhattan's west side. They would take Alfred and his elder sister, Charlotte, downtown to see their grandparents pretty regularly, especially on festive holidays like Passover in the spring or the festival of Sukkot in the fall, when, following a custom that recalls the lean-tos of the ancient Israelites during their long wanderings in the desert, the family would take their evening meal in a little shelter covered with branches that Grandpa Wieder had built in the backyard of No. 239. It was fun for the kids. Such colorful observances of Jewish tradition, as well as the iconic pushcarts that still lined Avenue C, and the slightly unsettling appearances of the homeless Ike the Wood Robber, known to tear the trim from buildings when no one was looking—these were novelties to a boy living uptown.

A photograph of No. 239 taken around 1940 as part of a city project to document property for tax purposes. The man on the stoop is not clear enough to be identified with confidence, but he bears a strong resemblance to Simon Wieder. (Courtesy of the New York City Municipal Archives.)

The toilet, Al recalls, was at the top of those steep stairs, on the landing. The front of the apartment was divided into three bedrooms, where his grandparents and three uncles, Max, Michael, and Morris, must have slept. Alfred rarely went into those rooms. The back room was the gathering place. Along one wall was a serving piece atop which sat a large radio, powered by enormous batteries. But the room was mostly taken up by a heavy dining table ringed with chairs. From his place facing the door beside Grandpa Wieder, Al would pass the time as a child does, letting the talk float over his head.

His uncles and father animatedly discussed local politics and judicial matters. His grandfather, Simon Wieder, laced his conversation with stories and lessons from the Torah and the Talmud. Al's grandmother, Gizella Wieder,[2] a large woman in contrast to her diminutive, angular husband, could often be found in the heart of the apartment, tending the great coal-fired iron stove. The place was kosher as long as Gizella held sway there. She made stuffed cabbage, Hungarian goulash, soups, roasts. Salads were not yet in vogue, Al tells me, unless it was chopped iceberg with Russian dressing, and for dessert, nothing elaborate, a little applesauce perhaps. Al considered Grandma Wieder's potato pancakes a particular treat, so much so that once, his grandmother and mother managed to feed their small boy a meat patty (something he didn't care for) by insisting against all evidence that it was a burned latke. They all spoke English, including Simon and Gizella. Al doesn't recall even an accent, although the term of course depends upon one's point of reference. They also could speak Hungarian and, in Simon's case at least, fluent Hebrew. Yiddish—"Jewish," as some East Siders called it—was the mother tongue of family members born in Europe. They talked Yiddish when the subject was one best kept from the children. In those days, the 1920s and '30s, a lot of subjects fell under that heading.

East 7th Street occupied a different place in the lives of Alfred's parents, Louis M. and Laura (Taubner) Wieder. It was where they felt the sap of youth running in their veins. Each had descended onto that stretch of sidewalk from a crowded apartment—he from No. 239, she from just down the block at No. 261—and come into each other's orbit. This was where they met. The East Side was the place where

they went to school, started working, and embraced American identity and the upward mobility so much a part of it. Going to one of the
neighborhood's public baths was no novelty to them, nor were its pro-
duce-laden pushcarts or barefoot boys selling papers in the park. The
East Side was the place they left to begin lives of their own, and to
which they would return with their children, mostly just to bring the
family together, I suppose, but no doubt in part to expose their kids to
a past that would always make a claim on their feelings, but that they
could no longer embody even if they'd wanted to.

And for Simon and Gizella, the place was something else again.
They had moved to No. 239 at age fifty-one and forty-five in 1907.
Louis, the oldest of their five sons, was already in his twenties, and
their youngest, American-born Morris, was thirteen. Seventh Street
was the place where Simon and Gizella put the finishing touches on
the world they'd built in America. And to some extent it held the shape
of the place they'd left behind, a Hungarian town called Nagymihály,
nestled against the foothills of the Eastern Carpathians. Simon crossed
7th Street every day to pray with other gray-haired men in the elegant
limestone-fronted shul built just a couple of years before the Wieders
moved to the block. Gizella, meanwhile, gave her time to the labors of
a devoted Jewish housewife and to the needs of her *landsleit*. She was
a member of the shul's women's auxiliary and active in the charitable
Vereinigte Ungarische Schwestern, or Hungarian Sisters Club. Pauline
Silberman, who with her husband, Philip, lived upstairs from the
Wieders in the '30s and '40s, came from a village just a few miles from
Nagymihály. She, too, had visits from her grandchildren, who came to
watch her light the candles on a Friday night while their parents went
to the movies or some such.

When, in a second-floor room of No. 239, Simon and Gizella closed
their eyes to the world, they took with them their memories of a particular corner of the Kingdom of Hungary in the latter half of the nineteenth century. Perhaps Gizella, the first of many children, gathered
mushrooms in the pine forests and kept chickens along with the two
long-horned cows noted by a census taker when Gizella was seven.
Maybe as a girl she played with gypsy children encamped at the edge
of town and heard folktales featuring great rabbis who worked deeds of

wonder amid simple everyday settings. Probably, as the Civil War began in America and the German Jew Abraham Weinstein moved into No. 239, Simon, at four or five, was taken to one of the local *chederim* to begin learning the Hebrew alphabet and studying first the Torah, then, a few years later, the commentaries and discussions of the Talmud, special mastery of which could earn the community's utmost esteem. Many years later, after the Nazi Holocaust had all but blotted out the Jewry of Nagymihály, one memorialist would recall that its boys had begun their Jewish education even before they'd learned to keep their pants dry.[3]

At thirty, Simon Wieder crossed the Atlantic on a steamship, arriving in New York in full summer, June 29, 1885. Gizella stayed behind with their three boys, the youngest, Max, only a few months old. That autumn, on the first day of Rosh Hashanah, the Jewish New Year, she must have taken them to the banks of the river that winds through Nagymihály to cast their sins into the moving water. And I don't doubt that Simon found his way to the oily current of the East River and did the same. The New Year begins a ten-day period of reckoning in the Jewish calendar. As the liturgy says, *On Rosh Hashanah it is written, on Yom Kippur it is sealed—who will live and who will die, who will rest and who will wander, who will be at peace and who will be harried, who will be impoverished and who made rich. But penitence, prayer, and charity temper the harshness of the decree.*[4] During that first year of yawning separation, the Wieders must have prayed and fasted with a special intensity, hoping that the momentous choice they'd made was the right one.

Mobility was the basic nature of the Jewish East Side. The neighborhood was less a fixed place than a great, clambering crossroads, a historic Jewish happening characterized by vigorous ingathering and equally vigorous dispersal. Between the years 1880 and 1920, Jews in their hundreds of thousands escaped the tightening anti-Semitic snare of tsarist Russia's Pale of Settlement, or the isolated, grindingly poor mountain shtetls of Galicia, or the population pressure and jarring economic changes taking place where the Wieders came from in northeastern Hungary. When they arrived in Manhattan, they encountered, among other astonishments, a more numerous congregation of their own people than any of them had seen in their lives.

Though its contours were somewhat different, the Jewish East Side more or less replaced Kleindeutschland, beginning, like the German neighborhood, in the narrow, irregular streets below Houston Street, and spreading north to encompass, by the early twentieth century, all the numbered grid streets up to 14th Street, from Tompkins Square east. Both neighborhoods were remarkable as ethnic agglomerations. But Kleindeutschland seems not to have had much significance beyond itself; when it passed into history, it sunk from view. Apart from the contemporary press, there's a single comprehensive history and precious little else to read about what the neighborhood was like.[5] By contrast, you could spend your life consuming the literature of the Jewish East Side, its novels and stories, memoirs and histories, plays, lyrics, political tracts, and newspaper articles.

One gets the impression that every little child growing up in the ghetto reached adulthood with a burning desire to testify. Some wax nostalgic, remembering the energy of streets where everyone knew each other, insisting poverty and hard work were ennobling, or at least left them not much the worse for wear. Other voices seem determined to take a sharp spade to this version of the East Side, to crack it like a crust of spun sugar. "There are enough pleasant superficial liars writing in America," Michael Gold caustically observes in his autobiographical novel, *Jews Without Money*. "I will write a truthful book of Poverty; I will mention bedbugs." The East Side he knew was a place of vulgarity and squalor, where children "stumbled over a gauntlet of whores' meaty legs" and his poor father swallowed the gall of watching other Jews get rich while he failed even to peddle bananas. "It's better to be dead in this country than not to have money," he told the boy. "Promise me you'll be rich when you grow up, Mikey!"

But even Gold's book is peopled by a few characters who throw off an otherworldly light, no one more than his own mother, a "buttinsky" who was always trying to "'reform' everybody, and fought people because they were 'bad.'" Coming home one day after joining other little boys in taunting a local prostitute with cries of "50 cents a night! 50 cents a night!" Mike is greeted by his mother with a swift slap across the face. "*Murderer!*" she screams. "Why did you make Rosie cry?" And when it comes to his mother, the author's own skepticism about what he saw on the East Side melts quite away. "Momma!" he writes. "I am still bound to you by the cords of birth. I cannot forget you. I must remain faithful to the poor because I cannot be faithless to you!" Finding Gold's socialist critique of American society a bit over the top and lacking in discernment, the literary critic Alfred Kazin, also a chronicler of New York Jewish life in the early twentieth century, had this to say about the author: "Gold—dare one say it?—was a monumentally injured soul but clearly not very bright."[6] This does seem an impertinent remark to make in a published introduction to the man's novel, but Kazin's directness (even if he himself grew up in Brownsville) captures something about the tenor of the East Side. It dared say. It was never cool or glib. Even its intellectualism was of the declamatory, talk-until-the-sun-comes-up variety. It wore its heart on its sleeve.

Whereas Kleindeutschland had been an essentially secular community—if the Phillipses and Harts were Jewish, that was their own business—this dense East Side settlement of Eastern Europeans was Jewish at its core. This is not to say that everyone adhered to Jewish law—far from it—but that most had to develop some posture in relation to it, often as one pole on a spectrum whose other extreme was assimilation. In the places the East Siders came from, the small local *kehilah* or congregation, though not impervious to change, changed as a body and established quite detailed prescriptions for how individuals would live. A Jew in the Hungary of Simon and Gizella's youth was compelled by the state to belong to a *kehilah* and pay taxes for the support of its institutions. Moreover, long custom created powerful inner constraints against, say, violating the Sabbath in public or exalting one's own opinion over that of a recognized authority.[7]

But in emigrating, families separated from their *kehilahs* and entered a society that was remarkably open, arguably much more so than America is today. Immigrants could in short order land a job (albeit an oppressive and low-paying one) and apartment (however foul a cave), attain citizenship, and enroll their children in free American schools, even colleges. Arriving with their feather pillows, peasant linens, and baggy underwear—manifestly greenhorns—in time they could vanish, if they chose, into the place whose organizing principle was summed up sometimes by the monikers *the free land* or *golden land*, other times by the labels *dollar land* or *thief America* for the old life it forced many to surrender abruptly and forever.[8]

For the Jewish immigrants and their progeny, nearly every aspect of daily life became a personal choice freighted with the question of identity. If a married woman, would you cover your hair with a wig or kerchief tied under the chin, or don the fashionable fruit- and flower-topped American millinery? If a man, would you shave the beard prescribed by Jewish law, but which bullies and anti-Semites the world over seemed so fond of yanking? Letters to the popular Yiddish daily the *Forward* were full of this intensely felt questioning. A cantor from Kovne in present-day Lithuania has read a great deal in America and finds he is no longer religious; should he find another occupation? A reader asks whether parents ought to eat nonkosher food when visiting their nonobservant children. And is it right for a progressive family to make their maid eat in the kitchen?[9]

With the opening of the Williamsburg (1903) and Manhattan (1909) bridges to Brooklyn and of a first subway line (1904) going uptown, the East Side's congestion began to ease. As some families left behind the acute struggles of their early years in America, naturally they left the ghetto, too. The hour for nostalgia about the East Side lay long in the future. Nobody told Louis Wieder he shouldn't peel off to a neighborhood where on a Sunday he could stroll with his small boy to the breezy banks of the Hudson, hopping the train weekday mornings to his municipal job in lower Manhattan. Certainly no one suggested to Al's aunt Anna Snyder, his mother's older sister, that she should stay on without so much as a full bathroom at No. 261 E. 7th St. instead of riding in a classy automobile and raising her family in a rambling Victorian in Yonkers with an elegant open porch and garden. The Snyders were the first in the family to attain this quintessentially American lifestyle. It had been a precipitous rise from the battered tenements of the East Side, and, in the estimation of Anna's son, Elmer Walter Snyder, who was ninety-five when I reached him by phone at his home in Florida, "it didn't hurt me at all."[10]

But as long as immigrants kept coming, pushed by intermittent re-
newals of mob violence in Eastern Europe and beckoned by relatives
already here—every tenement apartment was a Plymouth Rock, Gold
writes with an operatic flourish[11]—the East Side regenerated. For
decades it held together all their roiling worlds, in constant and intimate, sometimes too intimate, contact. "Talk about integration!" writes
East Side author Harry Golden. "The crotchety maiden aunt, Grandmother and Grandfather, the wild-eyed high school boy who had just
begun to study Marx, Uncle Boris from uptown and the boarder who
studied Spinoza and Shakespeare until late at night every night—all
sat at the same table and shared the same bread, soup and potatoes.
They also got involved in many-sided conversations and debates."[12] As
if they knew their time together was short, the East Siders fell into energetic mutual self-revelation and change. Though Jews lived all over
America at the turn of the twentieth century, it was hardscrabble New
York that came to be seen as the endlessly rocking cradle of Jewish-
American culture; it's the place I hear ringing ever so distantly in the
way Al, showing me around his Southern California home with his
wife, Judy, drops the final R from the word "oleander."

Simon, son of Moses and Sarah Wieder, and Gizella, daughter of Herman and Esther (Rosenbluth) Weinberger,[13] were born shortly after
the nineteenth century's midpoint and raised in an agrarian village
dominated by Christians, but with a long history of Jewish presence.
The 1869 Hungarian census finds a seven-year-old Gizella Weinberger
living with her extended kin in a one-story house on Selyem Lane in
Nagymihály. Each of three nuclear families shares a single bedroom.
Gizella, her parents, two little sisters, and a Greek Catholic maid form
one household. Another consists of her father's sister, Hani, who has
married a Wieder, Naftula; the couple has four children, the oldest a
girl of Gizella's age who shares her given name. The third family is
headed by Jakob and Mari Weinberger—probably another uncle and
aunt—and their two small children. The house on Selyem Lane also
includes a shop, of which Gizella's father is proprietor. He is a *röfös
kereskedó*, a term that translates roughly as haberdasher, meaning a
dealer in sewing "notions"—thread, buttons—and other small wares.

On another lane not far away lives a fourteen-year-old Jewish boy, the oldest of six children, listed in the census as Samu Vieder. Though I cannot extinguish doubt on the question, I suspect this is the youngster who will later be known as Simon Wieder. It seems he lives in more straitened circumstances than Gizella. His father, Mor (Moses), works as a *napszámos* (a "hand" or day laborer) in the produce market. The Vieders own no animals and share their single-story building—unlike the Weinbergers', it lacks a separate kitchen—with three other families. Two are Catholic households, a third that of another Jewish worker, a *rongy szedö*, or ragpicker. But there's something else I notice about the Vieders. Of the twenty-four people living in their house, only four can read and write. These include young Samu (or Simon), his father, and, most remarkably in the context of widespread illiteracy especially among women, his twelve-year-old sister, Rezi.[14]

On 7th Street, Simon Wieder was regarded as a keeper of tradition, markedly more devout than many around him. But in Nagymihály, a stronghold of Jewish Orthodoxy in a period when liberalizing winds blew across Hungary from the West, he may have occupied a somewhat different place on the spectrum. There are hints. He never shaved his beard in America, but did wear it neatly trimmed. His facility with languages implies secular education. And some years ago, his grandson, Alfred, came into possession of a perhaps telling artifact: a physics text with Simon's name on it. It came from a school in Maryland. On its blank work pages Grandpa Wieder had written out, in a meticulous hand, equations that describe universal order from a scientific point of view. But perhaps the most suggestive fact is that Simon Wieder chose to leave northeastern Hungary for America, where, as one Jewish mother who refused to make that journey lamented, "even the stones are *treyf*."*[15]

It is very possible that what motivated the Wieders to leave Hungary were not matters of faith at all but "affairs of the stomach," issues touching on "the nitty-gritty of existence,"[16] as an immigrant rabbi from the same region disapprovingly put it. It was a time of enormous economic change, population growth, and migration in that part of Eu-

---

Treyf: impure or unkosher.

rope. Erstwhile serfs, who after midcentury became free but often landless peasants, began emigrating from the northeastern parts of the country in large numbers. After an 1840 law lifted bans on Jewish settlement in many municipalities (and despite continued resistance by some local burghers), Jews began flocking into cities and towns. Not officially established until the emancipation of 1867, the Jewish community of Nagymihály burgeoned from a mere 170 in 1840 to more than 1,000 members, about a quarter of the town population, in 1880. Though Gizella and Simon both were born in Nagymihály, three of their four parents had moved there from tiny villages that lay within ten miles' distance. The town established linkages to a burgeoning railway system in the 1870s, which further accelerated growth. By 1888 the Jewish congregation was robust enough to erect a large synagogue. Meanwhile, other settlements dwindled or perished. As a group, Hungarian Jews were poised to prosper quite spectacularly in the latter decades of the century, playing a prominent role in the municipal and commercial affairs of Nagymihály. But in the midst of change, many were dislocated along with their non-Jewish neighbors, losing customers and livelihoods. America, they kept hearing, offered these in abundance.[17]

As for anti-Semitism, it was a fact of life. An incident that received world attention took place in April 1882 some fifty miles from Nagymihály, in Tiszaeszlár. There, a fourteen-year-old Christian servant girl disappeared three days before Passover, giving local authorities—the mayor, a priest—a pretext under which to revive an ancient blood libel: They accused Jewish villagers of murdering the girl and draining her blood for use in the baking of matzoh, the unleavened bread eaten at Passover. In August there followed riots in Budapest.

The Tiszaeszlár defendants were fully acquitted. Though the furor must have dimmed any expectations the Jews had that their rising fortunes in that part of the world would be untroubled by ethnic hatreds, they cannot have imagined what would unfold there a few decades hence.[18] After the First World War, the hamlet of Nagymihály would become known as Michalovce, and the surrounding countryside, the northern part of Austro-Hungary, would become Czechoslovakia. Czechoslovakia's fate was to be one of the first countries Herr Hitler would swallow in sating the Nazi appetite for *lebensraum*—living space. By March 1939, Germany occupied the western Czech lands, and the eastern Slovak portion broke away as a nominally independent Nazi collaborationist state under president Jozef Tiso, a Catholic priest and Slovak nationalist. In that corner of the former Kingdom of Hungary, exclusion of Jews from their professions and businesses began forthwith. Deportations soon followed.

When "the devils" came to Michalovce, one survivor would recall, "their boots glittered, their faces were strict and their pitiless hands were covered by white, bright gloves."[19] The young women were the first to be taken away. Many of the Jewish townspeople ended their days in death camps at Sobibor and Treblinka in the Lublin region of Poland.[20]

But this was a bestiality belonging to the twentieth century. In the 1880s, as Simon and Gizella made plans to raise their boys in a strange new world, they cannot have dreamed that the world of their own childhoods—not the pine forests or winding river, but the being-there of Jewish people—would soon be scrubbed from the map.

Though by inclination a studious person, Simon Wieder came to New York to work, save, establish a beachhead for his wife and sons, and, eventually, to purchase the steamship tickets that would bring them to his side. It took four years—four years of long hours at the cigarmaker's bench, working with his hands, cutting the fragrant leaves, rolling them, shaping them, feeling alone, or so I imagine, in the close company of so many strangers. He probably had little choice but to forgo Sabbath rest, the deepest rhythm of his life. In the shop, the boss was the boss. "He packs the cigars," as a contemporary short story describes the scene, "his mouth keeps moving like a windmill, grinding out one joke after another, at which the workers, naturally, laugh hilariously."[21]

What joy and tension they all must have felt when finally Simon went to meet Gizella and their sons at the immigration station at Manhattan's tip. Such travelers arrived weary and disoriented after weeks of sleeping in an unventilated steerage compartment pounded by the waves, eating little besides herring and black bread. The younger boys, Samuel, six, and Max, four, cannot have known their father. One guesses eight-year-old Louis had carried an image of Simon through the years, though perhaps it did not match the English-speaking person who appeared that day at Castle Garden. And for a married couple to reconstitute their partnership in a strange place after such a long separation, well, that surely had its anxious moments. But they knit themselves together again, and in 1891, Gizella gave birth to another boy, Michael, born in a tenement on Columbia Street—the very block where Clara and Levy Phillips had lived twenty-five years earlier. Morris followed in the spring of '94, by which time the Wieders lived on Cannon Street, the intensely crowded press of buildings among which the child Bella Spewack "learned to fear people."[22]

Al Wieder remembers hearing that his grandfather, retired by the time he knew him, had sold "yard goods"—fabric and the like—from a pushcart. Many Jews took up the pushcart, a chance to do business among their own people with little upfront investment. They sold everything from grapes for Passover wine to factory-damaged china, in many cases hoping to one day become proprietor of a storefront shop. In 1897, Simon stopped listing himself as a cigarmaker in the city directory and completed papers to become a U.S. citizen, a prerequisite, as it happens, for obtaining a pushcart license. By 1900 the family had moved north to 6th Street and Simon had a shop selling "trimmings." The next year he moved this shop to the location where it would remain for more than a decade, a storefront on Avenue C just below 3rd Street. It was a business bearing a more than passing resemblance to the shop his father-in-law had kept on Selyem Lane in Nagymihály, but the setting had changed dramatically, and so had the times.

Trimmings for hat and dress—artificial flowers, feathers, braid, fringe, lace, ribbon of every width and color—were a fashion mainstay for style-conscious but impecunious working girls of the East Side. For a few pennies they could sew a little flair onto an otherwise drab outfit. They could suss out patterns and ideas thumbing through Butterick's *The Delineator*, like little sister Mashah in the novel *Bread Givers*, who comes home one day having spent what little money she had on a bauble to pin on her headgear. "'I'm going to hear the free music in the park tonight,' she laughed to herself, with the pleasure before her, 'and these pink roses on my hat to match out my pink calico will make me look just the picture on the magazine cover.'"[23] So for years, Simon, a serious, slip of a man now in middle age, spent his days behind a counter on Avenue C, as one by one women of the East Side brought to him their plans for a dance or a concert, their hankering for an everyday touch of what was pretty and modern.

The boys apparently helped out from time to time.[24] But the sons' main duty through the '90s and beyond was to pitch themselves into that Americanizing cauldron of boys in knee pants and short-billed caps known as the New York City public school. There, you gained the vitally important favor of your teachers, writes Alfred Kazin in his memoir, "by sitting firmly at your wooden desk, hands clasped; by silence for the greatest part of the live-long day; by standing up obsequiously when it was so expected of you; by sitting down noiselessly when you had answered a question; by 'speaking nicely,' which meant reproducing their painfully exact enunciation; by 'showing manners,' or an ecstatic submissiveness in all things; by outrageous flattery; by bringing little gifts at Christmas, on their birthdays, and at the end of the term."[25] The East Side grammar schools were grossly overcrowded, their instruction uneven, but teachers not infrequently were charmed by the avidity of certain Jewish pupils, even "amazed at the evidences of precocity which they display[ed]."[26]

In any event, the Wieder boys did what was necessary. All except the oldest, Louis, who went to work, passed the exam for entrance to City College, then housed in a gloomy ramshackle building at 23rd and Lexington. The institution combined a one-year high school or "sub-freshman" year with four years of college. When Samuel and Max graduated in June 1902,[27] it was poised for a great flowering of intellectual life, a move uptown, expansion of the high school into three years, and the introduction of a progressive new president, changes that no doubt benefited Michael and Morris Wieder. While the older boys were at "City," the place was run with semi-military discipline by an old Civil War hero, Alexander Webb. Demerit books recording incidents of petty misconduct or lateness, a merit roll publicly listing each student's ranking, and mandatory attendance at chapel were the order of the day.[28] The kids, though, were lively enough. When, in Sam and Max's junior year, the student paper *The Review* published an attack on a Tammany political boss and a polemic against religion ("an imperfection of human nature," the student called it), Webb crammed all the copies he could find into his desk drawer and refused to speak further on the subject. The *Times* reported the story under the headline, "City College Review Not Wholly Suppressed; Students Have Copies and They Intend to Retain Them."[29]

By the time they moved into No. 239 E. 7th St. in 1907, the Wieders had climbed the steep learning curve of the new immigrant. They'd laid down twenty years of memories along the East Side streets, and belonged to them. In the mornings Simon had only to step over two curbs and climb a few stairs to pray with his *minyan* in the cool and dark of the limestone shul, then stroll four or five blocks south down Avenue C to open his shop. Gizella need only go downstairs to have a glass of tea and slice of honey cake with Mrs. Berkowitz, the Hungarian wife of a baker and mother of seven. The Wieders' own sons had grown up to resemble their mother, tall and well-fleshed, their educational attainment a veritable crown of laurels for Simon and Gizella, who'd not had to send *their* children to peddle papers in the park. The Wieders even had a Hungarian-born servant woman, Julie, although with seven in the family goodness knows where she laid her head at night.[30]

As the Wieder boys got older, they were drawn, after a pattern made familiar by their forebears, to an institution at once social and purposeful. It, too, had an embodiment on the block, the headquarters of the Jefferson Democratic Club, a handsome brick edifice that stood at No. 247, facing the family synagogue like some secular alternative, if not a rival. In fact, the assembly district's Republican clubhouse was on the block, too, and so were the homes of various bosses, judges, and other luminaries of the local political scene.* The Hungarian-born Samuel Koenig lived for many years with his wife, Sadie, and their children at No. 237, right next to the Wieders. A self-made man, Koenig

---

*The assembly district was the 16th until 1906, later the 6th. It was bounded roughly by Avenue B and Lewis streets from east to west, and by 8th and 2nd streets from north to south.

was Republican leader for the assembly district, rising (after a 1909–1910 stint as secretary of state) to the key position of Republican boss for all Manhattan. He had the ear of leaders in the statehouse and in Washington, and counted Teddy Roosevelt a friend.[31] A certain Patrick Keenan, meanwhile, "practically the father of the Jefferson Club" and the longtime Democratic leader of the assembly district, lived at No. 253 until his death in 1907. Keenan's history on the block went back fifty years, long enough for him to have done a stint caulking ship hulls along the riverbank. A gregarious bachelor born in County Tyrone, Keenan's death brought swarms of mourners to No. 253 to view his remains. He had ex-mayors, state supreme court justices, and U.S. congressmen for honorary pallbearers, and the Jefferson Club marched eight hundred strong behind Keenan's flower-bedecked coffin in a procession that passed No. 239 on its way west for a requiem mass at St. Brigid's overlooking Tompkins Square.

Far from meeting its doom at the turn of the century, as one news reporter had predicted, Political Row swung into the twentieth century in fullest regalia, the seat of local political power. Louis Wieder, an enthusiastic member of the Jefferson Club, addressed a billet-doux to the delightful girl down the block, "Miss Laura Taubner, Political Row, 261 E. 7th St., City." As if it were the very center of the world.

The Democratic Party of course meant the notorious Tammany Hall, the great "wigwam" whose "sachems" commanded a vast army of loyal braves. The trope was a vulgarization of Indian life but accurately expressed the tribal nature of a local political culture run on spectacle and small favors, on passionate personal loyalty to a district leader punctuated, at long intervals, by ferocious oedipal contests in which the young men of the district would rise up to replace an aging strongman. The Wieders could have chosen to pursue any number of paths into the heart of American life—the WASPish academy, the idealistic, Socialist-leaning and largely Jewish trade union, the multi-ethnic, pistol-toting gang. They were good boys who grew up in a tough neighborhood and chose to join an American club whose standards of mutual aid faintly recalled the *kehilah*, but that had long been the province of the immigrant Irish, whose own history had taught them to be skeptical of moralizing patrician authorities and to do for themselves.

Very early one day each summer, Keenan would lead a parade of hundreds from the clubhouse on 7th Street down to one of the East River piers, where they'd embark for some picnic spot in Connecticut or Long Island, there to pass the day in boat racing, small-stakes gambling, and other games, consuming quantities of cold beer, watermelon, beefsteak, as well as lobster, clams, and eels—a *treyf* repast if ever there was one. Later they'd return to Manhattan for more torchlight parading, fireworks, and late-night revelry in the clubhouse. In the fall came the equally visible electioneering. Placards went up in the windows of Political Row and great crowds overflowed from the clubhouse into the street, whipped up by speakers in the style of carnival barkers.[32]

In the years when Louis and his brothers began joining those crowds, occasionally a voice rose up to speak in the boisterous idiom of Tammany, but in the language of the Eastern European Jews. "There have been some anonymous letters written which charge that I am an Irishman," the Tammany candidate for city register teased an overflow Jefferson Club assemblage one October night in 1897, the year Louis was sixteen. "It's a calumny," Isaac Fromme continued, sprinkling his talk with Yiddish words, "and I'll put my nose in evidence of its falsity and I can give you cumulative evidence, too, but I'm too much of a gentleman to do it!" That night the club was circling the wagons to put up as mayor a rather lackluster character by the name Robert Van Wyck—anyone to replace William Strong, the anti-Tammany Fusion Party mayor who'd been insisting on straight-arrow enforcement of city ordinances, including some that harried the impoverished pushcart peddlers, others that banned drinking and, more important for Jews, opening shops on Sundays. These folk, who would come down to the East Side and earnestly (though not in Yiddish) make their case for honest and efficient government, Fromme colorfully denounced as "Puritans" and "hayseeders," as "a lot of blue-nosed, psalm-singing, sniveling idiots [whose] trade mark is cant, hypocrisy, and sham."[33] The crowd roared.

Tammany was reliably pro-immigrant because immigrants were its lifeblood. As for the East Side Jews, they leaned left in matters economic and political, a propensity stemming from their perennial experience as outsiders and tradition of finding duty and honor in caring for the poor, the aged, and the sick. No exception, Louis Wieder would later commit much of his free time to an East Side orphanage and a Jewish convalescent home; the latter work he shared not only with members of the old Jefferson Club crew, but with a sizeable contingent of Jewish progressives.[34] Indeed, unlike the Irish, the East Side Jews never were fully in Tammany's corner. They tended to alternate or split their vote, sometimes sympathizing more with Republican or Fusion efforts to stem graft and vice, or Socialist ideals of economic justice and workers' rights. It wasn't until Franklin Roosevelt came along that they coalesced behind the Democrats nationally.[35]

On the block, though, the wigwam knew the score, made its presence felt. In Jerome Weidman's 1970 reminiscence, *Fourth Street East: A Novel of How It Was*, the protagonist recalls that when the district boss came around in late August to speak to his mother, his father, a conscientious Socialist, would fold his paper and quietly leave the room. It was that old saw about not wanting to watch the sausage being made. The tenement mother would then barter her vote for exactly two tons of hard coal, their winter's fuel. "The things she wanted," recalled the son, "were always the things she needed."[36]

To the more active among the faithful, the party might deliver something far more valuable: a job. Contemporaries perceived not a whiff of impropriety in this. The Republican Sam Koenig explained in a late interview that when a rival stepped up to criticize party leaders, "we let him talk. It's a free country. . . . We may not give him his recognition as readily as we would to others, but that isn't necessarily punishment. He may not be deserving of it from the party standpoint—from the standpoint of ability, from the standpoint of mental equipment. Recognition, again, means patronage—not only jobs for himself, but in the case of a leader, jobs for his constituents."[37] Work was a principal concern of young Jewish Democrats like Louis Wieder. As one co-religionist complained during a Tammany bull session in the clubhouse of another East Side assembly district, "Everything goes to the Irish. Where do you see a Jewish copper, a Jewish fireman, a Jewish street-cleaner, a horse-car driver or conductor? . . . I have the slogan which will get out the vote for Tammany: 'Jobs for Jews.'"[38]

A changing of the guard was taking place on Political Row. At the Jefferson Club picnic in 1903, after a seafood breakfast, the neighborhood's Hungarians—they were Jewish Hungarians, though the *Times* doesn't mention this—presented Pat Keenan with an oil-on-silk portrait of himself. The leader, they said, "had been a wise father and had introduced them to the real idea of Americanism by seeing to it that they should become citizens as soon as possible" (and vote Tammany).[39] When Keenan died a few years later, there ascended the club's first Jewish leader, Benjamin Hoffman of No. 271, quickly followed by another Jew, David Lazarus of No. 267, who would lead the district for decades (until another fellow from the same building, Sol Eisler, led the charge against him). At the club's monthly meeting one June evening in 1913, a thirty-two-year-old Louis Wieder was one of four members to present Lazarus with *his* portrait—a life-size one.[40]

By that time the after-hours social annex to the clubhouses of Political Row was Papa Burger's Hungarian café at 20 Avenue C, just across from Simon's trimmings shop. If Keenan had celebrated his birthday on St. Patrick's Day, holding a banquet each year at the Jefferson Club, Papa marked his own with an equally festive uncorking of red, sparkling Szamorodni on the Jewish holiday of Purim, which happened to fall around the same time of year. He had taught his parrot to cry, "Papa was born on Purim! Ha ha ha! Look in the Luach!"* People of every political persuasion, including the Wieders, went to Burger's for the connection and the familiar relish of goulash, sweet paprikash, or a simple plate of franks and eggs. Burger often spoke about the time William Howard Taft greeted him at his own inauguration, hailing the restaurateur with a "Howdee-do, Brother Burger!" and hustling over to shake his hand. While Taft was war secretary, Sam Koenig, a regular customer, had brought him around for a midnight supper after a speech at Cooper Union. "Kishkes did that noble man eat," Burger would fondly recall.[41]

---

*This is the Hebrew calendar. Purim celebrates the story of how Esther, a Jewish queen of the ancient Persian Empire, foiled a plot by the villainous adviser Haman to destroy her people.

One day it would come time for Louis Wieder to be honored at a testimonial dinner, his eyes, keen as a bird's, looking out from behind a pince-nez on the program's cover. Louis's parents, brothers, and in-laws all would be there. And the Democrats of Political Row would be well represented, old friends whose loyalty represented life's greatest security. The women's leader and widow of former club leader Benjamin Hoffman, and the son of the club's current leader, David Lazarus, sat on the dais.

The dinner was to recognize Louis Wieder's work as treasurer of the Jewish Home for Convalescents north of the city (a place where he himself would pass a period of illness, plagued by liver disease associated with his hemophilia). It was January 1931. Bread lines were forming in New York. But the three oldest Wieders all were well established in municipal jobs. Louis had worked his way up at the Board of Water Supply, Gas, and Electricity and was responsible for the registration of water meters throughout the city. Samuel, the engineer, who lived with his family across the street from Louis in Washington Heights, was listed in a directory as "computer" at the city Board of Assessors, which assessed property owners for the cost of public improvements like sewers and roadwork.[42] Max Wieder, who set out for Essex Market Court in the mornings from the home he still shared with his parents and two younger brothers, was an assistant district attorney and perhaps the most politically prominent of the brothers. They belonged to a class of workers that would maintain very low unemployment in the years ahead, even as the city's manufacturing and trade ground to an agonizing halt.[43] They could be bread givers now.

For Louis, there had been something else about the Jefferson Club. Laura. She worked at the club—perhaps she did some of its bookkeeping—and that's how the two met. In photographs, Laura sparkles. In one, she stands knee-deep in surf, wearing a dark, skirted swimming costume with a nautical white tie at the neck. It may be Coney Island; the water is full of people. And she raises her arms straight up, clasping her hands as if to dive, her rather unruly brown hair tumbling around her face and shoulders. Smiling. When I remark to Al that she looks fun-loving and charming, he answers, "Yes, she was considered that," and then, more slowly, "Yes. She was considered that."

"Quite a dish," is how Al's cousin Walter describes her in a memoir.[44] A bookkeeper at a clothing shop, in her youth Laura would try on her big sister's finery—Anna worked for a milliner and made her own hats—and go forth from No. 261 the swellest girl on 7th Street. Louis was nearly thirty when they courted, Laura ten years younger. He was smooth-cheeked, with a dimpled chin and dark, wavy hair shaped in a widow's peak over a slightly furrowed brow. Even lying on the beach or at the oar of a rowboat—like everyone, they took pictures on holidays—Louis wore a serious expression.

Laura's mother, Fanny, was from Budapest. The family used to tease Fanny that she couldn't even butter toast, so obviously superior were her paper-thin noodles and strudel loaded with nuts and white raisins. Laura's father, Adolph Taubner, had been a traveling salesman; late one night somewhere in Pennsylvania, he'd been struck and killed by a train. Fanny had remarried a German-speaking (Austrian, according to the census) widower with a fiercely erect bearing. Max Gottlieb brought a son of his own, and together the couple had another boy, Benjamin, making nine in the Houston Street apartment of Laura's childhood. Fanny used the $1,000 insurance money paid out on Adolph's death to set up a cigar shop. Al remembers visiting the shop on Tompkins Square as a child; Walter remembers the cigars were awful—at least his mother thought so.

The Taubner-Gottlieb clan had a wild streak that must have seemed exotic to Louis Wieder. Fanny had one brother who sold stolen property. His son ran a jewelry business on the Bowery, meanwhile, according to Walter, serving as bagman for the Jewish mobster Meyer Lansky. This connection would bring young Walter such unforgettable experiences as plunging his hand into a suitcase full of bills, and attending a hoodlum bash on Long Island with "booze flowing like water . . . and wall-to-wall bimbos."[45] Grandma and Grandpa Gottlieb were religious, but they were up against a boisterous tide of young people at No. 261. Wrapped in a white prayer shawl, grandkids gathered around, Max Gottlieb would recline on a chaise to lead the Passover seder, only to find that a jokester son-in-law had clipped a few pages from the Haggadah to shorten the service.

So Laura was a working girl who had known scarcity and loss. From her pictures, the way she plants a fist at her waist and looks right into the camera, one gets the impression she now intended to get the most out of life. Women were changing, becoming freer, in those early years of the twentieth century. The East Side stood at the vanguard. When she wasn't in prison or on a cross-country tour lecturing about anarchist politics or the New Woman, Emma Goldman could be found stitching dresses on 4th Street or bunking with the long-suffering grandmother who kept two rooms and a grocery at 10th and Avenue B. On 3rd Street between Avenues C and D lived Clara Lemlich, the teenager who in 1909 pushed to the front of the crowd at Cooper Union, and, her small person vibrating like a tuning fork, gave voice to the labor struggle of her fellow shirtwaist makers. And down on Grand Street, in 1912, a married nurse named Margaret Sanger tended a young Russian Jewish mother who had begged her for the "secret" to preventing another pregnancy, and who now lay dying from an attempt at self-induced abortion. After that, Sanger would cry that secret from the rooftops. Even Pauline Silberman, the Wieders' neighbor at No. 239, won the disapproval of certain relatives (who felt she should devote more time to baking and cooking) by marching for women's suffrage and electioneering for the Republican Party.[46] Laura need not have experienced any of these events firsthand to sense the spirit of change they represented. Unimagined by former generations, possibilities rose up around the Taubner girls like the city's first skyscrapers.

Laura Taubner and Louis Wieder must have lingered, talking, on the stoop of No. 239, between those ornate iron railings, in the spring evenings of 1911, beneath the watchful tenement windows, the trees just beginning to leaf out. In April he wrote her one of his cards:

> *When life's strong clouds hang o'er us*
> *When my brightest dreams have fled;*
> *When the dear ones that once knew me*
> *Have been numbered with the dead—*
> *Will you still cling to me darling*
> *Will I find you staunch & true*

O'er will you be with the faithless
When I am trusting only you?

Hers to him, in a flowing script and signed "L.T.," was light and a little daring, one of the spirited gestures by which she must have drawn him to her pretty neck.

Dear Pal,
If I were you and you were me,
And in this world we were but two;
If I were shure that no one knew,
I would, would you?

They were impatient to be married. Propriety required that Laura's older sister, Anna, wed first, an impediment the couple set about removing by introducing Anna to Louis's best friend, Samuel L. Snyder, a funny, street-smart plumbing contractor and Tammany man who like Louis had spent his boyhood below Houston Street. The two hit it off, and Sam proposed to Anna while riding the Staten Island ferry across the Upper Bay, one of their favorite diversions. They met under a *chuppah* in one of the East Side halls, and by the end of 1913, Mr. and Mrs. Max Gottlieb were throwing a reception at the Vienna on 58th Street to make the happy announcement that their second daughter, Laura, was betrothed.

After marrying, both couples left the East Side, the Wieders moving to West 190th Street in Washington Heights, the Snyders to the Bronx, then Yonkers. But they maintained old friendships. Samuel Wieder, Louis's next-youngest brother, married and moved to Washington Heights, too, living nearby. The Snyders and the Wieders—two sisters paired with boyhood pals—vacationed together at Long Beach, Long Island, the Snyders renting a house and the Wieders staying at a kosher hotel owned by relatives. On Saturdays, when the barbers didn't work, Sam would shave Louis on the porch of the Snyders' suburban house; he liked to sneak a dab of ketchup onto his old friend's chin and exclaim, "Louie, I've cut you!" At dinner, Uncle Sam would occasionally delight the children (and annoy his wife) by placing a chunk of melted candle wax in his nose and gazing around the table nonchalantly.

Meanwhile, Louis's three youngest brothers stayed on at No. 239. This may have been based on economic imperatives, their client-driven livelihoods dependent on intricate connections made on the East Side. In the late '20s, Max often could be found in court prosecuting small-time fraudsters, errant landlords, and the like. In the 1930s he'd be assigned to homicides, and there were plenty. He'd prosecute a policeman who shot a woman in a tussle over a gun in a car, a crime the police commissioner chalked up to "these damnable petting parties in automobiles."[47] He'd handle the case of a beer-running gangster accused of murdering a former associate with a burst of pistol fire in front of a restaurant on Broome Street.[48] Then, by 1940, he'd turn this broad experience to effect as a defense attorney, telling the court, on behalf of a woman accused of stealing a baby from the hospital, that she was a poor, orphaned alcoholic herself, "addicted to drinking a concoction called 'Southern Comfort.'" "That is a very potent, dangerous drink," the judge quickly agreed.[49] Max's next-youngest brother, Michael, also was a lifelong bachelor and an attorney. He worked out of an office on Broadway, apparently on civil matters, although he didn't get as much work as Max. Morris, an accountant by training, was married briefly; his redheaded wife died young of pernicious anemia. He tried a clothing business that foundered. At one point he took a gig through his outlaw cousin running numbers, but when his brothers warned of a police crackdown, he backed out. Instead he found work unloading produce trucks.

In 1933, the Wieder family had to bury Louis. He died at fifty-two, his liver disease having progressed beyond remedy. Daughter Charlotte was a teenager, Alfred only ten. Far too soon the Sunday walks around upper Manhattan with his father, when Louis would buy the *Times* and Al would read the sepia-color illustrated page, had come to an end. The family—uncles and aunts and cousins—took special pains for the fatherless children. Uncle Charlie Stern—husband of Laura's vivacious younger sister, Sydonia, and the one who'd clipped pages from the seder service—lived on 168th Street and would come up to play gin rummy with Alfred. "If I cried," says Al, "he'd let me win. Then

I'd say, 'You let me win!'" Alfred was a conscientious kid, and in that perhaps he took after the father he lost.

A couple of years after Louis's death it came time for Alfred to prepare for his bar mitzvah. Laura sent him to an uptown Hebrew school, but it proved little more than a mass of rowdy boys tossing erasers. It wouldn't do, especially since Alfred's initiation to the full responsibilities of Jewish faith was to be entrusted to Grandpa Wieder's Beth Hamedrash Hagodol Anshe Ungarn, the Great House of Study of the People of Hungary, on 7th Street. Laura, who by then was working again, found a private tutor.

It was a very great distance for a boy of thirteen to travel, not just down the long spine of Manhattan to 7th Street, but all the way back to the world of his grandparents. The sturdiest plank of the bridge that linked Alfred to that place, Louis M. Wieder, had been swept away. "I remember the women all had to sit upstairs in the balcony, and I was on the dais or *bima* or whatever, and all these religious, including my grandfather, surrounded me," Alfred recalls. "You know, my grandfather spoke Hebrew and read Hebrew like I read English." Both sides of the family were represented. A teenage cousin Walter was there, wearing a tallis and a yarmulke, and, as he recalls, grasping not a word of the singsong Hebrew that floated out over the sanctuary that day. Alfred had learned the Torah portion phonetically—he didn't understand much of it, either—and, reading before the congregation, he struggled for the correct pronunciation. He was terribly nervous. "I stumbled over a few words," he says. "They didn't reprimand me. When I stumbled, they said the words." Afterward, Alfred felt he should have done better. No one made an issue of it, and that was a kind of lesson, too. "They were very tolerant people," says Al. There were macaroons and soda and other refreshments at a catering hall on 2nd Avenue. The bar mitzvah stood up and gave a little talk about how grateful he was for the help and support of the extended family after his father's death. His big sister, Charlotte, had written it for him. And thus did many hands lift another fine young person into the arms of America.

On September 21, 1939, having been ill since April and now very near death, Gizella Wieder gave her last will and testament to her son,

Michael, the next day signing it before two witnesses, the son and daughter-in-law of the Silbermans from upstairs. And it was a last expression of what mattered to her, a final opportunity to affirm the world she and Simon had helped create—helped re-create, in some sense—on 7th Street. "I desire to be buried pursuant to strictly Jewish Orthodox Law," she dictated, issuing a reminder to her offspring that her own mother would not have found necessary. Then, before getting to her sons, grandchildren, and husband, who would receive the bulk of her worldly estate, Gizella named the Hungarian Sisters ($25), the Beth Hamedrash Hagodol ($25), its women's auxiliary ($25), and the Hebrew school Ohel Torah on 6th Street ($50). She died at one a.m. on the 23rd, attended by Dr. Bergstein from two doors down.[50]

Simon, in his later years, was able to devote himself to the study and teaching of Jewish texts to which his heart had long inclined him. One of Al's pictures shows him ending a day at the limestone shul, a slight, bespectacled man, his beard gone mostly white, nattily dressed in coat and tie, pocket square, and dark fedora. Simon seems to be saying something to the several other men, likewise wearing fedoras and beards, who stand near—lean in, really, as if listening. One holds his chin in his hand, his head cocked in concentration toward Simon. Another holds out Simon's coat to him.

The literature of the East Side is full of stories about immigrant parents who feel lost in America, hurt and disgusted by their children's abandonment of tradition, and, on the other hand, about young people who scoff at their parents' way of life as ludicrously old-fashioned. It can't have been without tension that generations of the Wieder family parted ways on such matters as a kosher household. But the way they negotiated the chasm also was marked by a certain mutuality. It was Simon and Gizella, after all, who brought their sons to grow up in a place whose very stones were *treyf*, and it was around the same family table that the Talmud and the latest Tammany ticket were debated in turn. Each had his own role to play at the crossroads of the East Side. Al's was to pay his respects there on the way to adulthood, but then to raise a family on Long Island, his industry and entrepreneurial ambition helping him ride up, as an air conditioning and heating contractor, on a great postwar wave of prosperity and suburbanization. Simon's role, in the last years of his life, his adopted country at war and world Jewry cut to the bone, was to plant the Torah on 7th Street, to wrap his arms around that tree of life and hold fast.

Under the care of Dr. Bergstein from two doors down, Simon died at home on March 21, 1944. That November, Red Army troops slogged down the muddy trails of the Carpathians' southern foothills from positions just south of the Polish border and emerged to capture Michalovce and more than sixty other Czechoslovakian towns and villages. On May 8 the following year, finally the German surrender was made official. In New York, the streets went chockablock with happy people. Down on 7th Street, a pair of brothers sat on the stoop of No. 239, smacking spoons against pots and pans, joining in the block's clamorous jubilation that Nazism was at long last vanquished, driven from the earth.

This is the single instance where the chain of time bends in on itself, where the past came to find me while I lived at No. 239 in the late 1990s. The brothers, in their early sixties, I'd guess, rather tanned and healthy-looking, strolled by one day while we were out front, headed somewhere. They said they'd lived in the house as kids, on the parlor floor, if I recall correctly. They told their story about V-E Day. And they shook their heads over how upscale the neighborhood had become since those days. Then they were gone, and, much as I've tried, I never was able to find them again.

City of the Dead

I VISITED THE graves in chronological order. It took me a couple of weeks' worth of spring days, during which it rained a great deal. I wore rubber boots. I admired the drenched clover or the glistening silver boughs of a copper beech. I chatted up friendly grave keepers. When I found the stone I was looking for, I touched its rough and smooth surfaces. I brushed away vines and old mowings. I snapped a few pictures. I listened to the birdsong. Invariably, there came a faint sense of thwarted expectation. It was a kind of restlessness, a vague, roving hunger. I felt an impulse to eat, or drink, or smoke. Then: *Maybe if I came back another time?*

It seems that all those months I'd been planning a reunion. Some part of me had believed that, visiting their burial places, I finally was going to *meet* the former inhabitants of No. 239. A manifestation of the dead was to have been the reward for my diligence (hadn't I scrolled through the microfilm until my eyes crossed?) and good intentions (hadn't I tried to understand them on their own terms?).

I wonder if there can be a sadder moment in all of literature than when Adam and Eve, hearing footsteps in the garden, conceal themselves among the trees. Divinity itself seems to falter as the Lord God calls out to his creatures, *Where are you?* Certainly nothing *I* could do would summon them from their hiding places. And if I had possessed the power to call up the melancholic Rachel Hart and her long-lost Joseph, the peddler, it wouldn't be to thunder at them, *Who told you that you were naked?* and *Why did you eat?* All that's in the past. In life their necks were bent under humanity's curse, the struggle for bread, the bearing of children in pain and sorrow. I would have liked to spread a blanket under the catalpa tree that grows not far from Rachel's grave, its great, heart-shaped leaves stirring with light and wind. How I would have liked just to pass a quiet hour with them in our beautiful, fallen world.

I went back to the beginning, back to the earliest marked grave I could find, a DeLancey grave. James, the proprietor of the colonial-era farm on Bowery Lane, with its parterres and orchards and sliver of salt meadow, died, as one may recall, at Bath, England, in a rather diminished mood. But his youngest brother, John Peter, the same one who had befriended James's illegitimate children, slipped back to the United States of America after the War for Independence. "I am not yet become a citizen of America but suppose I soon must," he wrote his nephew in 1791.[1] It was not a question of blazing patriotism. Raised for a military career, John Peter had fought with the British and upon their defeat repaired to England. It was a professional row with the British army that sent him back to America to farm what was left of his mother's lands, an estate called Heathcote Hill north of Manhattan near the village of Mamaroneck. There, on the brow of a hill overlooking the road to Boston and an inlet of the Long Island Sound, he built the modest two-story house where he and his wife, Elizabeth, raised three sons and four daughters. One daughter, Susan Augusta, married the author James Fenimore Cooper in that house in 1811. Their daughter, also Susan, remembered Heathcote Hill fondly. The family, she wrote, lived and dined in a single room, attended by enslaved servants. At breakfast, she would sit in a high chair near her grandfather, John Peter DeLancey, who would crack open oyster shells and slip their contents onto little Susan's plate. She often was at his side as he drove his gig around the property, quizzing Susie on the names of the trees they saw; she would hop down and open the gates for him. There was a cluster of barns and a vegetable garden, a cider mill, and orchards of peach and apple trees. "And beyond all these orchards," Susan recalled, "there rose a beautiful wood, the remains of the ancient forest; within its shade there was an open enclosure, the family burying-ground, surrounded by a low stone wall; I have often been there."[2]

Both the house and the cemetery survive. The simple, white-shingled dwelling, five windows across, has been moved to the foot of the hill, where it now sits on the busy Boston Post Road facing the water. Across the facade, a bright sign announces its current function as La Piccola Casa Ristorante, which recently replaced another dining establishment known as Down By the Bay. The family burial site obviously remains in its original location, several blocks away on the crest of the hill. It simply rises up between two ample suburban houses, a hummock of stony ground shaded by a grove of old oaks. From across the street, one hardly notices the little blue sign, or the graying limestone tablets that lean out of the earth, rest against each other, or lie about broken and slimed with woodsy moisture. Their inscriptions are barely legible. One gathers that they are economical expressions, consisting mainly of names or even initials, and dates of birth and death. When Susie was small, she understood her aunt, Maria Frances, lay here, as did her grandfather's unmarried sister, Susan DeLancey. Before long her grandmother would join them, dead of typhoid fever. And so, in time, would John Peter, who died suddenly in his own bedroom after returning from a drive.[3] A person lived in the house and then went to dwell forever in the walled family ground. It was no great distance to travel. The Bee-Line bus that stops beside the burial place today goes farther—all the way to White Plains.

Humanity has been treading this path between house and grave for thousands of years. Diverse societies, with their different signs and symbols, have helped to forge a sturdy link between the places where the living dwell and those where the dead abide, so that the two might appear as mutually accessible people keepers, the twin cradles into which the generations lay each other in turn. The metaphor is now so powerful it is almost impossible to resist. So, not finding my people in the house, I expected, on some level beyond logic, to encounter them at the grave, only to be reminded that what separates the living from the dead is stronger even than metaphor. That's why the metaphor exists: to gird us in the confrontation with death's perfect majesty, its brute, absolute power.

Whereas many animals will treat a corpse precisely like the inanimate thing that it is, for perhaps hundreds of thousands and certainly tens of thousands of years, humans have been at pains to cache their dead in caves or shafts, sometimes sprinkling them with colorful ochre powder and provisioning them with a few of the ornaments and tools they used in life. But it wasn't until people became more sedentary and began to live in a marked-off world of their own construction, surrounded by the materiality of their houses and villages, that they began to express their connection to the dead by carefully situating their bodies within this human materiality, in places that in one way or another mirrored the communal lifescape. At Neolithic Jericho, perhaps 9,000 years ago, people kept, in the very rooms where they cooked and slept, the skulls of the deceased, fleshed out with plaster and made to gaze through cowrie-shell eyes. At Çatalhöyük in what is now Turkey, they stashed their dead beneath the house floors. And from the stone-built fishing and farming Neolithic village of Skara Brae in Orkney, a lowland road led through the mysterious and striking henge monuments known as the Ring of Brodgar and the Standing Stones of Stenness, then turned east along the shore of a loch to reach the great stone passage grave known as Maes Howe. Like the settlement at Skara Brae, the tomb was entered by a passage so low it required the visitor to stoop or kneel. The cairn's central corbelled chamber, its rear wall oriented to receive the light of the setting midwinter sun, produced a dramatic sense of interiority that must have recalled that of the fire-lit family dwelling. In the grave, side chambers were closed by massive blocking stones, just as each house in the village could draw and bolt its stone door against the covered passage outside.[4]

The archaeologist Ian Hodder argues that, in order to accept the new social constraints and long-term dependencies of a settled farming life, Neolithic people had to domesticate themselves inwardly. They did this, he says, by identifying the new social constraints with a realm of caring, safety, and fertility—"the domus"—and setting this safe place against an unstructured and potentially annihilating wild. The house itself, the control of spatial boundaries, and the monumental tomb all were potent ways of representing this newly conceived opposition. Indeed, the

metaphor involved managing the wild by bringing it within the domus—
by, among other things, literally housing the dead. This was an ideology
that served the powerful by helping them to intensify food production; it
also planted in individuals a desire so deep it seems to lie at the core of
our humanity.[5] We *want* to be kept beings. We want to feel located, contained against some beyond or other, held in place and time, in death no
less than in life. The alternative: endless wandering, our nameless bones
scattered to the beasts. Who doesn't shudder at the thought?

During my perambulations around the cemeteries of Westchester,
Brooklyn, and Queens, I saw suggestions everywhere of this keen desire
to be kept forever in one's allotted place within the human enclosure.
The early nineteenth-century gravestones of the DeLancey gentry are
simple and clean of line, like Heathcote Hill itself. At Ozone Park,
Queens, former tenement dwellers are represented by great, stolid
stones that stand shoulder to shoulder in rows. The prosperous Victori-
ans buried at Newark's Mount Pleasant Cemetery, who once might have
favored lushly carpeted and wallpapered rooms, in death are watched
over by weeping maids and cherubs with rosebud mouths. But what I
found really striking is that, even though Judaism and Christianity both
emphasize the trajectory of an individual soul, in the graveyards one
rarely finds an attempt to stand apart or express individuality; instead
the stones fix a state of belonging. Walking along the cemeteries' grassy
paths is very like browsing through the census, with many a "household"
enclosed by a low fence and marked by a large stone inscribed with the
family name; smaller markers are labeled "father," "mother," "beloved
sister," or, in the case of a child who died in 1926, "our adorable Jimmy."
Wealthy folk can be unmistakably located along millionaires' rows of
mausoleums built of rich materials to resemble both house and classical
temple. Rachel Hart is buried near a chain-link fence covered with hon-
eysuckle. On her side of the fence, many stones bear, like hers, the Hebrew inscription *May her soul be bound up in the bond of eternal life*. On
the other side of the fence, the cross appears in various iterations.

Today, the increasing popularity (at least in North America and Europe) of cremation and eco-friendly burials would seem to suggest that
people are learning to eschew this attachment to being "kept," even in
death, within some domesticated space. After all, the idea in scattering

ashes or burying a body in a biodegradable wicker casket is precisely that the corpse should dissipate, return to the natural world as wholly as possible. But look more closely at the imagery surrounding these funerary practices and you begin to suspect they are attempts merely to *re*locate the dead, to define, in the face of urban development, high family mobility, and religious agnosticism, new places where the beloved can be held close forever. The solutions people find aren't all that unlike the construction of megalithic tombs that create an enduring landmark, or indeed the storing of ancestral remains beneath house floors.

In a 2006 survey by the Cremation Association of North America examining more than 5,000 cremations, of the cremated bodies released to families, only about 22 percent were scattered on land or water.[6] When families do scatter ashes, they typically choose a spot for its promise of stable, long-term salience and identification with comfort and pleasure in life. As one professional ash scatterer told McClatchy-Tribune Newspapers in 2009, "I try to encourage families to consider a historical landmark or a protected place like a national park, so in 50 years you know it's not going to be a Wal-Mart."[7] Golf courses are apparently a popular scattering site. But, in the Cremation Association's survey, the preponderance of cremated dead—some 39 percent—were not scattered at all but kept *at home*. I know of a man who regularly visits his grandmother's ashes in his own garage. He sets up a folding chair, cracks a beer. A 2009 letter writer to the *Times* fretted over a friend who, after a year and a half, still kept his father's ashes in a cigar box on the old man's leather chair in the den.[8] And a 2008 piece in the British *Guardian* (whose author, by the way, kept her grandmother in the glove box of her Renault) quotes a widower explaining the disposition of his wife's ashes: "There was no plan, so I put her in the wardrobe in my bedroom," he said. "Now I find it comforting to know she is there, safe and, most important to me, warm. It might sound irrational—as a scientist, I know there's no logic in it and I'm not religious or superstitious—but on a winter's day when the weather's bad and I'm lying in bed, I'm just reassured to know that Pauline is not out there in the cold."[9]

I am also struck by the designs of various "green" caskets, which, on their way to speedy disintegration, take care to swaddle the dead in a particular cultural aesthetic—the frontiersman-like pine box, the space-age-looking "pod," the cardboard crate you can customize to look like a box of chocolates. Some are even meant to be used during life as domestic furniture; in effect, you go to eternal rest in the living room coffee table, bookshelf, or, believe it or not, wine rack. Forever Fernwood, a natural burial ground in Mill Valley, California, limits markers to indigenous rocks and plants; on the other hand, the exact location of each interment is pinned down for the ages using Global Positioning System (GPS) coordinates.[10]

All this cultural *stuff*—from the dwellings and cairns of prehistoric Orkney to the family plots of Brooklyn to coffins prepurposed as furniture—functions in a practical way, yes. It also means something. In a way, it tells us how to think. The psychologist Merlin Donald calls it "external symbolic storage." It's external because it resides not in the individual mind but in the cultural material that surrounds us, from houses and graves to written records. It's a sort of annex to personal memory that exponentially expands memory's capacity and lastingness. And Donald suggests that this man-made symbolic product, in turn, structures the individual thought process. The mind is functionally reliant on its storage, and invests heavily in the "decoding baggage" needed to interpret it. "This is more than a metaphor," he writes. "Each time the brain carries out an operation in concert with the external symbolic storage system, it becomes part of a network. Its memory structure is temporarily altered; and the locus of cognitive control changes."[11]

As one node in this vast and ancient network, I find myself equipped to "read" the local graveyards with their silent upright markers the same way I read houses with doors and windows—as emblems of human presence. It may be that I cannot read them otherwise. It's true my actual journey to the graves met with a certain disappointment, that startled question, *where are you?* But now that I'm back in my living room, I find, like the man who knows his wife is gone but can't help feeling she's in the wardrobe, that my mind mulishly re-peoples those gravesites. I see Rachel resting against the trunk of a catalpa tree. It may be that even to conceive of lost ones is to gather them once again into the fold.

Levi R. Barnard was one of the first people to live at No. 239. The eldest son of Elisha Barnard, the bookbinder turned agent, and his wife,

Frances, Levi moved there from Broome Street with his parents and two siblings in the late 1840s. He was not yet twenty. He got a job in a tea shop around the corner on Avenue C. The family lived there more than five years during the heyday of shipbuilding, sharing the building with a machinist and a locksmith, among others. Levi subsequently served in the Civil War; a photo shows him lean-cheeked, mutton-chopped, with ink-dark eyes. After the war he married Adrianna Mutter and lived in Newark, New Jersey, where his mother's family had a long presence. He went into chemicals, an early version of the pharmaceuticals business, perhaps; his brother-in-law was a pharmacist. After Levi died in 1915—he was in his eighties—Adrianna made a donation to the New Jersey Historical Society consisting of "a considerable number of Civil War books and relics and among the latter . . . flags carried through many engagements of the Civil War."[12] The war apparently had been a defining experience. The couple had no children.

Levi and Adrianna are buried in a landmark Victorian-era garden cemetery. Once a rural preserve where the Newark gentry went to rest, today its drip-castle sandstone gatehouse faces a gritty string of used-car dealerships. On the fine May morning when I passed through the gates, I soon ran across Scott Willman, a third-generation caretaker of Mount Pleasant. He let me into the office, where everything looked and smelled—not unpleasantly—old. There was dark wainscoting and, on a large desk, two ancient and clearly obsolete adding machines, their paper scrolls stained the color of tea. The bathroom was of marble and more wood, with chunky porcelain fixtures and a little wastebasket whose lid said "Sanette" in a jaunty script. Willman, himself rather boyish in appearance, consulted a large antique volume for the Barnards' burial location and walked with me to their stone, a granite block simply decorated with a braid and floral medallions, inscribed with the name Barnard, and accompanied by two small footstones. They are buried next to a Civil War surgeon, between two stately oaks.

Although many of Newark's old families have moved away and visitors are rather sparse at Mount Pleasant, the graveyard is lovely and immaculately kept. After Willman left me, I strolled. The rhododendrons were in bloom, the Japanese maples blood red in the sunlight. *Ye Shall Know the Truth*, said one stone. *Asleep in Jesus, blessed sleep/from which no one ever wakes to weep*, said another, the monument of a twenty-six-year-old. There were lilies of stone and doves on the wing. It was really quite mesmerizing. I mounted the little steps and peered through the brasswork doors of the mausoleums, ignoring the sheer marble sidewalls behind which the dead are entombed in order to focus on the stained-glass panels in the rear. I'd examined maybe a half dozen of these panels when, cupping my hands beside my face to minimize glare, I peered into a crypt whose right sidewall was busted at the bottom, exposing the rubble of a broken coffin sprouting torn white satin. It sent a bolt of energy through me.

It was a curious sensation I am tempted to describe as a thrill. I suppose this has to do with the violation of a taboo. It was as if a seam had separated in the known and sanctioned world, affording a glimpse of some forbidden landscape. Before leaving Mount Pleasant I ran into Willman again, the caretaker, and he told me that probably what I'd come across was the result of a grave robbing several years back, apparently to provide human bones to local practitioners of the Afro-Caribbean religion Palo Mayombe, who use them to invoke the spirit of the deceased in their rituals. This sort of thing came up from time to time, he said. Perhaps I'd noticed the plastic sack by the large central mausoleum? he queried apologetically. It contained a slaughtered chicken.[13]

Vandalism at graveyards is not in the least unusual. Toppling tombstones and the like can in fact be considered "a *traditional* [my emphasis!] form of juvenile malicious mischief," according to the *Handbook of Death & Dying*. "There are even cases of teenagers opening tombs and caskets to poke the body inside with a stick."[14] Indeed, the cemetery where Levy and Clara Phillips are buried, Bayside in Ozone Park, Queens, has more than once been desecrated by intruders who left human remains strewn on the floors of their crypts.[15] In 2003, three Long Island teens were accused of stealing a skeleton from a local cemetery and dressing it up as Darth Vader.[16] More recently, a young person pleaded guilty to abuse of a corpse after he and a couple of buddies allegedly retrieved the remains of an eleven-year-old boy from a snake-infested cemetery outside Houston, Texas, and used the skull as a bong.[17] One can scarcely imagine more outrageously transgressive behavior, and that, apparently, is the point.

But Willman, I'd noticed, had seemed unmoved by such lurid excitations. As the son and grandson of former caretakers of Mount Pleasant, he'd grown up around the cemetery, he told me during my visit. "Death is a part of life," he remarked as we stood near the Barnard stone, mowers buzzing dreamily in the distance. Then he added, as if the thought were somehow reassuring, "And it always will be."

Living with death and with the dead is a distinctly human accomplishment, but, let's not kid ourselves, it's also a terrible and persistent problem. We have an almost desperate need to keep the dead close, to honor the bonds of affection that are the source of our own continuity. At the same time there is an urgent necessity to put aside death and dead people in order to go on living. Nothing focuses this conflict like a corpse. As the utterly vulnerable remnant of a human being, wherein the body's ungovernable thingness is fully ascendant, it is widely afforded special protection in law, ethics, and religion. On the other hand it is garbage, ordure, and must be disposed of as such. "The great problem for survivors in all cultures," writes the psychiatrist Robert Jay Lifton, "is to convert 'homeless souls,' particularly those of the recent dead, into comfortably enshrined or immortalized souls. . . . *What is involved is the symbolic transformation of a threatening, inert image (of the corpse) into a vital image of eternal continuity (the soul)."*[18] Funeral rites of all kinds—including the apparently bizarre Neolithic practice of defleshing the corpse—facilitate this transformation, ushering the homeless soul into a state of purity and abstraction.

If death is a displacement, first from the body, also from the dwelling, the neighborhood, and the world, there's a widespread human impulse to serve and pacify the dead by giving them a new home, one that's nearby and permanent. But in New York City, where the living themselves jockey for a place to call their own, finding a suitably stable home for the dead is a particular challenge. In the years after terrorists made a pyre of the World Trade Center on September 11, 2001, for example, tension arose over how much turf to cede to memorialization of victims, retiring it from the many other uses city people make of space. A bitter episode came in 2005, when relatives of some 9/11 victims succeeded in excluding two cultural institutions from the site on the grounds that they might sponsor unpatriotic speech; the area should "tell the story of that fateful day—and that day alone," in the words of the opposition group.[19] One participant in the memorial planning process complained that these families were trying to claim Ground Zero as "their own personal property" and turn it into "a giant cemetery."[20] As it stands in 2010, the towers' footprints are to be preserved as pools in a six-acre memorial titled "Reflecting Absence," an extraordinary statement in a city whose every square inch is soaked with the blood and tears of the unremembered dead.

Manhattan, as a matter of fact, is well sown with physical remains. There once were something like a hundred burial grounds on this slender island. But as the bustling colonial town grew into a crowded world city, its dead were wedged ever more tightly into churchyard and family plots that, due to their suffocating stench and threat of contagion, made poor neighbors. Besides which, the land was worth a mint. In the mid-nineteenth century, when the city officially barred new interments below 86th Street, the dead were evicted en masse. Working mostly at night, gravediggers exhumed many thousands of bodies and carried them over the river to be re-interred in Brooklyn and Queens. Some 100,000 corpses were removed to Ward's Island from a single city cemetery at 50th Street between Park and 3rd avenues. It was a huge, physical job, and not always carried out with utmost fastidiousness. Both the African Burial Ground and Reformed Dutch Churchyard near the toe of Manhattan were sold, human remains and all, and developed. St. Marks in the Bowery at 2nd Avenue and 10th Street, founded in the Dutch period and long the resting place of the city's elite, kept its churchyard burial place, but over the years let it fall to ruin, until, in the late 1960s, it created new public space by covering the graves with a cobblestone pavement. Bodies rest, unmarked, under Central Park and James J. Walker Park in Greenwich Village. Likewise, nobody bothered to move the remains of the estimated 20,000 paupers and fever victims buried under Washington Square Park before turning it into a popular public gathering place in the mid-nineteenth century. Every so often a work crew unearths their bones, most recently in 2008.[21]

Buildings, and especially dwellings, are so full of life, so convincing as representations of human identity, that their dying also can provoke

anxieties and practical conflicts among the living. Their ruins can sometimes pose the same sort of difficulties as a corpse. There's evidence
that certain Neolithic societies even applied a kind of funerary rite to
houses at the end of their useful lives or upon the death of a significant
occupant, burning the dwelling to the ground in a purposeful—in fact,
spectacular and downright strenuous—act of destruction. The archaeologist Ruth Tringham has dubbed the practice "domithanasia." The
fire eliminated the unwanted (and perhaps disturbing, unhomelike)
house. But it also lit up the night in an unmistakable occasion, marking
the heart of many a thrilled witness, and marking the ground with a
long-lasting reminder that, as Tringham puts it, "a house had once lived
here."[22] This desire to mark out a place for the dead house, to avoid living upon its remains, also was expressed by Thoreau. "I am not aware
that any man has ever built on the spot which I occupy," he wrote with
satisfaction of his cabin at Walden. "Deliver me," he continued, "from
a city built on the site of a more ancient city, whose materials are ruins,
whose gardens cemeteries. The soil is blanched and accursed there."[23]

A Neolithic closure ritual is just the sort of thing I'd wanted for No.
239—to watch it go up in flames with everything it held, transformed
from a pile of rot to pure abstraction, something I could think about with
equanimity. Maybe I wouldn't have run around so frantically trying to locate its scattered contents, salvage bits and pieces, if there'd been a
scorch mark in its place, or a cool stone, something I could visit and
touch, as if I were touching my own lost youth and David's, the sweet
baby days of our children, the material plenty we'd enjoyed and expected
would continue, the way we'd thought our *lives* would go, every match-
less aspect of the era itself, even the city's own youthful boast of *first*
and *only*. But that's a luxury requiring an endless supply of virgin ground
or more money than God. Only in the most extraordinary circumstances
can New Yorkers afford to simply close our ruins. We must live in them.
So instead of torching the place, we watched from afar as the new owner
had No. 239 shrouded in scaffolding and reconstituted from the inside
out. Steel beams replaced its sagging wooden skeleton. The stove in
which we'd baked gingerbread men at Christmastime appeared on the
sidewalk, where it rusted. A new roof deck materialized, much tidier
than ours had been and a story higher. The new stoop, also perhaps a lit-

tle higher than the original, was similarly fitted out with an iron railing—
a straight, modern one. Gone are the graceful scrolls.

In this regard, it seems to me, New York arrives at a critical juncture. For all its buried history it is still a young city. In comparison to,
say, Damascus or Rome, it is only beginning to heave itself up on the
composted remains of the past. It is only beginning to shed the inno-
cence of Walden. No. 239, when it was built in 1845, *was* the first
building to occupy the spot—in the whole history of humanity and of
the world! The same can be said of any number of row houses all over
the city and especially uptown and in the so-called outer boroughs,
where urban density came later. They will disappear in due course,
though perhaps not for generations. And so will the tenements, with
their lattice of fire escapes. Even if today they are the very emblem of
New York, instantly evoking its urban culture, they are also an obsolete
housing form and will go the way of the little Dutch and Federal-style
row houses that once lined the riverfront. The painstakingly re-created
rooms of the Tenement Museum on Orchard Street will, I imagine,
remain to bear witness, but it won't be the same as living inside and
among the tenements, the buildings themselves wordlessly teaching
their occupants how to live and, by extension, how others lived. Some
other way of life will come to be, maybe sooner than we imagine. Will
a New York without stoops and fire escapes still be New York?

Pretty regularly, for the more than twenty years I've known David,
I've gone with him to a spot on the Canadian shore of Lake Erie where
he passed childhood summers, where indeed his father summered as
a youth. It doesn't change. Always the clinking of masts. The same
blue chickweed sprouting along the road. When I go there I feel young.
The peaches are sweet. I feel as if nothing at all separates me from the
twenty-year-old I was. But in the city, which ceaselessly transmogrifies,
I sometimes feel old, so terribly old, some vampire who's seen centuries and worlds slip away. I think of Veselka, the Ukrainian diner on
2nd Avenue. It keeps the memory of the day in late 1997 when I took
Lucy there as a baby, and she sat up, for the first time, and faced me
across the table, the marvel of her separate life unveiled in that instant. I can remember the way the light fell on us from the pastry case.
But Veselka doesn't just fail to bring forward but actively blots out the

times when David and I were kids ourselves and ate pierogies there in a dim back room, swatting at a fly, lighting a cigarette afterward. Those days, that girl, were overwritten, bricked over, in the 1996 renovation that made Veselka the bright, spick-and-span space it is today.

"No matter how long you have been here," claims the novelist Colson Whitehead in his 2003 *The Colossus of New York*, "you are a New Yorker the first time you say, That used to be Munsey's, or That used to be the Tic Toc Lounge. That before the internet café plugged itself in, you got your shoes resoled in the mom-and-pop operation that used to be there. You are a New Yorker when what was there before is more real and solid that what is here now."[24] A century earlier, Henry James, revisiting the New York of his childhood after decades abroad, lamented the towering new edifices that obscured the Gothic spire of old Trinity, once the pride of Broadway. He didn't really *see* the new structures at all, except as "buildings whose very first care is to deprive churches of their visibility." Equally dismayed by the spectacle of Castle Garden's concert hall dramatically demoted, after several intervening incarnations, to a "vague nonentity," James concluded, "This impact of the whole condensed past at once produced a horrible, hateful sense of personal antiquity."[25] It's a drag being ancient, watching your favorite places hurry along to their next appointment before you've finished living in them. Before you've had a chance to say goodbye. This is how the city, every day, confronts its people with the problem of death.

The crucial fiction of the house is permanence. Likewise, that of the grave. The Germans taught me that.

Abraham Weinstein, the German Jewish tailor whose clothing warehouse burned at the dawn of the Civil War just after he moved into No. 239 with his family, survived two wives and lived to an advanced age in the building two doors down. When he died, the kinsmen of his second wife, Caroline, came from Missouri to claim the house that had always been hers, and Abraham went to his rest in Union Field, the Queens burial yard of Rodeph Sholom, the synagogue he helped to found. His tombstone lies in a small section of old graves clustered beside a mausoleum on the main path. But it is unidentifiable among the white slabs, many of which are unreadable or lie in pieces despite obvious efforts—

metal braces and the like—at holding them up and together. They're like the pieces of a platter you mean to glue together but in the meantime stash in a cupboard. After all, life goes on.

Given the brouhaha surrounding Bayside Cemetery, where Levy and Clara Phillips were buried in 1884 and 1903, I figured I had even less of a chance of finding their markers than Weinstein's. An open lawsuit against the Upper West Side congregation that owns the graveyard accused it of failing to honor perpetual-care contracts. Intermittent cleanup efforts by, among others, a family-history-conscious Mormon from Salt Lake City and the Jewish motorcycle group Chai Riders, had proved only a temporary bulwark against nature's irrepressible will. This much I gathered from a lively online back-and-forth about the cemetery, complete with artistic photos posted by various urban adventurers. Among the posters' observations: "It's so beautiful, and so very very sad that so much damage has been done to it by douchebags." "Why agonize over maintaining a certain version—they're all dead anyway. Let nature take it back." "This reminds me of the Appian Way outside of Rome, not the catacombs and the romantic half standing buildings, but the overgrown old grave markers where the busted off pieces are still lying in the weeds where they landed."[26] Not promising.

But when I arrived at Bayside one wet spring morning, I right away ran into a deeply tanned, wiry man, faintly redolent of tobacco and wearing a forest-green Mets T-shirt and matching zippered sweatshirt, blue jeans, and bright white leather sneakers: Bob Martorano, the groundskeeper. He was happy to help. As he walked with me in the direction of the United Brothers section where, according to their file card, the Phillipses were interred, he explained that normally he likes visitors to call in advance so he can go hammer and tongs at the plot in question and make it presentable. "I'm really up against it here," he said, cataloguing the worst of it: these grasses, which are stringy as hell; that blue-flowered plant (I recognized it as Virginia dayflower), which wraps around the weed whacker, a soggy mash; and *that* stuff, he said, pointing to a thicket of chest-high, broad-leaved shrubs, that stuff Martorano hated for the sheer, monstrous, vegetable bulk of it, which seemed to double every time he turned his back. As we chatted and walked, at our right was a dense deciduous woods with an equally thick, viny undergrowth, amid which stood, all in a row, the most monumental tombstones—they reached maybe seven feet in height—here and there struck by a patch of penetrating light. It was a strange council of elders gathered there. The effect was of surpassing patience. Finally Martorano pointed me toward a rusted turnstile and headed back down the path.

United Brothers, a large section, proved very weedy but not impenetrable. The bigger problem was that many of the stones were toppled over facedown. In places you could hardly help stepping on them. I inspected every stone I could, pushing my way through the grass until my jeans were wet to the thigh. I had given up hope and was crouching under some vines in an adjacent section when I heard a voice. *Hello?* Martorano had returned with a plot map, a grid with a name in each rectangle. Using the readable stones, by this map we navigated our way to an empty place in the weeds. He stamped the ground, then stooped and brushed away some grass and dirt. He thought the stones were right here, underfoot. So he left me again, then returned lugging a large jug of water, a scrub brush, and a shovel. Soon—he insisted on doing the work himself—Martorano had laid bare the old glazier's battered, mottled, 125-year-old marker for the first time in who knows how long. Turned over on the grass, a thin plank of limestone with a scalloped top, it seemed almost to blink in the light. I could make out, in an arch at the top, the word *Sacred*, then underneath that, *to the memory of*, and further down, Levy's name, and, finally, his birthplace, *Hamburg, Germany*. Clara's stone, not as old but badly fissured and stained all along its face, was unreadable. I knew it was hers only by its placement, and the design, which mirrored Levy's. I returned a couple of weeks later to make a rubbing, at Martorano's suggestion. Now I could make out a few more words on Levy's stone—*my beloved husband and our dear father*, I'm pretty sure.

This time the daylilies were in bloom, a butterfly alighting here and there. I thought of the family—Clara, the matriarch, and her adult children, Rachel, Moses, and Isabella, and grandchildren, especially the young milliner, Clara, who had lived with her grandpa at No. 239 and probably watched him pass away—all standing there, saying goodbye. I wondered what it had accomplished, dragging their stones into view. Then I heard voices, and Martorano emerged from the thicket, busily conversing with a companion. He paused—"Well, well, well!" he called out from the path—but was soon on his way. They were planning an ambitious cleanup at Bayside.

Rachel and Clara Hart were (according to their death certificates) supposed to have been buried perhaps a mile away from the Phillipses, at Mount Hope Cemetery. But there wasn't any cemetery record for Clara, the working girl who died from tuberculosis. Lacking even a trailhead, all I could do was peer through the rusted, ivy-covered gates of Mount Hope and wonder. Rachel's record located her, not beside her daughter as I had assumed, but in the next cemetery over, Maimonides. I visited there on a steamy day after much rain. A small crew wielding the ubiquitous weed whacker was at work near the entrance. The head groundskeeper stopped his work to point the way. Maimonides is on a slope. Rachel is near the top of the hill, at the end of a row, a surprisingly significant white marker, up to my sternum and several inches thick, with a rounded top and a nice incised line all around its edge. It rests on a pedestal. I couldn't quite read the words, so I made a rubbing.

> *In memory of*
> *Rachel*
> *Relict of the late*
> *Joseph Hart*
> *Died Jun. 3, 1902*
> *Age 60 years*
> *May her soul rest in peace*

And underneath, in Hebrew, *May her soul be bound up in the bond of eternal life.*

I was startled. Joseph had been gone thirty-five years when Rachel died; their marriage had lasted three or four. But on her tombstone, it's his name that appears in full, at the center of the stone, and as large as her own, the other lines being slightly smaller. And that language—*relict* of the late Joseph Hart—was not so common even then. I recognized it as the phrase that had appeared in Rachel's death notice, which I'd supposed had been supplied by her brother, Moses, whose address also appeared there. I tugged the brittle, clinging remains of a dead vine from the stone and brushed away a bird dropping. The stone's message, I thought, was that Rachel's marriage had been the central relationship of her life. But was that an emotional truth or a social and economic fact? Could the two ever be separated? Maybe Moses, by emphasizing Rachel's husband, had simply meant to confer on his sister as proud a status as circumstances permitted. Maybe all those years she'd had to live alongside a more acceptable still image of herself, snapped in the short, upward arc of her early twenties. She would hardly be the only one.

The city's way of thrusting forward the problem of death has a parallel in nature, in the scream of the hare at night or the turning and dropping of autumn leaves. Like the natural world, the city is both terrible and sublime. It presents both the problem of death and, simultaneously, an answer.

New York is an answer to death not just for people who live here and experience its mysteries firsthand but for people all over America and maybe the world, although in a somewhat different way, as a great accretion of symbolic storage that must never be allowed to crumble, lest the light of civilization itself go out. Why else, after 9/11, would schoolchildren from Kentucky and Illinois send cookies and artwork to their counterparts at the Children's Workshop School on East 12th Street, where Lucy was a pre-kindergartner? Why would a Dutchman send enough bulbs to grow daffodils as far as the eye can see? They were claiming the city's dead, and that, most certainly, is to claim the city, if not as family ground, then as someplace important to their own symbolic continuation. Because, much as the feelings riot against such a concession, there is one thing worse than dying, and that's dying off, the extinction, not just of individual people, buildings, neighborhoods, or building types, but of their containers, the ultimate symbols.

It's ghastly to think of the city itself dying, its generations filing off into cold nothingness. The death of cities carries an inkling of the even more encompassing death of nature, of the wild that we draw into the human enclosure to tame it, as Hodder says, but also because we understand it is the source of all life. A dread of this kind of erasure comes across again and again in the futuristic movies that feature New York icons in tales of end days. In *Planet of the Apes*, the most disturbing moment comes at the end, when the camera pans across the Statue of

Liberty, a ruin half buried in the sand. In the 2004 movie *The Day After Tomorrow*, following a global environmental catastrophe, a human remnant hunkers down at the central branch of the New York Public Library, its famous stone lions gazing down on 5th Avenue; the survivors burn books for warmth. In a few years, if all goes well, we'll have another symbol we hope will outlast us. One World Trade Center is set to rise, higher than any rival, over the site of the former World Trade Center, resembling nothing so much as a megalithic tomb, with a small priestly class—the so-called 9/11 families—permitted special access to the nearby memorial's inner chamber. I happen to have preferred the first, asymmetric design for the tower, which seemed to stagger, broken but triumphant, to its feet, over the stout hypodermic the authorities settled on, which I "read" as an expression of, among other things, a dull militaristic form of nationalism, but so what? The point is, night after night for a hundred years we'll light the heavens with that spire. We'll all burn brighter and longer there.

Simon and Gizella Wieder are buried together at Union Field (around a corner from Abraham Weinstein, who, both here and at No. 239, predated them by several decades) under a weighty piece of gray granite whose long inscriptions are almost entirely in Hebrew.*

> *Here lies buried*
> *Chairman (to) disseminate Torah*
> *Acceptable guardian of Justice and righteousness*
> *He applied (himself) in the law in the straight way*
> *   (a straightforward manner)*
> *Straight and simple, may he be great in the congregation*
> *He disseminated his wellsprings with taste and consideration*
> *And his demise (was) very hard and bitter on us*

This is followed by his name, father's name, date of death, and the standard injunction, *May his soul be bound in the covenant of life.* And Gizella's inscription reads in part:

---

*I am indebted to Barbara Schmidt-Runkel for this translation.

Here lies buried
A dear and gentle soul
Many daughters did well
But you surpassed over all of them
The earnings of your righteousness will stand as a witness
Alas, your departure (is) hard for us
Your pure soul will intercede on our behalf . . .
She ascended to the heavens,
   to the suffering of her husband and her sons

Having taken a look at these inscriptions, Rabbi Joshua Segal, author of *A Field Guide to Visiting a Jewish Cemetery*,[27] points out that not only do the first letters of the lines in Simon's spell out his Jewish name (Yeshayahu or Isaiah), but the lines of Gizella's also form an acrostic spelling-out of Rosen, which may be a reference to her mother's family name, Rosenbluth. The third and fourth lines quoted above are from Proverbs 31, praise for a good woman, sometimes read in Jewish homes by a husband to his wife as they welcome the Sabbath. And finally, Rabbi Segal points out that Gizella's inscription uses different words for "soul" in lines two and seven. The "dear and gentle" soul is *nefesh*, the life force that animates the body and is bound to it, feeling its wants and needs. The part of Gizella that will intercede on behalf of her loved ones is *neshamah*; it outlives the body, the purest, highest aspect of soul, eternally connected to its divine source.

Their epitaphs are explicit and rather complete. More than sixty years after their deaths, no one need speak for Simon and Gizella Wieder. A tiny, starlike wildflower, little blue-eyed grass, it's called, blooms on their grave, an excellent source of nectar to pollinators.

The morning I'd set aside to drive out to Beth David Cemetery in eastern Queens, where a death notice located the burial of Simon and Gizella's son Max, the prosecutor, it poured down rain. I dashed into the cemetery office pushing my flimsy umbrella against the wind. There I was given a map revealing a neat grid of streets not unlike that of the East Side, with directions: right on Lincoln, left on Machpela, between Monroe & Jackson. Here I found snazzy Art Deco gateposts of smooth, highly polished pink granite, which gave entry to the plot of the Comac Club, a social club to which at least one of the leaders of 7th Street's Jefferson Democratic Club also had belonged. I walked up and down, up and down amid the rows, the rain splattering down in fat drops. At last I spotted the name Wieder and realized why I'd over-looked it before: This was not a single grave, but an unusual triple bur-ial, the family name in large letters across a broad stone, and below it, the names Max, Michael, and, not Morris—Moe. Moe finally quit No. 239 around 1960, after the other two had passed away. The brothers, whose deaths were spaced over more than thirty years, nevertheless ended the day under a single roof, as they so often had in life.

It's incredibly powerful as an expression of affinity, this lying side by side forever, maybe even more so than sharing the same rooms in life. I'd mostly pictured Louis and Laura Wieder falling in love on 7th Street, knocking around with Laura's sisters and their husbands in the early years of the twentieth century. I expected to be confronted with a starkly different image at their grave. Alfred Wieder had told me that his father was first buried in Queens, but that Laura, who outlived her husband by nearly twenty years, later had him relocated to a nonsec-tarian cemetery north of the city, not far from Yonkers. When I got there I could see why. They are all there together, Louie and Laura, Sam and Anna Snyder, Charlie and Syd Stern, in plots that look across from a grassy hillside to a mist-filled, wooded one. While I was there, at the perimeter of the cemetery, a coyote pup once or twice trotted on enormous paws out of the tree line, eyed me with that absence of recognition that so clearly distinguishes the wild thing, then faded back into the dusk from which he'd come.

I have made a strange habit of claiming ancestors who don't belong to me. It's not been lost on me that claiming them, creating a kind of false genealogy that links me with past inhabitants of No. 239, is a propri-etary act that has to do with place as well as people. Somewhere in there is an impulse to repossess the house. And every single day I've spent pawing through somebody else's vital records, I've been more or less troubled by the perversity of it. Good grief, hadn't we had enough of screw piles and tiebacks? Hadn't we indeed been delighted to es-cape that moldering heap of a house?

But sometimes, when you mean to look out at the world, you see into yourself. That's what happened in the graveyards. I never encountered the people I was looking for. I'll never know the expression in their eyes or the shape of their hands. But now that August is here, the city simmering in its own juices, I find my self-understanding is more flexible than before. I can see that the house itself has always been less important than everything it seemed to take with it into oblivion. At some point early on—maybe that moment in the municipal archives when I first discovered the Phillipses—the people and their stories became my object, not for what they could restore of the past, but for how they might accompany me into the future. Something about the beauty, the self-evident value of their ordinary days carries me through my own. My sense that they might actually materialize is a measure of the extent to which I *did* find them, first through the house, and then in bits and pieces preserved in the great containers of the city—our archives, our library guarded by noble and somnolent lions, our register of property conveyances. And they do appear to me, nearly every day, in a seemingly infinite parade of images. Never do I watch the river bearing itself along without thinking of one or the other of them.

All the documents in my box of files, all the records stored on paper or microfilm or in digital files, all the monuments of stone, all the inked and etched sayings are prompts—critical, to be sure, but merely prompts. They wait for us. We are the kept. And we are the keepers.

In family plots all along the border of Brooklyn and Queens, little benches are placed among the headstones. It's not logical exactly, but what could be more human? One wants to sit, for a moment or two, in the shade of an oak, near the place of disappearance.

On the Edge

ELEVEN

IN THE DECADES after the Second World War, cities lost population, drifting farther and farther from the center of American life. A hard-earned prosperity now permitted ordinary families to buy a Ford sedan, drive out along miles of freshly laid macadam, and settle, perhaps with the help of a federally financed loan, in a stand-alone house equipped with the basic amenities we know today: a yard, full plumbing and electricity, a refrigerator, central heat, not to mention a little privacy and room to stretch. By the time this postwar boom gave way to inflation and unemployment in the 1970s, the blocks of decaying tenements east of Avenue A seemed quite forsaken, as if perched at the very edge of the world.

Children growing up there developed a rare perspective. They saw wonderful things other people didn't get to see. In the meanest days of the '70s and '80s, they came to know things other people didn't want to know.

"There were a lot of Spanish kids, German kids, Jewish, Chinese," recalls Basil Hawryluk, who as a very small boy in the year 1950 moved into a tenement apartment across the street from No. 239 E. 7th St.[1] Hawryluk, whose parents had met in one of Europe's teeming displaced-persons camps, brought a Ukrainian heritage to the mix. To earn a living in New York, his father washed skyscraper windows. His mother worked the swing shift, cleaning office buildings. Basil meanwhile played stickball in the street with the other kids, sometimes lunching at their kitchen tables. Around age ten he and his sister Vera could go on their own to Tompkins Square Park, where in the summertime you could buy a slice of watermelon or a Spanish ice—a *piragua*, as the Puerto Ricans called it. Then, in the '60s, the hippies came traipsing through in their sandals, fringe- and feather-bedecked, half-naked sometimes. "It was interesting," says Hawryluk. "It was fun, and an education, that you could do anything you want in the United States."

In the late '60s, just as Hawryluk's family left the block for Astoria, Queens, another small boy, Milo Zwerling, moved into the same tenement on 7th Street with his mother and father, a merchant seaman who was often away. "Especially in the summertime, everyone was out on the stoop and the fire hydrants were open and a lot of salsa music was playing. There was a scene there," he says, "people playing conga drums." Just as vividly he remembers lying at night in his back bedroom—its window looked out on an airshaft piled with garbage—listening to the clanging of pots as his brave little cat, Corona, did battle with the rats that came scrambling out of the cupboards. After a few years the Zwerlings landed a place four critical blocks to the west, on 2nd Avenue. "That was a dream come true," says Zwerling. "Man, we were out of the slums."

In these same years, down at the eastern end of the block, young Migdalia Gonzalez would look down from her window at the other girls as they whiled away warm afternoons in a game called skelsies, shooting specially modified pop-bottle caps across a court they'd drawn in chalk on the sidewalk. But Migdalia had little connection to them. Her mother, Ada, raised in the impoverished coffee- and tobacco-growing interior of Puerto Rico, made sure of that. "You see, my mom was very strict," says Migdalia. "So I wasn't allowed to hang out with anyone, outside on the street, on the stoops. I would come from school straight home." Though the boy she would marry, Edwin Torres, lived not three blocks away, at 5th Street and Avenue C, she wouldn't meet him in the neighborhood, carrying his shoeshine box up and down on a Saturday, but in Central Park on a school field trip. Edwin was playing hooky. The two married young, Edwin joining Migdalia and her family at No. 282. That was the ark in which they'd raise their own children through turbulent times.

Philip Long was six years old when he moved onto 7th Street with his mom and sister in the early '70s. In an affecting unpublished memoir, he recalls the block as an early "paradise," the warmest and most racially integrated place he would ever know, where his mom would call from the window in the evenings to summon him and his sister to supper.[2] Often his cousins came too. And yet scenes of well-being are intercut with incidents of extreme brutality. Once he sat on his fire escape watching the sun come up, munching a slice of buttered bread, when an altercation erupted just below; he watched a man lift a shotgun to another man's face, and fire. Long went through a period of bedwetting and stammering; he would engage adversaries on the street in an explosion of fear, anger, and sometimes tears. Eventually he acquired the requisite steeliness. His adolescent years read like the memoir of any child soldier, a welter of blows and piercings. In the sixth grade he pulled a knife during a melee with kids from a rival school, disappointing a principal who'd taken a special interest in him. "I couldn't exactly find the right words," Long writes, "to express my sorrow."

Abandoned buildings became places to play. "Sometimes the doors would be open, or sometimes we'd climb through the windows in the back," recalls Eric Felisbret, who also came of age on the block in the 1970s, the son of an Italian-American mother from the west-side neighborhood of Chelsea and a black father from Cape Verde, off the west coast of Africa. "The ones that were burned were a little bit more dangerous, and we would probably just climb up on the fire escapes. Sometimes you'd be on the sixth floor and you could look all the way down to the basement because the floors had been burned out." There were times when, in order to get into his apartment, he'd have to literally step over some guy tying up and jabbing a needle in his arm. "As a kid," he says, "I guess the feeling was terror." Over the years Felisbret lived at four different addresses on the block. When he was about eleven, his parents took the family on a trip to Italy. "When I came back to my neighborhood," he says, "I saw how dirty and beaten up it was, and I saw that there were actually many people who were depressed and angry." This only complicated his steadfast identification with the place. Today Felisbret lives in New Jersey but writes in an e-mail, "I love 7th Street. My heart is there."

Different as their experiences were, the children "read" this block of 7th Street in much the same way. "It's amazing how that little street from one end to the other really was a bubble, a safe haven in a really rough neighborhood. You knew people, they knew you," says Philip Hof, who in the late '70s lived with his mother during the week in the prosperous, predominantly white town of Oyster Bay, Long Island, and on the weekends would visit his dad, Henry Hof III, on 7th Street. Donald Kearse lived on the block in a group home for runaway and homeless youth. As a gay black kid with a plump shape, he often found himself making a detour around certain threatening figures to avoid harassment or worse. "Once you left 7th Street, you had to run the gauntlet, that's all I can say," he recalls, laughing. "Not just me," he adds, "everyone did. You ran the gauntlet."

During these years, the children went to Rosie's, the block's little hole-in-the-wall candy store near Avenue D, for penny candy and egg creams. Rosie had a gruff manner and careworn oval face. She wore a faded housecoat. A big German shepherd drowsed in the back discouraging petty theft. The kids rode battered bicycles and, later, skateboards. As the years went by, their hair grew shaggier. Their A-line shifts and button-down shirts with long lapels turned to snug, high-waisted jeans and T-shirts with scoop necklines. They liked to fly kites from the roofs or out by the river. In the early days, they made them out of flour sacks and, if they were being bad, tied razors to the tails to slash their rivals out of the air. For years—decades—they loved to raise homing pigeons. Basil Hawryluk used to release his birds all the way up in Central Park; they'd get home before he did. Or the children would just send the birds wheeling up from their rooftop coops, as if flinging their own spirits into the sky. I myself remember seeing the pigeons when I lived on the block in the 1990s, how they'd circle over the tenement roofs in balletic unison, their breasts flashing pink when, all at once, they would tilt away from the setting sun.

What brought the grown-ups to establish households at the margin of the world was a mixed affair. For many—including Puerto Ricans, Ukrainians and Poles, African Americans originally from the South, Chinese—it was often a classic chain migration. Grandparents, an aunt, or a cousin had come first, and now the place offered the comfort and practical advantages of a kin network. Together, these family groups made culture and language communities that softened the shocks of migration to a forbidding city. Then there were working-class New Yorkers priced out of more stylish neighborhoods, and people who were "different" for any number of reasons. They were social activists or avant-garde artists. They were single mothers, gays and lesbians, biracial couples. There were those who found freedom in the very marginality of the place, its offer of a chance to live as one pleased, unsurveilled by a dominant culture that could seem at once harsh and bland. But if the organizing principle of the early nineteenth-century neighborhood had been work—the carpenters and machinists and even the shopkeepers were there to be near the manufactories lining the river—in the late twentieth century the common denominator linking the residents of 7th Street and environs was equally of an economic nature. They had no money to speak of. The place was cheap.

They were settled in the path of something destructive. Even with the benefit of hindsight it is difficult to say just what it was that was coming for them. A kind of war, a crisis of faintly apocalyptic tint, a plague? And that was part of the tension in it, as if they could hear the hoofbeats but couldn't see where they were coming from, couldn't even tell whether the threat came from within or without. Who lit the fires? Who sent the junkies with their skinny, scabby arms sneaking up the fire escapes to rob you? What devil invented AIDS? Tough as they were, people saw things that filled them with anguish and rage. Ann Feinstein, who lived on the block near Avenue D, once saw the man across the street punish his girlfriend by throwing her Siberian husky out an upstairs window. Later she saw the man himself shoved against a building and pumped full of bullets. Ani Sandoval, who lived just across Avenue D in the Jacob Riis projects, used to send notes to judges sentencing major drug dealers: "The sale of drugs in our neighborhood is not a victimless crime. Please do not be lenient with this person." When eventually her own son did some time in the drug world, she carried out a program of tough love—"call a lawyer, don't call me." What a heartache that was. When she heard gunshots at night, she'd pray it wasn't her child who had come to harm. "I would jump up," she says, "and just put on a robe and run out there."

The strongest, most discernible theme of these years was a spiraling-down into ruins. But there was always a counter-theme. The truth is, people set about rebuilding their world even as it crumbled around them. They never stopped. For some, it was as if the destruction itself stimulated an extraordinary burst of effort. There never came a time when people weren't literally picking up the pieces, stacking fallen bricks and sweeping away garbage, hauling buckets of slop from flooded basements and putting up new drywall. They never stopped arguing and discussing in dreary hours-long meetings how to engage this or that city agency in their cause. They learned to assess and min-imize personal risk with a brisk matter-of-factness, then go about their business. They never stopped making friends and taking lovers and bringing their babies to be baptized at the big yellow church overlook-ing the park. They never stopped drinking beers and smoking weed on the stoops of an evening, or roasting pigs on spits in the empty lots; one spit in a lot on Avenue D was jerry-rigged inside the shell of a burned-out car. In all the craziness, people found little ways to put things right. Ann Feinstein collected the broken husky from the side-walk and took him to a vet to be euthanized. She paid the bill herself. Ani Sandoval remembers the winter night after she'd managed, with an unrelenting volley of phone calls, to rescue a mother and her children from a dark, unheated tenement swarming with bugs. "I left her in a warm, clean, white apartment, with beds, with a stove, with pots and pans," she says. As Sandoval headed home in the dark, the first snow began to drift down. "It looked like diamonds were falling all around me. I felt so damn good."

It hardly seems surprising that the buildings reflected all this, that many sagged, went dark, and were reduced, finally, to rubble. So comely and well groomed is the neighborhood twenty-plus years later that people who were there during the rough years shake their heads in wonderment. To convey what it was like back then, they often invoke the wreckage of a major bombing campaign. It's an image that cap-tures the eeriness of the thing; what kind of bomb is it that falls and never makes a sound? "I'm still trying to understand," says Migdalia Torres. "I even asked the priest in church, I said, 'What happened? What went wrong? *Educate* me.'"

If it was a war that happened here, then the easternmost block of 7th Street was always a stronghold. It had been a relatively desirable block for generations, and perhaps it was because of the charming row houses miraculously preserved from the shipbuilding era that people with a little means still were attracted to it in the 1970s. The block remained more diverse, economically and ethnically, than the increasingly ghettoized surrounding area. It was in some ways an intensely close-knit community, a dense network of familiar faces lighting the way home. But I think it's also safe to say that at no time since the Revolution had the turf been more hotly contested. Plenty of people wanted to "save" the Lower East Side, but they often disagreed on just what that meant. By subdividing Manhattan into row upon row of roughly equal-size parcels, the American republic's inaugural generation had ensured that no party would take this place in a clean sweep. The struggle would be waged lot by city lot, building by building.

There were casualties. No. 239 was one. These years—the 1960s through the 1980s—compose the immediate backstory to my own time on the street in the '90s, and it was indeed during this period that the building sustained a killing wound. That's all I'd wanted to know about when I first asked, *What happened here?* But the answer to even that narrow question is more complex than I ever imagined.

During the '60s and '70s, No. 239 was operated as a rental building, initially with its longtime owners, David and Eva Bookman, in residence on the parlor floor. Mr. Bookman, as he was known, had apparently taken care of his fragile sister, Eva, all their adult lives. Or maybe it was dark-eyed, silent Eva who took care of him, going out to work as a cleaner while her brother, a small, somewhat portly man, stayed home. They slept in single beds in the same room, the apartment filled with the accumulated stuff of decades. There were shelves of liquor given as gifts at the Jewish holidays; Mr. Bookman didn't drink. The keys of former tenants, some of them long, old-fashioned skeleton keys, he kept, to no particular purpose, in an enamel pail. He doted on his very obese cat, Pancho. The cat was missing teeth and ate only baby food.

For two decades after Mr. Bookman purchased No. 239 from Simon Wieder in 1939, he'd rented to Jewish households—Goldstein,

Meisler, the Wieder brothers. By the '60s, though, the neighborhood had become more ethnically diverse. Bookman rented to a few Chinese, including Han Ding Hung, who spoke no English and had worked in the merchant marine; perhaps he was the same Han Ding Hung listed as "boy" in the 1952 manifest of aliens aboard the vessel SS *Hai Chang* arriving in the port of San Francisco out of Kobe, Japan. While Hung was on the top floor, Judith Harlan moved into the Wieders' old apartment on the second floor. She must have seemed a familiar type to Bookman. A reform Democrat, not long after she moved in, Harlan and her political partner, Humberto Aponte, defeated the regulars to fill the roles of male and female (and, not coincidentally, white and Puerto Rican) co-leaders of the assembly district that covered the Lower East Side.

Their job as leaders was not so much to deliver votes—there were essentially no Republicans in the district by now—but to get out constantly among the people and bring them what they needed. So they held "rat parties," rousing the health department and other city agencies to join in inspecting the most dangerously infested buildings. They advocated for a new subway line to service the East Side, because Hispanic and black people often couldn't flag down a taxi and had no way to get to the hospital in a hurry. Harlan attended the first great smoke-in at Tompkins Square Park, where one stoned participant gleefully told a television news reporter, "Trees grow in Brooklyn, but grass grows on the Lower East Side!" Harlan hailed from a middle-class family in Niagara Falls, New York. When she'd won the election, her mother had said, "That's wonderful, honey. Can you move now?"[3]

After about five years with the Bookmans, she did move, and was replaced on the second floor by a friend of a friend, another fervent pol named Jane Scheidler. "I was a nice white girl from the Midwest," says Scheidler, who now lives in Texas and works for the state environmental agency, "so I was okay with Mr. Bookman." She was very much a young woman of her time—graduate of the class of '68, freshly sprung from a brief early marriage, diving into work and politics (she'd soon be working full-time for the state senate campaign of feminist trailblazer Carol Bellamy), meeting interesting people, and staying up late. She was having a ball. The minute she turned her key in the door of No. 239 at night, Mr. Bookman would poke his head out to make sure she got in okay. And she liked that, too. Like Harlan, Scheidler grew fond of the man who plied them with kreplachs. The apartment, meanwhile, was lovely, with creamy, satin-finish walls, wood floors stained very dark, and a nicely tiled bathroom.

As it turned out, though, Scheidler's time at No. 239 would be short. Mr. Bookman had been sick when she moved in. By her last days in his building she was visiting him regularly at Bellevue Hospital, where he was dying from colon cancer. A few months after he died, Scheidler moved across the street to perhaps the first building on the block to become a "co-op," in which individuals purchase their apartments as shares in a housing corporation. She'd meanwhile been drawn deeper into block politics, heading up a survey that involved checking every window on the block for the metal gates then considered indispensable security equipment. It was while climbing up fire escapes and onto roofs and down into the yards of 7th Street that Scheidler and a neighbor from down the block, Otis Maclay, fell for each other. They moved in together at No. 248, the six-story tenement-turned-co-op. That was another project. Together they filled Dumpster after Dumpster with debris until they had a raw open space adjoined by a single separate room that became a repository for junk—"the bad room," they called it. They ate at a huge wooden dining table inherited from Mr. Bookman, and slept, at times, under the thin cotton blankets marked "Bellevue Hospital" he'd pressed on Scheidler during his final days. Scheidler and Maclay wed in 1974. That year Scheidler scrawled in red Crayola across the front of their tax return, "We use our own names but we are married."

In the rush of those days, Scheidler lost track of goings-on at No. 239, except to note a general decay in that section of the block, and that a cousin of the Bookmans had come from Queens to take charge of the building and, evidently, collect Eva. The cousin quickly sold the building to a couple by the name of Malek. The Maleks had a reputation as small-time speculators that endured long enough to reach my ear during the late 1990s. I never knew they once had owned our building. In fact, by the mid-'70s, they'd scooped up a generous handful of properties in the neighborhood, including all five buildings from No. 239 to the corner of Avenue C.[4]

What neighbors remember from those years is that the three little row houses next to No. 239 repeatedly burned and gradually emptied. One recalls an eccentric middle-age woman named Grace driven out of No. 237 by a fire, which killed her cat, Rowena. When another former resident showed me a picture of that building circa 1979, I was shocked, having expected at least some vestige of the attractive residence of Republican leader Sam Koenig, pictured in late-1930s tax photos; instead it showed a windowless shell crusted with pigeon shit. A discarded mattress lay beside the stoop.

For a long time I thought that No. 239 also went vacant during the last years of the 1970s. But I'd been relying on address directories, which are based on telephone numbers; not everyone had a telephone. Neighbors recall, on the second floor where Scheidler had lived, a Mrs. Perez and her several teenage children. A couple of residents also remember glimpsing, through the strange perceptual knotholes city living opens up, an Italian–Puerto Rican family that occupied the parlor floor in the late '70s. A boy from down the block paid particular attention to one of the kids in that family, a girl named Rosie. "She wasn't really pretty, it was just her mannerisms and her style," he explains. "She was sort of tomboyish, not a laid-back kind of girl but more of an action-oriented girl. And I think I found that kind of cute." He noticed that her father seemed to have an intransigent drinking problem. He used to watch Rosie talking with her boyfriend outside No. 239 and, more than once, saw the boy "take a little over-handed swing at her."

In the mid-twentieth century, a Spanish-speaking world began to rise like a sun over the blocks east of Avenue A, and by the 1970s, that world had a name: Loisaida. It was a Hispanicized and even distinctly New York–Puerto Rican way of evoking the old working class Lower East Side.* During the mass-migration years of the '50s and '60s,

---

*Though Dominicans already were settling there in increasing numbers (by 1990 they'd establish a major presence), for now this particular barrio was dominated by Puerto Ricans.

Puerto Ricans mixed with their Orthodox Jewish neighbors in the peculiar intimacy of the ghetto. Ani Sandoval remembers lighting stoves on Saturdays for observant Jewish families, collecting a nickel from each. Carlos "Chino" Garcia, a key leader in the neighborhood's Puerto Rican community, remembers Jewish pals stopping by his place after school (where they'd eat their fill of *treyf* delights). The Puerto Ricans shopped from the Jewish pushcarts that lined Avenue C into the '60s, snacked at their corner delis, and bought cheap clothes at their stands on Orchard Street.

As they settled in, they began to lay their own maps of home over the cityscape. They brought a new flavor to St. Brigid's, the Catholic church overlooking the park at Avenue B, which had been Irish, and to the Church of the Most Holy Redeemer on 4th Street, which had been German, arranging little outdoor shrines of the Virgin Mother or a favorite saint in brightly painted robes and ringed with artificial flowers. They opened tiny storefronts selling fried-pork *cuchifritos*, and bodegas where, in the early years, you could buy rice and beans in bulk from sacks, as well as the root vegetables and tropical fruits that are staples in the Caribbean diet. The *piraguero* appeared, pushing his cart with its block of ice and brightly colored syrups. Streets that in the nineteenth century had been filled with the sounds of German brass bands or Italian organ grinders now pulsed with Latin salsa. Sometimes it was just the percussive energy of congas and maracas played on a stoop; other times recorded music, topped with vocals and horns, poured from the popular new transistor radios.

Like quite a few earlier immigrants to the city, many Puerto Ricans had known a rural poverty more profound than the poverty they would know in New York, but that, emotionally, was inextricable from the place that had conditioned their childhood senses—a place, in this case, of blue waters, mountains thickly covered in vegetation, and balmy nights. They came to the great northern city for the same reason many a previous generation had come, to make a living.

For me, the image of this trajectory is a photograph of Carmen Pabon, an informal but widely recognized voice for the Lower East Side in its hardship years. The picture shows Pabon shortly after she arrived in the city in the late 1940s. She reclines on the stone perimeter wall of Central Park, her hair coiffed in soft waves. She wears a wool coat in a dressy, feminine cut, stockings, and ankle-strap heels. Pabon, now in her eighties, shows me a lot of family pictures as we talk in her longtime home in the Lillian Wald projects that run between Avenue D and East River Park from Houston Street to 6th Street, but this is the one that strikes me. With those long, elegant hands she'd snipped threads and glued toys together in factories around town, and considered it nice work if you could get it. She'd come from inland Puerto Rico, a town called Ciales. "I grew up in a country so poor," she tells me. "My mother used to work on the farm, with tobacco, and she used to take us to the farm to pick coffee." The little house where they lived was lit by oil lamps or the moon. Pabon learned some English in school, made her way to San Juan, where she worked in a health clinic, then came to New York. Here, she earned $25 a week, enough to pay her own living expenses and send regular money home to her mother and the small daughter she'd left behind. It was an old story.

As in parts of Europe during its mass emigrations of the nineteenth century, Puerto Rico's economy was shifting, fast, from a largely agricultural base to one driven by factory production in coastal cities. On average the shift would raise the local standard of living. But in the short run employment fell overall, and in certain regions opportunity all but evaporated. The United States—and this set the Puerto Rican migration apart—was as much implicated in these "push" factors spurring Puerto Ricans to leave the island as in the "pull" that drew them to New York. When the United States took over the island from the Spanish in 1898, the Puerto Rican economy became focused on creating products for the American marketplace—textiles sewn by women in their homes, tobacco products, and especially sugar, which now enjoyed favored, tariff-free entry into that market. This meant large-scale investment by North American companies in cane land and sugar mills on the island, and rising fortunes for a number of local landowning families. But it had a downside. Land that was now capitalized, taxed, and placed into sugar production was no longer available to the poor families who had used it, often informally, to raise their food. Agricultural workers' survival now depended on U.S.-imported staples purchased with a meager wage that dried up each year during the *tiempo muerto*. It was partly to address these problems that in 1947 the Puerto Rican government launched Operation Bootstrap, an initiative to attract investment in manufacturing on the island with tax breaks, cheap labor, and free access to the U.S. market. By the summer of 1950, eighty new manufactories were up and running. But during Bootstrap's first decade, manufacturing job gains were more than offset by losses in sugar and other industries.[5]

Wherever they came from, the people repopulating the East Side during these years found themselves facing another historic economic transition—a crisis, really—in New York City. Manufacturing, in steep decline, left urban areas. The city's factory work all but vanished, replaced by service and government jobs, the most coveted of which put a premium on education and fluency in English, the worst of which offered very low wages and little chance to rise—"assistant assistant/to the assistant's assistant/assistant lavaplatos [dishwasher]," as Pedro Pietri, cofounder of the Lower East Side's Nuyorican Poets Café, put it in his 1973 poem "Puerto Rican Obituary."[6] After a long period of growth, the American economy overall stalled; in the 1970s, New Yorkers' income fell in real terms for the first time since World War II. Meanwhile, the city's steady postwar loss of middle-class (and white) people to the suburbs reached a critical point; New York sustained a net loss of 800,000 residents during the 1970s. The city spiraled into its famous fiscal crisis, laying off thousands of employees, including the sanitation workers, police, and firemen who had helped make the city livable.[7]

It happened, in addition, that all this came at a critical juncture in the life cycle of the neighborhood's buildings. With their balky old boilers and leaking roofs, many were due for an infusion of cash. No. 239, for example, built without a great deal of care on shifty fill, was some 130 years old in 1970 but had received timely improvements by various buyers, most recently the Bookmans. In 1940 they had replaced the rickety wooden stair Al Wieder remembered from his boyhood with a steel one that helped support the building itself; in the '50s they added a new boiler and chimney. The Maleks made no such investments, nor, of course, were they alone in this.[8] During this period the cost of materials was rising. As a result of an embargo by oil-producing countries, energy costs spiked. But given their condition and the poverty of the neighborhood, getting more rent out of these buildings wasn't in the cards. Longtime landlords bailed out in droves, sending their buildings down the real-estate food chain to those who would manage them for the short term, ceasing maintenance, tax payments, and even basic services like heat, in order to consume their last drop of value—a little rent, some insurance money perhaps, the scrap value of their fixtures— and leave them for dead. Eventually, whole swaths of urban landscape were treated literally like garbage: torched, crushed, carted away for disposal. In the zone of greatest destruction, between Avenues B and D, Houston to 14th Street, the '70s saw the erasure of nearly half of all privately owned housing units and a correspondingly massive dispersal of the people who had lived there.[9]

In recalling our block's most trying years, people who were there will tend to mention the seemingly abrupt arrival in the late 1960s of dope. Suddenly it was everywhere. This, too, was connected to larger historical events. Even as Puerto Ricans and others were moving to New York after World War II, certain New York Italian crime syndicates were putting together the elements of an international trade in heroin, one that, until it was replaced by other schemes, joined Turkish poppy growers with Corsican gangsters in Marseilles (the "French Connection"), who would refine the drug and secret it into New York's busy port. At the same time, the mafia, facing law enforcement pressures, was withdrawing from direct dealing to the New York public (which had long included a preponderance of the country's heroin users).[10] Loisaida, with its idled labor force and marginal status, became host to an open-air, retail drug operation that catered, yes, to the neighborhood, but also to the whole city and even the region. When the police organized a massive crackdown in the early '80s, one law enforcement official told the *East Village Eye* that about half the arrestees were from outside Manhattan. Some had come from as far away as Boston to buy drugs near the top of the supply chain (where they were purer and cheaper) for resale at home.[11] In the '80s, heroin peddling was joined and to some extent replaced by cocaine (including crack) sales. The drug trade put money in some locals' pockets. But as a local industry it proved highly toxic, an accelerant to the spread of violence, addiction, and, by the mid-1980s, AIDS.

It was hard times for the people of Loisaida. Shut off from mainstream economic activity, some essentially scavenged whatever living they could. They collected the dregs from the milk cartons piled up outside the public school in the next block. They showed up outside local groceries and offered to carry patrons' bags for tips. In her study of thirty-six households living near a storefront at 4th Street and Avenue B in the 1970s, anthropologist Jagna Wojcicka Sharff describes mothers who work off the books for subminimum wage to supplement their welfare checks. One man commutes five hours per day to work in a Connecticut factory. One works as an extra in police lineups, while another breeds stolen purebred dogs and a third buys blue jeans wholesale and peddles them door to door.[12] Girls can make $10 to $15 a week for twenty to thirty hours bagging groceries at the Key Food on Avenue A, but the boys are such notorious thieves that the security guard, a large Jamaican man nicknamed Jumbo, won't even let them in the store.[13] Philip Long's younger sister, Ardell, recalls a day when residents of the block raced after a truck leaking food stamps. Her mother and others bleached off the ink marks that indicated the stamps had already been used and, for a while at least, delighted in foods they normally couldn't afford—steaks, pork chops, brand-name Froot Loops.

They lived in a world that was physically disintegrating—mailboxes and buzzer systems busted, garbage collecting in the potholed street, cockroaches swarming up through crumbling foundations. Even a hot shower wasn't an altogether reliable amenity in some buildings. I keep thinking about where *I* was in the 1970s—listening, with anxious longing, to the same Linda Ronstadt cover the Puerto Rican girls in Sharff's study would sing, again and again, in unison, a plaintive, homesick love song for a place called Blue Bayou.[14] I remember, looking down from the dome-shaped window on the stairs, how red the pyracantha berries looked against the drab midwinter yard. It's so strange. Were we even living in the same world?

In American life there always have been people who moved against the cultural traffic. During the second half of the twentieth century, a

steady stream of individuals loosely affiliated with various counterculture movements reversed the trajectory of the majority and headed into
the city to mingle with the urban poor. Many found their way to the
East Village.

Each group affected the development of the neighborhood and
telegraphed across the country an aesthetic that implied a whole set
of moods and values. Beatniks admired the city's black jazzmen, and
established, in the West Village but also the Lower East Side, smoky
hole-in-the-wall cafés where they'd take in long sets in dark, slim
clothes that gave them the appearance of silhouettes. They wrote outrageous poems. They swallowed or shot speed. The hippies grew mus-
taches and long hair. They explored Eastern religions, embraced the
civil rights movement, and protested the war in Vietnam. They lined
St. Marks Place just west of Tompkins Square with shops selling rock
and folk records, a dizzying array of drug paraphernalia, and flamboy-
ant personal adornments. During the hippie years, at the Paradox, a
popular restaurant specializing in macrobiotic foods a few blocks west
of No. 239, one young woman advised a reporter that plain brown rice
should be chewed at least twenty-five times to release its "flavors and
perfumes," while another, calling herself Sagittarius, remarked that
the names your parents give you aren't who you really *are*.[15] Advertisements in the alternative journal *East Village Other* announced opportunities for nude modeling, "Skiing for Swingers Only," and
consort with a guy named Ray, "Cunnilinguist." ("Anita," another ad
pleaded, "Please Contact Grandma and Grandpa—Very Urgent.")[16]
Then, in the '80s, New Wave and punk rockers came on the scene.
Vintage clothing shops sold sharkskin suits and cat's-eye glasses. You
had bleached-blond or jet-black spiky hair, zippered leather jackets,
leopard-skin prints, vinyl, fake fur, nylon, and fishnet. From a hip
apartment on our easternmost block of 7th Street, husband-and-wife
writers Joel Rose and Catherine Texier published a fiction magazine
whose title, *Between C & D*, proclaimed its avant-gardism by locating
itself in a place that had come to stand for extremity itself. The journal carried the tagline "Sex. Drugs. Violence. Danger. Computers,"
or, alternatively, "Romance. Risk. Rationale. Random Violence. Computers," or, indeed, "Death. Disease. Heartache. Subway crime. Com-

puters."[17] Each copy was individually printed in dot-matrix on computer paper with holes down the sides, and bound in a plastic ziplock
bag meant to evoke the tiny clear packets of dope purveyed on local
street corners. As one of Rose's own stories began, "New York's always been a tough town, bro."[18]

People didn't necessarily identify with any of these movements or
aesthetics. The point is simply that one model, already established in
the 1950s, made the blocks east of Avenue A the very nerve center of
American Otherness. There were those who self-consciously placed
themselves in that camp. And there were others who, enticed by the
promise of a bigger apartment, perhaps, discovered in themselves a
willingness to be there—which itself marked them as different.

Betty-Carol Sellen, a librarian at Brooklyn College, had been hunting for years for a place she could afford to buy when a friend saw an
ad in the *Village Voice* offering co-op apartments for sale at what
seemed a ludicrous price—roughly $500. Her partner balked at the lo-
cation. "'Forget it,' she says. 'Just forget it, I'm not going there!'" Sellen
recalls. "And I thought, well, let me just go look." Making a home on
the block did prove a grueling endeavor, between the major renovation
required to make the apartment itself attractive and the various block
projects Sellen took on, from raising funds for new high-intensity street
lights to tutoring local kids. In 1971, astonished by the brazen drug
operation that recently had come to the block—"just like a drug su-
permarket," she says, "everything right there"—Sellen raised a loud
hue and cry, drawing the attention of the *Daily News* and even the police commissioner himself.[19] So serious were the ensuing threats
against her person that Sellen was assigned a police escort for weeks.
"So it got kind of heavy duty," she says. "I also got very determined. I
mean, I was kind of surprised, but I thought, I've been working on this
apartment for eight months now, I want this apartment, I *want* to live
here, I'm fine with living on this block, and I'm not going to lose. I'm
just not going to lose."

The block's surprising human juxtapositions could feel redeeming, en-
larging. It was, as Sellen puts it, "the most *community* community I've
ever lived in." Former residents talk in the most personal terms about

heady days on this block where for the first time in their lives they encountered Puerto Rican people, or white people, or gay people, or people who made art, or people who were willing to build things with their own hands. They held regular block cleanups and hosted free lunch programs for kids. In the summer they threw fiestas in which residents danced in the street, a "mini Coney Island," Philip Long's memoir recalls, offering "Spanish food, Italian food, Jewish food, Indian food, Greek food, Jamaican food, and of course soul food." In the early 1970s a filmmaker living several doors from No. 239 went over to the boys' club at 10th and A to find young actors for a scruffy, feel-good "semi-documentary" called *Street of the Flower Boxes*, set and shot on the block. "Being kids of the ghetto persuasion," says one, Edwin Sepulveda, "we were real reluctant to talk to this guy. We were like, is he a pedophile? You know we were street smart." But before long they were hanging out in the filmmaker's row house, playing with his kids, getting paid, and having a blast. Urban density always has had its rewards, nowhere more than on this narrow piece of 7th Street.

But now, the stress of it—the mental and physical energy required just to get safely through another day—mounted steadily. Illicit economic activity, especially the drug trade that spread like an algae bloom beginning in the late '60s and early '70s, generated two kinds of crime. It elevated a few outlaws to positions of awe. They employed a targeted but ruthless application of force to deter would-be interlopers from their market space, silence witnesses, or collect debts. People in the neighborhood made up songs about some of these characters, remembers Edwin Torres. You didn't mess with them. Although there was plenty of ambivalence about the police in the community (sometimes expressed in bottle-chucking), as Awi Perkins, who grew up on 5th Street, puts it, "it didn't matter, because they didn't come anyway." So mostly people deferred to the tough guys. The Torreses, for example, lived above a social club where men would drink and play dominoes late into the night. Fed up, one local loudly told off the family that ran the place for its various offenses against law and neighborliness. "And one night," says Torres, "coming home in his truck—he used to deliver breads—right here on 7th Street, as he turned, they shot him. It was crazy. As he's turning on Avenue D coming down 7th

Street, *bam-bam-bam-bam-bam!*, and the truck just rolls, bam, it comes to a stop. Everybody saw who did it, and nobody knew nothing." Adds Migdalia Torres, "I mean, just getting into the building, we had to tell all these people, 'Excuse us, excuse us, excuse us.' You had to put on a different facade to survive."

Even so, you could avoid the heavyweights' crosshairs by keeping your head down. A more general problem was the swelling wave of muggings and break-ins. This, residents say, was fed especially by addicts whose cravings made their forays after a little cash frequent, desperate, and bold. Everything had to be locked down. After being mugged twice, Charles Levin, a trumpet player who lived at No. 278, took karate lessons, practicing for hours each day. He also arranged a plan with a neighbor, Tony Rivera, by which the latter would come running with a lead pipe if ever he heard Levin cry out the signal, "Hey, rube!" It worked, sort of, thwarting a robbery attempt but not before Levin was slashed across the wrist with a knife that looked to him like the one his dad, who owned a kosher deli in Bayonne, used to chop onions. He moved across town.[20] In 1974, a forty-year-old man from 6th Street was busted in the block's old synagogue while trying to rip off some relics and a section of brass railing.[21] As the '70s gave way to the '80s, block association newsletters became increasingly preoccupied with security. There were instructions on how to give a complete suspect description, safety tips for getting around ("Have the front door key READY when you approach your building"), and police-issued guidance on devices to thwart home invasion ("Hinges exposed on the outside of a door should always have non-removable hinge pins").[22]

By the time I moved onto the block in the early 1990s, murders, rapes, robberies, and burglaries in the precinct had each dropped by roughly half compared with ten years earlier, and crime rates continued to tumble.[23] Nobody ever hurt me or anyone in my family. Nobody ever took anything from us. I never heard gunshots or saw a dead body lying in the street, stashed between two buildings, or dangling from a tree, as earlier residents tell me they did. When I lived there, I couldn't really understand the old-timers' intermixture of relief and strained vigilance. Their confrontation with the problem of death had been frighteningly immediate. They also understood something I didn't about buildings; they knew what it was like to watch them die, too.

One of the first signs of ill health, property tax delinquency, wasn't always visible from the outside. By the end of the '70s, about a dozen properties on our block had entered foreclosure or had liens placed for tax arrears, including the Maleks' four buildings between No. 239 and the corner of Avenue C. Some of these were sold at public auction or by the owner before the opportunity for redemption closed. A few languished in a legal limbo that went on for years.

Dwindling human occupancy was a more obvious signal of a building's impending demise, and it both promoted and resulted from the surest, most vivid sign of all: fire. Eric Felisbret remembers standing on the rooftops of 7th Street watching fires nearly every week and worrying that, one day, his own place would burn. It was an understandable anxiety, because fire was not only ubiquitous, it was also, in its origins, mysterious and multivalent. In 1978, in a 1.7 square-mile area that stretches from 14th Street to the Brooklyn Bridge, there were 354 suspicious fires, 290 of them in occupied buildings. Fire officials pointed to landlords, who would inflate the paper value of their buildings by transferring ownership several times from one bogus entity to another, then have them torched to collect insurance. But sometimes, one city official told the *East Village Eye*, the landlord would just cut off services and rely on tenants to set the fire.[24] Being burned out moved you up the waiting list for a highly coveted place in the newer, cleaner public housing projects. Unsecured and vacant buildings furthermore invited random acts of malicious mischief, like the incident in July 1977 when a teenager set a fire on the fifth floor of a building just behind No. 239 on 8th Street and, once firefighters went to work there, set another on the second floor, trapping the men inside. Marty Celic of Ladder Company 15 fell to his death while trying to leap, loaded with gear, into a waiting cherry picker.[25] And finally, you had the drug users, homeless people, and assorted itinerants who occupied abandoned spaces and built fires there for warmth. Michael Diaz of No. 258 recalls getting word that an acquaintance of his, nicknamed Remache ("Rivet" or "Spike"), had lit himself a fire in a garbage can in one of the walk-ups near Avenue D, possibly because he'd been drinking and

In the late 1960s, these blocks between Avenues C and D were chockablock with tenements and other buildings. By 1983, they had the otherworldly look of a ruin or war zone. This image by photographer Marlis Momber looks north from a 4th Street roof onto 5th Street, 6th Street, and the exposed backs of buildings on 7th Street, still largely intact. At the center of the frame, the block's old Hungarian synagogue remains with its domed windows. At upper right are the high-rise brick housing projects and a large power plant. In the foreground, children seesaw in a makeshift playground. (Courtesy of Marlis Momber.)

wound up there, or maybe just seeking shelter for the night. Says Diaz, "We had to explain to him, 'You can't do that, you know. If you get cold, come over here. Don't do that, because you'll burn everybody to death!'" Stanley Valladares Smith of No. 249 remembers coming home from work one day and spotting, inside a window at the corner of 7th and D, a tall plume of flame.[26] It turned out the men camped out there were lighting an open gas line. People express a sense-memory of those fires. The curl of smoke. The roar that sounded like wind. The flash in the window at night. The crunch, crunch, crunch of charred timber underfoot.

Finally, there came demolition, a process that wiped out substantial portions of 6th and 8th streets between C and D, leaving 7th Street largely, but not entirely, intact. The first building on the block to go was a tenement on the north side, just off the corner of Avenue D. Then came No. 259, toward the middle of the block, and, in 1977, the twice-fired tenement No. 251. Typically there would be no official notice. Contractors for the city would simply turn up, sometimes hiring local volunteers on the spot. It was getting rid of a nuisance, that's all, and it was heavy work. "They took them down manually," explains Valladares Smith. "They paid people to just stand in the building with hammers and knock the bricks until it fell in on itself floor by floor. You could saw a few beams. Many of the beams had fallen in anyway. So the sixth floor would be knocked in and landed on the floor of the fifth, and then that floor would be knocked in and landed on the floor of the fourth. Then you wound up with like a two-story pile of bricks. And then the bulldozer came and shoveled it into dump trucks, then leveled the ground—because the basement is now full of bricks, they just leveled it as rubble—and put up a chain-link fence in the front. Finished."

On our block, in the 1960s, some of the houses in what had become Rabbis' Row or Judges' Row, rather than falling into the hands of slumlords, went to artists and other assorted lefties of middling means, who would live there as resident landlords in keeping with 7th Street's long tradition. One of the new owners was a college-educated landscape architect named Charles Bergemann, who, along with a couple of friends, purchased a row house on the south side of the street from a resident rabbi. Bergemann set himself apart by beginning a career as landlord and rental agent. By 1966 he owned three buildings on the street, whose eighty-nine units rented for between $40 and $60 a month. That fall, his tenants in a double tenement on the south side of the block—Nos. 248–252—actually picketed City Hall to protest "overzealous" enforcements against Bergemann for minor buildings code violations. It was an all but unheard of act of solidarity by "students and bearded budding artist types" who clearly saw their landlord as one of their own. Good vibes aside, it seems Bergemann was working hard for pretty slim margins; at the protest, he complained that he'd had to pay $43.01 for a city-ordered emergency repair to a stopped-up drain, when he could have had the problem fixed for $8.[27]

Soon, he began to formulate an alternative. Maybe he could turn around a faltering rental building by converting it to cooperative housing, long the province of more well-to-do New Yorkers. Essentially, you'd sell the apartments by the piece, not the bunch. While would-be landlords saw only headaches in these old heaps, the sweetener for the buyers of individual apartments was the dramatically lowered barrier to homeownership; the upfront cost of an apartment would be a trifling $500 to $1,000. Buyers would need to have some income, of course, because they'd have to pay monthly maintenance fees that would service a mortgage for the building's purchase price, as well as cover the cost of considerable renovations to wiring, plumbing, and other systems. A lot of the work they'd do themselves, so they'd do best if they had some of the practical skills Bergemann himself possessed. And they would need to proceed with a unity of purpose. The more financially and otherwise reliable owners a building could attract and keep, the better off it would be; each co-op building that succeeded on the block would make it that much easier for the others. And since Bergemann himself would have skin in the game—as no bank would come near these properties, he'd generally buy the buildings on credit from the seller—he, too, would have every reason to promote the co-ops' continued health. In an era when creating a co-op was a fairly obscure phenomenon even in much fancier neighborhoods, this model was a true innovation.

Bergemann launched himself into a project to preserve, beautify—and market—the whole block, serving refreshments at work parties, and driving his truck to the country to purchase the spring-flowering trees he loved and for which the block was known. Even thirty years later, some block residents assign him an almost mythic significance. He was, by all accounts, a compelling person, svelte and stylish, with long, dirty-blond hair, blue eyes, and a drooping mustache. One neighbor remembers he was the first person around to don one of the then-fashionable long sheepskin coats with embroidery on the outside. Another recalls his oft-worn work boots. In the early '60s he'd married Olivia Borrero, who'd come to New York from Puerto Rico's southern cane lands as a severely undernourished child of twelve. In her teenage years she'd gone to public night school, then worked as a bookkeeper. After marrying she went back to school and became a registered nurse. As Olivia Bergemann observed her husband interacting with the gay residents he'd helped bring to the block, she came to understand that his own sexual orientation made him "part of that group," though neither one of them articulated that, and she accepted it the same way she accepted his encompassing devotion to this project on 7th Street. "He was such a beautiful person," she says. "And he was very unusual. I thought he had such fantastic ideas. That's what I really loved about him." Chuck Bergemann was a man of wide-ranging and sophisticated tastes. In the summertime, say neighbors, he traveled to exotic places nobody else had ever been. He had a confidence so cool some found it arrogant. He picked out colors for other people's buildings. "He had this force in him," says Fred Seiden, a 7th Street neighbor who bought an apartment from him. "He was so sure of what he was doing. Not a lot of people have that feeling of being absolutely sure about the world."

By 1974, Bergemann had bought and converted six buildings on the block—"slum co-ops," he called them. As this project gained momentum and began to spread into the next block, some residents were disturbed by the spectacle of his buildings emptying of one population—poor people of color—and refilling with another—mostly white middle-class people. Their testimony today is that he made no bones about the sort of people he wanted to attract to the block, and it wasn't large, welfare-dependent families paying regulated rents that would scarcely keep a building's lights on. Indeed his habit was to place classifieds in the *Village Voice* with such specifications as "Prefer bus'n persons, Students o.k."[28] "He was contemptuous of other people, not of all other people but of people who got in his way," says Paul Broaddus, who moved into one of Bergemann's buildings in the late '60s, later purchasing an apartment. "Most of the people who got in his way were very poor people on welfare, one or two or three class levels below his own."

Broaddus, along with neighbor Ann Feinstein and Fred Seiden from the next block (who like Broaddus had purchased apartments from Bergemann), began investigating his methods. This was partly inspired by the former super of Nos. 272, 274, and 278, adjoining six-flight walk-ups Bergemann managed and, it was rumored, wanted to "co-op." A West Virginian with a strong Appalachian accent and several grown children (one of whom reportedly kept an impressive collection of firearms in the basement), this woman claimed Bergemann had fired her when she refused to aid him in underhanded eviction efforts. At the block fair in the summer of 1975, someone hung banners from the fire escape of one of these buildings: "We don't want Chuck Bergemann for our agent"; "No co-op speculators in our building." Some of Bergemann's opponents took to openly hectoring him when he brought people onto the block to show apartments.[29] Olivia Bergemann says there also were physical attacks and acts of vandalism on the couple's residence. Bergemann still had supporters—Jane Scheidler was one, having been persuaded by respected friends who were "big, unequivocal Chuck fans"—but the momentum was turning against him. "Chuck Bergemann was trying to rip off all the cribs on 7th Street," says Kwame Adansi-Bona, who would soon begin a decades-long residence at No. 272 himself. "Everybody talked about him like a dog."

The rumors and accusations flying around were myriad—that Bergemann had shut off tenants' heat and hot water, kept them in the dark about his plans to convert their buildings, refused to accept their rent, and then evicted them for nonpayment. But what were the facts? "It was all so apocryphal," says Otis Maclay. "It was this miasma."

An exposé by the *Soho Weekly News* on a co-op conversion under way by Bergemann in the next block offered as exhibit a certain Joey Mendez, who'd lived in the building in question, No. 184 E. 7th St., for nineteen years. Mendez had heard rumors that the building had a new owner, and said a man he'd never met before had told him he could stay if he paid $1,000, money he didn't have. "I don't think he wants Puerto Ricans living here," he told the *News*. "I'm not sure." Mendez, the article said, "figure[d] to move soon" from the building, which was more than half vacant, with two apartments burned out, its hallways "tight, dark, and littered with dogshit."[30]

The fact is, if someone wanted to dislodge Joey Mendez and others like him, it probably wouldn't have been very hard. Delivery of a co-op proposal sent even knowledgeable tenants in sounder neighborhoods into crisis mode. Co-op conversion often seemed like "a case of 'buy or else,'" one letter writer to the *Times* complained; it was a complex game of chicken in which "all the protagonists [were] lawyers," quipped *New York* magazine in 1980.[31] Legally, to go ahead with a conversion, the sponsor needed 35 percent of existing tenants to agree to buy in, an unlikely event in a slum tenement. But on the Lower East Side, where abandonment and displacement were so widespread anyway, it's easy to see how a dwindling, nonbuying tenancy might be encouraged to melt away before a co-op proposal was registered, as required by law, with the attorney general's office, or even announced.

Many poor residents were keen to get *out* of the tenements, not grapple and pay their way in. Why would Joey Mendez marshal whatever social and economic resources lay at his disposal, just to stay in a place that every day became more of a shit hole? Likewise, neighborhood housing activists facing a wholesale retreat of real estate capital from the area were not yet focused on redevelopment as another potential cause of displacement. Even a little later in the game, when the market began to perk and tenants received offers of cash to relinquish their rent-regulated apartments for co-op conversions or so the landlord could renovate and charge more rent, many low-income renters didn't foresee that their right of occupancy would one day prove highly valuable, in fact, all but irreplaceable. When they'd ask for his advice on such offers, says Edwin Torres, he'd tell them, "'No, hold on to it, that's home. They can't get you out. Forget the money, you got a home. That's more important.' I can't tell you how many people I advised like that," he says. But a buyout of, say, $10,000 looked like a fortune to some. "I am truly saddened by it," says Torres.

In any event, when Paul Broaddus conducted interviews with tenants in No. 184—the building under conversion in the next block—mainly what he heard was that Bergemann had applied "verbal pressure." "I didn't get the goods," he says, "because there weren't any goods to get." The block activists nonetheless brought their information to the attorney general's office, where officials launched their own investigation. In July 1975 a grand jury issued a forty-count indictment that included charges of grand larceny based in part on the fact that, during part of the time Bergemann and an associate were selling shares in the co-op (around the same time Joey Mendez was moving out), the building was actually owned by the City of New York, which had taken title to secure back taxes. But a few of the very buyers the partnership was accused of swindling gave affidavits supporting Bergemann, saying that he had been assured by his codefendant, Helen Barrera, that through her political connections she could get the taxes waived. "We took the gamble," wrote one couple, a dentist and a corporate law librarian, "as did Charles Bergemann himself."[32]

Bergemann was convicted on relatively minor charges involving a failure to register as a broker and to segregate purchase monies in a special account. The conviction, however, was soon followed by a broad injunction banning Bergemann from just about any activity having to do with co-op sales. So Nos. 272, 274, and 278 were, from one point of view, saved and, from another, lost. Their beleaguered landlord deeded them over to the super, who soon forfeited them, partially occupied, to tax foreclosure. They filled up with unofficial tenants who would live there at very low cost but without benefit of title or lease; the city called them squatters. Bergemann never would realize his aspiration to, as he put it to the *Soho News*, "do Sixth, Seventh and Eighth Streets between C and D." Upon his conviction, word got around fast. "So many people were sad," says Fred Seiden, who felt quite the opposite. "So many people were upset." Seiden says he actually heard one resident, an elderly woman, make the dramatic utterance,

"The great eagle has fallen." Maybe so. But the basic model was in place. If anyone wondered whether a middle-class co-op could ever fly in this place at the far edge of the world, well, they pretty much had their answer.

One day in 1979, Daniel Murray, a thirty-five-year-old freelance journalist from California, strolled east from his Greenwich Village apartment. He'd recently lost his father and inherited a modest sum of money, which he was looking to invest in real estate. Finally he approached Avenue C and descended along a slight incline onto the little tree-lined stretch where 7th Street comes to an end. "This was a block that had survived," he says. "Everything to the north and south was burnt out, was just redbrick rubble, like the South Bronx when presidential candidates used to have their pictures taken amid the devastation. It looked like a war had happened there."

Murray ran into Chuck Bergemann—"a lovely man," he recalls, "a bigger-than-life human being"—and it was Bergemann who put him in touch with Morris Malek, proprietor of No. 239 and at least a few other properties in danger of, or already in, foreclosure due to unpaid taxes. Murray then embarked upon protracted, difficult, and, it seemed to him, largely irrational negotiations with Malek to buy the property. He remembers the old man sitting in his cramped office in the rear of a storefront on Avenue B, where he also sold used pipes and other plumbing supplies. It was six months before Murray got a contract of sale, whereupon, according to his recollection, Malek went into the hospital and subsequently died, leaving the closing to his widow. There were more delays, and roundabout debate at the closing itself, says Murray, until one of the seller's advisers exclaimed, "If you don't close on this property today, it's going to be *tsuris* [trouble]!" And the deal was done. Murray's costs for the purchase, including the assumption of a mortgage, were about $22,000. It took place in June 1980.

In the interval between contract and closing, a critical event had taken place. The three little row houses immediately to the west of No. 239, two already deeded to the city and one under lien for tax arrears, all ruined, reached the end of the line. The city sent its demolition contractors to take them down, the last buildings on the block to go. One of the contractors told Murray that No. 239 was next. "In fact he actually pulled out from his wallet a photograph of a building whose entire sidewall, which is of course a supporting wall, had collapsed, exposing people—you know, like one of those old cartoons where the guy is in the bathtub?" But Murray, determined to close on the building and restore it, prevailed on the city to forgo condemning No. 239 and instead issue a so-called vacate order. Not that it took a lot of convincing. "When I walked in, they were like, here's some idiot Murray who's going to actually put up some money to take a building off their hands, get it off their desks."

Inside No. 239, Murray found a human presence typical of buildings sliding down the spiral to oblivion. On the second floor some energetic youths were erecting a warren of plywood partitions, apparently in preparation for some serious drug dealing. That was over, Murray told them, and with a few polite words they were gone. In the basement, a sixty-five-year-old man ran a shooting gallery, collecting a few dollars from drug users in exchange for a sheltered place to inject themselves. The floor was littered with needles. With no plumbing, the man was relieving himself in a bucket. Murray felt bad for him, though he also badly wanted him out. Finally the man's girlfriend carried him off to what Murray believes was some type of rehab (she and her family also had appeared in Sunday best to take him to church) and Murray took the occasion to clear out the place, throwing everything but a radio into the Dumpster. When the man returned several months later, looking well, he asked to move back in, but Murray demurred, instead giving him some money for his radio. Finally, in the building's single remaining habitable apartment—the parlor floor where the Bookmans had lived—was the Italian–Puerto Rican family, still paying rent. The vacate order meant they would have to leave, and they weren't happy about that. One of the teenage girls—maybe it was Rosie, the girl with the street-smart, action-oriented style—spat on Murray. Unable to bring their dog wherever it was they were going, they left the creature, a dark shepherd, to Murray. "Greatest dog," he says. "Best dog I ever had by far."

Then Murray moved into the parlor floor and began trying to save the building while living in it. No. 239 had shared a party wall with its neighbor, No. 237. For 135 years it had relied on that building's presence for structural support and protection from the elements. The demolition had shorn away that support, leaving No. 239's western wall "a gaping wound," says Murray. (Had it not been for the steel staircase, he thinks the building might have collapsed then and there.) So he had that wall weatherized, put on a new roof, and installed new wiring and plumbing supply lines, among other repairs. In the process, a bottle of nineteenth-century glass rolled out of a wall. He put in close to $40,000, he says. But after a couple of years, he'd had enough of the strain and returned to his old place in the Village, leaving No. 239 to some friends, aspiring theater people, with the minor request that they pay the utilities (which they did not).

It was a dispiriting time in the altered, depopulated streets of Alphabet City. And yet there rose, from either end of our block, a sad, sweet, ragtag whistle of a song nearly mad with defiance.

In a city-owned vacant lot on Avenue C, Carmen Pabon made a garden full of flowers and vegetables she named El Bello Amanecer Boriqueño, the Beautiful Puerto Rican Dawn. She made it a gathering place for the neighborhood's proliferating homeless, a place where they could be fed, find some donated clothing or blankets, or even sleep in the bright blue casita a neighbor had built there. She knew what it was like to have your little house shattered by a storm, to stand in line for food. "As long as you have a piece of bread in your stomach," she tells me with emphasis, "it makes no difference. I say for *me*." Carmen Pabon was the piping of the fife.

At the other end of the block, on the corner of Avenue D, Brian Lippel, having bought from a well-known slumlord the dilapidated tenement that housed his family's pharmacy, entombed it, bricking in and boarding up everything but the corner storefront. He would stay hunkered down that way, selling medication to the people of Avenue D in a store that seemed to cower beneath an enormous pigeon roost spattered with guano, for twenty years. Why? His grandfather had once had his barbershop across the street. His father had been born next door. "My roots are here," he says. "Every time I open the door I look at the ground that my father was born on." Brian Lippel was the rattle of the drum.

Soon there came along a local real estate man who'd recently delved into the business of co-op sponsorship, wanting to buy No. 239, "quick," as Murray says. The deal, financed largely with a mortgage to Murray, closed in April 1984, with Murray roughly doubling his money. Rafael Sassouni embarked upon renovations of a nonstructural nature, including the installation of new oak floors that were raised by a foot or more, apparently to correct a significant tilt. He nudged the building's four units into a booming mid-'80s real estate market that brought shoppers all the way to Avenue C. One buyer, who purchased the second-floor unit, paid more than $110,000 for his apartment and actually lost money when he resold it in the 1990s—to me and David. A second buyer owned a restaurant on Avenue A. And then there were Gary and Oren with the wives we would never meet. Needless to say, whatever Murray and Sassouni did to dress the wounds sustained by this now-leaning old house, its feet sunk in mud, its rooms echoing with the lost lexicons of men who earned their living building ships and women who went marketing with a basket on their arms, it wasn't enough—it wasn't enough to keep it standing much longer.

What on earth happened here?

The boy who'd had a crush on Rosie didn't see her for a few years, and then he hardly recognized her. "It looked like she had hit really tough times," he says. There were plenty of stories of like that, stories of addiction, early death by violence.

But Edwin and Migdalia Torres prospered in the paper business and became proprietors on the block, purchasing, in 1984, the double building where Migdalia was raised, and where the couple and all but one of their grown children live. There's a bodega on the ground floor, once Rosie's candy store. Sixty-two-year-old retiree José M. Cruz, who lives down Avenue D in a limited-equity co-op, likes to sit on a folding chair in front, like everyone did in the old days, greeting customers as they come and go, shooting the breeze. "We're friendly," he says, when I approach him there. "There's nothing funny here. We talk, and that's it." In fact, he's been coming to the block since he was a kid. "Now this block is the most beautiful block," he says. "You know how much it costs to get an apartment here? Two thousand dollars. You know what they pay there for a studio?" he asks, gesturing across the street to the building where the Lippels still run their pharmacy. "Fifteen hundred dollars." When I meet the Torreses at the little Italian place on Avenue C, I learn that they took in Felicia, the cat feeder, when she lost her place. "We took her in because we just felt compelled," Edwin Torres explains. "I wouldn't allow her to just be out on the streets. How could I do that?"

The block association made a garden where the three little row houses had been, ordering a truckload of soil, planting trees, putting up an iron fence. Much later, in the '90s, two of the lots were sold by the city at auction. One was purchased by neighbors (including me and David) and remained an open space inhabited, eventually, by a haunting and beautiful sculpture of a female figure holding before her in an oddly stiff posture a doe, apparently dead. The middle lot was bought by the man with more money than God. The week he broke ground there, I learned he'd once pleaded guilty to bid rigging at foreclosure auctions in Queens. Ah, well, there's a new building there now, a sliver of garden on either side.

The old Hungarian synagogue went condo in the '80s. "A once-somber sanctuary takes on a modern exhibitionist look," the *Times* Home Section said in 2009, referring to how the dwelling's glass walls, though "fritted for privacy near the toilet," offered neighbors a view of the inhabitants' king-size platform bed and egg-shaped tub.[33]

The son of the people who made the film *The Street of the Flower Boxes* returned to the block and built a spectacular glass-sheathed condominium with self-watering planters called the Flowerbox Building—an "Alphabet City gamechanger," according to the real estate website Curbed.com—whose penthouse sold in 2009 for $5.75 million.[34] By that time, the kid who'd played the lead in the film held an executive job with an international discount retailer, according to his pal and costar Thomas Brasuell, while Brasuell himself had become Major League Baseball's urbane vice president of community affairs. Eddie Sepulveda, another young actor in the film, had moved to Ohio with his family and become a buyer for a food distribution company.

Chuck Bergemann died of AIDS in the autumn of 1985. The disease was poorly understood and greatly feared, but Olivia, who was nursing at a city hospital, had experience with it. She took care of him, moving him, toward the end, from 7th Street to a place in Midtown. "I was angry at everyone on the block," she says. "Because I felt that he really gave his life to create that, people were benefiting from that, and when he was ill down there, there was absolutely no one that came to ask how he was doing. I wasn't about to let him die there." He left his Spanish Mission table to a museum in Miami, a Tiffany table lamp to Cornell University, and, to his widow, Olivia—his *Puerto Rican* widow, as she herself pointedly remarks—an apartment or partial interest in each of six buildings on 7th Street.[35]

Near Avenue D, Nos. 272, 274, and 278, abandoned, partially emptied, and taken for back taxes during the 1970s, stood for decades as a holdover from that time, neither returning to the private marketplace nor being legitimized by the city as tenant-run rentals or low-income co-ops.* According to some sources, the reason the city refused to admit the buildings to its self-management program was that the super—who had become the owner of record and therefore the tax defaulter—had been among the petitioners. In any event, the buildings filled up with people who never held a lease but kept their homes intact (no mean feat) with their own labor and materials. Over the years, apartments turned over by extralegal mechanisms that, in some cases at least, involved money changing hands. Finally, in 2002, two of the buildings, Nos. 274 and 278, joined the neighborhood's nine other squats in inking a deal with the city to become official low-income co-ops for a nominal fee, although they'd have to take on debt to bring the buildings up to code, and seven years later the process still was far from complete.[36]

No. 272 was the only squat to refuse participation in the program; it fell prey to an internal disputatiousness involving leadership run

---

*A modest number of city-owned rental buildings eventually were transferred to their tenants and, with the help of neighborhood housing groups, became low-income co-ops. And in 1987, the city approved a plan to effectively yoke the provision of affordable housing to the horsepower of private redevelopment; it would sell some of the neighborhood's lots and buildings to developers of market-rate apartments, but use the proceeds to rehabilitate an equal number of units for low- and moderate-income households.

amok, a coup and countercoup, police reports, screaming matches, etc., that, when I read through the documents provided to me by one major participant, reminded me all too painfully of what had happened in my house, at the other end of the block, a few years earlier. "I told you that I would go to Home Depot to buy bags and bldg. supplies and you agreed," went the e-mail one resident dropped to another under the subject line "expenses." "You told me to buy things in bulk such as soap for the floors, garbage bags, light bulbs (fluorescent ones). You agreed to this. Getting you to do work on the bldg. is like pulling teeth." And here the writer veers toward the subjective. "You are a gross liar and a great perpetrator of fraudulence. . . . I think there is something mentally wrong with you." It's as if they, like us, found themselves trapped in the unsound structures—physical, legal, financial, political—hammered together as little more than expedients in a chaotic time. Judge if you will; it's not easy setting things right.

I think of that day when David and I stood in the sunshine on the roof of No. 239, our first child on the way, impatient to begin our lives there. I suppose it's just as well I couldn't see then how the moment was colored by all the moments leading up to it, no such thing as a fresh start. Everything I found on 7th Street, in the instant I encountered it, filtered down from a depthless past, not just the wreck of a house or the unworkable co-op, but the crepe myrtles and fruit trees, the painted murals and crazily soldered fences, the purple facade of the squat and the bright casitas with their swept yards and curious figurines. It was a place nobody planned but many had made with their own hands, building and planting and spray-painting amid the ruins. Both the push of gentrification and the pushback against it had made the place exactly what it was, most hospitable to a person like me, an educated white woman who wanted to plant daffodils and push her child in the Mercedes of prams through a world that seemed vivid, real, even good. There was nothing to fear there. Lucy would frown when the old man with his big knuckles pressed a peppermint into her hand, and I'd laugh, coaxing her to see it for just what it was—a gift. The industrious young drug dealers were still busy working the next block, standing on the stoops clutching wads of cash like ticket sellers at a carnival, but there was only one who occasionally harassed me with a coke-addled exclamation. When David had a few words with him, he looked stricken. I didn't really get why. But Awi Perkins does. "The dealers would protect you," he says, "because they don't want to bring police down on them because somebody got robbed or somebody got hurt. So they're like, *you don't do that over here*. It's almost like you were walking through a protected area, because they're not going to let any noise be made on their territory. That's it: no noise."

What is it that happened? The incident that led inexorably to the demise of No. 239 could not be found in the records of its own past but lay in the unrecorded history of No. 237, the ancient support so roughly kicked away in 1980. If there isn't any such thing as an isolated moment, I've discovered, telling this story, that there's no way to talk about buildings and people without telling about other buildings and other people. This is a feature of city life whose instruction we often resist. Haven't I preferred the fiction of the little storybook house that begins its life with nothing to contend with but the stars, whose nature is somehow violated by the presence of other buildings as the city rises around her? That was wrong. No. 239 never did sit on a hill, sending a curl of smoke from her chimney and watching the countryside spill before her. And maybe I've been wrong to quote Heidegger, that old Nazi, with his seductive allusions to elemental forms. "Let us think for a while of a farmhouse in the Black Forest," he writes.[37] Let's not! Let us think instead of the city dwelling, which holds the neighbor so close you imagine you can hear the sound of his breathing all through the long summer nights. Maybe you believe he is everything wrong with the world. Maybe you smile and nod as you pass. Little matter. What happens to him happens to you.

The Living

I set out on this ground, which I suppose to be self evident, *'that the earth belongs in usufruct to the living'*; that
the dead have neither powers nor rights over it.
　　—Thomas Jefferson to James Madison, Paris, September 6, 1789[1]

NOT LONG AFTER we finally sold No. 239, we bought a two-
bedroom apartment on the fourth floor of a twelve-story building
that sits on high ground near where the East River bends around Corlear's Hook, less than a mile south of 7th Street. To keep our monthly
costs low, we funneled nearly all the sale proceeds from the old
place—very nearly everything we had—into the new place, doubling
down on Manhattan and the life we'd had to choose, again and again.
It was perhaps less like a renewal of vows than like plunking more
quarters into a parking meter. Still, at the closing, David loudly blew
his nose into his knit hat, a breach of decorum for which I adored him,
and that has always seemed to me the mystical sequel to that moment
when he stomped the crystal glass at our wedding, acknowledging in
our joy the destruction of the Temple, etc., etc.

At the time, we were living in the tiny box on 8th Street. Fewer
than six hundred square feet total, the children's bedroom was a
cramped cell wholly taken up by a bunk bed that went mostly unused,

the kids, at two and five, often preferring to pile onto our bed, a queen-size mattress on the floor. In that apartment, we were instantly alerted each time the cat defecated, and we always knew just when the super had come to empty our wine bottles, with a mortifying, unholy racket, from the recycling bin on the landing. The place was never anything but temporary to us; I more stored myself than lived there.

Then there was our *stuff*, enduring its long exile in two literal storage spaces, one on 10th Street and another in Long Island City, Queens. Opening them after nearly two years was ghastly. We found two rooms full of stone-cold, dusty objects, the accoutrements of our own household rendered inert with disuse. There was my grandmother's old sideboard, missing a plank in back. Our children's wooden blocks. A washer and dryer we wouldn't need. Though many of these objects provoked an instant surge of emotion, we were not about to yoke ourselves to the enormous heft of it all; we were done weighting ourselves down with possessions that did nothing but memorialize loss. Hardly any of it seemed to have any *utility*. So the days after the closing were filled with painting our new rooms in the intense colors I'd chosen—wild daisy in the living room, blue iris in the bedroom, fireball orange in the kitchen—and also with a great, almost violent casting off of the old. In one breakneck overnight haul, David and a friend drove a truckload up to my folks' roomy farmhouse in Vermont. The washer and dryer and some toys and furniture went to a church in Brooklyn. And plenty of things—things we'd been carrying to and fro and housing at some expense for years—completed their absurd journey in the garbage.

The first night we spent in the new place was a revelation. We were amazed to peer through our southwest-facing windows at a city turning moody and purple in the darkness, but sprinkled with lights. Distant buildings we hadn't quite noticed announced themselves in dramatic fashion, while others slipped into shadow. It was so different from the close-up street of the tenement blocks, and I nearly swooned with happiness when we gathered the children at the kitchen table to eat the chicken and rice that Cameron and Lalou had cooked and brought to us still hot in the pots, as if they'd kept something of ours burning all this time, carried it to us over the blocks from Suffolk Street on a flaming branch. Our hearth relit, I could have wept with gratitude for its brightness and warmth.

That was six winters ago now. It's December once again. I work here in the quiet until late afternoon, bands of light traveling across the living room rug. David returns in the evenings wearing the cold on his cheeks like a perfume. On his side of our bedroom, he keeps clothes, lotions, colognes, vitamins, candy wrappers, sticky spoons, bags of dried fruit, books, marked-up manuscripts, loose change, receipts, paper clips, etc., in the apparently (he would argue otherwise) disorderly ag-glomeration we call "man heap." I have my tidy spaces no one would dream of interfering with—two red geraniums go in and out of bloom on the kitchen windowsill, and on the sunny living room sill, the theme is aloe and other blue-green succulents in clay pots. My disorder is kept in drawers, especially my top dresser drawer, where I harbor, among other items, hotel soaps from a childhood vacation, a drawing of a rooster-like creature with the label "crackpot" Byron made in first grade, and a tin containing our deceased pet's ashes. I'm learning—perhaps you've figured this out already—that the drawer and the sill are one. I'm even getting comfortable with the spot in the hall, halfway between our bedroom door and the bathroom, where, stumbling along in the deep of night, I am routinely ambushed by the thought *this is it, this shabby, narrow space of a life!* which then, like a cat assured of its prey, toys with me for hours. Lucy, the baby we were expecting when we moved into No. 239, is nearly thirteen. She isn't much for washing her hair or trimming her fingernails, and yet, slung in her accustomed posture over an armchair with a book, she is a perfect beauty. She sits there like an orchid. She is furthermore in the know; Lucy, with her fresh ways of seeing, brings us the news. And Byron? During unhappy times, in my mind, I've always held our youngest child out of the fray; he was the place in my heart where all was well. Today, at nine, he's the sweet spirit we call House Elf, because he likes to change into his loungewear the minute he crosses the threshold, because he's always leaving his doodles, computer passwords, and experiments—a plum drilled full of screws, let's say—for us to discover in the oddest places. Sometimes, as a family, we discuss the gingko tree outside our living room window, whether it's a good shape or not, whether it's best when green, or nicer when the fan-shaped leaves turn yellow and drop, to be collected by Chinese women for medicinal tea, meanwhile revealing our winter view. In short, we inhabit this place.

Not long after we moved in, a large, balding man of perhaps sixty walked through the door calling a woman's name. *Irene!* I think that was the name. *Irene!* Catching sight of Byron playing naked on the floor, and me, emerging from the bedroom, he called out once again, but weakly this time, *Irene?* while sort of reeling back—not turning around but reversing his steps like a film rewinding. Without another word he was gone. I know this place has a history. I've seen the layers of paint. There is a death certificate in our ownership documents, and I recall the heir's testy impatience at the closing. But you know what? I don't care. Let it rest. This place is ours now. These rooms belong to the living.

In 1789 Thomas Jefferson wrote to his friend and protégé bursting with the political implications of an idea that was old even then—that the earth beneath our feet is a gift each generation has a right to receive whole, free and clear. A purist version of this notion might mean an end to history, each of us born to a world innocent of culture, stripped even of words. What Jefferson had in mind, during the opening months of the French Revolution, was whether a society could purge itself of the hereditary institutions that "charge [the earth] with debt." These included perpetual land grants to the church, hospitals, colleges, and orders of chivalry; the incursion of long-term debt to wage expensive wars; and the long catalog of ecclesiastical and feudal privileges attached to soil. Once the makers of these arrangements passed from the earth, so, too, said Jefferson, should their ancient claims on the land, lest the living be held in a kind of peonage to the dead. "The earth belongs always to the living generation," he insisted. "They may manage it then, and what proceeds from it, as they please, during their usufruct."[2]

Usufruct means the right to use the land and enjoy its fruits, but not to sell, bequeath, or destroy it. This recalls the basic relation of the Lenape to their environment before people like Van Corlear or De-Lancey landed on its shores. The arrival of Europeans with their surveying equipment doomed the Lenape's way to extinction. And yet their way reflected a truth about the human condition that no society can overturn. The magic of inhabitation depends upon the living body. Possession of place—no matter what the faded documents say—is the province of those who live and breathe. It is therefore provisional, like the body itself.

The good news is this: So long as the heart beats, a person may yet inhabit and possess the world, is able to renew the creative process of being there. Indeed, my very first self-instruction in purple marker reflected nothing more than a blind instinct to return to square one, the living body, in its first raw encounter with space. *1. Take a deep breath.* I found out you can breathe your way back to the place that feels so natural it disappears, falls away. You can breathe your way home again.

And you can take the old places with you. Not even time can snatch them away. Ardell LongTemple, who grew up on 7th Street in the 1970s, told me that what she liked to remember about those days was different from what her older brother, Philip, remembered; she liked to think of the nights when, hanging her head out the window, she could look up and down the block and see the faces of her friends doing the same. The children had developed a fantasy that aliens would descend from a distant planet and bring more trees to the block; they watched the night sky for saucers. Who can ever take that particular world from Ardell LongTemple? Settled down with a family of her own in Brooklyn, she may indeed be its sole possessor.

Memory is a strong potion. It can be a source of vital continuity, charging the moment with texture and meaning. It also can bring a form of blindness, obscuring the present, preventing a person from seeing what lies right before her eyes.

No. 239 was the first dwelling, the first structure, ever to occupy its place on earth. And during a century and a half it sent forth who knows how many images of itself, fragmentary and panoramic, clouded and Windex-clear, my own included. Yet it seems right and good that no image from the past be permitted to lie like a dead hand over the life that unfolds in that spot at this hour. When I lived in the house with my young family, we never felt the presence of Elisha Barnard or Clara

Hart—not in a shadow across the floor, not in the lifting of a curtain on the breeze. Nor would I wish to place any lien against the plain, steel-beamed, four-story structure that replaces the first No. 239, or cast an oppressive shadow over its inhabitants.

Which brings me to the old house with its decorative iron railing. I've been rebuilding it, haven't I, out of salvaged bits and pieces. And you have been helping me build, as surely as if you'd been laying the timbers. The job, such as it was, is done. Surely the time has come, not to re-inhabit the house, but to finally bid a proper farewell to all the life it held, subject its decaying hulk to a tremendous, bright, purifying heat, and set free, in a burst of sparks, some immortalized spirit.

Night has fallen on that house. So come, take a torch, and we'll burn it down together. Let nothing remain, when morning comes, but what's lighter than a cinder, what anyone can carry away.

ACKNOWLEDGMENTS AND
NOTES ON SOURCES

Several quite different kinds of information went into making this book, and I owe a debt of gratitude to the people and institutions that helped me gather that material.

During the course of my research I contacted, usually by letter, dozens of people who had lived on 7th Street; many responded with great warmth and openness, sharing impressions and details from their lives and times. I thank them all. I want to express special appreciation for Alfred and Judy Wieder, who extended their welcome during a trip I made to California, and to Al for sharing photographs and other personal mementos.

A particular thanks goes to Stephen C. Barto, who was generous enough to give me access to field notes he made during the summer of 1975 for a graduate social-science paper on 7th Street's block association; also to Philip Long, who let me read parts of his well-wrought unpublished memoir, and Betty-Carol Sellen, who provided me with block-association newsletters I could not have found elsewhere. Barbara Schmidt-Runkel and Rabbi Joshua Segal translated and interpreted Hebrew grave inscriptions for me. Thanks to them.

Because my subject was local and New York is so richly endowed with archival institutions, I was able to do most of my research close to home, returning again and again to the same reading rooms and municipal offices. I am deeply grateful for these institutions and their staffs and supporters. They include the New York City Municipal Archives, City Hall Library, New York County Surrogate's Court records department, the City Register's office, the National Archives Northeast Region repository in downtown Manhattan, the American Jewish Historical Society, and various historic houses open to the public, including Clermont and Staatsburgh in the Hudson River valley, and, in Manhattan, the Merchant's House Museum and Fraunces Tavern. The New-York Historical Society and Museum of the City of New York were irreplaceably valuable sources of primary materials; their amiable and knowledgeable curators helped me find my way.

I spent many contented days at various branches of the New York Public Library, especially at its main branch on 5th Avenue at 42nd Street, now known as the Stephen A. Schwarzman Building (the Irma and Paul Milstein Division of U.S. History, Local History & Genealogy being my habitual haunt). I came to believe this library is the jewel of our civilization. The extraordinary scale and beauty of its landmark building, and the unfailing courtesy of its staff, express a profound respect for culture, for learning, and for human beings. I never needed any special status there but was very happy to receive the same careful guidance I saw extended to the tourist dropping in to find out about a forebear who immigrated through Ellis Island, the nattily dressed scholar plumbing and plumbing a single collection, or indeed the unwashed and possibly mentally ill patron filling page after page with tiny script. I was just one more individual in the grip of a curiosity that might or might not lead anywhere. The New York Public Library honors curiosity in all its forms, and for that it deserves veneration.

This book could not have been written without extensive use of digital databases and online resources. These resources, though no substitute for more traditional materials and methods, make history accessible in ways it never has been before—in fact render certain details from the past more accessible to today's researchers than they were to contemporaries. The digitized, searchable *New York Times* from the mid-nineteenth century to the present allowed me not only to study lifestyles of bygone eras, but also to locate proverbial needles in a haystack—references to individuals in my narrative that I never could have found scrolling through microfilm. Ancestry.com allowed for quick, repeated examination of federal census returns, a peek inside virtually any household in the country at various points in history. Google Books, although the bête noire of some who are concerned—and rightly so—for the interests of publishers and impecunious scribes, is a game changer, too. I was able to simply Google the name of one mid-nineteenth-century resident of No. 239, and up popped a crusty old volume of genealogy, made available for digitization by Harvard University. The book's title contained a different family name than the one I was interested in, so without the digital search function I never would have uncovered it—not in a million years. I made wide use of an array of databases of scholarly (JSTOR and Project MUSE) and historical (HarpWeek) materials, as well as online digital-image galleries of the U.S. Library of Congress, the New York Public Library, and others. Acknowledgment is due to all the scanners, curators, and other contributors to these projects.

The circle of those who helped me turn this material into a book is a much smaller one. One of my first readers was a good friend, Nina Collins, who coached me on how to assemble a book proposal and put me in touch with the editor of the *New York Times* City Section, which published an essay that was the seed of this book, as well as with my agent, Ann Rittenberg. Ann embraced the project with the confidence and appreciation every writer longs for. She has been a wise and convivial ally ever since.

Likewise, the publisher of this book, PublicAffairs, led by Susan Weinberg and Peter Osnos, jumped in with both feet, allowing me to pack off to the library with the heartening notion that somewhere over the rainbow was a reader. I count myself exceptionally fortunate that the manuscript came into the hands of editor Clive Priddle, whose editing has been close and highly skilled, but leavened by an easygoingness that made the whole process downright pleasant. A hearty thanks goes to copy editor Antoinette Smith, who undertook the strenuous and important task of imposing stylistic consistency on the manuscript, and to project editor Melissa Veronesi for her admirably efficient, ever friendly oversight of the book-production process.

A number of friends and family members talked over aspects of this book with me and gave enormously helpful encouragement along the way. No one offered more attentive listening or generous response than my parents, Linda Greider and William Greider. Their sensibilities as writers and as people deeply inform my own. My children, Lucy Greider-Andrews and Byron Greider-Andrews, brought fascinating perspectives to my work, yet their joyful presence constantly reminded me that there's much more to life than books. David Andrews, my husband, also a writer and editor, read and gave invaluable feedback on portions of the manuscript. He also lived this story with me, but from the beginning encouraged me to tell it my way. Though quietly proffered, that was no small gift.

NOTES

PROLOGUE

1. Kevin Lynch, *The Image of the City* (Cambridge, MA: MIT Press, 1960), 2.

CHAPTER ONE

1. Paul E. Cohen and Robert T. Augustyn, *Manhattan in Maps: 1527–1995* (New York: Rizolli International Publications, 1997), 138–139.

2. Egbert L. Viele, *Topographical Atlas of the City of New York, Including the Annexed Territory, Showing Original Water Courses and Made Land* (New York: E. L. Viele, 1874).

3. Egbert L. Viele, *The Topography and Hydrology of New York* (New York: Robert Craighead, 1865), 10. This booklet was published in connection with Viele's map, *Sanitary & Topographical Map of the City and Island of New York Prepared for the Council of Hygiene and Public Health of the Citizens Association* (New York: Ferd. Mayer & Co., lithographers, 1865).

4. Viele, *Topography*, 4–5.

5. Ibid., 7.

6. Ibid., 12.

7. New York City Office of Emergency Management, "Ready New York: Hurricanes and New York City," flyer, undated.

8. U.S. Army Corps of Engineers, New York District, www.nan.usace.army .mil/harbor/deep.htm.

9. U.S. Army Corps of Engineers, New York District, et al., "Stemming the Tide of Marsh Loss in Jamaica Bay With $13M Urban Wetlands Project," news release, July 6, 2006; U.S. Army Corps of Engineers, New York District, "Elders Point, Jamaica Bay, Salt Marsh Islands, NY: Project Facts," undated, www.nan .usace.army.mil/project/newyork/factsh/pdf/elders.pdf; Richard Hake, "An Island Shrinks in Brooklyn: The Fight to Save the Jamaica Bay Salt Marshes," broadcast on WNYC radio August 24, 2006, podcast at www.wnyc.org/news/articles/ 63567.

10. John Hay, *In the Company of Light* (1998), excerpted in *The Way to the Salt Marsh: A John Hay Reader* (Hanover, NH: University Press of New England, 1998), 246.

11. Salt marshes grow and change even without human interference. So we can't know exactly what this particular marsh looked like hundreds of years before it was first mapped in the colonial era. The topography described here is based on examination of the Viele maps (see notes 2 and 3), as well as an earlier map by Bernard Ratzer, *Plan of the City of New York in North America: Surveyed in the years 1766 & 1767* (London: Jefferys & Faden, 1776). The basic ecology of any New England or Middle Atlantic salt marsh follows a similar pattern. See, for example, John Teal and Mildred Teal, *Life and Death of the Salt Marsh* (Boston: Little, Brown, and Co., 1969); Kimberly R. Sebold, *From Marsh to Farm: The Landscape Transformation of Coastal New Jersey* (Washington, DC: National Park Service, 1992); Elizabeth Barlow, *The Forests and Wetlands of New York City* (Boston: Little, Brown, and Co., 1969).

12. John Bierhorst, *Mythology of the Lenape: Guide and Texts* (Tucson: University of Arizona Press, 1995), 28. This is one of a few different Lenape origin myths, but it was one of the first Lenape stories told to and recorded by a European—the Dutch traveler Jaspar Danckaerts, in 1679.

13. This comparison between the Lenape origin story and scholarly descriptions of the last ice age I owe to Anne-Marie Cantwell and Diana diZerega Wall, *Unearthing Gotham: The Archaeology of New York City* (New Haven, CT: Yale University Press, 2001), 25–38. Also see Herbert C. Kraft, *The Lenape: Archaeology, History, and Ethnography* (Newark: New Jersey Historical Society, 1986), 31–57.

14. Robert S. Grumet, "Munsee Country," in *Historic Contact: Indian People and Colonists in Today's Northeastern United States in the Sixteenth Through Eighteenth Centuries* (Norman: University of Oklahoma Press, 1995), 211. On first European birth, see Joseph Dillaway Sawyer, *History of the Pilgrims and Puritans: Their Ancestry and Descendants: Basis of Americanization*, ed. William Elliot Griffis, 3 vols. (New York: Century History Co., 1922), 2:42.

15. See Kraft, *The Lenape*, xiii–xvi; Robert S. Grumet, *The Lenapes* (New York: Chelsea House Publishers, 1989), 13.

16. Kraft, *The Lenape*, 162.

17. Quoted in Reginald Pelham Bolton, *Indian Life of Long Ago in the City of New York* (New York: Joseph Graham/Schoen Press, 1934), 162.

18. John Heckewelder, *History, Manners, and Customs of the Indian Nations Who Once Inhabited Pennsylvania and the Neighbouring States* (1876; New York: Arno Press and the New York Times, 1971), 103.

19. Nicolaes Van Wassenaer, "From the 'Historisch Verhael,' By Nicolaes Van Wassenaer, 1624–1630," in *Narratives of New Netherland, 1609–1664*, ed. J. Franklin Jameson (New York: Charles Scribner's Sons, 1909), 70; Kraft, *The Lenape*, 136.

20. Johannes Megapolensis Jr., "A Short Account of the Mohawk Indians," in Jameson, *Narratives of New Netherland*, 174.

21. Adriaen Van der Donck, "Representation of New Netherland," in Jameson, *Narratives of New Netherland*, 302. On marriage: Margaret M. Caffrey, "Complementary Power: Men and Women of the Lenni Lenape," *American Indian Quarterly* 24, no. 1 (Winter 2000): 48–50. On the mayapple, see August C. Mahr, "Semantic Analysis of Eighteenth-Century Delaware Indian Names for Medicinal Plants," *Ethnohistory* 2, no. 1 (Winter 1955): 21–22.

22. Adriaen Van der Donck, *The Representation of New Netherland, Concerning Its Location, Productiveness and Poor Condition, Presented to the States General of the United Netherlands, and printed at The Hague, in 1650* (New York: Bartlett & Welford, 1849), 18.

23. Isaack de Rasieres, "Letter of Isaack de Rasieres to Samuel Blommaert, 1628(?)," in Jameson, *Narratives of New Netherland*, 106.

24. Kraft, *The Lenape*, 129–130; Grumet, *The Lenapes*, 16.

25. See for example Lynn Ceci, "Radiocarbon Dating for 'Village' Sites in Coastal New York: Settlement Pattern Change in the Middle to Late Woodland," *Man in the Northeast* 39 (Spring 1990): 2. An elucidating discussion of this issue can be found in Cantwell and Wall, *Unearthing Gotham*, 93–116.

26. Grumet, *The Lenapes*, 14.

27. A map of these trails is found in Robert S. Grumet, *Native American Place Names in New York City* (New York: Museum of the City of New York, 1981), 68.

28. See Grumet, *Native American Place Names*, 68.

29. Other scholars seem to have placed the site farther west. See Grumet, *Native American Place Names*, 68. Bolton quotation is in Bolton, *Indian Life of Long Ago*, 53. "Schepmoes" seems demonstrably Dutch and indeed was the name of a prominent family, that of tavern keeper Jan Jansen Schepmoes, that owned Manhattan property (albeit not at that site) in early colonial days.

30. Names were based on events or personal characteristics and might change in life; after death, it was considered disrespectful to utter the name of the deceased. See Heckewelder, *History, Manners, and Customs*, 141–142; Julian Harris Salomon, *Indians of the Lower Hudson Region: The Munsee* (New City, NY: Historical Society of Rockland County, 1982), 29.

31. Heckewelder, *History, Manners, and Customs*, 102. It should be noted that by this time, neither the Native American who purportedly uttered these words nor the missionary who reported them did so naively but would have understood the different land-use cultures in question, and the implications of these differences for the Indian way of life.

32. Bierhorst, *Mythology of the Lenape*, 33.

33. From a survey made by Evert Bancker Jr., around the time of the Revolution; original is in Bancker plans, 1770–1815, box 2, folder 73–75, Manuscripts and Archives Division, New York Public Library. Astor, Lenox, and Tilden Foundations.

34. This is the last time the land was conveyed as more than one lot. Robert and Emily Gibbes to Gilbert Speir, January 21, 1845.

35. Heckewelder, *History, Manners, and Customs*, 102.

36. Van der Donck, *Representation of New Netherland*, 13.

37. Ibid., 24.

38. Bartlett Burleigh James and J. Franklin Jameson, eds., *Journal of Jasper Danckaerts, 1679–1680* (New York: Charles Scribner's Sons, 1913), 229.

39. The chronology of the James DeLancey Farm, including the portion known as Corlear's Hook, is given in I. N. Phelps Stokes, *The Iconography of Manhattan Island, 1498–1909*, 6 vols. (New York: Robert H. Dodd, 1915–1928), 6:86–94. The early history of the meadow parcels is given in 6:120–121.

40. All the former governors except Peter Minuit had served very short terms. See Jameson, *Narratives of New Netherland*, 66.

41. William Elliot Griffis, *The Story of New Netherland: The Dutch in America* (Boston: Houghton Mifflin Company, 1909), 93.

42. On Van Corlear's career, see a letter translated by and published in Jaap Jacobs, "A Troubled Man: Director Wouter van Twiller and the Affairs of New Netherland in 1635," *New York History* 85, no. 3 (Summer 2004): 232. On his parentage, see Arnold J. F. Van Laer, trans. and ed., *Van Rensselaer Bowier Manuscripts: Being the Letters of Kiliaen Van Rensselaer, 1630–1643, and Other Documents Relating to the Colony of Rensselaerswyck* (Albany: University of the State of New York, 1908), 78n.

43. Griffis, *The Story of New Netherland*, 101, 94.

44. John Fiske, *The Dutch and Quaker Colonies in America* (Boston: Houghton Mifflin, 1902), 154–155.

45. Stokes, *Iconography of Manhattan Island*, 4:85.

46. James and Jameson, eds. *Journal of Jasper Danckaerts*, 64.

47. Grumet, *The Lenapes*, 25; "Letter of Jonas Michaelius, 1628," in Jameson, *Narratives of New Netherland*, 128.

48. James Riker, *Revised History of Harlem (City of New York): Its Origins and Early Annals*, revised by Henry P. Toler (New York: New Harlem Publishing Co., 1904), 119.

49. David Pietersz de Vries, *Voyages from Holland to America, A.D. 1632 to 1644*, trans. Henry C. Murphy (New York: Billin and Brothers, 1853), 161; A. J. F. Van Laer, *Van Rensselaer Bowier Manuscripts*, 428.

50. See Van Twiller's letter in Jaap Jacobs, "A Troubled Man," 232.

51. Berthold Fernow, ed., *The Records of New Amsterdam from 1653 to 1674 Anno Domini*, 7 vols. (New York: Knickerbocker Press, 1897), 5:51.

52. G. R. L. Marriott, *Primitive Property*, trans. Emile De Laveleye (London: Macmillan and Co., 1878), 187–288. For regional settlement patterns in the Netherlands, see Audrey M. Lambert, *The Making of the Dutch Landscape: An Historical Geography of the Netherlands* (London: Harcourt Brace Jovanovich, 1985), 55, 57, 78.

53. Joan Thirsk, *Fenland Farming in the Sixteenth Century, with an Introduction by R. H. Tawney* (Leicester, UK: University College of Leicester, 1953), 13.

54. Roger J. P. Kain, "The Tithe Commutation Surveys in Kent," *Archaeologia Cantiana* 89 (1974): 110.

55. John Deitz, *Brookhaven and South Haven Hamlets*, at BrookhavenSouth Haven.org, "History of Brookhaven Village, a Paper Written by Mr. Osborn Shaw

of Bellport for the Fireplace Literary Club, and Read by Him at the Brookhaven Free Library, October 5th, 1933," http://BrookhavenSouthHaven.org/history/OsborneShaw.htm; also see Three Village Historical Society, *The Three Villages* (Charleston, SC: Arcadia Publishing, 2008), 37, 61.

56. Bernice Schultz Marshall, *Colonial Hempstead: Long Island Under the Dutch and English*, 2nd ed. (1937; Port Washington, NY: Ira J. Friedman Inc., 1962), 144–147.

57. John Romeyn Brodhead, *Documents Relative to the Colonial History of the State of New-York: Procured in Holland, England, and France*, ed. Berthold Fernow and F. B. O'Callaghan, 15 vols. (Weed, Parsons, 1853–1887) 14:460, 474.

58. John Bierhorst, *The White Deer and Other Stories Told by the Lenape* (New York: William Morrow and Co., 1995), 11.

59. Jan Folkerts, "The Failure of West India Company Farming on the Island of Manhattan," published online at www.let.rug.nl/~usa/E/wic/wicxx.htm by the Department of Alfa-informatica, University of Groningen, 1996, 6.

60. In Jaap Jacobs, "A Troubled Man," 232.

61. John Greenleaf Whittier, *Snow-bound: A Winter Idyl* (Boston: James R. Osgood and Company, 1877), 23.

62. Riker, *History of Harlem*, 131.

63. The so-called Manatus Map, "Manatus Gelegen op de Noort Rivier, 1639," or "Manhattan Situated on the North River," drawn for the Dutch West India Company.

64. Cornelis Van Tienhoven, "Answer to the Representation of New Netherland, 1650," in Jameson, *Narratives of New Netherland*, 67.

65. Riker, *History of Harlem*, 131.

66. Ira Berlin and Leslie M. Harris, *Slavery in New York* (New York: New Press, 2005), 31.

67. Ibid., 51.

68. *NIH Record*, April 22, 1997, http://nihrecord.od.nih.gov/newsletters/04_22_97/story01.htm.

69. William Cronon, *Changes in the Land: Indians, Colonists, and the Ecology of New England* (New York: Hill & Wang, 1983), 48.

70. For an introduction to Tchen's work on port culture, see John Kuo Wei Tchen, *New York Before Chinatown: Orientalism and the Shaping of American Culture, 1776–1882* (Baltimore: Johns Hopkins University Press, 1999), 71–74.

71. The matter is recorded in the minutes of the court of burgomasters and schepens: Fernow, ed., *The Records of New Amsterdam*, 1:255–258.

72. *Year Book of the Holland Society of New York*, 1900, 75.

73. Grumet, *Native American Place Names*, 27.

74. De Vries, *Voyages from Holland to America*, 167–171.

75. Lysbet Van Hoogvelt had been the lover of company secretary Cornelis Van Tienhoven, a controversial figure disparaged by Van der Donck for his "lust after the prostitutes" (*Representation of New Netherland*, 57). Apparently she came with Van Tienhoven to New Amsterdam in 1651, only to discover he was already married with three children. See Riker, *History of Harlem*, 132n. Also

Henri and Barbara Van Der Zee, *A Sweet and Alien Land: The Story of Dutch New York* (New York: Viking Press, 1978), 200.

76. Grumet, "Munsee Country," 220. Also see Grumet, *Native American Place Names*, iv.

77. Bierhorst, *Mythology of the Lenape*, 5.

78. Grumet, *The Lenapes*, 60. For a map showing the various westward-rolling purchases of Indian land by the government, see William James McKnight, *A Pioneer Outline History of Northwestern Pennsylvania* (Philadelphia: J. B. Lippincott Company, 1905), 59.

79. C. A. Weslager, *The Delaware Indian Westward Migration* (Wallingford, PA: Middle Atlantic Press, 1978), 27.

80. Salomon, *Indians of the Lower Hudson*, 59–60.

81. Stephen Jarvis, [forage book], 1782 July–1783 June (BV Revolutionary War), New-York Historical Society.

CHAPTER TWO

1. Stevan E. Hobfoll, *The Ecology of Stress* (Washington, DC: Hemisphere, 1988), 25–26.

2. Whether dispersal of the so-called Neolithic package occurred by the expansion and migration of farming people or through cultural diffusion is a matter for debate.

3. In the fertile belt along the Mediterranean, the optimal area would have been 300 to 600 square kilometers, with more territory—from 500 to 2,000 square kilometers—required in desert or steppe. See Ofer Bar-Yosef, "The Natufian Culture in the Levant, Threshold to the Origins of Agriculture," *Evolutionary Anthropology* 6, no. 5 (1998): 161.

4. Peter Bellwood reports "clear signs of relatively independent agricultural origins" in western Asia, central China, the New Guinea highlands, Mesoamerica, the central Andes, the Mississippi basin, and "possibly" western Africa and southern India. See Peter Bellwood, *The First Farmers: Origins of Agricultural Societies* (Malden, MA: Blackwell, 2005), 2.

5. Jacques Cauvin, *The Birth of the Gods and the Origins of Agriculture*, trans. Trevor Watkins (Cambridge: Cambridge University Press, 2000; first published as *Naissance des Divinités, Naissance de L'Agriculture: La Révolution Des Symboles Au Néolithique*, Paris: CNRS Éditions, 1994), 22.

6. Anne-Marie Cantwell and Diana diZerega Wall, *Unearthing Gotham: The Archaeology of New York City* (New Haven, CT: Yale University Press, 2001), 109.

7. See Kent V. Flannery, "The Origins of the Village as a Settlement Type in Mesoamerica and the Near East: A Comparative Study," in *Man, Settlement, and Urbanism: Proceedings of a Meeting of the Research Seminar in Archaeology and Related Subjects Held at the Institute of Archaeology, London University*, ed. Peter J. Ucko, Ruth Tringham, and G. W. Dimbleby (Cambridge, MA: Schenkman, 1972), 27.

8. "Hog-back-brick people" is the shorthand of British archaeologist Kathleen Kenyon, who excavated Jericho in the 1950s. See Kathleen M. Kenyon, *Digging Up Jericho* (London: Ernest Benn, 1957), 75.

9. This inferred or reconstructed language is known as Proto-Indo-European, or PIE. It is the hypothetical (never recorded) precursor of all Indo-European languages, including English.

10. Calvert Watkins, *The American Heritage Dictionary of Indo-European Roots*, 2nd ed. (Boston: Houghton Mifflin, 2000), 20–21.

11. Kenyon, *Digging up Jericho*, 55. Kenyon posited that this was a hostile breaching of the defensive wall by the plastered-floor people. Later arguments held that the change was the result of in-migration by people from Syria who mixed with the existing population and gave it new cultural traits. See Cauvin, *The Birth of the Gods*, 104.

12. Emma Goldman, *Living My Life*, 2 vols. (1931; New York: Dover Publications, 1970), 1:3.

13. See Ian Hodder, "This Old House," *Natural History* (June 2006), online at www.naturalhistorymag.com/htmlsite/index_archive.html; Ian Hodder, "The Spatio-Temporal Organization of the Early 'Town' at Çatalhöyük," in *(Un)settling the Neolithic*, ed. Douglass Bailey, Alasdair Whittle, and Vicki Cummings (Oxford: Oxbow Books, 2005), 128–131; Michael Balter, "The Seeds of Civilization," *Smithsonian Magazine*, May 2005, www.smithsonianmag.com/history-archaeology/seeds_civilization.html; Ian Hodder and Shashina Fahid, "Season Review: A Season of Great Finds and New Faces at Çatalhöyük," *Çatal News: The Newsletter of the Çatalhöyük Research Project* 11 (December 2004), www.catalhoyuk.com/newsletters/11/index.html.

14. Hodder, "This Old House."

15. Michael Balter, *The Goddess and the Bull: Çatalhöyük: An Archaeological Journey to the Dawn of Civilization* (New York: Free Press, 2005), 27.

16. Ian Hodder, "Çatalhöyük in the Context of the Middle Eastern Neolithic," *Annual Review of Anthropology* 36 (2007): 109. Also see Hodder, *The Leopard's Tale: Revealing the Mysteries of Çatalhöyük* (London: Thames & Hudson, 2006), 143.

17. Balter, *The Goddess and the Bull*, 30.

18. See D. V. Clarke and Niall Sharples, "Settlements and Subsistence in the Third Millenium BC," in *The Prehistory of Orkney*, ed. Colin Renfrew (Edinburgh: Edinburgh University Press, 1985), 60–66.

19. Flannery, "Origins of the Village," 30–31, 39, 42.

20. Margaret M. Caffrey, "Complementary Power: Men and Women of the Lenni Lenape," *American Indian Quarterly* 24, no. 1 (Winter 2000): 50.

21. Sarah Blaffer Hrdy, *Mother Nature: A History of Mothers, Infants, and Natural Selection* (New York: Pantheon, 1999), 202–203.

22. Kenyon, *Digging Up Jericho*, 62–63.

23. Balter, *The Goddess and the Bull*, 1.

24. Flannery, "Origins of the Village," 29.

25. J. P. Mallory and D. Q. Adams, eds., *Encyclopedia of Indo-European Culture* (Chicago: Fitzroy Dearborn, 1997), 283, 622.

26. Ibid., 171.

27. Mark Epstein, *Thoughts Without a Thinker: Psychotherapy from a Buddhist Perspective* (New York: Basic Books, 1995), 137–138, 145, 154.

28. John Heckewelder, *History, Manners, and Customs of the Indian Nations Who Once Inhabited Pennsylvania and the Neighbouring States* (1876; New York: Arno Press and the *New York Times*, 1971), 140.

29. "The agricultural system is a form of settlement that depends upon, and gives rise to, the most pervasive form of nomadism," writes the anthropologist Hugh Brody. "Townspeople and country people live and make their decisions within the same cultural and economic tradition: they move, they settle, they create a home, and they find—or their children or their children's children find—that they must move on. Exile is the deep condition." Hugh Brody, *The Other Side of Eden: Hunters, Farmers, and the Shaping of the World* (New York: North Point Press, 2001), 34–35.

30. Lewis Mumford refers to these properties of the city as those of the "magnet" and the "container." Lewis Mumford, *The City in History: Its Origins, Its Transformations, and Its Prospects* (New York: Harcourt, Brace & World, 1961), 9.

31. Yi-Fu Tuan, *Space and Place: The Perspective of Experience* (Minneapolis: University of Minnesota Press, 1977), 6.

CHAPTER THREE

1. This house is known today as Fraunces Tavern for Samuel Fraunces, who bought the building in 1762 and operated the Queen's Head Tavern there through the Revolution. While the DeLanceys occupied it, its address was 49 Great Dock Street. See *54 Pearl Street: If These Walls Could Talk . . .* (New York: Fraunces Tavern Museum, 2006), 1, 4–7.

2. This was one of thirteen toasts, one for each colony, reprinted from *Rivington's Gazette*, November 26, 1783, in James Parton, *Famous Americans of Recent Times* (Boston: Tichnor and Fields, 1867), 394–395.

3. John Fiske and James Grant, eds., *Appletons' Cyclopaedia of American Biography*, 6 vols. (New York: D. Appleton and Co., 1900), 2:129.

4. Edward Countryman, "The Uses of Capital in Revolutionary America: The Case of the New York Loyalist Merchants," *William and Mary Quarterly* 49, no. 1 (January 1992): 13. Countryman applies Max Weber's term "capitalistic adventurers" to New York merchants in general. He quotes from and elaborates on Weber's characterization of a social type whose wealth is based on "'the acquisition of booty, whether directly in war or in the form of continuous fiscal booty by exploitation of subjects.' Speculation, entrepreneurship, and the running of plantations 'with slaves, or directly or indirectly forced labour' were also among their characteristic activities."

5. *Ships and Shipping of Old New York* (New York: Bank of Manhattan Co., 1915), 24.

6. P. Bradley Nutting, "The Madagascar Connection: Parliament and Piracy, 1690–1701," *American Journal of Legal History* 22, no. 3 (July 1978): 211.

7. Cathy Matson, "The 'Hollander Interest' and Ideas about Free Trade in Colonial New York: Persistent Influences of the Dutch, 1664–1764," in *A Beautiful and Fruitful Place: Selected Rensselaerswijck Seminar Papers*, ed. Nancy Anne McClure Zeller (Albany, NY: New Netherland Publishing, 1991), 257–258.

8. Cathy Matson, *Merchants & Empire: Trading in Colonial New York* (Baltimore: Johns Hopkins University Press, 1998), 76.

9. Countryman, "The Uses of Capital," 13.

10. E. B. O'Callaghan, *The Documentary History of the State of New-York*, 4 vols. (Albany, NY: C. Van Benthuysen, 1851), 4:1038.

11. Elizabeth DeLancey to Anne DeLancey, undated, in DeLancey Family Reminiscences, DeLancey Family Papers, Museum of the City of New York. This letter is in a book of copies and labeled "Miss Elizabeth DeLancey to her sister Anne DeLancey." I believe this must have been Elizabeth (Colden) De-Lancey, who had married Peter DeLancey in 1737, to Peter's sister, Anne DeLancey, who would later wed the merchant John Watts. If so, the letter seems to have been written in a light-hearted spirit. In a later letter in the same collection, written by "Mrs. Peter DeLancey" to "Miss Anne DeLancey," Elizabeth expresses terrible grief over the loss of her husband: "I trust you in particular will recollect that your Brother held me dear as life. . . . Alas my dear, you have lost him and I have lost him."

12. Sung Bok Kim, *Landlord and Tenant in Colonial New York: Manorial Society 1664–1775* (Chapel Hill: University of North Carolina Press, 1978), 242–247. Dixon Ryan Fox, *Caleb Heathcote, Gentleman Colonist* (New York: Charles Scribner's Sons, 1926), 107, 115.

13. From genealogical notes made by John Watts in 1784 on his arrival in England as a Loyalist, in the DeLancey Family Papers, Museum of the City of New York.

14. William Smith Jr., *The History of the Province of New York, Vol. 2, 1732–1762*, ed. Michael Kammen (Cambridge, MA: Harvard University Press, 1972), 247.

15. Ibid., 245.

16. This and numerous other details of the DeLancey genealogy are from D. A. Story, *The deLanceys, A Romance of a Great Family* (London: T. Nelson, 1931), 18.

17. See I. N. Phelps Stokes, *The Iconography of Manhattan Island, 1498–1909*, 6 vols. (New York: Robert H. Dodd, 1915–1928), 6:94–95 on the Oliver De-Lancey farm, and 6:88–89 on the James DeLancey farm.

18. Martha J. Lamb, "Historic Homes and Landmarks, Their Significance and Present Condition," *Magazine of American History with Notes and Queries* 21, no. 3 (March 1889): 191–192.

19. Ample evidence that the DeLanceys employed a small army of craftsmen and other workers can be found among the bills and receipts in box 1 of the James DeLancey Papers, New-York Historical Society.

20. Stokes, *Iconography*, 6:139.

21. Thomas Joseph Davis, *A Rumor of Revolt: The "Great Negro Plot" in Colonial New York* (Amherst: University of Massachusetts Press, 1990), 145, 180,

188, 190. Also Jill Lepore, *New York Burning: Liberty, Slavery, and Conspiracy in Eighteenth-Century Manhattan* (New York: Alfred A. Knopf, 2005), 172.

22. Maura A. Henry, "The Making of Elite Culture," in *A Companion to Eighteenth-Century Britain*, ed. H. T. Dickinson (Malden, MA: Blackwell Publishing, 2002), 315–320.

23. This quotation from DeLancey's missive is found in Philip Ranlet, "Richard B. Morris's James DeLancey: Portrait in Loyalism," *New York History* 80 (April 1999): 195. Morris's essay, printed here in full, was written in 1939 as a brochure to accompany the sale of a portrait of James DeLancey Jr. It is the most complete biography of the man and is provided with editing and an introduction by Ranlet.

24. John Watts wrote of his experience in 1787, quoted in J. Thomas Scharf, *History of Westchester County, New York, including Morrisania, Kings Bridge and West Farms, Which Have Been Annexed to New York City*, 2 vols. (Philadelphia: L. E. Preston & Co., 1886), 1:865

25. A map of this plan can be found in Thomas Jones, *History of New York During the Revolutionary War*, ed. Edward Floyd Delancey, 2 vols. (New York: New-York Historical Society, 1879), 2:559. For DeLancey's claims vis-à-vis his father's income, "Transcript of the manuscript books and papers of the Commission of Enquiry into the losses and services of the American Loyalists held under Acts of Parliament of 23, 25, 26, 28 and 29 of George III," transcribed for the New York Public Library, 1898–1903, on microform in its manuscripts division, 41:295–296. For his calculations about the future growth of the city and value of his land, see Loyalist transcripts, 41:311–312. For his ground and other rents from the city property, Loyalist transcripts, 41: 307–312. For a general description of the era's system of ground, building, and other leases, see Elizabeth Blackmar, *Manhattan for Rent: 1785–1850* (Ithaca, NY: Cornell University Press, 1989), 9–10.

26. Jones, *History of New York*, 2:544.

27. See Francis Barnum Culver, *Blooded Horses of Colonial Days: Classic Horse Matches in America Before the Revolution* (Virginia: by author, 1922), 144–155. Also Avalyn Hunter, *American Classic Pedigrees, 1914–2002* (Lexington, KY: Blood-Horse Publications, 2003), 62.

28. *New-York Gazette* or *Weekly Post-Boy*, June 6, 1757.

29. Remonstrance quoted from Ross J. S. Hoffman, *Edward Burke, New York Agent: With His Letters to the New York Assembly and Intimate Correspondence with Charles O'Hara, 1761–1776* (Philadelphia: American Philosophical Society, 1956), 159.

30. Jones, *History of New York*, 1:103.

31. Evert Bancker Jr.'s Ms. Survey Book, March 1780–October 1788 (BV Bancker, Evert, Jr.), New-York Historical Society.

32. Julia Delafield, *Biographies of Francis Lewis and Morgan Lewis, By Their Granddaughter, Julia Delafield*, 2 vols. (New York: Anson D. F. Randolph and Co., 1877), 1:33–34.

33. Ibid., 1:75.

34. Abstract of letter from John Forbes to James Murray, original sent to Forbes's wife, Dorothy Forbes, in cartel of September 29, 1780, in Murray Family Papers, box 4, New-York Historical Society.

35. Hugh Edward Egerton, ed., *The Royal Commission on the Losses and Services of American Loyalists, 1783 to 1785, Being the Notes of Mr. Daniel Parker Coke, MP, One of the Commissioners During that Period* (1915; New York: Burt Franklin, 1971), 145. On colonial-era pay, see Jackson Turner Main, *The Social Structure of Revolutionary America* (Princeton, NJ: Princeton University Press, 1965), 95, 104.

36. David Colden to Mrs. Henrietta Maria Colden, September 15, 1783. In E. Alfred Jones, "Letter of David Colden, Loyalist, 1783," *American Historical Review* 25, no. 1 (October 1919): 82.

37. Story, *The deLanceys*, 21–24. He claims the relationship was a "morganatic" or "left-hand" (because the groom offered the bride his left rather than right hand) marriage, recognized by the church but without the right of inheritance. According to Story, James's youngest brother, John Peter, saw to it that these children, rejected by Margaret Allen DeLancey, were "carefully brought up and educated."

38. Loyalist transcripts, 41:334.

39. Statement by George Stanton and Samuel Magee, house carpenters, and Abraham Russell, bricklayer, on damages to James DeLancey's estate, June 11, 1779, in James DeLancey Papers, box 1, folder 4, New-York Historical Society.

40. Henry Onderdonk, *Documents and Letters Intended to Illustrate the Revolutionary Incidents of Queens County* (New York: Leavitt, Trow, 1846), 153–154.

41. Anne Charlotte DeLancey to her father, John Peter DeLancey, December 22, ca. 1821, in the DeLancey Family Papers, Museum of the City of New York.

42. Except where noted, the letters that follow, from Stanton and other agents to DeLancey, from DeLancey to the Office of American Claims, and from John Forster to DeLancey, are found in the James DeLancey Papers, box 2, folders 4 and 1, New-York Historical Society. The letter from DeLancey himself is apparently a copy or draft.

43. Loyalist transcripts, 11:128–129. Records of his claim and its hearing are in 41:269–342. Also invaluable on the disposition of the estate in America is Harry Yoshpe, "The DeLancey Estate: Did the Revolution Democratize Landholding in New York?" *New York History* 17, no. 2 (April 1936): 167–179.

44. Quote from memorial and description of the event are from Egerton Ryerson, *The Loyalists of America and their Times: From 1620 to 1816*, 2 vols. (Toronto: W. Briggs, 1880), 2:180–181.

45. Lt. John DeLancey to his brother James DeLancey, October 1, 1789, in the DeLancey Family Papers, Museum of the City of New York.

46. John Peter DeLancey to Lt. John DeLancey, January 18, 1791, in the DeLancey Family Papers, Museum of the City of New York.

47. Letters from James DeLancey to Lt. John DeLancey, January 2 and 30, 1792, in the DeLancey Family Papers, Museum of the City of New York. According to Story, John did obtain a captaincy in 1793, served in the West Indies,

and married the daughter of a wealthy Guernsey merchant, Caroline Carey, in 1797. See Story, *The deLanceys*, 24, 25.

48. Jane Austen, *Persuasion* (1817; New York: Barnes & Noble Books, 2003), 14, 126–127.

49. Delafield, *Biographies*, 1:180.

50. In a letter of September 4, 1795, from Anne Robertson to her brother Morgan Lewis, in Morgan Lewis Papers, New-York Historical Society, she thanks him for sending money to England to help her pay rent and expresses concern over the financial condition of her father and oldest brother, Francis.

51. Delafield, *Biographies*, 1:180.

52. Clare Brandt, *The Livingstons: An American Aristocracy* (Garden City, NY: Doubleday & Co., 1986), 136.

53. Copy of a letter from Francis Lewis to Anne Robertson, March 8, 1785. Morgan Lewis Papers, New-York Historical Society.

54. Delafield, *Biographies*, 2:165.

55. The petition, submitted by "Morgan Lewis and other proprietors of the Marsh or meadow land lying East of north St. between Avenue B, and the East river," apparently was first filed in 1822, but not acted upon until later. See *Minutes of the Common Council of the City of New York, 1784–1831*, 19 vols. (New York: Dodd, Mead, 1917), 12:188. The history is reviewed in *Documents of the Board of Aldermen of the City of New-York*, Vol. 1, Document 8, June 9, 1834. The petition included a request to abolish the marketplace sited just above 7th Street on the East River under the Commissioners Plan of 1811. This space apparently was never used as a market.

56. Register of Conveyances, New York County, located at 66 John Street. Lewis's purchase is recorded in 48:277. His conveyance to the Lewis Association (183:423) is missing, but the transaction is referred to in 194:214 and 216:289.

57. Clermont and Staatsburgh, the latter expanded to a monstrous size by Morgan and Gertrude Lewis's Gilded Age descendants, are open to the public today.

58. Delafield, *Biographies*, 2:182.

59. Ibid., 2:141–142.

60. Rem Koolhaas, *Delirious New York: A Retroactive Manifesto for Manhattan* (Rotterdam: 010 Publishers, 1994), 123.

61. On the grid plan in history, see Spiro Kostof, *The City Shaped: Urban Patterns and Meanings Through History* (New York: Bullfinch Press, 1991), 95–157. The design of Washington, DC, is discussed on 113 and 209–210. For the quotation from the commissioners' report, see William Bridges, "Map of the City of New York and Island of Manhattan: With Explanatory Remarks and References (New York: T. & J. Swords, 1811), 24.

62. Adams to Jefferson and Thomas McKean, July 30, 1815, and Jefferson to Adams, August 10–11, 1815, in *The Adams-Jefferson Letters: The Complete Correspondence Between Thomas Jefferson and Abigail and John Adams*, ed. Lester J. Cappon, 2 vols. (Chapel Hill: University of North Carolina Press, 1959), 2:451–454.

63. Bridges, *Map of the City of New York*, 24.

64. Koolhaas, *Delirious*, 18–19.

65. Lewis Association articles recorded July 22, 1825, in Register of Conveyances, New York County, 194:214.

66. Lewis Association partition deed, recorded November 2, 1827, executed June 13, 1826, Register of Conveyances, New York County, 227:163. The Lewis Association lands also included a small strip to the north bought from Peter Stuyvesant, a descendant of the Dutch governor.

67. *Minutes of the Common Council*, 15:556.

68. Ibid., 16:284.

69. *Documents of the Board of Aldermen and Board of Assistants of the City of New-York*, Vol. 1, Document 15, January 23, 1832.

70. Ibid.

71. *Proceedings of the Board of Aldermen and Assistant Aldermen, and Approved by the Mayor*, Vol. 1, 302, December 7, 1832.

72. *Documents of the Board of Aldermen of the City of New-York*, Vol. 1, Document 8, June 9, 1834. The sewer and stench traps were proposed in 1832 as well. See Note 69.

73. Register of Conveyances, New York County, 216:289, 216:334, 220:94.

74. Register of Conveyances, 347: 606, 609, also recorded in 337:6. See also *Map of 150 Lots of Ground Situated in the Eleventh Ward of New York Belonging to the Estate of John Flack, Decd.* (New York: Mesier's Lith, 1833), New York Public Library Map Division. On James B. Murray, see James B. Murray to his wife, Maria Bronson Murray, October 16, 1828, and the *Autobiography of the late Col. James B. Murray of New York*, both in Murray Family Papers, box 4, New-York Historical Society.

75. Register of Conveyances, New York County, 337:6. This indenture of May 25, 1835 also mentions the $40,000 mortgage to John Flack's estate.

76. *Harper's Weekly*, November 22, 1873.

77. Assessed Valuation of Real Estate, 1789–1979, New York City Municipal Archives, for the year 1845.

78. 106 West 11th, according to *Doggett's New York City Directory*, 1849–1850.

79. Richard Plunz remarks that in the middle decades of the nineteenth century, New York "became a city not of 'houses,' but of 'housing.'" See Richard Plunz, *A History of Housing in New York City: Dwelling Type and Social Change in the American Metropolis* (New York: Columbia University Press, 1990), 4.

80. Andrew Lipscomb and Albert Bergh, eds., *The Writings of Thomas Jefferson*, 20 vols. (Washington, DC: Thomas Jefferson Memorial Association of the United States, 1904), 19:17–18.

81. This is the title of Ellis's book on Jefferson. Joseph J. Ellis, *American Sphinx: The Character of Thomas Jefferson* (New York: Alfred A. Knopf, 1997).

CHAPTER FOUR

1. Ernst Jentsch, "On the Psychology of the Uncanny" (1906), trans. Roy Sellars, *Angelaki* 2, no. 1 (November 1995): 11, 15.

2. Sigmund Freud, "The 'Uncanny'" (1919), in *The Standard Edition of the Complete Psychological Works of Sigmund Freud*, ed. and trans. James Strachey, 24 vols. (London: Hogarth, 1955), 17: 219–252.

3. Gaston Bachelard, *The Poetics of Space*, trans. Maria Jolas (Boston: Beacon Press, 1969), 5.

4. *Structural Engineer*, March 2000, 3.

5. Virginia Lee Burton, *The Little House* (New York: Houghton Mifflin, 1942), 1.

6. Luce Irigaray, "Place, Interval: A Reading of Aristotle, *Physics IV*," in *An Ethics of Sexual Difference*, trans. Carolyn Burke and Gillian C. Gill (Ithaca, NY: Cornell University Press, 1993), 35.

7. The term was coined by the British psychoanalyst D. W. Winnicott and the concept elaborated in numerous mid-twentieth-century essays. See "Ego Integration in Child Development" (1962), in D. W. Winnicott, *The Maturational Processes and the Facilitating Environment: Studies in the Theory of Emotional Development* (London: Hogarth, 1965), 56–63, and, in the same volume, "The Capacity to Be Alone" (1958), 29–36, and "The Theory of the Parent-Infant Relationship" (1960), 37–55.

8. *Time* magazine, June 3, 2008, www.time.com/time/nation/article/0,8599 ,1820028,00.html.

9. Irigaray, "Place, Interval," 40.

10. Manhattan average co-op size from the chart "Manhattan Average Co-op/Condo Square Foot Trend," at www.millersamuel.com. The average new single-family home size is from the chart "Median and Average Square Feet of Floor Area in New Single-Family Houses Completed by Location," U.S. Census Bureau, www.census.gov/const/C25Ann/sftotalmedavgsqft.pdf. The chart covers the years 1973 to 2009. Also see "A Century of Progress: America's Housing 1900–2000," National Association of Home Builders, April 2003, www.ewcupdate .com/fckeditor/userfiles/baec_net/A%20Century%20of%20Progress(1).pdf.

11. The inner workings of the Tredwell house are gleaned from several site visits, as well as the excellently detailed *Merchant's House Museum Tour Book* (New York: Merchant's House Museum, 2006).

12. "The Newly Housed," *New York Times*, May 15, 1872. The word "Daily" and a hyphen between "New" and "York" were dropped from the paper's title in the nineteenth century. For simplicity, I will refer to it as the *New York Times* throughout.

CHAPTER FIVE

1. *New York Times*, May 1, 1866. Further references to this columnist's advice, given in italics, are from the same piece.

2. I can't say for sure that the Barnards moved on May 1, but as they were renters, it's a very good bet. This material and other information about residents of the block and their movements, unless otherwise noted, are drawn from extensive examination of city directories, especially *Doggett's New York City Street Directory* for 1851, a reverse directory giving the names and occupations of resi-

dents by address; federal censuses for 1850, 1860, and 1870 and the state census for 1855; and tax assessment records at the New York City Municipal Archives, which give the names of owners or occupants each year.

3. Elisha's genealogy is given in Royal R. Hinman, *A Catalogue of the Names of the Early Puritan Settlers of the Colony of Connecticut* (Hartford, CT: Tiffany and Co., 1852), 134. That of Frances is given in Bethuel C. Dodd and John R. Burnet, *Genealogies of the Male Descendants of Daniel Dod, of Branford, Conn., a Native of England: 1646–1863* (Newark, NJ: self-published, 1864), 46.

4. *New York Times*, May 2, 1863.

5. Ibid., May 2, 1854.

6. His name was Joshua Beebe Pendleton; genealogy given in Everett Hall Pendleton, *Brian Pendleton and His Descendants, 1599–1910: With Some Account of the Pendleton Families of Orange County, N.Y., Otsego County, N.Y., and Luzerne County, Pa., etc.* (self-published, 1910), 440.

7. *New York Tribune*, May 2, 1845.

8. This description is cobbled from *Doggett's New York City Street Directory* for 1851 and examination of a detailed map, William Perris, *Maps of the City of New York, Surveyed Under Directions of Insurance Companies of Said City* (New York: Perris & Browne, 1852–1854), plate 42.

9. This description of the riverfront layout is taken from maps—Matthew Dripps, *City of New York Extending Northward to Fiftieth Street, Surveyed and Drawn by John F. Harrison, C.E.* (New York: M. Dripps, 1852), William Perris's 1852–1854 maps mentioned in note 8, and slightly later versions, William Perris, *Maps of the City of New York* (New York: Perris & Browne, 1857–1863), plates 31, 34, and 38. Also directory listings for James R. Steers and J. A. Secor, proprietors who lived on our block, *New York Times* obituaries for James R. Steers and John Englis (April 19, 1896, and April 3, 1915), as well as a detailed description of the establishments in 1857 in reporting on layoffs due to that year's economic depression (October 7, 1857). It should be understood this is something of a moving target. For example, Westervelt & Mackey started in business around the hook at Houston Street in 1841 and moved to 7th Street and Lewis in 1844, where the firm continued through at least 1851. Dripps 1852 shows the yard at both sites. Around 1856, the firm was "financially embarrassed" but was continued "in their interest" and "at the old yard" by S. G. Bogert, according to John Harrison Morrison's *A History of New York Ship Yards* (New York: W. F. Sametz & Co., 1909), 95, 111. Perris 1857–1863 shows the Bogert name between Houston and 3rd.

10. *Niles' National Register*, November 9, 1839.

11. Register of Conveyances, New York County, 505:533.

12. Sean Wilentz calls an 1815 bindery of three or four workers a "rough norm" for New York artisan working arrangements of that time. Sean Wilentz, *Chants Democratic: New York City and the Rise of the American Working Class, 1788–1850*, 20th anniversary ed. (Oxford: Oxford University Press, 2004), 28. The bookbinding factory of later years is described in detail in C. T. Hinceley, "A Day at the Bookbindery of Lippincott, Grambo & Co.," *Godey's Lady's Book*, November

1852, pp. 403–412. "We were completely lost in astonishment," says the author, "as we passed through room after room peopled with workmen engaged in the various branches to which the rooms were devoted." Edward Walker, who had a bookbindery on Fulton Street in the mid-nineteenth century, refers to being able to produce 10,000 volumes "in an incredibly short space of time" through "an admirable distribution of labor." Edward Walker, *The Art of Book-Binding, Its Rise and Progress; Including a Descriptive Account of the New York Book-Bindery*, ed. Paul S. Koda (1852; New Castle, DE: Oak Knoll Books, 1984), 81.

13. *New York Times*, May 2, 1856.

14. *Young America*, May 3, 1845.

15. From the diaries of George Templeton Strong, March 21, 1865, in *Writing New York: A Literary Anthology*, ed. Philip Lopate (New York: Library of America, 1998), 235.

16. *New York Times*, May 3, 1887.

17. *New York Herald*, March 29, 1846.

18. *New York Tribune*, August 3, 1861.

19. *New York Herald*, September 13, 1861.

20. Elizabeth Blackmar discusses the sharing of housing in *Manhattan For Rent, 1785–1850* (Ithaca, NY: Cornell University Press, 1989), 68–71. Also see Elizabeth Collins Cromley, *Alone Together: A History of New York's Early Apartments* (Ithaca, NY: Cornell University Press, 1990), 25–27.

21. Blackmar, *Manhattan For Rent*, 128.

22. May 8, 1845, and September 1841, respectively.

23. *New York Times*, May 2, 1856.

24. Ibid., May 2, 1863.

25. James R. Steers's obituary in the *New York Times* (April 19, 1896) says the brothers' firm, opened in 1850 near the foot of 12th, built *America*. George Steers was widely feted for his work on the yacht. However, according to Morrison, it was designed by George Steers but built by William H. Brown, whose yard was in the same area. John Harrison Morrison, *A History of New York Ship Yards*, 125. Whatever the case, James R. Steers's career unfolded within the glorious penumbra cast by *America*.

26. Richard C. McKay, *South Street: A Maritime History of New York*, 2nd ed. (Riverside, CT: 7C's Press, 1969), 178.

27. *New York Times*, November 30, 1852.

28. Quoted in Edwin L. Dunbaugh and William duBarry Thomas, *William H. Webb: Shipbuilder* (Glen Cove, NY: Webb Institute of Naval Architecture, 1989), 112. The letter was also addressed to Webb's accountant, Hugh McClellan.

29. The *Times*, in 1854, gives the local weekly pay of shipwrights (skilled carpenters), ship caulkers, and ship fasteners (or joiners) as $18 a week, compared with $12 to $20 for boilermakers, $10 for a harness maker, and as little as $5 for a "slop" tailor. *New York Times*, June 20, 1854. Wilentz cites the account books of a journeyman ship carpenter earning up to $2.75 a day between 1830 and 1852, and gives the average monthly wage in shipbuilding as $48.27. Wilentz, *Chants Democratic*, 135, 405.

30. For the mechanics of building wooden ships, see Samuel Orchart Beeton, *Beeton's Dictionary of Industries and Commerce* (1888; New York: Elibron Classics, 2006), 231. On ship workers see John V. Goff, "Shipyard Owners and Workers," in *This American River: Five Centuries of Writing about the Connecticut*, ed. W. D. Wetherell (Lebanon, NH: University Press of New England), 112–115.

31. These hours given by Dunbaugh and Thomas, *William H. Webb*, 18. Morrison, in *A History of New York Ship Yards*, 69, says breakfast was at eight, dinner at noon.

32. *Boston Daily Atlas*, June 16, 1851. Transcribed by Lars Bruzelius, *The Maritime History Virtual Archives*, www.bruzelius.info/nautica/Nautica.html.

33. Descriptions of these particular ironworks are contained in J. Leander Bishop, *A History of American Manufactures from 1608 to 1860*, 3 vols. (Philadelphia: E. Young, 1868), 3:124–128, 130–132. Also contains descriptions of major shipyards.

34. *Scrapbook of New York City Views*, 9th Street, New York Public Library.

35. Edward K. Spann, *The New Metropolis: New York City, 1840–1857* (New York: Columbia University Press, 1981), 404. Advertisements in New York City directories for 1860s.

36. Graham Russell Hodges, *New York City Cartmen, 1667–1850* (New York: New York University Press, 1986). On "close living patterns," including in the eleventh ward, see page 130. Hodges develops a portrait of the cartmen as politically astute, independent, familiar with every aspect of the city—and often attracting the ire of other citizens for reckless driving and other transgressions.

37. *New York Times*, March 1, 1860.

38. For a lively account, see Isaac S. Lyon, *Recollections of an Old Cartman* (1872; New York: New York Bound, 1984).

39. These statistics were collected in the context of a dispute between the city and the man contracted to collect dead horses and other offal from city streets and deposit them on Barren Island. *New York Times*, March 8, 1855.

40. Graham Hodges, "'Desirable Companions and Lovers': Irish and African Americans in the Sixth Ward, 1830–1870," in *The New York Irish*, ed. Ronald H. Bayor and Timothy J. Meagher (Baltimore: Johns Hopkins University Press, 1996), 121. Black and Irish domestics "shared equally poor chances for marriage and family life," writes Hodges.

41. Citizens' Association of New York Council of Hygiene and Public Health, *Report of the Council of Hygiene and Public Health of the Citizens' Association of New York Upon the Sanitary Condition of the City*, 1866, 172. This report goes over the condition of the streets and buildings neighborhood by neighborhood.

42. On details of housekeeping, see Susan Strasser, *Never Done: A History of American Housework* (New York: Pantheon Books, 1982); on stoves, 36–42; on hauling water for various uses, 86–97; on laundry, 104–108.

43. Abraham Jacobi, a physician in New York's German dispensary, described visiting children dying from "summer cholera" and the advice given him by older colleagues to withhold milk, probably a wise choice since the unpasteurized and unrefrigerated milk might be contaminated. Teething itself was thought to be a

cause of sickness and death in infants because of its coincidence with the dangerous period of weaning, when babies were exposed to new and potentially harmful weaning foods. Purging and cutting the gums were common practices, but doctors like Jacobi, called the father of American pediatrics, railed against them. He told the milk story in an address at the twenty-fifth anniversary of the German Dispensary, in *Dr. Jacobi's Works,* 8 vols. (New York: Critic and Guide Company, 1909), 8:59. Also see Abraham Jacobi, *Dentition and Its Derangements: A Course of Lectures Delivered in the New York Medical College* (New York: Balliere Brothers, 1862), and Henry Hanks, *On Teething of Infants: Its Prevalent Errors, Neglects, and Dangers; Their Influence on the Health, and As Causes of Death of Children: including The Dangers of Teething Powders, Soothing Powders, Soothing Syrups, etc., etc.* (London: J. W. Davies, 1861). Ads for Mrs. Winslow's Soothing Syrup, which contained morphine, were common during these decades. This one was found in the *Tribune,* May 1, 1861.

44. Details on the school are from the *New York Times,* March 14, 1856. "The singing was good," the reporter says of the primary department's examination by school officials, a description the students' parents would no doubt have considered faint praise.

45. This number is from the eighth enumeration district, eleventh ward, 1855 New York State census. The enumeration district comprises two regular-size and three short blocks that are residential, a fairly small area where so many deaths of young children surely would have been keenly felt.

46. The deaths of Eliphant, Foesh, Francis, and Burgess are recorded in the register of deaths for the year 1855, New York City Municipal Archives.

47. Walt Whitman, "A Song for Occupations," written in 1855. Quoted from *Leaves of Grass,* ed. Sculley Bradley and Harold W. Blodgett (New York: W. W. Norton & Co., 1973), 217.

48. James B. Murray to Maria (Bronson) Murray, April 29, 1841. Murray Family Papers, box 4, New-York Historical Society. This letter, in a book of typescripts, omits a word where Murray describes the type of conveyance he has taken to Le Havre. I'm assuming it was a stage, considering the dust, the fact the journey took fifteen and a half hours, and the number of people accommodated. Maria was addressed at Hotel Messina in Paris.

49. I refer to Greenfield Hill, the country seat of Maria's father, the banker Isaac Bronson; she and the Murray children spent a good deal of time there.

50. The 1870 federal census lists his birthplace as Hesse. The 1880 federal census lists it as Bavaria. According to the Battery Conservancy's database of immigrants through New York, searchable at www.castlegarden.org, a twenty-seven-year-old Abraham Weinstein, tailor, sailed out of Bremen on the barque *Republic,* arriving in New York June 29, 1839.

51. For discussion of the German migration in these years, see Stanley Nadel, *Little Germany: Ethnicity, Religion, and Class in New York City, 1845–80* (Urbana: University of Illinois Press, 1990), 16–26. Some authors emphasize the economic as opposed to religious reasons for German emigration (see Roger Daniels, "Nineteenth-Century German Immigrants Sought Economic Prosperity," in *Com-*

ing to America: The Germans, ed. Jacquelyn Landis [Detroit, MI: Greenhaven Press, 2006], 56–61), but those writing on Jewish life in Germany at the time document additional "push" factors that applied to this group, especially in the southwest German states. See for example, James F. Harris, *The People Speak! Anti-Semitism and Emancipation in Nineteenth Century Bavaria* (Ann Arbor: University of Michigan Press, 1993), 20–24; Marion A. Kaplan, *Jewish Daily Life in Germany, 1618–1945* (Oxford: Oxford University Press, 2005), 93, 131. "The issue of citizens' rights at commune level remained a key problem above all in the South and South West German states, since these rights involved many aspects of communal life, notably the benefits of communal resources as well as contribution to poor relief, the right to settle and opportunities of earning a livelihood," writes Reinhard Rürup, "European Revolutions and Emancipation," in *Revolution and Evolution: 1848 in German-Jewish History,* ed. Werner E. Mosse, Arnold Paucker, and Reinhard Rürup (Tübingen: Mohr Siebeck, 1981), 10–11.

52. In fact, the 1900 federal census, which finds the Weinsteins' firstborn in St. Louis, Missouri, says he was born in New York in May 1839—the month *before* his father's arrival there. Abraham and Regina, in the 1855 state census, both report being in the country sixteen years, and Samuel here gives his age as fifteen. At this distance, it's impossible to tell where the error lies, but the family's basic trajectory is clear—immigration, marriage, and first birth came in a rush.

53. Nathaniel Parker Willis, "Open-Air Musings in the City, 1843–4," in *Writing New York,* 82.

54. City directories for the early '40s list the congregation and the Weinsteins at 156 Attorney St. That Abraham was a founder and trustee is from an unfinished manuscript by former Senior Rabbi Lewis I. Newman, *History of Rodeph Sholom,* made available by W. W. Chuck Weiss, chairman of the synagogue's archives committee.

55. Hyman B. Grinstein, *The Rise of the Jewish Community of New York, 1654–1860* (Philadelphia: Jewish Publication Society of America, 1947), 32, 173–174, 233–234, 272, 395–396. Grinstein provides a quite detailed account of the rise of the first synagogues. Rodeph Sholom was the seventh to be formed. The congregation built a sanctuary at 11 Clinton St. in the 1850s and later moved to the Upper West Side. In 1901 the congregation joined the Reform movement (www.rodephsholom.org).

56. *New York Times,* October 9, 1857.

57. "A tailor is nothing without a wife and very often a child," one of Weinstein's contemporaries, a German tailor, told a Senate committee later in the century. Quoted in Edith Abbott, *Women in Industry: A Study in American Economic History* (North Stratford, NH: Ayer Co., 1970), 223.

58. Michael Zakim explores and emphasizes the emerging distinctions between tailors and clothiers in "A Ready-Made Business: The Birth of the Clothing Industry in America," *Business History Review* 73, no. 1 (Spring 1999): 70. In newspaper accounts of the fire in Murray Street (see below), Weinstein was variously described as a wholesale clothier, a dealer in clothing, and a manufacturer of clothing. These terms make him a boss and a merchandiser; what's not certain is

whether his workers were outworkers or labored in a shop at the Murray Street address. I think the reference to wholesaling implies the former. Also useful is Zakim's "Customizing the Industrial Revolution: The Reinvention of Tailoring in the Nineteenth Century," *Winterthur Portfolio* 33, no. 1 (Spring 1998).

59. David S. Reynolds, *Walt Whitman's America: A Cultural Biography* (New York: Knopf, 1995), 406.

60. Assessed Valuation of Real Estate, 1789–1979, New York City Municipal Archives. This abatement began the year he moved in, in 1860, so it doesn't necessarily imply service in the Civil War. The Sellecks at No. 275 also got an abatement, as did the Littles and a few other families on the block.

61. State of New York, *Annual Report of the Adjutant-General* (Albany: 1858), 5.

62. William S. Stryker, New Jersey Adjutant-General's Office, *Record of Officers and Men of New Jersey in the Civil War, 1861–1865* (Trenton, NJ: John L. Murphy, Steam Book and Job Printer, 1876), 1256, 1257, 1284, 1288. From a digitized, searchable version on the website of the New Jersey State Library, www.njstatelib.org.

63. On Germans' support for Lincoln's policies, a feeling not shared by all the neighborhood's mechanics, some of whom participated in riots against the draft in 1863, see Edward K. Spann, *Gotham At War: 1860–1865* (Wilmington, DE: Scholarly Resources, 2002), 110–112. On the depression among clothiers preceding the war, see Spann, *Gotham At War*, 7, 52, 137.

64. Coverage of the fire is found in the *New York Times*, September 10, 11, and 17, 1864; the *New York Herald*, September 10 and 11; and the *New York Tribune*, September 10, 11, and 12. On the 11th the *Tribune* reported that there was "almost another big fire in Murray Street," with what looked like a large quantity of camphene, a highly flammable lamp fuel, thrown under a door and lit. I could not find any other follow-up to the arson charge.

65. *New York Times*, July 18, 1865.

66. See Henry Hall, Department of the Interior, Census Office, *Report on the Ship-Building Industry of the United States* (Washington, DC: Government Printing Office, 1884), 118; Dunbaugh and Thomas, *William H. Webb*, 117–118; *New York Times*, January 29, 1867, in which William Webb gives his own explanation of the industry's demise; McKay, *South Street*, 420–424.

67. *New York Tribune*, May 16, 1870. Here, in an argument over protectionism, the *Tribune* seems to be quoting the *Evening Post* quoting itself.

68. *New York Times*, July 28, 1858.

69. Dunbaugh and Thomas, *William H. Webb*, 230.

70. Marriage certificate #1937, March 22, 1868. Steinberg's first husband, Morris, had acquired No. 243 on August 17, 1862, from Jonas Straus, who had bought it from the oil dealer Leonard L. Johnson (Register of Conveyances, New York County, 863:96). Morris died after 1865. Abraham Weinstein sold No. 239 in 1867 but evidently lived there until his marriage the following year. Caroline and Abraham were married by a Rev. Herman Hoffman, who lived on Clinton Street near the new site of Rodeph Sholom and was probably affiliated with the synagogue. A dealer in wines who lived at No. 239 served as witness.

71. The cabin of the steamer *China*, which served in the transpacific trade, survives at Belvedere, California. Having been used as a private residence and clubhouse, it's now open to the public. Dunbaugh and Thomas, *William H. Webb*, 228–229.

72. Archaeologists commissioned by the New York City Landmarks Preservation Commission, Grossman & Associates Inc., made two reports: "The Archaeology of Civil War Era Water Control Systems on the Lower East Side of Manhattan, New York: Data Recovery and Mitigation of the Mid 19th Century Cistern Complex" and "Addendum to Archaeological Data Recovery Results: Economic and Ethnic Land Use History of Lot 58: The Human Face of Lot 58," both dated 1995. The artifacts were moved to the New York State Museum, Albany, in 2008.

73. From "A Song for Occupations," in *Leaves of Grass*, 215.

CHAPTER SIX

1. "The young child's world . . . is animated and consists of vivid, sharply delineated objects in a weakly structured space," writes Yi-Fu Tuan in *Topophilia: A Study of Environmental Perception, Attitudes, and Values* (New York: Columbia University Press, 1990), 56.

2. Summarizing Jean Piaget and other theorists, Lynn S. Liben and Roger M. Downs describe "a developmental progression [in children] that moves from a focus on (a) spatial properties of individual objects or local groups of objects, (b) objects in space in relation to the viewer, and (c) objects in space in relation to some specified, viewer-independent system (such as Cartesian coordinates)." "Geography for Young Children: Maps as Tools for Learning Environments," in *Psychological Perspectives on Early Childhood Education: Reframing Dilemmas in Research and Practice*, ed. Susan L. Golbeck (Philadelphia: Lawrence Erlbaum Associates, 2001), 239. The process by which grown-ups develop knowledge about a given environment is not dissimilar. As summarized by M. Raubal and M. J. Egenhofer, "The mental map develops from a mental landmark map to a mental route map and should eventually result in a mental survey map. The last state is closest to a cartographic map, though it still contains inaccuracies and distortions." In "Comparing the Complexity of Wayfinding Tasks in Built Environments," *Environment and Planning B: Planning and Design* 25, no. 6 (1998): 897.

3. Quoted in Yi-Fu Tuan, *Space and Place: The Perspective of Experience* (Minneapolis: University of Minnesota Press, 1977), 160.

4. Martin Heidegger, "The Thing," in *Poetry, Language and Thought*, trans. Albert Hofstadter (New York: Harper & Row, 1971), 166. "What about nearness?" he continues. "How can we come to know its nature? Nearness, it seems, cannot be encountered directly. We succeed in reaching it rather by attending to what is near."

5. Passive experiences of a place result in less richly differentiated cognitive maps; people who know a city only by public transit develop "notoriously fragmented"

mental schemes of the place, according to Donald Appleyard, "Notes on Urban Perception and Knowledge," in *Image and Environment: Cognitive Mapping and Spatial Behavior*, ed. Roger M. Davis and David Stea (Chicago: Aldine, 1973), 112. Also see Davis and Stea, *Maps in Mind: Reflections on Cognitive Mapping* (New York: Harper & Row, 1977), 236–237.

6. A review of this literature, still somewhat controversial, can be found in Jennifer L. Black and James Macinko, "Neighborhoods and Obesity," *Nutrition Reviews* 66, no. 1 (January 2008): 2–20.

7. Kevin Lynch, *The Image of the City* (Cambridge, MA: MIT Press, 1960), 9.

8. Justice L.A. Giegerich, "Reminiscences of the Old Eleventh Ward," in *Valentine's Manual of Old New York*, ed. Henry Collins Brown (New York: Valentine's Manual Inc., 1921), 211–215; *The Sun*, September 1, 1895; *New York Times*, May 11, 1902. The documentaries mentioned here are *Street of the Flower Boxes*, directed by David Tapper (Wilmette, IL: Films Inc., 1973), based on a book by Peggy Mann; and *7th Street*, directed by Josh Pais, who grew up on the block (Paradise Acres Productions, 2003). The thesis quotation is from Stephen C. Barto, "A Study of the Lower East Side Block's Block Association," in *The Structure and Function of Block Associations as Emerging Urban Phenomena: June 8–Aug. 31, 1975*, Stephen C. Barto, project director; Owen Lynch, faculty adviser (New York University, 1975), 2.

9. The poem is "Loisaida," in *Aloud: Voices from the Nuyorican Poets Café*, ed. Miguel Algarín and Bob Holman (New York: Henry Holt, 1994), 361.

10. Grant Hildebrand, *Origins of Architectural Pleasure* (Berkeley: University of California Press, 1999), 18.

11. Stephen Kaplan, "Aesthetics, Affect, and Cognition: Environmental Preference from an Evolutionary Perspective," *Environment and Behavior* 19, no. 1 (January 1967): 20.

12. "Legibility" is a term Kevin Lynch first used in *The Image of the City*. Jay Appleton first espoused the prospect-refuge idea, arguing that "the strategic value of a landscape" continues to be "apprehended aesthetically" even though survival is no longer at issue. Jay Appleton, *The Experience of Landscape*, rev. ed. (1975; Chichester, West Sussex, UK: John Wiley & Sons, 1996), 67. "Making sense" and "involvement" are terms used by Stephen Kaplan and Rachel Kaplan in *Cognition and Environment: Functioning in an Uncertain World* (New York: Praeger, 1982), 81. Their chapter "Evaluation, Preference, and Human Needs" (pp. 73–95) provides a detailed discussion.

13. On historical demographics, see Kenneth T. Jackson, ed., *The Encyclopedia of New York City* (New Haven, CT: Yale University Press, 1995), 921; and Wendell Cox Consultancy, "New York (Manhattan) Wards: Population & Density, 1800–1910," www.demographia.com. For demographics as of 2000, see New York City Department of City Planning, Population Division, "Map PL-1: Population Density by Census Tract" (2000) and *The Newest New Yorkers: 2000*, Appendix Table 5–1, "Population Density and Percent Foreign-born New York Metropolitan Region by Subregion and County." On U.S. population density

overall, see U.S. Census Bureau, "Population, Housing Units, and Density for Counties: 2000," www.census.gov and www.nyc.gov/dcp.

14. E. S. Martin, "East Side Considerations," in *Harper's New Monthly Magazine,* reprinted in *Tales of Gaslight New York,* ed. Frank Oppel (Edison, NJ: Castle Books, 2000), 95.

15. For a summary of research on density and crowding, see Paul A. Bell, Thomas Greene, Jeffrey D. Fisher, and Andrew S. Baum, *Environmental Psychology,* 5th ed. (Hove, East Sussex, UK: Psychology Press, 2005), 305–327. Elevator study mentioned on page 316. Tony Cassidy also treats the subject in *Environmental Psychology: Behaviour and Experience in Context* (Hove, East Sussex, UK: Psychology Press, 1997), 141–152.

16. Bella Spewack, *Streets: A Memoir of the Lower East Side* (New York: Feminist Press at the City University of New York, 1995), 3, 56, 66.

17. Ibid., from the introduction by Ruth Limmer, xiv.

18. In borrowing this concept of the familiar stranger, I may be violating the definition Milgram intended. He stressed that the relationship between familiar strangers is a "frozen" one; "a barrier has developed that is not readily broken." Of his own experience standing on a train platform with familiar strangers he'd seen for years but never addressed, Milgram said, "I found a peculiar tension in this situation, when people treat each other as properties of the environment rather than as individuals to deal with." In the nine years I lived on the block I watched certain children grow up without ever acknowledging them directly. I never found this disturbing; sometimes another "individual to deal with" is exactly what neither party wants or needs. I suspect this difference both in the way the familiar-stranger relationship feels and in how rigidly anonymity is maintained may have to do with the setting; what place could be colder or more anonymous than a suburban commuter rail station at rush hour? Rather than emphasize the barrier between familiar strangers on the platform, you could marvel that they (wordlessly) helped each other to "dwell," to find a sense of home, even in a landscape defined by unceasing mobility. Milgram's quotes and paper on the familiar stranger are published in his book, *The Individual in a Social World: Essays and Experiments* (Reading, MA: Addison-Wesley Publishing Company, 1977), 3–4, 51–53.

19. Jane Jacobs, *The Death and Life of Great American Cities* (New York: Random House, 1961), 56.

20. See Eric Paulos and Elizabeth Goodman, "The Familiar Stranger: Anxiety, Comfort, and Play in Public Places," Conference on Human Factors in Computing Systems, April 24–29, 2004, Vienna, Austria. Available on the Web at www.paulos.net/research/intel/familiarstranger. This is part of a fascinating effort by researchers at Intel to elaborate the familiar-stranger concept with a system of personal mobile devices that emit unique signals recognizable and recordable by similar devices when they come into proximity. The devices also could be affixed to specific locations. Thus, write Paulos and Goodman, "As individuals traverse an urban landscape, they simply infuse their path with a unique and detectable digital redolence. Similarly, fixed places/objects can also emit

unique 'scents' once they are 'digitally tagged.'" You could figure out that someone you cross paths with at the bus stop also frequents your favorite falafel place. It's strange—but cool!—to imagine that what I've always thought of in metaphorical and even mystical terms could be represented digitally.

21. Paulos and Goodman report that prevalence—reappearance frequently in one place or occasionally in many places—could confer sociometric-star status on otherwise unremarkable characters. See above, note 20.

22. Meyer Liben, who grew up uptown, writes of an athletic contest one afternoon in June 1924 that pitted "up-the-blocks" against "down-the-blocks," with "middle-of-the-blocks" joining with up-the-blocks for the day's events. "These internecine struggles can be the bitterest of all," he writes. Meyer Liben, *New York Street Games and Other Stories and Sketches* (New York: Schocken Books, 1984), 56–57.

23. Sophie Ruskay, *Horsecars and Cobblestones*, 1948, excerpted in *How We Lived: 1880–1930*, ed. Irving Howe and Kenneth Libo (New York: Richard Marek Publishers, 1979), 54.

24. *New York Times*, June 5, 1931.

25. Ibid., July 6, 1913.

26. The boys' games are discussed in Robert Dunn, "Games of the City Street," 1904, in *Tales of Gaslight New York*, 129–137. Horseshoe-the-mare quotes, 132–133.

27. P.-H. Chombart de Lauwe, *Paris et l'agglomération Parisienne, Vol. 1: L'espace social dans une grande cité* (Paris: Presses Universitaires de France, 1952), 106–107.

28. Guy Debord, "Theory of the Dérive," in the *Situationist International Anthology*, rev. and expanded ed., ed. and trans. Ken Knabb (Berkeley, CA: Bureau of Public Secrets, 2006), 63. In a dérive, Debord explains, "one or more persons during a certain period drop their relations, their work and leisure activities, and all their other usual motives for movement and action, and let themselves be drawn by the attractions of the terrain and the encounters they find there."

29. Lights in the subway: Lettrist International, October 1955, "Proposals for Rationally Improving the City of Paris," in *Situationist International Anthology*, 12. Equestrian statues: Guy Debord quotes Marcel Mariën in "Introduction to a Critique of Urban Geography," *Situationist International Anthology*, 11.

30. Kenneth A. Scherzer has argued that among nineteenth-century New Yorkers, "most meaningful social interaction was rooted in the 'unbounded community': the widely dispersed network of friends and relations beyond the neighborhood or its institutions." Scherzer, *The Unbounded Community: Neighborhood Life and Social Structure, 1830–1875* (Durham, NC: Duke University Press, 1992), 169. For the twentieth century, Jane Jacobs also rejects the metaphor of the village as a description of city neighborhoods. "The lack of either economic or social self-containment is natural and necessary to city neighborhoods—simply because they are parts of cities," she writes in *The Death and Life of Great American Cities*, 117. Interestingly, though, Scherzer found in the Dry Dock wards a partial exception to the pattern he described, with residents more likely to marry within the neighborhood and choose neighbors to witness bap-

tisms and weddings (169, 181). My own rather narrow and unscientific study convinces me that while of course inhabitants of No. 239 and of the block interacted widely across the city—indeed many had relations outside the city or even across the ocean—the immediate neighborhood was for the most part a very meaningful, densely connected locus of social life. It was no village, but it was, for lack of a better term, a world.

31. "The individual differences among cognitive maps emerge primarily from subtle variations in spatial activity patterns, variation which can have striking effects on such maps," according to Downs and Stea in *Image and Environment*, 21. "Repeated exposure to everyday environments leads to increasingly differentiated cognitive maps of those environments," writes Lynn S. Liben in "Environmental Cognition through Direct and Representational Experience: A Life-Span Perspective," in *Environment, Cognition, and Action: An Integrated Approach*, ed. Tommy Gärling and Gary W. Evans (New York: Oxford University Press, 1991), 259.

CHAPTER SEVEN

1. These details are taken from the *New York Times*, July 4 and 6, 1865.

2. New York City register of births, 1865, in New York City Municipal Archives.

3. From "Address at the Twenty-Fifth Jubilee of the German Dispensary of New York," in *Dr. Jacobi's Works: Collected Essays, Addresses, Scientific Papers and Miscellaneous Writings of A. Jacobi*, ed. William J. Robinson, 8 vols. (New York: Critic and Guide Company, 1909), 8:59–64.

4. *New York Times*, June 24, 1883.

5. Professional care of the newborn is described in "Infant Hygiene," *Dr. Jacobi's Works*, 3:41–138. Treatment of the cord is described on page 44.

6. On peddling, see Hasia R. Diner, *A Time for Gathering: The Second Migration, 1820–1880* (Baltimore: Johns Hopkins University Press, 1992), 66–73. Diner calls peddling "an almost universal male Jewish experience in nineteenth-century America."

7. Samuel Cohen, *Transplanted* (Hoboken, NJ: self-published, 1937), 107.

8. Information on diphtheria symptoms and first paper are from Abraham Jacobi, *A Treatise on Diphtheria* (New York: William Wood & Co., 1880), 77, 162.

9. John Watson, *American Medical Times*, vol. 2 (January 12, 1861): 32.

10. These and other treatments are discussed by Abraham Jacobi in a letter to the *American Medical Times*, vol. 2 (January 26, 1861): 69. See also Jacobi, *A Treatise on Diphtheria*, 178.

11. Tracheotomy was often resorted to in cases where asphyxiation seemed imminent due to "obstruction somewhere in the larynx." See, for example, the *American Medical Times* 3 (July 6, 1861): 10.

12. *New York Times*, May 6, 1900.

13. His death certificate can be found with others of the year 1867 on microfilm at the New York City Municipal Archives. The number of the certificate has been either cut off or lost.

14. There was at least the opportunity of doing well in the glazier's trade, especially if the workingman graduated to making contracts with builders or opening a storefront shop. Abraham Abrahamsohn, a German Jewish immigrant, reported in his memoirs having earned as a glazier a profit of $1,200 in just the second half of 1850; he was working under contract with a man building six houses on speculation. During the 1850s, Levy was one of only several men listed as glaziers in business directories and described himself in the 1880 census as a "retired merchant," which makes me think he met with some success in the business while at 257 Delancey St.; possibly he had a glass shop there. See Abraham Abrahamsohn, *Interesting Accounts of the Travels of Abraham Abrahamsohn to America and Especially to the Gold Mines of California and Australia*, prepared from the oral account by Friedrich Mihn; Marlene P. Toeppen, trans.; Norton B. Stern, ed., in *Western States Jewish History* 1, no. 3 (April 1969); originally published Ilmenau, Germany: Carl Friedrich Trommsdorf, 1856. Downloaded from the Western States Jewish History website at www.wsjh.com. On glaziers in New York also see Tyler Anbinder, *Five Points: The 19th-Century New York City Neighborhood That Invented Tap Dance, Stole Elections, and Became the World's Most Notorious Slum* (New York: Free Press, 2001; New York: Plume, 2002), 113, 118; Diner, *A Time for Gathering*, 74–75; Irving Howe, *World of Our Fathers: The Journey of the East European Jews to America and the Life They Found and Made*, 30th anniversary ed. (New York: New York University Press, 2005), 79.

15. Register of Conveyances, New York County, 997:665.

16. "Year's End" by Ellen Bryant Voigt is published in her volume *The Forces of Plenty* (Pittsburgh: Carnegie Mellon University Press, 1996), 42–43.

17. *New York Times*, January 12, 1896. See also *New York Times*, January 13, 1891; Clare Brandt, *The Livingstons: An American Aristocracy* (Garden City, NY: Doubleday & Co., 1986), 206–207; website of the Staatsburgh State Historic Site, www.staatsburgh.org.

18. On tenement-house law, see Robert W. DeForest and Lawrence Veiller, eds., *The Tenement House Problem: Including the Report of the New York State Tenement House Commission of 1900*, 2 vols. (New York: Macmillan Company, 1903), 2:319. Water-closet figures are from *Report of the Tenement House Committee as Authorized by Chapter 479 of the Laws of 1894* (Albany, NY: James B. Lyon, state printer, 1895), 115.

19. Jacob A. Riis, *How the Other Half Lives: Studies Among the Tenements of New York*, preface by Charles A. Madison (New York: Charles Scribner's Sons, 1890; New York: Dover Publications, 1971), 2.

20. Ibid., 17.

21. On the emergence of "apartments," see Richard Plunz, *A History of Housing in New York City* (New York: Columbia University Press, 1990), 62–87. In his chapter on nineteenth-century tenement-house life, James D. McCabe Jr., author of the contemporary *Lights and Shadows of New York Life,* identified tenement folk as both the very poor and the laboring class, meaning "all those who are forced to pursue some regular occupation for their support." He allowed that the

latter group lived in better tenements, "immense, but spruce looking," yet in his estimation all "suffer[ed] from the evils incident to and inseparable from such close packing." James D. McCabe Jr., *Lights and Shadows of New York Life; Or, the Sights and Sensations of the Great City*, a facsimile edition (Philadelphia: National Publishing Co., 1872; New York: Farrar, Straus & Giroux, 1970), 683, 686.

22. "Infected houses," see *The Tenement House Problem*, 1:463. For "saturated with bodily emanations" quote, see *Report of the Tenement House Committee as Authorized by Chapter 479 of the Laws of 1894*, 30.

23. Though the decline in infectious disease deaths began around 1870, it accelerated after 1900, dropping from 797 per 100,000 that year to 36 per 100,000 in 1980. See G. L. Armstrong, "Trends in Infectious Disease Deaths in the United States During the Twentieth Century," *Journal of the American Medical Association* 218, no. 1 (January 6, 1999): 61–66. At the turn of the twentieth century, the difference between urban and rural life expectancy was ten years; it dropped steadily thereafter.

24. *Report of the Tenement House Committee as Authorized by Chapter 479 of the Laws of 1894*, 158.

25. *New York Times*, September 29, 1892.

26. An 1894 investigation of dilapidated houses found that of 3,984 inspected, 2,055 had water supply in the halls. Because of poor lighting, the housewife was sometimes forced to "wholly or partially feel her way" there. *Report of the Tenement House Committee as Authorized by Chapter 479 of the Laws of 1894*, 93, 115.

27. Riis, *How the Other Half Lives*, 5, 2.

28. McCabe, *Lights and Shadows*, 697.

29. Helen Campbell, *Darkness and Daylight; or, Lights and Shadows of New York Life* (Hartford, CT: Hartford Publishing Co., 1899), 106.

30. During a smallpox outbreak in 1872, for example, the board instituted house-to-house inspections for "secreted" victims in the section east of 3rd Avenue and south of 14th Street, and found forty-three cases. City sanitary inspector Moreau Morris reassured the public that removal to the hospital "is not enforced" when "circumstances surrounding the patient will warrant his remaining" at home, i.e., when the patient could be reasonably well isolated there. See *New York Times*, March 28, 1872. "The board of health, in its practical enforcement of the law, has not required its obedience in, nor made a regular inspection of, the better class of what the law defines as tenements" (those more popularly known as flats or apartment houses), noted a state Tenement House Committee report in the 1890s. *Report of the Tenement House Committee as Authorized by Chapter 479 of the Laws of 1894*, 12.

In his study of the typhus and cholera epidemics of 1892, Howard Markel shows how Eastern European Jewish victims were seen as the source of contagion and were treated quite differently than the native born; this included "searches and roundups" targeting immigrants or immigrant neighborhoods, and policies for detaining arriving steamer passengers that focused on steerage passengers, assuming that cabin-class ticket holders led, as one paper put it, a "charmed life and [were] incapable of transmitting contagious diseases." Howard Markel, *Quarantine! East European Jewish Immigrants and the New York City Epidemics of 1892* (Baltimore: Johns Hopkins University Press, 1999), 127, 98.

31. *Report of the Tenement House Committee as Authorized by Chapter 479 of the Laws of 1894*, 86–87. There was a law for semi-annual whitewashing in tenements, but it was widely flouted.

32. This was the United Hebrew Charities. *New York Times*, August 5, 1883.

33. The nurse-reformer Lillian Wald sagely counseled her colleagues that while, yes, the sickbed might be full of crumbs and overhung by an unpleasant odor, "if you go in and make it apparent immediately that you perceive the air to be bad, that you do not approve of all the children lying upon the bed with the sick mother, that you wish to educate and reform, you will not be able to approach the matter of close air, dirt, and disorder without hurt feelings and bad temper." Lillian D. Wald, "The Treatment of Families in Which There Is Sickness," *American Journal of Nursing* 4, no. 6 (March 1904): 429–430.

34. Lillian W. Betts, *The Leaven in a Great City* (New York: Dodd, Mead and Company, 1902), 202–203.

35. *New York Sun*, September 1, 1895.

36. *New York Times*, May 11, 1902.

37. This expenditure is according to the permit application, alteration No. 121, February 26, 1875.

38. Alteration No. 73, January 22, 1904, was submitted by Dr. Emanuel Kleinman, presumably a near relative of Morris Kleinman, the neighbor who bought No. 239 after Clara Phillips's death.

39. Quotes in this paragraph from the *New York Sun*, September 1, 1895.

40. Campbell, *Darkness and Daylight*, 318.

41. Stanley Nadel, *Little Germany: Ethnicity, Religion, and Class in New York City, 1845–80* (Urbana: University of Illinois Press, 1990), 1.

42. Karl Theodor Griesinger, from *Land und Leute in America: Skizzen aus dem Amerikanischen Leben* (*Land and People in America: Sketches of American Life*), in *Empire City: New York Through the Centuries*, ed. Kenneth T. Jackson and David S. Dunbar (New York: Columbia University Press, 2002), 241–242.

43. Eric Homberger, *The Historical Atlas of New York City: A Visual Celebration of Nearly 400 Years of New York City's History* (New York: Henry Holt, 1994), 98.

44. Griesinger, *Land und Leute*, in *Empire City*, 242.

45. Nadel, *Little Germany*, 105.

46. Ibid., 109.

47. Their club memberships are from their obituaries in the *New York Times*, September 2, 1925, and July 10, 1928.

48. McCabe Jr., *Lights and Shadows*, 551.

49. Hutchins Hapgood, *Types from City Streets* (New York: Funk & Wagnalls, 1910), 117.

50. A thousand native-born and naturalized citizens of the eleventh ward signed a petition to the board of education asking for German-language instruc-

tion in 1869. *New York Times*, September 27, 1869. Also see *New York Times*, October 5, 1865, and February 29, 1870.

51. Griesinger, *Land und Leute*, in *Empire City*, 242.

52. *New York Times*, July 10, 1882.

53. The congregation was Mischan Israel. New York City marriages, certificate #1982, May 1, 1877. On Wasserman, see his obituary, *New York Times*, January 13, 1901.

54. Charges against Moses and his hearing covered in the *New York Times*, June 2 and 25, 1885.

55. Her will, dated July 16, 1894, along with two codicils signed October 26, 1894, and May 18, 1898, are found in New York County Surrogate's Court records, 714:321.

56. Based on estimates for girls' annual clothing needs in Robert Coit Chapin, *Standard of Living Among Workingmen's Families in New York City*, a report of an investigation conducted under the auspices of a special committee of the eighth New York State Conference of Charities and Corrections (New York: Russell Sage Foundation, 1909), 166.

57. Ibid., 198.

58. Ibid., 210.

59. *New York Times*, June 22, 1871; image from *Leslie's*, published in 1876, is in the New York Public Library's digital gallery, online at www.digitalgallery .nypl.org, image #805722.

60. *Harper's Weekly*, August 17, 1889.

61. *New York Times*, August 15 and 23, 1857.

62. Ibid., November 6 and 9, 1857.

63. Samuel Gompers, *Seventy Years of Life and Labor: An Autobiography*, ed. and with an introduction by Nick Salvatore (E. P. Dutton, 1925; Ithaca, NY: ILR Press, 1984), 32, 34.

64. *New York Times*, September 5, 1879.

65. *Harper's Weekly*, August 17, 1889.

66. New York City births, #26032, June 16, 1879.

67. New York City deaths, #41932, April 16, 1882.

68. Transfer of the house from Clara and Levy Phillips to Rachel Hart and vice versa: Register of Conveyances, New York County, 1411:423 and 1697:467.

69. Lillian W. Betts, "Tenement-House Life and Recreation," *Outlook*, February 11, 1899, 365.

70. Wendy Gamber, *The Female Economy: The Millinery and Dressmaking Trades, 1860–1930* (Urbana: University of Illinois Press, 1997). "Female Aristocracy of Labor" is the title of a chapter on workers in the dressmaking and millinery trades, 55–95. Much of my characterization of the social significance of millinery work is based on Gamber's work.

71. The "Michnieicz-Tuvee" hat, described in *Illustrated Milliner* 1, no. 3 (March 1900): 33.

72. *Millinery Trade Review* 15, no. 8 (August 1890): 17.

73. *Illustrated Milliner* 1, no. 3 (March 1900): 71.

74. Ibid., no. 1 (January 1900): 71.

75. Mary Van Kleeck, *A Seasonal Industry: A Study of the Millinery Trade in New York* (New York: Russell Sage Foundation, 1917), 35.

76. These photos are in a collection of Hine's work at the New York Public Library, unit III, Women at Work, ca. 1907–ca. 1933; several are reproduced in Van Kleeck, *A Seasonal Industry*.

77. This description of the division of labor in millinery shops, including quotes, from Lorinda Perry, *Millinery as a Trade for Women* (New York: Longmans, Green, and Company, 1916), 18–22.

78. *Illustrated Milliner* 1, no. 6 (June 1900): 30.

79. Betty Smith, *A Tree Grows in Brooklyn* (Philadelphia: Blakiston Company, 1943), 27.

80. "Jewish asthma": Harry Golden, in preface to Hutchins Hapgood, *The Spirit of the Ghetto* (New York: Funk & Wagnalls, 1902; New York: Funk & Wagnalls Company, 1965), xiv. "Tailors' disease": Lillian D. Wald, *The House on Henry Street* (New York: Henry Holt and Company, 1915), 54. Rate of TB among Jews: See, for example, Irving Howe, *World of Our Fathers: The Journey of the East European Jews to America and the Life They Found and Made*, 30th anniversary ed. (New York: New York University Press, 2005), 149–150; Maurice Fishberg, "The Relative Infrequency of Tuberculosis Among Jews," reprinted from *American Medicine*, November 2, 1901; and Maurice Fishberg, *Tuberculosis Among the Jews* (New York: William Wood & Co., 1908). The largely Russian-Jewish eleventh, tenth, and seventh wards had some of the lowest death rates from tuberculosis in 1890, according to Fishberg. This fact he said might be attributable to their different housecleaning habits (they wiped instead of swept), their moderate consumption of alcohol, or perhaps to the kosher laws that required close inspection of meats.

81. Edward J. Bermingham, ed., *An Encyclopaedic Index of Medicine and Surgery* (New York: Bermingham & Co., 1882), 629.

82. *New York Times*, June 12, 1892.

83. C. E. A. Winslow, *The First 50 Years of the New York Tuberculosis and Health Association* (New York: New York Tuberculosis Association, 1952). No page numbers.

84. *New York Times*, February 22, 1893.

85. *The Delineator* 44, no. 6 (December 1894): 31, and *The Delineator* 43, no. 5 (May 1894): 21.

86. DeForest and Veiller, *The Tenement House Problem*, 2:448.

87. Fishberg, "The Relative Infrequency of Tuberculosis Among Jews," 18.

88. Reproduced in Riis, *How the Other Half Lives*, 127.

89. According to Clara's death certificate, the doctor began treating her October 1, 1893. His name is all but illegible. It was not Dr. Michaelis, who had died. New York City deaths, #3423, January 27, 1893.

90. *New York Herald*, May 6, 1894.

91. *New York World*, January 18, 1893.

92. *New York Times*, February 26, 1893.

93. Riis, *How the Other Half Lives*, 2.

94. Her diagnosis is according to her death certificate, which listed chronic melancholia as a secondary cause of death. New York City deaths, #17035, June 3, 1902. For a contemporary description of melancholia, see Archibald Church, *Nervous and Mental Diseases* (Philadelphia: W. B. Saunders Company, 1914), 789–792. Though in Rachel's time people tended to see mental illness as coming in the form of an "attack"—one was either sane or a "lunatic"—the description of Rachel's affliction otherwise closely resembles what today is known as depression.

95. Ellen Dwyer, *Homes for the Mad: Life Inside Two Nineteenth-Century Asylums* (New Brunswick, NJ: Rutgers University Press, 1987), 87.

96. *New York Times*, December 22, 1892.

97. This and subsequent references to the *Herald* exposé are in the *New York Herald*, May 13, 1894.

98. Church, *Nervous and Mental Diseases*, 769.

99. Bly's reportage was published in a book, *Ten Days in a Mad-House* (New York: Ian L. Munro, c. 1887). It can be read online at the University of Pennsylvania's digital library, http://digital.library.upenn.edu/women/bly/madhouse/madhouse.html. The same year Bly published her story in the *World*, a report by the State Board of Charities on the men's asylum on Ward's Island showed "that fifteen hundred insane persons are half starved, and that they are intrusted to the care of brutal keepers" (*Harper's Weekly*, September 10, 1887). The *Herald's* 1894 exposé refers to a mayoral investigation in 1892 and regular reports since 1888 by the state Commissioners in Lunacy, all of which found the city asylums to be badly overcrowded and dilapidated.

100. Petition, Certificate of Lunacy and Orders for a forty-five-year-old New York woman, dated January 10, 1910, in Gustav Scholer Papers, box 3, Manuscripts and Archives Division, New York Public Library. Astor, Lenox, and Tilden Foundations.

101. *New York Times*, December 22, 1892.

102. New York State Commission in Lunacy, *Report Relating to the Conduct and Management of the New York City Asylum for the Insane* (Albany, 1894), 9.

103. These details are from the *Herald* exposé, May 6, 1894; *New York Times*, April 3, 1897; Dwyer's description of asylum routines in *Homes for the Mad*, 14–17. The band concert is pictured in *Sixth Annual Report of the Managers of the Manhattan State Hospitals at New York to the State Commission in Lunacy for the Year Ending September 30, 1901—Manhattan State Hospital, East—Ward's Island*, 64.

104. MacDonald was nominally the top official for all the city asylums but had day-to-day responsibility for the East Branch (the men's side of Ward's Island), where he lived. Emmett C. Dent, who had been superintendent of the women's asylum when Nelly Bly was there in 1887, continued in that capacity until his death in 1906.

105. *Seventh Annual Report of the Managers of the Manhattan State Hospitals at New York to the State Commission in Lunacy for the Year Ending September 30, 1902—Manhattan State Hospital, East—Ward's Island*, 45, 39, 31–32.

106. Ibid., 53.

107. Ibid., 57.

108. Ibid., 32.

109. New York Commission in Lunacy, *Report Relating to the Conduct and Management of the New York City Asylums for the Insane*, 9.

110. New York City deaths, #17035, June 3, 1902.

111. *New York Times*, June 8, 1902.

112. New York City deaths, #9167, March 21, 1903.

113. The conveyance to a Morris Kleinman took place in December 1903; Register of Conveyances, New York County, 119:94; *New York Times*, November 18, 1903.

114. *New York Sun*, September 1, 1895.

115. New York City deaths, #12331, April 9, 1896.

116. Tenement House Department of the City of New York and the Tenement House Committee of the Charity Organization Society, New York City, "For You. It is hard to get money. It is harder to spend it right. Health is wealth," 1914.

CHAPTER EIGHT

1. I'm quoting the Carl Sandburg poem "Fog."

2. Georg Simmel, *The Philosophy of Money*, 2nd enlarged ed.; David Frisby, ed.; Tom Bottomore and David Frisby, trans. (London: Routledge, 1990), 309, 329–330.

3. Ibid., 210–211.

4. Quoted in *Time* magazine, March 9, 2009.

5. Chairman's message in "Understanding America's Homeownership Gaps: 2003 Fannie Mae National Housing Survey," Fannie Mae, 2.

6. This propaganda is reproduced in Paul C. Luken and Suzanne Vaughan, "' . . . Be a Genuine Homemaker in Your *Own* Home': Gender and Familial Relations in State Housing Practices, 1917–1922," *Social Forces* 83, no. 4 (June 2005): 1615, 1613, 1617.

7. Remarks on the National Homeownership Strategy, June 5, 1995, quoted from transcript by John T. Woolley and Gerhard Peters, The American Presidency Project (www.presidency.ucsb.edu); Santa Barbara, University of California (hosted); Gerhard Peters (database).

8. Remarks by President George W. Bush at the White House Conference on Minority Homeownership, George Washington University, Washington, D.C., October 15, 2002, http://georgewbush-whitehouse.archives.gov/news/releases/2002/10/20021015-7.html.

9. Register of Conveyances, New York County, 806:66; January 10, 1860.

10. Ibid., 271:1915; March 19, 1973.

11. I'm using the consumer price index—how much it costs to buy a typical basket of goods and services—as a measure of inflation. Official data go back only to the early twentieth century, but economists Lawrence H. Officer and

Samuel H. Williamson have modified these data and linked them with other data series in their calculator of relative value, http://measuringworth.org.

12. Register of Conveyances, New York County, 997:665.

13. Simmel, *The Philosophy of Money*, 220.

14. M. K. Gandhi, *Non-Violent Resistance* (New York: Schocken Books, 1961; Mineola, NY: Courier Dover Publications, 2001), 45–47.

15. "When I consider how our houses are built and paid for, or not paid for, and their internal economy managed and sustained," Thoreau wrote in 1854, "I wonder that the floor does not give way under the visitor while he is admiring the gewgaws upon the mantelpiece. . . . I cannot but perceive that this so-called rich and refined life is a thing jumped at, and I do not get on in the enjoyment of the *fine* arts which adorn it, my attention being wholly occupied with the jump." Henry David Thoreau, *Walden*, in *The Portable Thoreau*, ed. Carl Bode (New York: Penguin Books, 1982), 293.

16. Quotations from legal documents are taken from our affirmation in answer to the plaintiff's motion to show cause for an injunction, a memorandum of law submitted by Gary's attorneys in support of that motion, and our notice of motion for summary judgment (which summarized all the foregoing litigation, including quotations from documents). I have also made use of my own thirteen-page chronology of events, written in 2003.

CHAPTER NINE

1. These recollections are based on a series of interviews with Al Wieder, in December 2005 on the telephone, in June 2006 on Long Island, and in May 2008 in Southern California.

2. I've chosen the spelling of Gizella that appears on her will and death certificate. In three separate censuses—1910, 1920, and 1930—she gave her name as Kate or Katy, a name Al had not heard in connection with his grandmother.

3. Mordechay Ben-Zeev, ed., *The Book of Michalovce* (Tel Aviv: Committee of Michalovce Emigrants in Israel, 1969), 29. This and other Holocaust memorial books are made available online by the New York Public Library at http://yizkor.nypl.org.

4. This is a condensed version of the prayer, adapted from various translations. *Teshuvah*, traditionally translated as "repentence," means literally a "return"—to oneself, to God, to the right way. *Tzedakah*, a key concept in Judaism, is traditionally translated as "charity" but more broadly means righteous or just action.

5. I'm referring to Stanley Nadel's *Little Germany: Ethnicity, Religion, and Class in New York City, 1845–80* (Urbana: University of Illinois Press, 1990). There are other histories, of course, that tell the story of Kleindeutschland with a particular focus, for example, Tom Goyens's *Beer and Revolution: The German Anarchist Movement in New York City, 1880–1914* (Urbana: University of Illinois Press, 2007).

6. These quotations are from Gold's *Jews Without Money*, 3rd ed., with an introduction by Alfred Kazin (New York: Carroll & Graf Publishers, 2004), 71, 15, 301, 160, 18, 158, 4.

7. The nineteenth-century Hungarian rabbi Moses Weinberger, on immigrating to New York, lamented the lack of any Jewish obligation to support their congregations, as well as the fact that the "less consequential members of our people, who never previously held opinions of their own, and who prior to their emigration had always been forced to answer an 'amen' of assent to every idea that other people had put into their heads, have here earned the right to express their opinions publicly." See Jonathan D. Saran, ed. and trans., *People Walk on Their Heads: Moses Weinberger's Jews and Judaism in New York* (New York: Holmes & Meier Publishers, 1982), 44.

8. The locution "Dollar Land" is from Samuel Ornitz's novel *Haunch, Paunch and Jowl* (Garden City, NY: Garden City Publishing, 1923), 43. The others make frequent appearances in East Side literature.

9. Examples are from *A Bintel Brief: Sixty Years of Letters from the Lower East Side to the Jewish Daily Forward*, ed. and with an introduction by Isaac Metzker, foreword and notes by Harry Golden (Garden City, NY: Doubleday, 1971; New York: Schocken Books, 1990), 124–125, 181, 139.

10. I interviewed E. Walter Snyder by phone on a few occasions in December 2005 and March–April 2009, at which point he was about to turn ninety-six. Elmer is his given name—that's the name he went by as a kid—but for many years he has used his middle name, Walter, so that's the name I use in this narrative. Much of the information about the Taubners and Gottliebs, as well as Walter's direct quotations, except where otherwise noted, are from personal interviews.

11. Gold, *Jews Without Money*, 78.

12. This quotation is from Golden's foreword to *A Bintel Brief*, 22.

13. The names of their parents are from Simon's and Gizella's death certificates, New York City Municipal Archives, #7031 (Simon, died March 21, 1944) and #19658 (Gizella, died September 23, 1939). Simon was the informant for Gizella's certificate, so I consider it very reliable. Son Michael provided the names for Simon's certificate and apparently could not give his paternal grandmother's maiden name.

14. Magyar Statisztikai Hivatal, *Népszámlálás: Zemplén (megye)*, 1869, on microfilm at the Family History Library of the Church of Jesus Christ of Latter-day Saints, Salt Lake City. Film 722754#1. The Weinbergers are house #67, the Vieders house #214. Gizella's family is fairly readily identifiable, since her mother's maiden name was Rosenbluth, given as Rozenblut in the census, and her father's name, Herman, likewise appears. Simon Wieder's identity is slightly more problematic, since I have no other mention of his mother's maiden name, Friedmann, to cross-reference, and the first names are slightly off. However, it would not be at all unusual for Moses to give his name as Mor (Moritz, Morris, Maurice, etc., were often substituted for Moses) and even for Sarah to give hers as Rozi, considering that in America, Gizella gave her name as Kate or Katy—a moniker her grandchildren never heard—in three separate censuses, and Simon Wieder listed his name as Widder in a city directory during years when his sons were listed in the same directory under the spelling Wieder. On the other hand,

Simon's birthday is given as December 10, 1855, on both his death certificate and naturalization record, and this Nagymihály family includes one of only two Jewish Wieder (Vieder, Widder, etc.) boys recorded in the Hungarian census as having been born that year. The other is a Salomon Widder, who lived in Nagy-Surány, a town northwest of Budapest that is separated from Nagymihály by more than 150 miles of mostly mountainous terrain.

15. Quoted from Sydney Stahl Weinberg, *The World of Our Mothers: The Lives of Jewish Immigrant Women* (Chapel Hill: University of North Carolina Press, 1988), 77.

16. Saran, ed., *People Walk on their Heads*, 61.

17. On population figures, see *Encyclopedia Judaica*, 2nd ed., 14:172–173. On the economics of this part of Hungary and the role of Jews there, useful sources are Ben-Zeev, *The Book of Michalovce*; Michael K. Silber, "The Entrance of Jews into Hungarian Society in *Vormärz*: The Case of the 'Casinos,'" in *Assimilation and Community: The Jews in Nineteenth-Century Europe*, ed. Jonathan Frankel and Steven J. Zipperstein (Cambridge: Cambridge University Press, 2004), 288–289; Robert Perlman, *Bridging Three Worlds: Hungarian-Jewish Americans, 1848–1914* (Amherst: University of Massachusetts Press, 1991), 34–46; T. D. Kramer, *From Emancipation to Catastrophe: The Rise and Holocaust of Hungarian Jewry* (Lanham, MD: University Press of America, 2000), 7–13. Also see the town website, www.michalovce.sk, although its short history makes no mention of Jewish people.

18. See Kramer, *From Emancipation to Catastrophe*, 13–19.

19. Senesh Erzi, in Ben-Zeev, *The Book of Michalovce*, 14.

20. Testimony on the deportation of young women from Michalovce was given in the trial in Jerusalem of Nazi leader Adolf Eichmann, Session #53, May 25, 1961. The Eichmann trial transcripts are online courtesy of the Nizkor Project, www.nizkor.org.

21. Here I must confess to taking a small liberty with Simon's story, because he was not listed in the city directory at all until 1891, when he was listed as a cigarmaker. His naturalization in 1897 (U.S. District Court, New York, New York, vol. 56, 666–667) also lists him as a cigarmaker, and his witness, tenement neighbor Eugene Krow, is a cigarmaker who testifies to having personally known Simon since mid-1890. I think it likely they worked in the same shop. It may be Simon didn't list himself in the directory from his immigration in 1885 to 1890 because he was living with roommates or as a boarder. It seems safe to assume that he was then employed as a cigarmaker or in some comparable job. Quotation is from Leon Kobrin's short story, "Little Souls," in *Pushcarts and Dreamers: Stories of Jewish Life in America*, ed. Max Rosenfeld (Philadelphia: Sholom Aleichem Club Press, 1967), 54.

22. Bella Spewak, *Streets: A Memoir of the Lower East Side* (New York: Feminist Press at the City University of New York, 1995), 3.

23. Anzia Yezierska, *Bread Givers: A Struggle Between a Father of the Old World and a Daughter of the New World* (New York: Doubleday, 1925; New York: George Braziller, 1975), 3.

24. One William Widder, who lived with the Wieders on 6th Street at the time and was undoubtedly a relative, worked with Simon as a trimmings maker in 1901, and son Samuel was the one to report a small fire in the shop one afternoon in February 1904. Fire: *New York Times*, February 13, 1904.

25. Alfred Kazin, *A Walker in the City* (San Diego and New York: Harvest Books, 1951), 19.

26. *New York Tribune*, September 18, 1898.

27. Their names are listed among the graduates in the *New York Times*, June 19, 1902, Sam with a bachelor of science degree, Max a bachelor of arts. I'm not certain when Michael and Morris graduated, but Alfred Wieder recalls they all attended City College.

28. See Eileen F. Lebow, *The Bright Boys: A History of Townsend Harris High School* (Westport, CT: Greenwood Press, 2000), 10–14; and Irving Howe, *World of Our Fathers: The Journey of the East European Jews to America and the Life They Found and Made*, 30th anniversary ed. (New York: New York University Press), 280–286.

29. *New York Times*, May 4, 1901.

30. The Berkowitzes, who like the Wieders had moved up from below Houston Street (their youngest, Ida, was born on Georck Street), appear in the 1910 federal census, as does the maid, Julie Janka(?), who had a husband and four-year-old child, although they apparently did not live with her.

31. Koenig's location is from federal censuses of 1910, 1920, and 1930. He discusses his political career and contacts in late interviews given through the Oral History Project of Columbia University: Reminiscences of Samuel S. Koenig, February and March 1950, especially 5–33, in the Oral History Collection of Columbia University.

32. Keenan's annual outings were covered by the *Times*. The papers of May 6, 8, and 9, 1907, feature details of his life and funeral.

33. *New York Times*, October 22, 1897.

34. This characterization draws from the program for the testimonial dinner, which includes scores of names, including that of the Honorable Morris D. Reiss, who'd run for local office on the Progressive ticket (and sat on the dais), as well as representatives of the "Progressive League" of the convalescent home itself.

35. See, for example, Irving Howe's discussion of Jewish politics in *World of Our Fathers*, 360–374; Ronald Sanders, *The Downtown Jews: Portraits of an Immigrant Generation* (New York: Harper & Row, 1969), 319–322; Moses Rischin, *The Promised City: New York Jews, 1870–1914* (Cambridge, MA: Harvard University Press, 1962), 228–235; Thomas M. Henderson, *Tammany Hall and the New Immigrants: The Progressive Years* (New York: Arno Press, 1976), esp. 284–285.

36. Jerome Wiedman, *Fourth Street East: A Novel of How it Was* (New York: Random House, 1970), 82.

37. Reminiscences of Samuel S. Koenig, Oral History Collection of Columbia University, 43.

38. S. L. Blumenson, *Commentary*, March 1956. Accessed from the magazine's online archive, http://commentarymagazine.com.

39. *New York Times*, August 12, 1903.

40. Ibid., June 4, 1913.

41. The Purim/birthday parties were reported in the *Times*. See March 15, 1911, and March 22, 1913. When Burger died, the *Times* recapped his career, including his contacts with Taft. *New York Times*, May 4, 1933.

42. Trow's General Directory of the Boroughs of Manhattan and Bronx, City of New York, 1933–34 Emergency Unemployment Relief Committee Edition. Alfred Wieder recalled his uncle had worked for the Board of Estimate, an administrative body also closely involved in public works and related assessments.

43. In fact, in 1930 only 2.3 percent of public-service workers in the city were collecting relief, compared with a whopping 35.3 percent of manufacturing and mechanical workers, and 24.1 percent of trade workers. Statistics from the federal Works Progress Administration, quoted in Ronald H. Bayor, *Neighbors in Conflict: The Irish, Germans, Jews and Italians*, 2nd ed. (Urbana: University of Illinois Press, 1988), 11.

44. This quotation is from E. Walter Snyder's autobiography, *Daddy, Tell Us About When You Were a Little Boy: 89 Years and Most of Them Fun* (New York: Writers Club Press, 2003), 3. Certain other details were mentioned both in this lively narrative and in interviews, so I have only cited cases of direct quotation.

45. Ibid., 59.

46. Telephone interview with a granddaughter of Pauline's, Judith Margolis, June 2009.

47. *New York Times*, August 10, 1937.

48. Ibid., October 27 and November 10, 1931.

49. Ibid., November 14, 1944.

50. Gizella's will is found in New York County Surrogate's Court records, 1670:412.

CHAPTER TEN

1. John Peter DeLancey to Lieutenant John DeLancey, January 18, 1791, in the DeLancey Family Papers, Museum of the City of New York.

2. Susan Fenimore Cooper, "Small Family Memories," in *Correspondence of James Fenimore Cooper*, ed. James Fenimore Cooper, 2 vols. (New Haven, CT: Yale University Press, 1922), 1:24, 26, 25.

3. Ibid., 1:26, 45, 69.

4. See Rodney Castleden, *The Stonehenge People: An Exploration of Life in Neolithic Britain, 4700–2000 BC* (London: Routledge & Kegan Paul, 1987), 117, 32–36, 174–177.

5. For quotations, see Ian Hodder's extended discussion of this idea, *The Domestication of Europe: Structure and Contingency in Neolithic Societies* (Oxford, UK, and Cambridge, MA: B. Blackwell, 1990), 41. For a synopsis of the concept, see Ian Hodder, *Theory and Practice in Archaeology* (1992; New York: Routledge, 1995), 208–218.

6. Cremation Association of North America, "2006 CANA Cremation Container, Disposition, and Service Survey Final Results," 19.

7. *St. Petersburg Times*, June 21, 2009.

8. *New York Times*, September 29, 2009.

9. Claire Seeber, *The Guardian*, November 8, 2008.

10. From the company website, www.foreverfernwood.com.

11. See Merlin Donald, "Précis of *Origins of the Modern Mind: Three Stages in the Evolution of Culture and Cognition*," *Behavior and Brain Sciences* 16, no. 4 (1993): 737–748. For final quotation, see Merlin Donald, *Origins of the Modern Mind: Three Stages in the Evolution of Culture and Cognition* (Cambridge, MA: Harvard University Press, 1991), 312.

12. New Jersey Historical Society, *Proceedings of the New Jersey Historical Society* 4, no. 1–4 (January–October 1919): 184.

13. See, for example, the Associated Press, April 14, 2004.

14. Clifton D. Bryant, "'Thanatological Crime': Some Conceptual Notes on Offenses Against the Dead as a Neglected Form of Deviant Behavior," in *Handbook of Death & Dying*, ed. Clifton D. Bryant, 2 vols. (Thousand Oaks, CA: Sage Publications, 2003), 2:979.

15. See *Jewish Week*, June 13, 1997, and June 6, 2003; *Queens Chronicle*, January 29, 2009.

16. *New York Times*, January 30, 2003.

17. *Houston Chronicle*, May 9, 2008, and August 26, 2008.

18. Robert Jay Lifton, *The Broken Connection: On Death and the Continuity of Life* (Washington, DC, and London: American Psychiatric Press, 1979), 95.

19. From the group's website, www.takebackthememorial.org.

20. David Stanke, "Freedom Requires Standing Up to 9/11 Family Leaders," *Downtown Express*, August 5–11, 2005.

21. See Carolee R. Inskeep, *The Graveyard Shift: A Family Historian's Guide to New York City Cemeteries* (Orem, UT: Ancestry, 2000), esp. xi–xiv. On bones found during a renovation of Washington Square Park: *New York Times* blog "City Room," January 23, 2008.

22. Ruth Tringham, "Weaving House Life and Death into Places: A Blueprint for a Hypermedia Narrative," in *(Un)settling the Neolithic*, ed. Douglass Bailey, Alasdair Whittle, and Vicki Cummings (Oxford, UK: Oxbow Books, 2005), 107. Also see Mirjana Stevanovic, "The Age of Clay: The Social Dynamics of House Destruction," *Journal of Anthropological Archaeology* 16, no. 4 (December 1997): 334–395.

23. Henry David Thoreau, from *Walden*, in *The Portable Thoreau*, ed. Carl Bode (New York: Penguin Books, 1982; New York: Viking Penguin, 1947), 507.

24. Colson Whitehead, *The Colossus of New York* (New York: Doubleday/Random House, 2003), 5.

25. Henry James, "The American Scene," in *Writing New York: A Literary Anthology*, ed. Phillip Lopate (New York: Library of America, 1998), 374–375.

26. Online at www.citynoise.org/article/8696.

27. *A Field Guide to Visiting a Jewish Cemetery: A Spiritual Journey to the Past, Present and Future* (Nashua, NH: Jewish Cemetery Publishing, LLC, 2005). Publisher's website: www.cemeteryjewish.com.

CHAPTER ELEVEN

1. A note on sources for this chapter: This chapter is based primarily on interviews with people who remember the time and place under observation. Most lived on 7th Street. A few were neighborhood housing or other community activists. The bulk of the interviews took place in 2009, from August through December, although a few were conducted as early as 2006. Individuals interviewed include the following: Kwame Adansi-Bona, Stephen Barto, Olivia Bergemann, Thomas Brasuell, Paul Broaddus, Wilfredo Cacquia, José M. Cruz, Michael Diaz, Ann Feinstein, Eric Felisbret, Carlos Garcia, Fred Good, Suzan Shown Harjo, Judith Harlan, Basil Hawryluk, Bill Heine, Herman Hewitt, Henry Hof III, Philip Hof, Stanley Karanewski, Donald Kearse, Omar Kharem, Brian Lippel, Ardell LongTemple, Otis Maclay, Daniel Murray, Regis Obijiski, Carmen Pabon, Awi Perkins, Ani Sandoval, Jane Scheidler, Sandra Scoppettone, Fred Seiden, Betty-Carol Sellen, Edwin Sepulveda, Stanley Valladares Smith, Anne Spitzer, Edwin Torres, Migdalia Torres, Clarence Williams, Harriet Zwerling, and Milo Zwerling. Quotations in the text are from these interviews except where otherwise noted.

Another key source was the extensive field notes made by researcher Stephen Barto during the summer of 1975, which he very generously shared with me. A graduate student at New York University at the time, Barto was conducting research for a study on block associations funded by the National Science Foundation SOS Program: Stephen C. Barto, "A Study of the Lower East Side Block's Block Association," in *The Structure and Function of Block Associations as Emerging Urban Phenomena: June 8–Aug. 31, 1975*, Stephen C. Barto, project director; Owen Lynch, faculty adviser (New York University, 1975). Barto's field notes describe interviews he conducted, as well as conversations, meetings, and events he observed during three summer months on the block of East 7th Street between Avenues C and D.

A third important resource has been block-association newsletters from the early 1970s through the early '80s, kindly provided to me by Betty-Carol Sellen, a former president of the association.

2. The memoir is titled *Below the Color Line*, a reference to Long's fair, freckled complexion, which made him feel, as an African American, especially pressed to prove himself.

3. *New York Times*, December 1, 1967.

4. In a couple of cases, the Maleks had apparently purchased the mortgage, not the building itself. From property records available at the New York City Online Register, www.nyc.gov/html/dof/html/jump/acris.shtml. Block 377, lots 11 and 68–72; block 353, lot 33; block 378, lot 49; block 385, lot 4; block 389, lot 46; block 398, lots 29, 34, and 35; block 437, lot 19.

5. See César J. Ayala and Rafael Bernabe, *Puerto Rico in the American Century: A History Since 1898* (Chapel Hill: University of North Carolina Press, 2007), 33–38, 189–194.

6. The poem was published as a book by the same name by Monthly Review Press in 1973.

7. See New York City Urban Coalition Inc., *The New York City In Rem Housing Program: A Report*, January 1985.

8. From buildings department records for No. 239, New York City Municipal Archives.

9. Christopher Mele, *Selling the Lower East Side: Culture, Real Estate, and Resistance in New York City* (Minneapolis: University of Minnesota Press, 2000), 196.

10. See President's Commission on Organized Crime, *America's Habit: Drug Abuse, Drug Trafficking & Organized Crime: Report to the President and Attorney General* (Washington, DC: The Commission, 1986), 105–107; Eric C. Schneider, *Smack: Heroin and the American City* (Philadelphia: University of Pennsylvania Press, 2008), 8–14; Christopher Mele, *Selling the Lower East Side*, 147.

11. *East Village Eye*, March 1984.

12. Jagna Wojcicka Sharff, "The Underground Economy of a Poor Neighborhood," in *Cities of the United States: Studies in Urban Anthropology*, ed. Leith Mullings (New York: Columbia University Press, 1987), 21, 27–30.

13. Jagna Wojcicka Sharff, *King Kong on 4th Street: Families and the Violence of Poverty on the Lower East Side* (Boulder, CO: Westview Press, 1998), 10, 36.

14. Ibid., 96–97. The song is "Blue Bayou" by Roy Orbison and Joe Melson.

15. *New York Times*, April 17, 1966, and February 9, 1971.

16. Ads are from *East Village Other*, November 15, 1967.

17. The taglines, in order, are from Winter 1984, Spring/Summer 1985, and Winter 1985 issues.

18. Joel Rose, "The Sunshine of Paradise Alley," republished in *Between C & D: New Writing from the Lower East Side Fiction Magazine*, ed. Joel Rose and Catherine Texier (New York: Penguin Books, 1988), 183.

19. *New York Daily News*, April 10 and 13, 1971.

20. *New York Times*, September 23, 1969.

21. Ibid., May 10, 1974.

22. *Alphabet Soup*, October 1981, November 1981, and March 1982.

23. In Emily Zimmerman, Hongsook Eu, and David Daykin, *The Lower East Side, Community District 3, Manhattan* (New York: United Way of New York City, 1993), 26.

24. *East Village Eye*, May 1979.

25. The details of this incident are told in New York City Department of Parks & Recreation historical sign for the Firemen's Garden at the site, www.nycgovparks.org/sub_your_park/historical_signs/hs_historical_sign.php?id=12184.

26. This is the same Stanley who later became our co-op's attorney and a personal friend.

27. *New York Times*, September 14, 1966.

28. Quoted in a letter from Bergemann himself to the attorney general's office, dated March 31, 1975. In court documents, *People of the State of New York v. Helen Barrera and Charles Bergemann Jr.*, indictment 3556/75.

29. The accusation by the super and events at the block fair of 1975 are from Stephen Barto's field notes. See note 1.

30. *Soho Weekly News*, November 21, 1974.

31. *New York Times*, December 6, 1970; *New York*, March 31, 1980.

32. In *People v. Barrera and Bergemann*, 3556/75.

33. *New York Times*, April 2, 2009.

34. Online at http://curbed.com/archives/2009/08/31/10_million_living_on _avenue_d_gets_a_discount.php#more.

35. In New York County Surrogate's Court records, #5358–1985.

36. *City Limits*, September/October 2002; *The Villager*, December 31–January 6, 2009.

37. Martin Heidegger, "Building Dwelling Thinking," in *Poetry, Language, Thought*, trans. Albert Hofstadter (New York: Harper & Row, 1971), 160.

EPILOGUE

1. *The Papers of Thomas Jefferson*, ed. Julian P. Boyd, 36 vols. (Princeton, NJ: Princeton University Press, 1958), 15:392.

2. Julian P. Boyd, ed., *Papers of Thomas Jefferson*, 15:393, 396.

AUTHOR PHOTO BY LALOU DAMMOND

Katharine Greider is a writer living in New York City. She got her start in journalism at an alternative newsweekly and then a small-town daily newspaper. As a freelancer she has written on health and medicine, culture, and other topics for many local and national newspapers, magazines, and non-profit organizations, from the *New York Times* to the *AARP Bulletin*. Her first book was *The Big Fix: How the Pharmaceutical Industry Rips Off American Consumers* (PublicAffairs, 2003).

PublicAffairs is a publishing house founded in 1997. It is a tribute to the standards, values, and flair of three persons who have served as mentors to countless reporters, writers, editors, and book people of all kinds, including me.

I.F. STONE, proprietor of *I. F. Stone's Weekly*, combined a commitment to the First Amendment with entrepreneurial zeal and reporting skill and became one of the great independent journalists in American history. At the age of eighty, Izzy published *The Trial of Socrates*, which was a national bestseller. He wrote the book after he taught himself ancient Greek.

BENJAMIN C. BRADLEE was for nearly thirty years the charismatic editorial leader of *The Washington Post*. It was Ben who gave the *Post* the range and courage to pursue such historic issues as Watergate. He supported his reporters with a tenacity that made them fearless and it is no accident that so many became authors of influential, best-selling books.

ROBERT L. BERNSTEIN, the chief executive of Random House for more than a quarter century, guided one of the nation's premier publishing houses. Bob was personally responsible for many books of political dissent and argument that challenged tyranny around the globe. He is also the founder and longtime chair of Human Rights Watch, one of the most respected human rights organizations in the world.

.   .   .

For fifty years, the banner of Public Affairs Press was carried by its owner Morris B. Schnapper, who published Gandhi, Nasser, Toynbee, Truman, and about 1,500 other authors. In 1983, Schnapper was described by *The Washington Post* as "a redoubtable gadfly." His legacy will endure in the books to come.

Peter Osnos, *Founder and Editor-at-Large*